OECD Research and Development Expenditure in Industry 2016

ANBERD

This work is published under the responsibility of the Secretary-General of the OECD. The opinions expressed and arguments employed herein do not necessarily reflect the official views of OECD member countries.

This document and any map included herein are without prejudice to the status of or sovereignty over any territory, to the delimitation of international frontiers and boundaries and to the name of any territory, city or area.

Please cite this publication as:
OECD (2017), *OECD Research and Development Expenditure in Industry 2016: ANBERD*, OECD Publishing.
http://dx.doi.org/10.1787/anberd-2016-en

ISBN: 978-92-64-27454-9 (print)
ISBN: 978-92-64-22479-7 (PDF)

The statistical data for Israel are supplied by and under the responsibility of the relevant Israeli authorities. The use of such data by the OECD is without prejudice to the status of the Golan Heights, East Jerusalem and Israeli settlements in the West Bank under the terms of international law.

Corrigenda to OECD publications may be found on line at: *www.oecd.org/about/publishing/corrigenda.htm*.
© OECD 2017

You can copy, download or print OECD content for your own use, and you can include excerpts from OECD publications, databases and multimedia products in your own documents, presentations, blogs, websites and teaching materials, provided that suitable acknowledgment of the source and copyright owner is given. All requests for public or commercial use and translation rights should be submitted to *rights@oecd.org*. Requests for permission to photocopy portions of this material for public or commercial use shall be addressed directly to the Copyright Clearance Center (CCC) at *info@copyright.com* or the Centre français d'exploitation du droit de copie (CFC) at *contact@cfcopies.com*.

Table of contents

Australia	8
Austria	10
Belgium	12
Canada	16
Chile	18
Czech Republic	20
Denmark	24
Estonia	26
Finland	28
France	32
Germany	36
Hungary	38
Israel	40
Italy	42
Japan	46
Korea	48
Mexico	50
Netherlands	52
New Zealand	54
Norway	56
Poland	58
Portugal	60
Slovak Republic	64
Slovenia	66
Spain	68
Sweden	70
Switzerland	72
Turkey	74
United Kingdom	76
United States	80
China	82
Romania	84
Singapore	86
Chinese Taipei	88

Readers' guide

Main features

This publication includes business R&D data in ISIC Rev. 4 for 31 OECD member economies and four non-member economies. The reported data follow the International Standard Industrial Classification, Revision 4 (ISIC Rev. 4).

The data according to different versions of ISIC classification are published in the following database:

- OECD (2017), "STAN R&D: Research and development expenditure in industry – ISIC Rev. 4", STAN: OECD Structural Analysis Statistics (database), *http://dx.doi.org/10.1787/data-00689-en*.

Signs and abbreviations

- ..   Not available.
- .   Decimal point.
- n.e.c.   not elsewhere classified.

Sources and methods

- Documentation (PDF): *www.oecd.org/sti/inno/ANBERD_full_documentation.pdf*.
- Industry coverage (XLS): *www.oecd.org/sti/inno/ANBERDcoverage.xls*.

Contact details

- For any enquiries, please contact *oecdilibrary@oecd.org* or *RDSurvey@oecd.org*.

Classification

- The International Standard Industrial Classification (ISIC) Rev. 4 is available online at *http://unstats.un.org/unsd/cr/registry/isic-4.asp*.

ISIC Rev. 4 classification

Section	Divisions	Description
A-U	01-99	**TOTAL BUSINESS ENTERPRISE**
A	01-03	**AGRICULTURE, FORESTRY AND FISHING**
B	05-09	**MINING AND QUARRYING**
C	10-33	**MANUFACTURING**
	10-12	Manufacture of food products, beverages and tobacco
	13-15	
	13	Manufacture of textiles
	14	Manufacture of wearing apparel
	15	Manufacture of leather and related products
	16-18	
	16	Manufacture of wood and of products of wood and cork, except furniture; manufacture of articles of straw and plaiting materials
	17	Manufacture of paper and paper products
	18	Printing and reproduction of recorded media
	19-23	
	19	Manufacture of coke and refined petroleum products
	20-21	
	20	Manufacture of chemicals and chemical products
	21	Manufacture of basic pharmaceutical products and pharmaceutical preparations
	22	Manufacture of rubber and plastics products
	23	Manufacture of other non-metallic mineral products
	24-25	
	24	Manufacture of basic metals
	25	Manufacture of fabricated metal products, except machinery and equipment
	26-30	
	26	Manufacture of computer, electronic and optical products
	27	Manufacture of electrical equipment
	28	Manufacture of machinery and equipment n.e.c.
	29	Manufacture of motor vehicles, trailers and semi-trailers
	30	Manufacture of other transport equipment
	31-33	
	31	Manufacture of furniture
	32	Other manufacturing
	33	Repair and installation of machinery and equipment
D+E	35-39	**ELECTRICITY, GAS, WATER AND WASTE MANAGEMENT**
D	35-36	Electricity, gas and water
E	37-39	Sewerage, waste management, remediation activities
F	41-43	**CONSTRUCTION**
G-U	45-99	**TOTAL SERVICES**
G-N	45-82	Business sector services
G	45-47	**Wholesale and retail trade; motor vehicles and motorcycles repairs**
H	49-53	**Transportation and storage**
I	55-56	**Accommodation and food service activities**
J	58-63	**Information and communication**
	58-60	
	58	Publishing activities
	59-60	
	59	Motion picture, video and television programme production, sound recording and music publishing activities
	60	Programming and broadcasting activities
	61	Telecommunications
	62-63	
	62	Computer programming, consultancy and related activities
	63	Information service activities
K	64-66	**Financial and insurance activities**
L-N	68-82	**Real estate activities; professional, scientific and technical activities; administrative and support service activities**
L	68	Real estate activities
Mx72	69-75x72	Professional, scientific and technical activities, except scientific R&D
	72	Scientific research and development
N	77-82	Administrative and support service activities
O-U	84-99	Community, social and personal services
O-P	84-85	Public administration and defence; compulsory social security and education
Q	86-88	Human health and social work activities
R	90-93	Arts, entertainment and recreation
S-U	94-99	Other service activities; activities of households as employers; undifferentiated goods- and services-producing activities of households for own use; extraterritorial bodies, activities of extraterritorial organizations and bodies

R&D expenditure in industry

AUSTRALIA

R&D expenditure in industry by main activity of the enterprise, current prices
ISIC Rev. 4

Million USD PPP

		2007	2008	2009	2010	2011	2012	2013	2014
	TOTAL BUSINESS ENTERPRISE	10 547.0	11 690.6	11 629.2	11 983.0	12 124.9	..	13 027.6	..
01-03	**AGRICULTURE, FORESTRY AND FISHING**	83.3	98.9	127.5	122.5	125.5	..	167.7	..
05-09	**MINING AND QUARRYING**	2 410.6	2 937.2	2 576.5	2 554.5	2 716.1	..	1 956.1	..
10-33	**MANUFACTURING**	3 078.6	2 980.2	2 968.8	3 210.5	2 978.7	..	3 373.9	..
10-12	Food products, beverages and tobacco	292.1	302.5	340.3	401.3	362.9	..	476.2	..
13-15	Textiles, wearing apparel, leather and related products	23.1	23.7	20.1	30.7	34.9	..	31.8	..
13	Textiles	14.0	14.5	11.6	14.6	16.8	..	..	..
14	Wearing apparel	4.6	5.0	4.5	5.4	4.6	..	..	..
15	Leather and related products, footwear	4.6	4.2	4.0	10.7	13.6	..	..	..
16-18	Wood and paper products and printing	99.5	90.4	181.0	144.6	68.7	..	68.6	..
16	Wood and wood products, except furniture	36.0	38.6	39.9	41.5	25.3	..	..	..
17	Paper and paper products	49.8	36.4	..	..	32.0	..	..	..
18	Printing and reproduction of recorded media	13.8	15.4	..	..	11.4	..	..	..
19-23	Chemical, rubber, plastic, non-metallic mineral products	665.6	695.0	660.6	688.8	712.9	..	857.0	..
19	Coke and refined petroleum products	74.8	68.1	53.8	60.8	59.9	..	115.0	..
20-21	Chemical and pharmaceutical products	454.1	498.6	455.5	489.0	517.9	..	571.0	..
20	Chemicals and chemical products	230.3	221.3	189.2	237.0	250.6	..	204.6	..
21	Pharmaceuticals, medicinal, chemical and botanical products	223.7	277.3	266.3	252.0	267.2	..	366.3	..
22	Rubber and plastic products	55.2	52.3	50.5	65.7	67.6	..	75.0	..
23	Other non-metallic mineral products	81.5	76.1	100.8	73.2	67.6	..	96.1	..
24-25	Basic metals, metal products, except machinery and equipment	556.5	553.3	434.8	533.0	482.6	..	..	..
24	Basic metals	432.7	439.4	304.1	346.6	334.5	..	229.0	..
25	Fabricated metal products, except machinery and equipment	123.9	113.9	130.7	186.5	148.1	..	..	..
26-30	Computer, electronic, optical products; electrical machinery, transport equipment	1 282.5	1 156.0	1 173.7	1 229.2	1 110.8	..	..	..
26	Computer, electronic and optical products	225.3	272.3	254.9	248.8	237.9	..	..	..
27	Electrical equipment	64.2	52.6	64.6	62.6	86.8	..	..	..
28	Machinery and equipment n.e.c.	306.7	256.6	263.9	288.0	239.2	..	..	..
29	Motor vehicles, trailers and semi-trailers	529.3	425.3	452.3	469.8	440.7	..	..	..
30	Other transport equipment	157.0	149.2	138.0	160.0	106.2	..	..	..
31-33	Furniture; repair, installation of machinery and equipment	159.1	159.4	158.2	182.9	205.9	..	240.4	..
31	Furniture	4.7	5.7	6.7	7.9	12.2	..	11.5	..
32	Other manufacturing	141.3	140.4	138.8	162.0	175.8	..	203.1	..
33	Repair and installation of machinery and equipment	13.1	13.3	12.7	13.0	17.9	..	25.8	..
35-39	**ELECTRICITY, GAS, WATER AND WASTE MANAGEMENT**	169.6	243.3	281.9	280.8	250.2	..	218.0	..
35-36	Electricity, gas and water	111.8	170.6	202.1	185.1	173.7	..	129.2	..
37-39	Sewerage, waste management and remediation activities	57.8	72.6	79.8	95.7	76.6	..	88.7	..
41-43	**CONSTRUCTION**	527.1	627.8	600.6	669.3	542.3	..	597.2	..
45-99	**TOTAL SERVICES**	4 277.8	4 803.2	5 073.9	5 144.5	5 512.0	..	6 714.7	..
45-82	**Business sector services**	4 195.6	4 697.5	4 961.8	5 026.8	5 362.8	..	6 507.5	..
45-47	Wholesale and retail trade; motor vehicle and motorcycle repairs	667.2	664.1	616.1	550.6	573.1	..	847.1	..
49-53	Transportation and storage	155.0	158.3	179.2	194.4	193.8	..	250.9	..
55-56	Accommodation and food service activities	12.0	18.1	15.4	10.4	14.2	..	16.8	..
58-63	Information and communication	1 266.6	1 256.1	1 067.4	1 114.5	1 215.2	..	1 656.1	..
58-60	Publishing, audiovisual and broadcasting activities	153.3	143.4	118.7	123.4	119.4	..	189.5	..
58	Publishing activities	138.4	116.8	79.7	82.7	84.6	..	132.4	..
59-60	Motion picture, video and TV programme production; broadcasting activities	14.9	26.6	39.0	40.7	34.7	..	57.1	..
59	Motion picture, video and TV programme production; sound and music	7.3	9.5	13.3	13.5	13.4	..	..	..
60	Programming and broadcasting activities	7.6	17.2	25.7	27.2	21.4	..	..	..
61	Telecommunications	399.4	400.3	203.0	234.0	319.0	..	164.8	..
62-63	IT and other information services	714.0	712.5	745.7	757.0	776.7	..	1 301.8	..
62	Computer programming, consultancy and related activities	695.7	696.2	728.8	737.5	751.1	..	1 258.8	..
63	Information service activities	18.2	16.3	16.9	19.6	25.6	..	42.9	..
64-66	Financial and insurance activities	1 021.6	1 425.4	1 814.4	1 842.3	1 975.6	..	2 137.6	..
68-82	Real estate; professional, scientific and technical; administrative and support	1 073.2	1 175.4	1 269.4	1 315.6	1 391.0	..	1 599.1	..
68	Real estate activities	7.1	30.0	11.8	9.2	15.2	..	32.8	..
69-75x72	Professional, scientific and technical activities, except scientific R&D	449.5	559.3	575.2	636.6	668.0	..	..	..
72	Scientific research and development	493.0	489.6	464.2	427.2	454.9	..	..	..
77-82	Administrative and support service activities	123.5	96.5	218.2	242.6	252.9	..	..	..
84-99	**Community, social and personal services**	82.2	105.7	112.1	117.7	149.2	..	207.2	..
84-85	Public administration and defence; compulsory social security and education	4.9	10.3	10.9	13.4	17.5	..	23.1	..
86-88	Human health and social work activities	39.7	50.6	53.6	53.1	62.5	..	50.9	..
90-93	Arts, entertainment and recreation	18.7	22.2	23.5	27.3	47.9	..	77.9	..
94-99	Other services; household-employers; extraterritorial bodies	18.9	22.6	24.2	23.9	21.2	..	55.3	..

.. Not available

Note: Detailed metadata at: http://metalinks.oecd.org/anberd/20170419/301f.
   Information on data for Israel: http://oe.cd/israel-disclaimer.

Disclaimer: http://oe.cd/disclaimer

AUSTRALIA

R&D expenditure in industry by main activity of the enterprise, constant prices
ISIC Rev. 4

2010 USD PPP

		2007	2008	2009	2010	2011	2012	2013	2014
	TOTAL BUSINESS ENTERPRISE	11 269.1	12 341.7	11 842.7	11 983.0	11 946.7	..	12 136.9	..
01-03	**AGRICULTURE, FORESTRY AND FISHING**	89.0	104.4	129.9	122.5	123.7	..	156.3	..
05-09	**MINING AND QUARRYING**	2 575.6	3 100.8	2 623.8	2 554.5	2 676.1	..	1 822.4	..
10-33	**MANUFACTURING**	3 289.4	3 146.2	3 023.3	3 210.5	2 934.9	..	3 143.2	..
10-12	Food products, beverages and tobacco	312.1	319.3	346.5	401.3	357.5	..	443.6	..
13-15	Textiles, wearing apparel, leather and related products	24.7	25.0	20.5	30.7	34.4	..	29.6	..
13	Textiles	15.0	15.3	11.8	14.6	16.6	..	..	..
14	Wearing apparel	4.9	5.3	4.6	5.4	4.5	..	..	..
15	Leather and related products, footwear	4.9	4.4	4.1	10.7	13.4	..	..	..
16-18	Wood and paper products and printing	106.3	95.4	184.4	144.6	67.7	..	63.9	..
16	Wood and wood products, except furniture	38.4	40.8	40.6	41.5	24.9	..	..	..
17	Paper and paper products	53.2	38.4	..	..	31.5	..	..	..
18	Printing and reproduction of recorded media	14.8	16.3	..	..	11.3	..	..	..
19-23	Chemical, rubber, plastic, non-metallic mineral products	711.2	733.7	672.8	688.8	702.5	..	798.4	..
19	Coke and refined petroleum products	79.9	71.9	54.8	60.8	59.0	..	107.1	..
20-21	Chemical and pharmaceutical products	485.1	526.3	463.9	489.0	510.2	..	531.9	..
20	Chemicals and chemical products	246.1	233.6	192.7	237.0	246.9	..	190.7	..
21	Pharmaceuticals, medicinal, chemical and botanical products	239.1	292.7	271.2	252.0	263.3	..	341.3	..
22	Rubber and plastic products	59.0	55.2	51.4	65.7	66.6	..	69.9	..
23	Other non-metallic mineral products	87.1	80.3	102.7	73.2	66.6	..	89.5	..
24-25	Basic metals, metal products, except machinery and equipment	594.6	584.1	442.8	533.0	475.5	..	..	..
24	Basic metals	462.3	463.9	309.6	346.6	329.6	..	213.4	..
25	Fabricated metal products, except machinery and equipment	132.3	120.3	133.1	186.5	145.9	..	..	..
26-30	Computer, electronic, optical products; electrical machinery, transport equipment	1 370.4	1 220.4	1 195.2	1 229.2	1 094.5	..	..	..
26	Computer, electronic and optical products	240.6	287.4	259.6	248.8	234.4	..	..	..
27	Electrical equipment	68.6	55.5	65.8	62.6	85.5	..	..	..
28	Machinery and equipment n.e.c.	327.6	270.9	268.7	288.0	235.7	..	..	..
29	Motor vehicles, trailers and semi-trailers	565.6	449.0	460.6	469.8	434.2	..	..	..
30	Other transport equipment	167.8	157.5	140.5	160.0	104.7	..	..	..
31-33	Furniture; repair, installation of machinery and equipment	170.0	168.2	161.1	182.9	202.9	..	223.9	..
31	Furniture	5.0	6.1	6.9	7.9	12.0	..	10.8	..
32	Other manufacturing	151.0	148.2	141.3	162.0	173.3	..	189.2	..
33	Repair and installation of machinery and equipment	14.0	14.0	12.9	13.0	17.6	..	24.0	..
35-39	**ELECTRICITY, GAS, WATER AND WASTE MANAGEMENT**	181.2	256.9	287.1	280.8	246.5	..	203.1	..
35-36	Electricity, gas and water	119.5	180.2	205.8	185.1	171.1	..	120.4	..
37-39	Sewerage, waste management and remediation activities	61.7	76.7	81.3	95.7	75.5	..	82.7	..
41-43	**CONSTRUCTION**	563.2	662.8	611.6	669.3	534.4	..	556.4	..
45-99	**TOTAL SERVICES**	4 570.7	5 070.7	5 167.1	5 144.5	5 431.0	..	6 255.6	..
45-82	**Business sector services**	4 482.8	4 959.1	5 052.9	5 026.8	5 284.0	..	6 062.6	..
45-47	**Wholesale and retail trade; motor vehicle and motorcycle repairs**	712.9	701.1	627.4	550.6	564.7	..	789.1	..
49-53	**Transportation and storage**	165.7	167.2	182.5	194.4	190.9	..	233.7	..
55-56	**Accommodation and food service activities**	12.8	19.1	15.7	10.4	14.0	..	15.6	..
58-63	**Information and communication**	1 353.4	1 326.1	1 087.0	1 114.5	1 197.3	..	1 542.9	..
58-60	Publishing, audiovisual and broadcasting activities	163.8	151.4	120.9	123.4	117.6	..	176.6	..
58	Publishing activities	147.8	123.3	81.2	82.7	83.4	..	123.4	..
59-60	Motion picture, video and TV programme production; broadcasting activities	16.0	28.1	39.7	40.7	34.2	..	53.2	..
59	Motion picture, video and TV programme production; sound and music	7.8	10.0	13.5	13.5	13.2	..	..	..
60	Programming and broadcasting activities	8.2	18.1	26.2	27.2	21.1	..	..	..
61	Telecommunications	426.7	422.5	206.7	234.0	314.3	..	153.5	..
62-63	IT and other information services	762.8	752.2	759.4	757.0	765.3	..	1 212.8	..
62	Computer programming, consultancy and related activities	743.4	735.0	742.2	737.5	740.1	..	1 172.8	..
63	Information service activities	19.5	17.2	17.2	19.6	25.2	..	40.0	..
64-66	**Financial and insurance activities**	1 091.5	1 504.7	1 847.7	1 842.3	1 946.5	..	1 991.4	..
68-82	**Real estate; professional, scientific and technical; administrative and support**	1 146.7	1 240.9	1 292.7	1 315.6	1 370.5	..	1 489.8	..
68	Real estate activities	7.6	31.7	12.0	9.2	14.9	..	30.5	..
69-75x72	Professional, scientific and technical activities, except scientific R&D	480.3	590.4	585.7	636.6	658.2	..	..	..
72	Scientific research and development	526.8	516.8	472.7	427.2	448.2	..	..	..
77-82	Administrative and support service activities	132.0	101.9	222.2	242.6	249.2	..	..	..
84-99	**Community, social and personal services**	87.8	111.6	114.2	117.7	147.0	..	193.0	..
84-85	Public administration and defence; compulsory social security and education	5.2	10.8	11.1	13.4	17.3	..	21.5	..
86-88	Human health and social work activities	42.5	53.5	54.6	53.1	61.6	..	47.5	..
90-93	Arts, entertainment and recreation	20.0	23.4	23.9	27.3	47.2	..	72.6	..
94-99	Other services; household-employers; extraterritorial bodies	20.1	23.9	24.7	23.9	20.9	..	51.5	..

.. Not available

Note: Detailed metadata at: http://metalinks.oecd.org/anberd/20170419/301f.
Information on data for Israel: http://oe.cd/israel-disclaimer.

Disclaimer: http://oe.cd/disclaimer

AUSTRIA

R&D expenditure in industry by main activity of the enterprise, current prices
ISIC Rev. 4

Million USD PPP

		2007	2008	2009	2010	2011	2012	2013	2014
	TOTAL BUSINESS ENTERPRISE	5 574.1	6 124.2	6 043.6	6 567.0	6 847.5	7 734.4	8 511.7	..
01-03	**AGRICULTURE, FORESTRY AND FISHING**	1.6	1.6	1.7	2.0	2.4	3.3	4.4	..
05-09	**MINING AND QUARRYING**	8.8	7.3	5.3	6.3	7.2	6.3	3.7	..
10-33	**MANUFACTURING**	3 891.3	4 212.5	4 076.7	4 301.3	4 361.2	4 844.0	5 281.1	..
10-12	Food products, beverages and tobacco	26.3	33.9	38.1	37.5	34.5	42.1	54.4	..
13-15	Textiles, wearing apparel, leather and related products	35.8	33.4	26.8	24.7	23.3	24.9	26.3	..
13	Textiles	21.3	19.0	14.2	12.9	12.8	14.8	16.8	..
14	Wearing apparel	10.6	10.3	8.7	8.1	7.3	6.8	5.9	..
15	Leather and related products, footwear	3.9	4.1	3.9	3.7	3.2	3.3	3.6	..
16-18	Wood and paper products and printing	52.0	55.9	63.8	68.8	65.3	68.9	72.8	..
16	Wood and wood products, except furniture	15.3	17.4	21.6	21.5	18.4	20.5	25.2	..
17	Paper and paper products	16.2	15.4	17.1	23.8	28.4	30.2	28.2	..
18	Printing and reproduction of recorded media	20.4	23.2	25.2	23.5	18.6	18.1	19.4	..
19-23	Chemical, rubber, plastic, non-metallic mineral products	711.4	734.5	670.2	708.2	745.5	854.1	951.6	..
19	Coke and refined petroleum products	18.7	18.1	15.3	14.4	12.9	12.0	10.5	..
20-21	Chemical and pharmaceutical products	486.0	485.6	432.4	446.0	462.9	530.3	594.5	..
20	Chemicals and chemical products	163.8	190.0	203.9	243.5	258.0	260.6	237.0	..
21	Pharmaceuticals, medicinal, chemical and botanical products	322.2	295.5	228.5	202.5	204.8	269.7	357.5	..
22	Rubber and plastic products	123.0	139.8	135.6	146.3	157.6	191.4	227.9	..
23	Other non-metallic mineral products	83.7	91.0	86.9	101.4	112.1	120.5	118.8	..
24-25	Basic metals, metal products, except machinery and equipment	268.9	298.8	306.7	319.3	325.8	403.4	503.9	..
24	Basic metals	134.9	151.8	155.8	149.0	145.6	202.5	288.4	..
25	Fabricated metal products, except machinery and equipment	134.0	147.0	150.9	170.3	180.2	200.9	215.5	..
26-30	Computer, electronic, optical products; electrical machinery, transport equipment	2 652.0	2 896.2	2 814.9	2 957.9	2 962.4	3 232.5	3 459.2	..
26	Computer, electronic and optical products	609.6	529.6	625.5	673.8	630.1	687.6	773.0	..
27	Electrical equipment	859.3	1 097.5	979.7	944.9	885.0	888.1	863.9	..
28	Machinery and equipment n.e.c.	562.7	636.5	647.0	739.7	817.6	972.9	1 117.4	..
29	Motor vehicles, trailers and semi-trailers	479.2	492.9	437.3	463.2	489.4	545.1	581.5	..
30	Other transport equipment	141.2	139.7	125.5	136.4	140.3	138.9	123.4	..
31-33	Furniture; repair, installation of machinery and equipment	145.0	159.9	156.2	184.9	204.3	218.1	212.7	..
31	Furniture	33.1	31.9	19.9	20.6	24.1	23.0	16.4	..
32	Other manufacturing	91.6	108.5	111.0	116.5	111.1	111.6	108.1	..
33	Repair and installation of machinery and equipment	20.3	19.4	25.3	47.8	69.1	83.6	88.2	..
35-39	**ELECTRICITY, GAS, WATER AND WASTE MANAGEMENT**	15.7	15.9	15.4	20.4	24.4	25.5	22.9	..
35-36	Electricity, gas and water	10.1	11.1	12.6	16.8	19.2	20.1	18.5	..
37-39	Sewerage, waste management and remediation activities	5.6	4.8	2.8	3.6	5.2	5.4	4.4	..
41-43	**CONSTRUCTION**	23.2	26.0	34.5	49.5	57.1	57.9	50.4	..
45-99	**TOTAL SERVICES**	1 633.6	1 860.9	1 909.9	2 187.5	2 395.3	2 797.4	3 149.3	..
45-82	**Business sector services**	1 631.8	1 858.8	1 906.7	2 182.6	2 389.7	2 791.7	3 144.2	..
45-47	Wholesale and retail trade; motor vehicle and motorcycle repairs	259.7	291.3	303.6	343.3	361.3	400.3	426.9	..
49-53	Transportation and storage	9.1	9.5	7.9	6.8	6.6	9.1	12.7	..
55-56	Accommodation and food service activities	0.0	0.0	0.0	0.0	0.0	0.0	0.0	..
58-63	Information and communication	346.6	328.8	264.2	327.0	415.9	496.4	535.6	..
58-60	Publishing, audiovisual and broadcasting activities	50.4	39.8	14.0	13.7	26.4	37.8	44.8	..
58	Publishing activities	45.6	36.1	12.7	12.7	24.7	35.6	42.5	..
59-60	Motion picture, video and TV programme production; broadcasting activities	4.8	3.7	1.3	1.0	1.7	2.2	2.3	..
59	Motion picture, video and TV programme production; sound and music	..	..	..	..	..	..	..	..
60	Programming and broadcasting activities	..	..	..	..	..	..	..	..
61	Telecommunications	49.9	54.7	53.6	59.7	60.3	57.6	48.3	..
62-63	IT and other information services	246.3	234.2	196.6	253.6	329.2	400.9	442.4	..
62	Computer programming, consultancy and related activities	185.7	189.8	174.6	194.5	223.1	281.7	342.3	..
63	Information service activities	60.7	44.4	21.9	59.1	106.1	119.2	100.2	..
64-66	Financial and insurance activities	10.0	27.2	53.6	54.9	36.0	23.5	14.5	..
68-82	Real estate; professional, scientific and technical; administrative and support	1 006.4	1 202.0	1 277.3	1 450.6	1 569.7	1 862.4	2 154.5	..
68	Real estate activities	1.5	1.0	0.3	0.2	0.7	1.6	2.8	..
69-75x72	Professional, scientific and technical activities, except scientific R&D	475.4	522.4	508.6	572.4	625.3	721.0	797.2	..
72	Scientific research and development	526.2	673.6	760.8	866.6	931.0	1 128.5	1 347.1	..
77-82	Administrative and support service activities	3.3	5.1	7.6	11.3	12.8	11.4	7.3	..
84-99	Community, social and personal services	1.8	2.1	3.3	4.9	5.6	5.8	5.1	..
84-85	Public administration and defence; compulsory social security and education	1.4	1.4	2.0	2.8	3.1	3.0	2.3	..
86-88	Human health and social work activities	0.1	0.2	0.2	0.4	0.8	1.3	1.9	..
90-93	Arts, entertainment and recreation	0.0	0.3	0.6	0.7	0.6	0.4	0.3	..
94-99	Other services; household-employers; extraterritorial bodies	0.3	0.3	0.4	0.9	1.2	1.1	0.6	..

.. Not available

Note: Detailed metadata at: http://metalinks.oecd.org/anberd/20170419/301f.
Information on data for Israel: http://oe.cd/israel-disclaimer.
Disclaimer: http://oe.cd/disclaimer

AUSTRIA

R&D expenditure in industry by main activity of the enterprise, constant prices
ISIC Rev. 4

2010 USD PPP

		2007	2008	2009	2010	2011	2012	2013	2014
	TOTAL BUSINESS ENTERPRISE	**6 041.0**	**6 406.7**	**6 119.1**	**6 567.0**	**6 646.4**	**7 203.9**	**7 638.5**	..
01-03	AGRICULTURE, FORESTRY AND FISHING	1.7	1.6	1.8	2.0	2.3	3.0	3.9	..
05-09	MINING AND QUARRYING	9.5	7.7	5.4	6.3	7.0	5.9	3.3	..
10-33	MANUFACTURING	4 217.3	4 406.8	4 127.6	4 301.3	4 233.1	4 511.7	4 739.2	..
10-12	Food products, beverages and tobacco	28.5	35.5	38.6	37.5	33.5	39.2	48.8	..
13-15	Textiles, wearing apparel, leather and related products	38.8	35.0	27.1	24.7	22.7	23.2	23.6	..
13	Textiles	23.1	19.8	14.4	12.9	12.5	13.7	15.1	..
14	Wearing apparel	11.5	10.8	8.8	8.1	7.1	6.3	5.3	..
15	Leather and related products, footwear	4.2	4.3	4.0	3.7	3.1	3.1	3.2	..
16-18	Wood and paper products and printing	56.3	58.5	64.6	68.8	63.4	64.1	65.3	..
16	Wood and wood products, except furniture	16.6	18.2	21.8	21.5	17.8	19.1	22.6	..
17	Paper and paper products	17.6	16.1	17.3	23.8	27.5	28.2	25.3	..
18	Printing and reproduction of recorded media	22.1	24.2	25.5	23.5	18.0	16.8	17.4	..
19-23	Chemical, rubber, plastic, non-metallic mineral products	771.0	768.3	678.6	708.2	723.6	795.6	854.0	..
19	Coke and refined petroleum products	20.3	18.9	15.5	14.4	12.6	11.2	9.4	..
20-21	Chemical and pharmaceutical products	526.7	508.0	437.8	446.0	449.3	493.9	533.5	..
20	Chemicals and chemical products	177.5	198.8	206.4	243.5	250.5	242.7	212.7	..
21	Pharmaceuticals, medicinal, chemical and botanical products	349.2	309.2	231.3	202.5	198.8	251.2	320.8	..
22	Rubber and plastic products	133.3	146.2	137.3	146.3	152.9	178.3	204.5	..
23	Other non-metallic mineral products	90.7	95.2	88.0	101.4	108.8	112.2	106.6	..
24-25	Basic metals, metal products, except machinery and equipment	291.4	312.6	310.5	319.3	316.3	375.7	452.2	..
24	Basic metals	146.2	158.8	157.7	149.0	141.4	188.6	258.8	..
25	Fabricated metal products, except machinery and equipment	145.2	153.8	152.8	170.3	174.9	187.1	193.4	..
26-30	Computer, electronic, optical products; electrical machinery, transport equipment	2 874.2	3 029.8	2 850.1	2 957.9	2 875.4	3 010.8	3 104.3	..
26	Computer, electronic and optical products	660.7	554.1	633.3	673.8	611.6	640.4	693.7	..
27	Electrical equipment	931.3	1 148.1	991.9	944.9	859.0	827.1	775.3	..
28	Machinery and equipment n.e.c.	609.9	665.9	655.0	739.7	793.6	906.1	1 002.8	..
29	Motor vehicles, trailers and semi-trailers	519.3	515.6	442.8	463.2	475.1	507.7	521.9	..
30	Other transport equipment	153.0	146.1	127.1	136.4	136.2	129.4	110.7	..
31-33	Furniture; repair, installation of machinery and equipment	157.1	167.2	158.2	184.9	198.3	203.1	190.9	..
31	Furniture	35.8	33.4	20.2	20.6	23.4	21.4	14.7	..
32	Other manufacturing	99.3	113.6	112.4	116.5	107.9	103.9	97.0	..
33	Repair and installation of machinery and equipment	22.0	20.3	25.6	47.8	67.0	77.8	79.2	..
35-39	ELECTRICITY, GAS, WATER AND WASTE MANAGEMENT	17.0	16.6	15.6	20.4	23.7	23.8	20.6	..
35-36	Electricity, gas and water	10.9	11.6	12.7	16.8	18.7	18.7	16.6	..
37-39	Sewerage, waste management and remediation activities	6.1	5.0	2.8	3.6	5.0	5.1	4.0	..
41-43	CONSTRUCTION	25.1	27.1	35.0	49.5	55.4	53.9	45.2	..
45-99	**TOTAL SERVICES**	**1 770.4**	**1 946.8**	**1 933.8**	**2 187.5**	**2 324.9**	**2 605.5**	**2 826.2**	..
45-82	**Business sector services**	**1 768.5**	**1 944.6**	**1 930.5**	**2 182.6**	**2 319.5**	**2 600.2**	**2 821.6**	..
45-47	Wholesale and retail trade; motor vehicle and motorcycle repairs	281.5	304.8	307.4	343.3	350.7	372.8	383.1	..
49-53	Transportation and storage	9.8	10.0	8.0	6.8	6.4	8.5	11.4	..
55-56	Accommodation and food service activities	0.0	0.0	0.0	0.0	0.0	0.0	0.0	..
58-63	Information and communication	375.6	343.9	267.5	327.0	403.7	462.3	480.6	..
58-60	Publishing, audiovisual and broadcasting activities	54.6	41.7	14.2	13.7	25.7	35.2	40.2	..
58	Publishing activities	49.5	37.8	12.9	12.7	24.0	33.2	38.2	..
59-60	Motion picture, video and TV programme production; broadcasting activities	5.2	3.9	1.3	1.0	1.7	2.1	2.0	..
59	Motion picture, video and TV programme production; sound and music	..	..	..	..	..	..	..	..
60	Programming and broadcasting activities	..	..	..	..	..	..	..	..
61	Telecommunications	54.0	57.2	54.2	59.7	58.6	53.7	43.4	..
62-63	IT and other information services	267.0	245.0	199.0	253.6	319.5	373.4	397.0	..
62	Computer programming, consultancy and related activities	201.2	198.6	176.8	194.5	216.5	262.4	307.1	..
63	Information service activities	65.7	46.4	22.2	59.1	103.0	111.0	89.9	..
64-66	Financial and insurance activities	10.9	28.4	54.3	54.9	35.0	21.9	13.0	..
68-82	Real estate; professional, scientific and technical; administrative and support	1 090.7	1 257.5	1 293.2	1 450.6	1 523.6	1 734.6	1 933.4	..
68	Real estate activities	1.6	1.0	0.3	0.2	0.6	1.5	2.5	..
69-75x72	Professional, scientific and technical activities, except scientific R&D	515.2	546.5	514.9	572.4	606.9	671.5	715.4	..
72	Scientific research and development	570.3	704.6	770.3	866.6	903.7	1 051.0	1 208.9	..
77-82	Administrative and support service activities	3.6	5.3	7.7	11.3	12.4	10.6	6.6	..
84-99	Community, social and personal services	1.9	2.2	3.3	4.9	5.4	5.4	4.6	..
84-85	Public administration and defence; compulsory social security and education	1.5	1.5	2.0	2.8	3.0	2.7	2.1	..
86-88	Human health and social work activities	0.1	0.2	0.2	0.4	0.8	1.2	1.7	..
90-93	Arts, entertainment and recreation	0.0	0.3	0.7	0.7	0.6	0.4	0.3	..
94-99	Other services; household-employers; extraterritorial bodies	0.3	0.3	0.4	0.9	1.1	1.0	0.6	..

.. Not available

Note: Detailed metadata at: http://metalinks.oecd.org/anberd/20170419/301f.
      Information on data for Israel: http://oe.cd/israel-disclaimer.

Disclaimer: http://oe.cd/disclaimer

BELGIUM

R&D expenditure in industry by main activity of the enterprise, current prices
ISIC Rev. 4

Million USD PPP

		2007	2008	2009	2010	2011	2012	2013	2014
	TOTAL BUSINESS ENTERPRISE	5 022.2	5 363.7	5 388.0	6 021.0	6 747.6	7 898.1	8 375.0	..
01-03	**AGRICULTURE, FORESTRY AND FISHING**	32.4	31.0	31.9	29.8	31.1	18.6	20.4	..
05-09	**MINING AND QUARRYING**	2.2	2.0	1.9	6.0	7.7	1.5	2.3	..
10-33	**MANUFACTURING**	3 413.4	3 470.7	3 480.9	3 611.7	4 246.0	4 887.6	5 150.1	..
10-12	Food products, beverages and tobacco	106.8	109.5	120.0	134.0	146.3	132.7	138.5	..
13-15	Textiles, wearing apparel, leather and related products	58.7	53.3	54.2	60.2	68.0	59.7	67.8	..
13	Textiles	47.6	44.5	45.8	49.9	52.4	40.6	46.3	..
14	Wearing apparel	4.8	2.5	2.7	6.2	6.4	7.4	8.7	..
15	Leather and related products, footwear	6.3	6.4	5.6	4.1	9.2	11.6	12.8	..
16-18	Wood and paper products and printing	17.6	20.2	22.2	19.5	23.4	32.3	36.5	..
16	Wood and wood products, except furniture	6.6	5.7	6.1	6.0	6.8	14.9	17.0	..
17	Paper and paper products	9.3	10.0	10.7	9.8	12.5	13.2	14.6	..
18	Printing and reproduction of recorded media	1.7	4.5	5.4	3.6	4.1	4.3	4.9	..
19-23	Chemical, rubber, plastic, non-metallic mineral products	1 794.6	1 826.5	1 858.3	1 899.4	2 331.7	2 924.5	3 068.3	..
19	Coke and refined petroleum products	20.8	13.9	14.9	6.8	7.9	11.5	12.1	..
20-21	Chemical and pharmaceutical products	1 590.1	1 655.1	1 674.8	1 717.8	2 137.4	2 733.2	2 874.8	..
20	Chemicals and chemical products	339.2	341.4	325.8	348.9	421.0	458.4	461.1	..
21	Pharmaceuticals, medicinal, chemical and botanical products	1 250.9	1 313.8	1 349.1	1 368.9	1 716.4	2 274.8	2 413.7	..
22	Rubber and plastic products	129.4	98.8	96.4	102.8	109.6	111.9	113.0	..
23	Other non-metallic mineral products	54.2	58.8	72.2	72.0	76.9	68.0	68.3	..
24-25	Basic metals, metal products, except machinery and equipment	193.5	178.6	184.8	237.0	276.0	299.5	288.1	..
24	Basic metals	111.2	113.2	111.6	136.0	169.0	171.7	155.3	..
25	Fabricated metal products, except machinery and equipment	82.3	65.5	73.3	101.0	107.0	127.9	132.8	..
26-30	Computer, electronic, optical products; electrical machinery, transport equipment	1 200.3	1 246.4	1 200.4	1 224.8	1 359.4	1 378.5	1 482.5	..
26	Computer, electronic and optical products	532.7	544.0	533.1	489.6	511.4	555.7	593.9	..
27	Electrical equipment	198.0	251.9	231.8	241.7	266.7	169.4	170.5	..
28	Machinery and equipment n.e.c.	273.9	248.2	227.5	260.2	289.0	359.7	376.3	..
29	Motor vehicles, trailers and semi-trailers	95.0	101.7	99.2	106.4	136.2	153.6	183.8	..
30	Other transport equipment	100.6	100.5	108.9	127.0	156.2	140.1	157.9	..
31-33	Furniture; repair, installation of machinery and equipment	41.8	36.1	40.9	36.8	41.1	60.4	68.5	..
31	Furniture	..	9.5	10.7	9.7	10.4	12.5	12.6	..
32	Other manufacturing	..	11.9	15.1	14.2	16.2	21.1	25.0	..
33	Repair and installation of machinery and equipment	..	14.8	15.1	12.9	14.5	26.8	30.9	..
35-39	**ELECTRICITY, GAS, WATER AND WASTE MANAGEMENT**	10.7	29.0	19.5	60.7	68.8	107.3	127.5	..
35-36	Electricity, gas and water	..	21.1	11.6	41.9	51.7	91.3	105.0	..
37-39	Sewerage, waste management and remediation activities	..	7.9	7.9	18.9	17.2	15.9	22.5	..
41-43	**CONSTRUCTION**	64.3	51.7	58.6	76.3	67.6	44.0	48.7	..
45-99	**TOTAL SERVICES**	1 499.2	1 779.0	1 795.1	2 236.3	2 326.4	2 839.0	3 026.0	..
45-82	**Business sector services**	1 486.0	1 772.3	1 787.5	2 224.9	2 311.9	2 833.5	3 020.4	..
45-47	Wholesale and retail trade; motor vehicle and motorcycle repairs	88.1	128.3	128.1	167.0	162.1	339.3	353.7	..
49-53	Transportation and storage	15.7	14.5	19.6	14.5	18.1	17.0	21.5	..
55-56	Accommodation and food service activities	1.5	1.1	1.3	0.0	0.0	0.1	0.0	..
58-63	Information and communication	445.1	427.8	441.0	592.5	670.6	659.9	673.8	..
58-60	Publishing, audiovisual and broadcasting activities	..	23.0	22.1	27.4	31.9	51.1	55.9	..
58	Publishing activities	..	15.0	14.9	20.2	22.1	44.8	47.9	..
59-60	Motion picture, video and TV programme production; broadcasting activities	..	8.0	7.1	7.2	9.8	6.2	8.0	..
59	Motion picture, video and TV programme production; sound and music	..	2.7	2.2	5.3	7.5	3.6	4.5	..
60	Programming and broadcasting activities	..	5.2	4.9	1.9	2.3	2.6	3.5	..
61	Telecommunications	179.6	142.0	140.5	206.9	249.7	112.4	94.6	..
62-63	IT and other information services	..	262.8	278.5	358.1	389.0	496.5	523.3	..
62	Computer programming, consultancy and related activities	..	228.9	240.9	319.8	353.3	460.9	486.0	..
63	Information service activities	..	33.9	37.6	38.3	35.7	35.6	37.3	..
64-66	Financial and insurance activities	97.4	118.9	122.7	120.7	125.9	214.1	218.5	..
68-82	Real estate; professional, scientific and technical; administrative and support	838.3	1 081.5	1 074.8	1 330.3	1 335.2	1 603.2	1 752.9	..
68	Real estate activities	..	0.2	0.3	0.9	0.9	1.4	1.5	..
69-75x72	Professional, scientific and technical activities, except scientific R&D	..	505.6	496.9	661.0	682.0	743.2	831.7	..
72	Scientific research and development	485.6	439.5	461.2	637.0	618.6	809.7	870.6	..
77-82	Administrative and support service activities	..	136.3	116.4	31.3	33.7	48.8	49.1	..
84-99	Community, social and personal services	13.1	6.6	7.6	11.4	14.5	5.5	5.6	..
84-85	Public administration and defence; compulsory social security and education	..	0.9	1.0	0.9	1.0	..	..	..
86-88	Human health and social work activities	..	5.1	5.2	9.2	12.0	4.1	4.0	..
90-93	Arts, entertainment and recreation	..	0.0	0.4	0.0	0.0	..	..	..
94-99	Other services; household-employers; extraterritorial bodies	..	0.6	1.0	1.3	1.5	0.6	0.7	..

.. Not available

Note: Detailed metadata at: http://metalinks.oecd.org/anberd/20170419/301f.
   Information on data for Israel: http://oe.cd/israel-disclaimer.
Disclaimer: http://oe.cd/disclaimer

BELGIUM

R&D expenditure in industry by main activity of the enterprise, constant prices
ISIC Rev. 4

2010 USD PPP

		2007	2008	2009	2010	2011	2012	2013	2014
	TOTAL BUSINESS ENTERPRISE	5 545.9	5 722.3	5 584.4	6 021.0	6 590.4	7 468.5	7 670.1	..
01-03	**AGRICULTURE, FORESTRY AND FISHING**	35.7	33.1	33.0	29.8	30.3	17.6	18.7	..
05-09	**MINING AND QUARRYING**	2.5	2.1	2.0	6.0	7.6	1.4	2.1	..
10-33	**MANUFACTURING**	3 769.4	3 702.8	3 607.8	3 611.7	4 147.1	4 621.8	4 716.7	..
10-12	Food products, beverages and tobacco	117.9	116.8	124.4	134.0	142.9	125.5	126.8	..
13-15	Textiles, wearing apparel, leather and related products	64.8	56.9	56.1	60.2	66.5	56.5	62.1	..
13	Textiles	52.6	47.4	47.5	49.9	51.2	38.4	42.4	..
14	Wearing apparel	5.3	2.6	2.8	6.2	6.2	7.0	8.0	..
15	Leather and related products, footwear	7.0	6.8	5.8	4.1	9.0	11.0	11.7	..
16-18	Wood and paper products and printing	19.5	21.6	23.0	19.5	22.9	30.6	33.4	..
16	Wood and wood products, except furniture	7.3	6.1	6.3	6.0	6.7	14.1	15.6	..
17	Paper and paper products	10.3	10.7	11.0	9.8	12.2	12.4	13.3	..
18	Printing and reproduction of recorded media	1.9	4.8	5.6	3.6	4.0	4.0	4.4	..
19-23	Chemical, rubber, plastic, non-metallic mineral products	1 981.8	1 948.7	1 926.0	1 899.4	2 277.4	2 765.5	2 810.0	..
19	Coke and refined petroleum products	23.0	14.8	15.4	6.8	7.7	10.8	11.1	..
20-21	Chemical and pharmaceutical products	1 756.0	1 765.8	1 735.9	1 717.8	2 087.6	2 584.6	2 632.9	..
20	Chemicals and chemical products	374.6	364.2	337.6	348.9	411.2	433.4	422.3	..
21	Pharmaceuticals, medicinal, chemical and botanical products	1 381.3	1 401.6	1 398.3	1 368.9	1 676.4	2 151.1	2 210.6	..
22	Rubber and plastic products	142.9	105.4	99.9	102.8	107.0	105.8	103.5	..
23	Other non-metallic mineral products	59.9	62.7	74.8	72.0	75.1	64.3	62.6	..
24-25	Basic metals, metal products, except machinery and equipment	213.7	190.6	191.6	237.0	269.5	283.2	263.9	..
24	Basic metals	122.8	120.7	115.7	136.0	165.1	162.3	142.2	..
25	Fabricated metal products, except machinery and equipment	90.9	69.8	75.9	101.0	104.5	120.9	121.6	..
26-30	Computer, electronic, optical products; electrical machinery, transport equipment	1 325.5	1 329.8	1 244.2	1 224.8	1 327.8	1 303.5	1 357.7	..
26	Computer, electronic and optical products	588.3	580.4	552.5	489.6	499.5	525.5	543.9	..
27	Electrical equipment	218.6	268.7	240.3	241.7	260.4	160.1	156.2	..
28	Machinery and equipment n.e.c.	302.5	264.8	235.8	260.2	282.2	340.2	344.6	..
29	Motor vehicles, trailers and semi-trailers	104.9	108.5	102.8	106.4	133.1	145.3	168.3	..
30	Other transport equipment	111.1	107.2	112.9	127.0	152.5	132.4	144.6	..
31-33	Furniture; repair, installation of machinery and equipment	46.2	38.6	42.4	36.8	40.1	57.1	62.8	..
31	Furniture	..	10.2	11.1	9.7	10.2	11.8	11.5	..
32	Other manufacturing	..	12.7	15.6	14.2	15.8	20.0	22.9	..
33	Repair and installation of machinery and equipment	..	15.7	15.6	12.9	14.2	25.3	28.3	..
35-39	**ELECTRICITY, GAS, WATER AND WASTE MANAGEMENT**	11.8	31.0	20.2	60.7	67.2	101.4	116.8	..
35-36	Electricity, gas and water	..	22.5	12.1	41.9	50.5	86.4	96.1	..
37-39	Sewerage, waste management and remediation activities	..	8.4	8.1	18.9	16.8	15.1	20.6	..
41-43	**CONSTRUCTION**	71.0	55.2	60.8	76.3	66.0	41.6	44.6	..
45-99	**TOTAL SERVICES**	1 655.5	1 897.9	1 860.6	2 236.3	2 272.2	2 684.6	2 771.3	..
45-82	**Business sector services**	1 641.0	1 890.8	1 852.7	2 224.9	2 258.0	2 679.4	2 766.2	..
45-47	Wholesale and retail trade; motor vehicle and motorcycle repairs	97.3	136.9	132.8	167.0	158.3	320.8	323.9	..
49-53	Transportation and storage	17.3	15.5	20.4	14.5	17.7	16.1	19.7	..
55-56	Accommodation and food service activities	1.7	1.2	1.3	0.0	0.0	0.1	0.0	..
58-63	Information and communication	491.5	456.4	457.1	592.5	655.0	624.0	617.1	..
58-60	Publishing, audiovisual and broadcasting activities	..	24.5	22.9	27.4	31.2	48.3	51.2	..
58	Publishing activities	..	16.0	15.5	20.2	21.6	42.4	43.8	..
59-60	Motion picture, video and TV programme production; broadcasting activities	..	8.5	7.4	7.2	9.6	5.9	7.3	..
59	Motion picture, video and TV programme production; sound and music	..	2.9	2.3	5.3	7.3	3.4	4.1	..
60	Programming and broadcasting activities	..	5.6	5.1	1.9	2.2	2.5	3.2	..
61	Telecommunications	198.3	151.5	145.6	206.9	243.8	106.3	86.6	..
62-63	IT and other information services	..	280.4	288.7	358.1	379.9	469.5	479.3	..
62	Computer programming, consultancy and related activities	..	244.2	249.7	319.8	345.1	435.8	445.1	..
63	Information service activities	..	36.2	39.0	38.3	34.9	33.6	34.2	..
64-66	Financial and insurance activities	107.5	126.9	127.2	120.7	122.9	202.4	200.1	..
68-82	Real estate; professional, scientific and technical; administrative and support	925.7	1 153.8	1 113.9	1 330.3	1 304.1	1 516.0	1 605.3	..
68	Real estate activities	..	0.2	0.3	0.9	0.9	1.3	1.4	..
69-75x72	Professional, scientific and technical activities, except scientific R&D	..	539.4	515.0	661.0	666.1	702.8	761.7	..
72	Scientific research and development	536.2	468.9	478.0	637.0	604.2	765.7	797.3	..
77-82	Administrative and support service activities	..	145.4	120.7	31.3	32.9	46.2	45.0	..
84-99	Community, social and personal services	14.5	7.1	7.9	11.4	14.1	5.2	5.1	..
84-85	Public administration and defence; compulsory social security and education	..	1.0	1.1	0.9	0.9	..	..	..
86-88	Human health and social work activities	..	5.5	5.4	9.2	11.7	3.8	3.6	..
90-93	Arts, entertainment and recreation	..	0.0	0.4	0.0	0.0	..	..	..
94-99	Other services; household-employers; extraterritorial bodies	..	0.6	1.0	1.3	1.4	0.6	0.6	..

.. Not available

Note: Detailed metadata at: http://metalinks.oecd.org/anberd/20170419/301f.
Information on data for Israel: http://oe.cd/israel-disclaimer.

Disclaimer: http://oe.cd/disclaimer

BELGIUM

R&D expenditure in industry by product field, current prices
ISIC Rev. 4

Million USD PPP

		2007	2008	2009	2010	2011	2012	2013	2014
	TOTAL BUSINESS ENTERPRISE	5 022.2	5 363.7	5 388.0	6 021.0	6 747.6	7 898.1	8 375.0	..
01-03	**AGRICULTURE, FORESTRY AND FISHING**	78.2	78.2	92.5	96.9	104.3	79.0	89.9	..
05-09	**MINING AND QUARRYING**	2.2	1.9	1.9	6.1	7.8	6.8	6.0	..
10-33	**MANUFACTURING**	3 824.4	3 909.0	3 937.5	4 463.6	5 071.8	6 143.2	6 481.2	..
10-12	Food products, beverages and tobacco	134.2	143.8	149.9	182.4	180.8	200.7	202.2	..
13-15	Textiles, wearing apparel, leather and related products	56.5	52.9	54.1	62.0	71.0	74.6	84.3	..
13	Textiles	45.5	44.2	45.9	49.5	52.0	50.3	56.9	..
14	Wearing apparel	4.7	2.3	2.5	6.3	6.5	12.6	14.6	..
15	Leather and related products, footwear	6.3	6.4	5.6	6.2	12.4	11.6	12.8	..
16-18	Wood and paper products and printing	20.6	25.2	25.5	17.9	21.9	32.8	37.6	..
16	Wood and wood products, except furniture	6.6	5.5	6.0	5.5	6.3	14.6	17.2	..
17	Paper and paper products	12.9	17.3	17.0	9.8	12.5	14.0	15.6	..
18	Printing and reproduction of recorded media	1.1	2.4	2.5	2.6	3.1	4.2	4.8	..
19-23	Chemical, rubber, plastic, non-metallic mineral products	2 088.7	2 222.7	2 271.7	2 593.0	3 016.1	3 688.1	3 862.5	..
19	Coke and refined petroleum products	22.0	12.3	13.1	7.2	8.0	12.0	12.4	..
20-21	Chemical and pharmaceutical products	1 858.8	2 001.9	2 041.1	2 345.7	2 756.5	3 454.1	3 626.0	..
20	Chemicals and chemical products	430.8	522.9	500.5	605.9	688.2	774.8	779.1	..
21	Pharmaceuticals, medicinal, chemical and botanical products	1 428.0	1 478.9	1 540.6	1 739.8	2 068.3	2 679.4	2 846.9	..
22	Rubber and plastic products	147.7	141.4	135.7	155.3	160.0	129.7	130.1	..
23	Other non-metallic mineral products	60.2	67.1	81.8	84.8	91.5	92.2	94.1	..
24-25	Basic metals, metal products, except machinery and equipment	228.4	250.8	252.8	286.5	345.9	342.8	333.4	..
24	Basic metals	121.7	118.2	117.5	162.2	199.3	210.1	193.9	..
25	Fabricated metal products, except machinery and equipment	106.7	132.6	135.3	124.3	146.5	132.7	139.5	..
26-30	Computer, electronic, optical products; electrical machinery, transport equipment	1 270.3	1 191.8	1 158.6	1 289.9	1 401.2	1 747.1	1 894.5	..
26	Computer, electronic and optical products	750.2	667.0	646.8	520.6	541.4	643.7	685.7	..
27	Electrical equipment	57.1	82.3	78.4	176.6	201.6	172.5	173.9	..
28	Machinery and equipment n.e.c.	224.3	240.5	222.3	266.6	295.4	371.9	389.8	..
29	Motor vehicles, trailers and semi-trailers	140.0	94.4	94.3	194.5	201.8	400.1	461.0	..
30	Other transport equipment	98.6	107.6	116.7	131.7	161.0	158.9	184.3	..
31-33	Furniture; repair, installation of machinery and equipment	25.8	21.8	24.8	32.0	35.0	57.1	66.6	..
31	Furniture	..	..	..	8.7	9.2	13.8	14.3	..
32	Other manufacturing	..	..	..	21.2	23.3	39.6	48.5	..
33	Repair and installation of machinery and equipment	..	..	..	2.1	2.5	3.7	3.9	..
35-39	**ELECTRICITY, GAS, WATER AND WASTE MANAGEMENT**	21.1	31.2	17.4	62.1	70.0	132.2	155.1	..
35-36	Electricity, gas and water	..	..	..	42.5	52.1	113.7	129.7	..
37-39	Sewerage, waste management and remediation activities	..	..	..	19.6	17.9	18.5	25.4	..
41-43	**CONSTRUCTION**	68.1	52.4	57.7	80.4	73.7	79.2	84.9	..
45-99	**TOTAL SERVICES**	1 028.2	1 290.9	1 280.9	1 312.0	1 420.0	1 457.6	1 558.0	..
45-82	**Business sector services**	1 007.1	1 276.7	1 266.7	1 295.2	1 399.8	1 407.4	1 499.0	..
45-47	Wholesale and retail trade; motor vehicle and motorcycle repairs	78.7	46.2	51.2	83.5	75.7	63.8	75.6	..
49-53	Transportation and storage	15.5	14.0	19.0	15.1	18.4	16.3	20.0	..
55-56	Accommodation and food service activities	1.5	1.8	2.1	0.0	0.0	0.1	0.1	..
58-63	Information and communication	497.5	715.0	705.4	700.6	775.2	748.6	773.3	..
58-60	Publishing, audiovisual and broadcasting activities	..	..	..	27.4	31.7	29.8	31.1	..
58	Publishing activities	..	..	..	20.2	21.9	22.7	22.1	..
59-60	Motion picture, video and TV programme production; broadcasting activities	..	..	..	7.2	9.8	718.9	742.2	..
59	Motion picture, video and TV programme production; sound and music	..	..	..	..	..	..	..	..
60	Programming and broadcasting activities	..	..	..	..	..	..	..	..
61	Telecommunications	179.7	259.7	254.2	310.0	350.2	161.4	145.7	..
62-63	IT and other information services	..	..	..	363.1	393.2	557.5	596.6	..
62	Computer programming, consultancy and related activities	..	..	..	324.3	356.8	512.0	549.0	..
63	Information service activities	..	..	..	38.8	36.5	45.6	47.6	..
64-66	**Financial and insurance activities**	61.5	78.0	82.2	114.3	119.5	111.5	106.6	..
68-82	**Real estate; professional, scientific and technical; administrative and support**	352.4	421.7	406.8	381.8	411.0	467.0	523.3	..
68	Real estate activities	..	..	..	0.9	0.9	2.9	3.0	..
69-75x72	Professional, scientific and technical activities, except scientific R&D	..	..	..	345.0	370.1	446.2	500.5	..
72	Scientific research and development	1.8	6.9	8.8	4.9	6.2	7.4	7.6	..
77-82	Administrative and support service activities	..	..	..	30.9	33.8	10.5	12.2	..
84-99	**Community, social and personal services**	21.1	14.3	14.3	16.8	20.1	50.2	59.0	..
84-85	Public administration and defence; compulsory social security and education	..	..	..	1.0	1.1	4.3	4.5	..
86-88	Human health and social work activities	..	..	..	15.5	18.7	44.3	52.8	..
90-93	Arts, entertainment and recreation	..	..	..	0.0	0.0	0.2	0.2	..
94-99	Other services; household-employers; extraterritorial bodies	..	..	..	0.3	0.4	1.5	1.6	..

.. Not available

Note: Detailed metadata at: http://metalinks.oecd.org/anberd/20170419/301f.
   Information on data for Israel: http://oe.cd/israel-disclaimer.
Disclaimer: http://oe.cd/disclaimer

BELGIUM

R&D expenditure in industry by product field, constant prices
ISIC Rev. 4

2010 USD PPP

		2007	2008	2009	2010	2011	2012	2013	2014
	TOTAL BUSINESS ENTERPRISE	**5 545.9**	**5 722.3**	**5 584.4**	**6 021.0**	**6 590.4**	**7 468.5**	**7 670.1**	..
01-03	**AGRICULTURE, FORESTRY AND FISHING**	86.4	83.4	95.9	96.9	101.9	74.7	82.3	..
05-09	**MINING AND QUARRYING**	2.5	2.1	2.0	6.1	7.6	6.5	5.5	..
10-33	**MANUFACTURING**	4 223.2	4 170.4	4 081.0	4 463.6	4 953.7	5 809.1	5 935.7	..
10-12	Food products, beverages and tobacco	148.2	153.5	155.4	182.4	176.6	189.7	185.1	..
13-15	Textiles, wearing apparel, leather and related products	62.3	56.4	56.1	62.0	69.3	70.5	77.2	..
13	Textiles	50.2	47.2	47.6	49.5	50.8	47.6	52.1	..
14	Wearing apparel	5.2	2.5	2.6	6.3	6.4	12.0	13.3	..
15	Leather and related products, footwear	7.0	6.8	5.8	6.2	12.1	11.0	11.7	..
16-18	Wood and paper products and printing	22.8	26.8	26.5	17.9	21.4	31.0	34.5	..
16	Wood and wood products, except furniture	7.3	5.9	6.2	5.5	6.1	13.8	15.8	..
17	Paper and paper products	14.3	18.4	17.7	9.8	12.2	13.2	14.3	..
18	Printing and reproduction of recorded media	1.2	2.6	2.6	2.6	3.0	4.0	4.4	..
19-23	Chemical, rubber, plastic, non-metallic mineral products	2 306.5	2 371.3	2 354.5	2 593.0	2 945.8	3 487.5	3 537.4	..
19	Coke and refined petroleum products	24.3	13.1	13.6	7.2	7.8	11.4	11.4	..
20-21	Chemical and pharmaceutical products	2 052.6	2 135.7	2 115.5	2 345.7	2 692.3	3 266.3	3 320.8	..
20	Chemicals and chemical products	475.7	557.9	518.7	605.9	672.2	732.6	713.5	..
21	Pharmaceuticals, medicinal, chemical and botanical products	1 576.9	1 577.8	1 596.8	1 739.8	2 020.1	2 533.7	2 607.3	..
22	Rubber and plastic products	163.1	150.9	140.7	155.3	156.3	122.7	119.1	..
23	Other non-metallic mineral products	66.5	71.6	84.8	84.8	89.4	87.2	86.2	..
24-25	Basic metals, metal products, except machinery and equipment	252.2	267.6	262.1	286.5	337.8	324.2	305.3	..
24	Basic metals	134.4	126.1	121.8	162.2	194.7	198.7	177.6	..
25	Fabricated metal products, except machinery and equipment	117.8	141.4	140.2	124.3	143.1	125.5	127.8	..
26-30	Computer, electronic, optical products; electrical machinery, transport equipment	1 402.7	1 271.5	1 200.8	1 289.9	1 368.6	1 652.1	1 735.1	..
26	Computer, electronic and optical products	828.5	711.6	670.4	520.6	528.8	608.7	628.0	..
27	Electrical equipment	63.0	87.9	81.3	176.6	196.9	163.1	159.2	..
28	Machinery and equipment n.e.c.	247.7	256.5	230.4	266.6	288.6	351.6	357.0	..
29	Motor vehicles, trailers and semi-trailers	154.6	100.7	97.8	194.5	197.1	378.3	422.2	..
30	Other transport equipment	108.9	114.8	121.0	131.7	157.2	150.3	168.7	..
31-33	Furniture; repair, installation of machinery and equipment	28.4	23.3	25.7	32.0	34.1	54.0	61.0	..
31	Furniture	..	..	..	8.7	9.0	13.0	13.1	..
32	Other manufacturing	..	..	..	21.2	22.7	37.5	44.4	..
33	Repair and installation of machinery and equipment	..	..	..	2.1	2.4	3.5	3.5	..
35-39	**ELECTRICITY, GAS, WATER AND WASTE MANAGEMENT**	23.3	33.3	18.0	62.1	68.3	125.0	142.0	..
35-36	Electricity, gas and water	..	..	..	42.5	50.9	107.5	118.8	..
37-39	Sewerage, waste management and remediation activities	..	..	..	19.6	17.5	17.5	23.2	..
41-43	**CONSTRUCTION**	75.2	55.9	59.9	80.4	72.0	74.9	77.7	..
45-99	**TOTAL SERVICES**	**1 135.4**	**1 377.2**	**1 327.6**	**1 312.0**	**1 386.9**	**1 378.3**	**1 426.9**	..
45-82	**Business sector services**	**1 112.1**	**1 362.0**	**1 312.8**	**1 295.2**	**1 367.2**	**1 330.8**	**1 372.8**	..
45-47	Wholesale and retail trade; motor vehicle and motorcycle repairs	86.9	49.3	53.1	83.5	73.9	60.4	69.3	..
49-53	Transportation and storage	17.1	15.0	19.7	15.1	18.0	15.4	18.3	..
55-56	Accommodation and food service activities	1.7	1.9	2.2	0.0	0.0	0.1	0.1	..
58-63	Information and communication	549.4	762.8	731.1	700.6	757.2	707.9	708.2	..
58-60	Publishing, audiovisual and broadcasting activities	..	..	..	27.4	31.0	28.1	28.5	..
58	Publishing activities	..	..	..	20.2	21.4	21.4	20.2	..
59-60	Motion picture, video and TV programme production; broadcasting activities	..	..	..	7.2	9.6	679.8	679.8	..
59	Motion picture, video and TV programme production; sound and music	..	..	..	..	..	..	..	..
60	Programming and broadcasting activities	..	..	..	..	..	..	..	..
61	Telecommunications	198.4	277.0	263.5	310.0	342.1	152.6	133.4	..
62-63	IT and other information services	..	..	..	363.1	384.1	527.2	546.4	..
62	Computer programming, consultancy and related activities	..	..	..	324.3	348.4	484.1	502.8	..
63	Information service activities	..	..	..	38.8	35.6	43.1	43.6	..
64-66	**Financial and insurance activities**	67.9	83.2	85.2	114.3	116.7	105.4	97.6	..
68-82	**Real estate; professional, scientific and technical; administrative and support**	389.1	449.9	421.6	381.8	401.4	441.6	479.3	..
68	Real estate activities	..	..	..	0.9	0.9	2.7	2.8	..
69-75x72	Professional, scientific and technical activities, except scientific R&D	..	..	..	345.0	361.5	421.9	458.3	..
72	Scientific research and development	2.0	7.4	9.1	4.9	6.0	7.0	7.0	..
77-82	Administrative and support service activities	..	..	..	30.9	33.0	10.0	11.2	..
84-99	Community, social and personal services	23.3	15.2	14.8	16.8	19.7	47.5	54.0	..
84-85	Public administration and defence; compulsory social security and education	..	..	..	1.0	1.0	4.0	4.1	..
86-88	Human health and social work activities	..	..	..	15.5	18.2	41.9	48.3	..
90-93	Arts, entertainment and recreation	..	..	..	0.0	0.0	0.2	0.2	..
94-99	Other services; household-employers; extraterritorial bodies	..	..	..	0.3	0.4	1.4	1.4	..

.. Not available

Note: Detailed metadata at: http://metalinks.oecd.org/anberd/20170419/301f.
Information on data for Israel: http://oe.cd/israel-disclaimer.

Disclaimer: http://oe.cd/disclaimer

CANADA

R&D expenditure in industry by main activity of the enterprise, current prices
ISIC Rev. 4

Million USD PPP

		2007	2008	2009	2010	2011	2012	2013	2014
	TOTAL BUSINESS ENTERPRISE	13 813.9	13 483.6	13 348.1	12 941.2	13 625.3	13 417.9	13 113.7	12 841.8
01-03	**AGRICULTURE, FORESTRY AND FISHING**	147.6	108.6	105.7	107.3	116.9	77.9	66.3	68.8
05-09	**MINING AND QUARRYING**	643.8	793.9	773.2	803.4	1 118.6	1 292.0	1 296.5	1 166.3
10-33	**MANUFACTURING**	6 982.3	6 291.0	6 496.0	6 032.9	5 973.0	5 782.5	5 542.6	5 506.5
10-12	Food products, beverages and tobacco	150.9	161.2	167.3	158.9	136.3	126.9	115.7	122.1
13-15	Textiles, wearing apparel, leather and related products	73.0	68.8	67.4	59.8	66.9	48.1	34.4	38.8
13	Textiles	42.2	38.9	39.1	36.0	35.0	25.7	21.3	24.3
14	Wearing apparel	..	..	25.0	20.5	28.7	19.1	9.8	10.9
15	Leather and related products, footwear	..	..	3.3	3.3	3.2	3.2	3.3	3.6
16-18	Wood and paper products and printing	373.4	350.0	211.4	244.9	234.7	214.5	211.9	213.5
16	Wood and wood products, except furniture	92.3	177.4	85.7	71.2	71.0	70.7	63.0	60.7
17	Paper and paper products	233.3	122.3	65.8	123.7	121.8	105.3	110.4	108.0
18	Printing and reproduction of recorded media	47.7	50.2	59.9	49.1	41.9	38.6	38.4	44.9
19-23	Chemical, rubber, plastic, non-metallic mineral products	1 398.1	1 126.0	1 269.2	1 297.2	953.3	791.6	695.7	745.7
19	Coke and refined petroleum products	183.3	170.4	246.4	271.1	71.8	56.4	60.9	88.2
20-21	Chemical and pharmaceutical products	956.5	754.1	804.0	835.3	675.9	543.9	474.4	494.2
20	Chemicals and chemical products	152.7	207.3	245.5	288.3	258.1	180.0	144.8	145.6
21	Pharmaceuticals, medicinal, chemical and botanical products	803.8	546.8	558.5	547.0	417.8	364.0	329.6	348.6
22	Rubber and plastic products	191.0	145.5	146.5	126.1	140.3	138.2	109.6	114.0
23	Other non-metallic mineral products	67.3	55.9	72.4	64.7	65.3	53.0	50.7	49.3
24-25	Basic metals, metal products, except machinery and equipment	581.6	560.7	531.0	413.5	409.7	384.9	398.4	328.4
24	Basic metals	289.4	273.8	221.4	155.6	172.6	167.1	194.7	107.6
25	Fabricated metal products, except machinery and equipment	292.3	286.9	309.6	258.0	237.1	217.7	203.7	220.8
26-30	Computer, electronic, optical products; electrical machinery, transport equipment	4 190.4	3 808.6	4 041.6	3 657.3	3 989.8	4 035.8	3 936.1	3 898.6
26	Computer, electronic and optical products	2 367.6	2 008.3	2 120.7	1 739.4	1 980.8	2 012.7	1 815.1	1 813.4
27	Electrical equipment	215.2	132.0	135.7	130.2	118.6	117.3	132.5	127.0
28	Machinery and equipment n.e.c.	440.9	446.3	526.8	436.5	516.2	472.4	450.7	451.3
29	Motor vehicles, trailers and semi-trailers	346.5	281.4	208.1	209.6	162.1	149.4	131.7	153.7
30	Other transport equipment	820.2	940.5	1 051.2	1 141.6	1 212.2	1 283.9	1 406.1	1 353.2
31-33	Furniture; repair, installation of machinery and equipment	215.0	215.8	208.1	201.5	182.3	180.8	150.5	159.3
31	Furniture	33.2	38.1	39.9	34.4	29.0	23.3	17.2	17.8
32	Other manufacturing	..	..	134.8	140.0	125.8	131.8	110.4	122.1
33	Repair and installation of machinery and equipment	..	..	33.3	27.0	27.4	25.7	22.9	19.4
35-39	**ELECTRICITY, GAS, WATER AND WASTE MANAGEMENT**	237.4	175.8	155.6	154.0	160.5	171.1	189.8	171.5
35-36	Electricity, gas and water	..	..	..	..	..	..	..	..
37-39	Sewerage, waste management and remediation activities	..	..	..	..	..	..	..	..
41-43	**CONSTRUCTION**	80.0	98.8	112.4	92.5	127.4	88.4	55.6	61.5
45-99	**TOTAL SERVICES**	5 722.9	6 015.5	5 706.1	5 751.2	6 128.7	6 005.9	5 963.0	5 866.4
45-82	**Business sector services**	5 344.7	5 762.8	5 574.6	5 639.0	6 019.8	5 904.7	5 861.6	5 755.6
45-47	Wholesale and retail trade; motor vehicle and motorcycle repairs	849.7	1 182.8	1 121.9	1 111.3	1 198.5	1 255.8	1 146.0	1 151.8
49-53	Transportation and storage	65.9	99.6	139.8	55.7	49.2	50.6	67.1	59.9
55-56	Accommodation and food service activities	4.9	4.7	5.0	6.6	2.4	2.4	1.6	1.6
58-63	Information and communication	2 276.9	2 134.7	1 954.2	2 112.0	2 171.9	2 076.2	2 148.0	2 133.7
58-60	Publishing, audiovisual and broadcasting activities	..	..	473.6	480.7	494.4	593.8	544.8	553.2
58	Publishing activities	..	..	456.9	459.4	470.2	563.2	511.2	515.2
59-60	Motion picture, video and TV programme production; broadcasting activities	..	..	16.6	21.3	24.2	30.5	33.5	37.2
59	Motion picture, video and TV programme production; sound and music	..	..	..	20.5	23.4	28.9	31.1	34.8
60	Programming and broadcasting activities	..	..	..	0.8	0.8	1.6	2.5	2.4
61	Telecommunications	..	..	441.9	470.1	347.6	322.2	383.6	338.9
62-63	IT and other information services	..	..	1 038.7	1 161.2	1 329.9	1 161.0	1 219.6	1 242.4
62	Computer programming, consultancy and related activities	1 060.1	1 016.7	980.4	1 100.6	1 254.9	1 079.9	1 126.3	1 136.4
63	Information service activities	..	..	58.3	60.6	75.0	81.2	93.2	106.0
64-66	Financial and insurance activities	402.7	376.7	349.6	255.5	260.5	278.0	371.4	329.2
68-82	Real estate; professional, scientific and technical; administrative and support	1 744.5	1 964.2	2 004.1	2 098.0	2 337.3	2 241.7	2 128.4	2 079.5
68	Real estate activities	..	..	9.2	6.6	6.5	6.4	6.5	6.5
69-75x72	Professional, scientific and technical activities, except scientific R&D	..	..	482.7	488.9	575.0	555.2	..	..
72	Scientific research and development	1 067.6	1 335.1	1 395.7	1 504.3	1 641.3	1 564.3	1 501.8	1 474.5
77-82	Administrative and support service activities	..	..	116.5	97.5	114.5	115.7	..	..
84-99	Community, social and personal services	378.2	252.7	131.5	112.2	108.9	101.2	101.4	110.8
84-85	Public administration and defence; compulsory social security and education	..	..	21.6	9.8	10.4	11.2	11.5	12.1
86-88	Human health and social work activities	289.4	188.8	95.7	80.3	79.0	72.3	71.2	77.6
90-93	Arts, entertainment and recreation	..	..	4.2	4.1	4.0	4.0	4.1	4.0
94-99	Other services; household-employers; extraterritorial bodies	..	..	10.0	18.0	15.4	13.7	14.7	17.0

.. Not available

Note: Detailed metadata at: http://metalinks.oecd.org/anberd/20170419/301f.
Information on data for Israel: http://oe.cd/israel-disclaimer.
Disclaimer: http://oe.cd/disclaimer

CANADA

R&D expenditure in industry by main activity of the enterprise, constant prices
ISIC Rev. 4

2010 USD PPP

		2007	2008	2009	2010	2011	2012	2013	2014
	TOTAL BUSINESS ENTERPRISE	14 345.4	13 700.0	13 511.2	12 941.2	13 400.2	13 086.5	12 367.0	12 019.5
01-03	**AGRICULTURE, FORESTRY AND FISHING**	153.2	110.3	107.0	107.3	115.0	76.0	62.5	64.3
05-09	**MINING AND QUARRYING**	668.6	806.7	782.6	803.4	1 100.2	1 260.1	1 222.7	1 091.7
10-33	**MANUFACTURING**	7 250.9	6 392.0	6 575.3	6 032.9	5 874.4	5 639.7	5 227.0	5 153.9
10-12	Food products, beverages and tobacco	156.7	163.8	169.3	158.9	134.0	123.8	109.2	114.3
13-15	Textiles, wearing apparel, leather and related products	75.8	69.9	68.2	59.8	65.8	46.9	32.4	36.3
13	Textiles	43.8	39.5	39.6	36.0	34.4	25.1	20.1	22.7
14	Wearing apparel	..	..	25.3	20.5	28.3	18.7	9.3	10.2
15	Leather and related products, footwear	..	..	3.4	3.3	3.2	3.1	3.1	3.4
16-18	Wood and paper products and printing	387.7	355.6	214.0	244.9	230.8	209.2	199.8	199.9
16	Wood and wood products, except furniture	95.9	180.3	86.8	71.2	69.8	69.0	59.4	56.8
17	Paper and paper products	242.3	124.3	66.6	123.7	119.8	102.7	104.1	101.1
18	Printing and reproduction of recorded media	49.6	51.0	60.7	49.1	41.2	37.6	36.3	42.0
19-23	Chemical, rubber, plastic, non-metallic mineral products	1 451.8	1 144.0	1 284.7	1 297.2	937.6	772.0	656.1	698.0
19	Coke and refined petroleum products	190.4	173.2	249.4	271.1	70.6	55.0	57.5	82.5
20-21	Chemical and pharmaceutical products	993.3	766.2	813.8	835.3	664.7	530.5	447.4	462.6
20	Chemicals and chemical products	158.6	210.6	248.5	288.3	253.8	175.5	136.5	136.3
21	Pharmaceuticals, medicinal, chemical and botanical products	834.7	555.6	565.3	547.0	410.9	355.0	310.9	326.3
22	Rubber and plastic products	198.3	147.8	148.3	126.1	138.0	134.8	103.4	106.7
23	Other non-metallic mineral products	69.9	56.8	73.3	64.7	64.2	51.7	47.8	46.2
24-25	Basic metals, metal products, except machinery and equipment	604.0	569.7	537.5	413.5	402.9	375.4	375.7	307.4
24	Basic metals	300.5	278.2	224.1	155.6	169.7	163.0	183.6	100.7
25	Fabricated metal products, except machinery and equipment	303.5	291.5	313.4	258.0	233.2	212.4	192.1	206.7
26-30	Computer, electronic, optical products; electrical machinery, transport equipment	4 351.7	3 869.1	4 090.9	3 657.3	3 923.9	3 936.1	3 712.0	3 648.9
26	Computer, electronic and optical products	2 458.7	2 040.5	2 146.6	1 739.4	1 948.1	1 963.0	1 711.7	1 697.3
27	Electrical equipment	223.4	134.2	137.3	130.2	116.6	114.4	125.0	118.9
28	Machinery and equipment n.e.c.	457.9	453.4	533.3	436.5	507.6	460.8	425.0	422.4
29	Motor vehicles, trailers and semi-trailers	359.8	285.9	210.6	209.6	159.4	145.8	124.2	143.8
30	Other transport equipment	851.8	955.6	1 064.0	1 141.6	1 192.2	1 252.2	1 326.0	1 266.5
31-33	Furniture; repair, installation of machinery and equipment	223.2	219.3	210.6	201.5	179.3	176.3	141.9	149.1
31	Furniture	34.5	38.7	40.4	34.4	28.6	22.7	16.2	16.7
32	Other manufacturing	..	..	136.5	140.0	123.7	128.5	104.1	114.3
33	Repair and installation of machinery and equipment	..	..	33.7	27.0	27.0	25.1	21.6	18.2
35-39	**ELECTRICITY, GAS, WATER AND WASTE MANAGEMENT**	246.6	178.6	157.5	154.0	157.8	166.9	179.0	160.5
35-36	Electricity, gas and water	..	..	..	..	..	..	..	..
37-39	Sewerage, waste management and remediation activities	..	..	..	..	..	..	..	..
41-43	**CONSTRUCTION**	83.0	100.4	113.7	92.5	125.3	86.2	52.5	57.5
45-99	**TOTAL SERVICES**	5 943.1	6 112.0	5 775.8	5 751.2	6 027.5	5 857.6	5 623.5	5 490.8
45-82	**Business sector services**	5 550.3	5 855.3	5 642.7	5 639.0	5 920.4	5 758.9	5 527.8	5 387.1
45-47	Wholesale and retail trade; motor vehicle and motorcycle repairs	882.4	1 201.8	1 135.6	1 111.3	1 178.7	1 224.8	1 080.7	1 078.0
49-53	Transportation and storage	68.5	101.2	141.5	55.7	48.4	49.4	63.3	56.0
55-56	Accommodation and food service activities	5.1	4.8	5.1	6.6	2.4	2.4	1.5	1.5
58-63	Information and communication	2 364.5	2 168.9	1 978.1	2 112.0	2 136.1	2 024.9	2 025.7	1 997.1
58-60	Publishing, audiovisual and broadcasting activities	..	..	479.4	480.7	486.2	579.1	513.8	517.8
58	Publishing activities	..	..	462.5	459.4	462.4	549.3	482.1	482.2
59-60	Motion picture, video and TV programme production; broadcasting activities	..	..	16.8	21.3	23.8	29.8	31.6	34.8
59	Motion picture, video and TV programme production; sound and music	..	..	..	20.5	23.0	28.2	29.3	32.6
60	Programming and broadcasting activities	..	..	..	0.8	0.8	1.6	2.3	2.3
61	Telecommunications	..	..	447.3	470.1	341.9	314.2	361.8	317.2
62-63	IT and other information services	..	..	1 051.4	1 161.2	1 308.0	1 132.3	1 150.2	1 162.8
62	Computer programming, consultancy and related activities	1 100.9	1 033.0	992.4	1 100.6	1 234.2	1 053.2	1 062.2	1 063.6
63	Information service activities	..	..	59.0	60.6	73.8	79.1	87.9	99.2
64-66	Financial and insurance activities	418.2	382.7	353.8	255.5	256.2	271.1	350.2	308.1
68-82	Real estate; professional, scientific and technical; administrative and support	1 811.6	1 995.7	2 028.6	2 098.0	2 298.7	2 186.3	2 007.2	1 946.4
68	Real estate activities	..	..	9.3	6.6	6.3	6.3	6.2	6.1
69-75x72	Professional, scientific and technical activities, except scientific R&D	..	..	488.6	488.9	565.5	541.5	..	..
72	Scientific research and development	1 108.6	1 356.5	1 412.8	1 504.3	1 614.2	1 525.7	1 416.3	1 380.1
77-82	Administrative and support service activities	..	..	117.9	97.5	112.6	112.8	..	..
84-99	Community, social and personal services	392.7	256.7	133.1	112.2	107.1	98.7	95.7	103.7
84-85	Public administration and defence; compulsory social security and education	..	..	21.9	9.8	10.2	11.0	10.8	11.4
86-88	Human health and social work activities	300.5	191.8	96.9	80.3	77.7	70.5	67.1	72.7
90-93	Arts, entertainment and recreation	..	..	4.2	4.1	4.0	3.9	3.9	3.8
94-99	Other services; household-employers; extraterritorial bodies	..	..	10.1	18.0	15.2	13.3	13.9	15.9

.. Not available

Note: Detailed metadata at: http://metalinks.oecd.org/anberd/20170419/301f.
Information on data for Israel: http://oe.cd/israel-disclaimer.
Disclaimer: http://oe.cd/disclaimer

CHILE

R&D expenditure in industry by main activity of the enterprise, current prices
ISIC Rev. 4

Million USD PPP

		2007	2008	2009	2010	2011	2012	2013	2014
	TOTAL BUSINESS ENTERPRISE	..	..	..	..	..	..	541.6	515.5
01-03	**AGRICULTURE, FORESTRY AND FISHING**	..	..	..	..	..	..	91.4	70.5
05-09	**MINING AND QUARRYING**	..	..	..	..	..	..	94.9	53.4
10-33	**MANUFACTURING**	..	..	..	..	..	..	119.1	155.1
10-12	Food products, beverages and tobacco	..	..	..	..	..	..	..	..
13-15	Textiles, wearing apparel, leather and related products	..	..	..	..	..	..	..	..
13	Textiles	..	..	..	..	..	..	..	..
14	Wearing apparel	..	..	..	..	..	..	..	..
15	Leather and related products, footwear	..	..	..	..	..	..	..	..
16-18	Wood and paper products and printing	..	..	..	..	..	..	..	..
16	Wood and wood products, except furniture	..	..	..	..	..	..	..	..
17	Paper and paper products	..	..	..	..	..	..	..	..
18	Printing and reproduction of recorded media	..	..	..	..	..	..	..	..
19-23	Chemical, rubber, plastic, non-metallic mineral products	..	..	..	..	..	..	..	..
19	Coke and refined petroleum products	..	..	..	..	..	..	..	..
20-21	Chemical and pharmaceutical products	..	..	..	..	..	..	..	..
20	Chemicals and chemical products	..	..	..	..	..	..	..	..
21	Pharmaceuticals, medicinal, chemical and botanical products	..	..	..	..	..	..	..	..
22	Rubber and plastic products	..	..	..	..	..	..	..	..
23	Other non-metallic mineral products	..	..	..	..	..	..	..	..
24-25	Basic metals, metal products, except machinery and equipment	..	..	..	..	..	..	..	..
24	Basic metals	..	..	..	..	..	..	..	..
25	Fabricated metal products, except machinery and equipment	..	..	..	..	..	..	..	..
26-30	Computer, electronic, optical products; electrical machinery, transport equipment	..	..	..	..	..	..	..	..
26	Computer, electronic and optical products	..	..	..	..	..	..	..	..
27	Electrical equipment	..	..	..	..	..	..	..	..
28	Machinery and equipment n.e.c.	..	..	..	..	..	..	..	..
29	Motor vehicles, trailers and semi-trailers	..	..	..	..	..	..	..	..
30	Other transport equipment	..	..	..	..	..	..	..	..
31-33	Furniture; repair, installation of machinery and equipment	..	..	..	..	..	..	..	..
31	Furniture	..	..	..	..	..	..	..	..
32	Other manufacturing	..	..	..	..	..	..	..	..
33	Repair and installation of machinery and equipment	..	..	..	..	..	..	..	..
35-39	**ELECTRICITY, GAS, WATER AND WASTE MANAGEMENT**	..	..	..	..	..	..	12.6	7.2
35-36	Electricity, gas and water	..	..	..	..	..	..	..	..
37-39	Sewerage, waste management and remediation activities	..	..	..	..	..	..	..	..
41-43	**CONSTRUCTION**	..	..	..	..	..	..	2.6	3.3
45-99	**TOTAL SERVICES**	..	..	..	..	..	..	220.9	226.1
45-82	**Business sector services**	..	..	..	..	..	..	210.7	220.7
45-47	Wholesale and retail trade; motor vehicle and motorcycle repairs	..	..	..	..	..	..	40.6	60.2
49-53	Transportation and storage	..	..	..	..	..	..	1.7	8.5
55-56	Accommodation and food service activities	..	..	..	..	..	..	0.6	0.5
58-63	Information and communication	..	..	..	..	..	..	47.9	28.6
58-60	Publishing, audiovisual and broadcasting activities	..	..	..	..	..	..	..	..
58	Publishing activities	..	..	..	..	..	..	..	..
59-60	Motion picture, video and TV programme production; broadcasting activities	..	..	..	..	..	..	..	..
59	Motion picture, video and TV programme production; sound and music	..	..	..	..	..	..	..	..
60	Programming and broadcasting activities	..	..	..	..	..	..	..	..
61	Telecommunications	..	..	..	..	..	..	..	..
62-63	IT and other information services	..	..	..	..	..	..	..	..
62	Computer programming, consultancy and related activities	..	..	..	..	..	..	15.5	25.3
63	Information service activities	..	..	..	..	..	..	..	..
64-66	Financial and insurance activities	..	..	..	..	..	..	25.0	28.8
68-82	Real estate; professional, scientific and technical; administrative and support	..	..	..	..	..	..	94.9	94.1
68	Real estate activities	..	..	..	..	..	..	3.6	0.0
69-75x72	Professional, scientific and technical activities, except scientific R&D	..	..	..	..	..	..	50.2	49.8
72	Scientific research and development	..	..	..	..	..	..	38.3	42.6
77-82	Administrative and support service activities	..	..	..	..	..	..	2.8	1.7
84-99	Community, social and personal services	..	..	..	..	..	..	10.2	5.4
84-85	Public administration and defence; compulsory social security and education	..	..	..	..	..	..	0.0	2.0
86-88	Human health and social work activities	..	..	..	..	..	..	5.1	2.2
90-93	Arts, entertainment and recreation	..	..	..	..	..	..	2.0	0.0
94-99	Other services; household-employers; extraterritorial bodies	..	..	..	..	..	..	3.1	1.3

.. Not available

Note: Detailed metadata at: http://metalinks.oecd.org/anberd/20170419/301f.
Information on data for Israel: http://oe.cd/israel-disclaimer.
Disclaimer: http://oe.cd/disclaimer

CHILE

R&D expenditure in industry by main activity of the enterprise, constant prices
ISIC Rev. 4

2010 USD PPP

		2007	2008	2009	2010	2011	2012	2013	2014
	TOTAL BUSINESS ENTERPRISE	..	..	..	..	..	..	492.6	465.1
01-03	**AGRICULTURE, FORESTRY AND FISHING**	..	..	..	..	..	..	83.1	63.6
05-09	**MINING AND QUARRYING**	..	..	..	..	..	..	86.3	48.1
10-33	**MANUFACTURING**	..	..	..	..	..	..	108.3	139.9
10-12	Food products, beverages and tobacco	..	..	..	..	..	..	..	..
13-15	Textiles, wearing apparel, leather and related products	..	..	..	..	..	..	..	..
13	Textiles	..	..	..	..	..	..	..	..
14	Wearing apparel	..	..	..	..	..	..	..	..
15	Leather and related products, footwear	..	..	..	..	..	..	..	..
16-18	Wood and paper products and printing	..	..	..	..	..	..	..	..
16	Wood and wood products, except furniture	..	..	..	..	..	..	..	..
17	Paper and paper products	..	..	..	..	..	..	..	..
18	Printing and reproduction of recorded media	..	..	..	..	..	..	..	..
19-23	Chemical, rubber, plastic, non-metallic mineral products	..	..	..	..	..	..	..	..
19	Coke and refined petroleum products	..	..	..	..	..	..	..	..
20-21	Chemical and pharmaceutical products	..	..	..	..	..	..	..	..
20	Chemicals and chemical products	..	..	..	..	..	..	..	..
21	Pharmaceuticals, medicinal, chemical and botanical products	..	..	..	..	..	..	..	..
22	Rubber and plastic products	..	..	..	..	..	..	..	..
23	Other non-metallic mineral products	..	..	..	..	..	..	..	..
24-25	Basic metals, metal products, except machinery and equipment	..	..	..	..	..	..	..	..
24	Basic metals	..	..	..	..	..	..	..	..
25	Fabricated metal products, except machinery and equipment	..	..	..	..	..	..	..	..
26-30	Computer, electronic, optical products; electrical machinery, transport equipment	..	..	..	..	..	..	..	..
26	Computer, electronic and optical products	..	..	..	..	..	..	..	..
27	Electrical equipment	..	..	..	..	..	..	..	..
28	Machinery and equipment n.e.c.	..	..	..	..	..	..	..	..
29	Motor vehicles, trailers and semi-trailers	..	..	..	..	..	..	..	..
30	Other transport equipment	..	..	..	..	..	..	..	..
31-33	Furniture; repair, installation of machinery and equipment	..	..	..	..	..	..	..	..
31	Furniture	..	..	..	..	..	..	..	..
32	Other manufacturing	..	..	..	..	..	..	..	..
33	Repair and installation of machinery and equipment	..	..	..	..	..	..	..	..
35-39	**ELECTRICITY, GAS, WATER AND WASTE MANAGEMENT**	..	..	..	..	..	..	11.5	6.5
35-36	Electricity, gas and water	..	..	..	..	..	..	..	..
37-39	Sewerage, waste management and remediation activities	..	..	..	..	..	..	..	..
41-43	**CONSTRUCTION**	..	..	..	..	..	..	2.4	3.0
45-99	**TOTAL SERVICES**	..	..	..	..	..	..	200.9	204.0
45-82	**Business sector services**	..	..	..	..	..	..	191.6	199.1
45-47	**Wholesale and retail trade; motor vehicle and motorcycle repairs**	..	..	..	..	..	..	36.9	54.3
49-53	**Transportation and storage**	..	..	..	..	..	..	1.6	7.7
55-56	**Accommodation and food service activities**	..	..	..	..	..	..	0.5	0.4
58-63	**Information and communication**	..	..	..	..	..	..	43.6	25.8
58-60	Publishing, audiovisual and broadcasting activities	..	..	..	..	..	..	..	..
58	Publishing activities	..	..	..	..	..	..	..	..
59-60	Motion picture, video and TV programme production; broadcasting activities	..	..	..	..	..	..	..	..
59	Motion picture, video and TV programme production; sound and music	..	..	..	..	..	..	..	..
60	Programming and broadcasting activities	..	..	..	..	..	..	..	..
61	Telecommunications	..	..	..	..	..	..	..	..
62-63	IT and other information services	..	..	..	..	..	..	..	..
62	Computer programming, consultancy and related activities	..	..	..	..	..	..	14.1	22.8
63	Information service activities	..	..	..	..	..	..	..	..
64-66	**Financial and insurance activities**	..	..	..	..	..	..	22.8	26.0
68-82	**Real estate; professional, scientific and technical; administrative and support**	..	..	..	..	..	..	86.3	84.9
68	Real estate activities	..	..	..	..	..	..	3.2	0.0
69-75x72	Professional, scientific and technical activities, except scientific R&D	..	..	..	..	..	..	45.7	44.9
72	Scientific research and development	..	..	..	..	..	..	34.8	38.4
77-82	Administrative and support service activities	..	..	..	..	..	..	2.5	1.5
84-99	**Community, social and personal services**	..	..	..	..	..	..	9.3	4.9
84-85	Public administration and defence; compulsory social security and education	..	..	..	..	..	..	0.0	1.8
86-88	Human health and social work activities	..	..	..	..	..	..	4.6	2.0
90-93	Arts, entertainment and recreation	..	..	..	..	..	..	1.8	0.0
94-99	Other services; household-employers; extraterritorial bodies	..	..	..	..	..	..	2.9	1.1

.. Not available

Note: Detailed metadata at: http://metalinks.oecd.org/anberd/20170419/301f.
Information on data for Israel: http://oe.cd/israel-disclaimer.
Disclaimer: http://oe.cd/disclaimer

CZECH REPUBLIC

R&D expenditure in industry by main activity of the enterprise, current prices
ISIC Rev. 4

Million USD PPP

		2007	2008	2009	2010	2011	2012	2013	2014
	TOTAL BUSINESS ENTERPRISE	**2 055.2**	**2 101.7**	**2 110.1**	**2 239.7**	**2 601.4**	**2 917.1**	**3 298.2**	**3 763.7**
01-03	**AGRICULTURE, FORESTRY AND FISHING**	**8.1**	**7.1**	**7.4**	**8.4**	**8.5**	**10.0**	**11.4**	**11.8**
05-09	**MINING AND QUARRYING**	**4.6**	**5.9**	**4.8**	**3.8**	**1.4**	**1.5**	**1.1**	**2.4**
10-33	**MANUFACTURING**	**1 154.3**	**1 192.8**	**1 180.9**	**1 251.2**	**1 462.7**	**1 603.4**	**1 898.7**	**2 123.3**
10-12	Food products, beverages and tobacco	14.8	22.7	22.2	24.3	24.6	22.8	25.0	18.1
13-15	Textiles, wearing apparel, leather and related products	19.2	15.1	18.2	18.4	32.9	15.7	24.7	27.1
13	Textiles	13.0	10.8	12.8	14.8	16.8	12.9	22.0	24.8
14	Wearing apparel	5.0	3.4	3.9	2.6	14.8	1.7	1.3	0.8
15	Leather and related products, footwear	1.2	0.9	1.5	1.1	1.4	1.1	1.5	1.5
16-18	Wood and paper products and printing	1.0	1.3	1.2	3.5	6.1	3.2	2.7	4.0
16	Wood and wood products, except furniture	0.4	0.8	1.0	1.3	3.1	0.4	0.8	1.6
17	Paper and paper products	0.1	0.1	0.2	0.2	2.4	2.1	1.0	1.1
18	Printing and reproduction of recorded media	0.5	0.4	0.0	2.0	0.5	0.7	0.9	1.3
19-23	Chemical, rubber, plastic, non-metallic mineral products	203.3	213.5	222.9	226.5	239.5	243.0	281.3	305.3
19	Coke and refined petroleum products	0.8	0.8	0.7	0.8	0.8	0.5	0.5	0.6
20-21	Chemical and pharmaceutical products	128.0	130.6	153.7	147.7	156.4	155.9	165.3	178.4
20	Chemicals and chemical products	51.1	52.6	66.3	70.5	75.7	72.0	88.2	93.5
21	Pharmaceuticals, medicinal, chemical and botanical products	76.9	77.9	87.3	77.2	80.7	83.9	77.0	84.9
22	Rubber and plastic products	43.4	47.1	44.6	49.4	52.0	51.4	66.6	83.9
23	Other non-metallic mineral products	31.1	35.0	23.9	28.6	30.2	35.2	49.0	42.4
24-25	Basic metals, metal products, except machinery and equipment	60.8	67.0	59.8	75.3	79.8	92.4	86.6	113.8
24	Basic metals	29.7	24.0	14.9	17.7	22.0	23.6	17.8	23.6
25	Fabricated metal products, except machinery and equipment	31.1	43.0	44.9	57.6	57.8	68.8	68.8	90.2
26-30	Computer, electronic, optical products; electrical machinery, transport equipment	705.4	748.8	699.1	733.7	874.8	1 004.9	1 245.3	1 378.9
26	Computer, electronic and optical products	131.3	115.3	96.8	87.3	86.1	92.7	119.2	148.1
27	Electrical equipment	62.1	64.1	78.6	102.7	121.3	154.1	147.3	239.9
28	Machinery and equipment n.e.c.	165.5	172.3	167.1	183.1	219.7	289.1	335.6	331.4
29	Motor vehicles, trailers and semi-trailers	284.3	306.6	260.5	252.5	298.3	345.4	508.9	513.5
30	Other transport equipment	62.2	90.5	96.1	108.1	149.3	123.6	134.3	146.0
31-33	Furniture; repair, installation of machinery and equipment	149.8	124.4	157.5	169.4	205.0	221.5	233.0	276.2
31	Furniture	1.9	1.8	2.8	3.0	5.4	4.0	3.7	3.1
32	Other manufacturing	17.6	19.8	19.3	21.2	26.8	34.0	27.0	28.2
33	Repair and installation of machinery and equipment	130.3	102.8	135.4	145.2	172.8	183.5	202.3	244.9
35-39	**ELECTRICITY, GAS, WATER AND WASTE MANAGEMENT**	**9.3**	**9.5**	**11.1**	**11.0**	**10.6**	**10.5**	**14.8**	**13.0**
35-36	Electricity, gas and water	4.7	4.9	3.1	2.2	3.1	3.7	7.6	5.1
37-39	Sewerage, waste management and remediation activities	4.6	4.6	8.0	8.7	7.4	6.7	7.2	7.9
41-43	**CONSTRUCTION**	**23.8**	**24.7**	**27.6**	**29.7**	**27.2**	**31.7**	**41.3**	**53.3**
45-99	**TOTAL SERVICES**	**855.2**	**861.7**	**878.2**	**935.7**	**1 091.0**	**1 259.9**	**1 330.8**	**1 560.0**
45-82	**Business sector services**	**816.9**	**822.0**	**831.7**	**894.3**	**1 047.0**	**1 214.2**	**1 261.0**	**1 497.2**
45-47	Wholesale and retail trade; motor vehicle and motorcycle repairs	47.8	61.3	62.5	67.6	69.8	69.1	75.1	71.0
49-53	Transportation and storage	0.5	0.4	0.1	0.1	0.4	1.5	1.7	1.8
55-56	Accommodation and food service activities	0.0	0.0	0.0	0.0	0.1	0.1	0.1	0.1
58-63	Information and communication	228.1	274.2	280.2	300.3	371.5	421.2	458.7	610.0
58-60	Publishing, audiovisual and broadcasting activities	19.9	19.9	15.6	18.1	16.0	18.3	18.1	21.6
58	Publishing activities	19.9	19.9	15.6	18.1	16.0	18.0	17.6	21.1
59-60	Motion picture, video and TV programme production; broadcasting activities	0.0	0.0	0.0	0.0	0.1	0.3	0.5	0.5
59	Motion picture, video and TV programme production; sound and music	0.0	0.0	0.0	0.0	0.1	0.3	0.4	0.5
60	Programming and broadcasting activities	0.0	0.0	0.0	0.0	0.0	0.0	0.1	0.0
61	Telecommunications	31.6	31.4	29.7	38.1	41.1	45.7	46.3	47.7
62-63	IT and other information services	176.7	223.0	234.9	244.2	314.4	357.2	394.3	540.7
62	Computer programming, consultancy and related activities	134.0	168.5	177.2	194.8	229.7	267.5	288.2	415.9
63	Information service activities	42.7	54.5	57.8	49.4	84.7	89.6	106.1	124.9
64-66	**Financial and insurance activities**	**123.3**	**66.0**	**35.9**	**36.7**	**35.2**	**45.8**	**60.2**	**58.4**
68-82	**Real estate; professional, scientific and technical; administrative and support**	**416.6**	**420.1**	**453.0**	**489.5**	**570.0**	**676.6**	**665.2**	**755.9**
68	Real estate activities	1.3	1.0	2.1	5.6	9.4	23.4	37.5	15.6
69-75x72	Professional, scientific and technical activities, except scientific R&D	75.8	93.4	114.9	132.7	183.0	182.2	161.4	182.3
72	Scientific research and development	339.5	324.7	335.4	350.6	376.2	466.1	458.5	550.4
77-82	Administrative and support service activities	0.0	1.0	0.6	0.7	1.4	4.9	7.8	7.7
84-99	**Community, social and personal services**	**38.4**	**39.7**	**46.5**	**41.4**	**44.0**	**45.7**	**69.9**	**62.7**
84-85	Public administration and defence; compulsory social security and education	0.3	0.5	0.4	0.3	1.0	2.0	12.1	9.8
86-88	Human health and social work activities	31.6	29.4	33.8	34.0	36.4	37.1	48.1	44.0
90-93	Arts, entertainment and recreation	4.4	6.6	9.0	5.1	3.6	3.4	3.7	3.3
94-99	Other services; household-employers; extraterritorial bodies	2.1	3.1	3.3	1.9	3.1	3.2	5.9	5.6

Note: Detailed metadata at: http://metalinks.oecd.org/anberd/20170419/301f.
Information on data for Israel: http://oe.cd/israel-disclaimer.
Disclaimer: http://oe.cd/disclaimer

CZECH REPUBLIC

R&D expenditure in industry by main activity of the enterprise, constant prices
ISIC Rev. 4

2010 USD PPP

		2007	2008	2009	2010	2011	2012	2013	2014
	TOTAL BUSINESS ENTERPRISE	2 219.1	2 168.0	2 075.7	2 239.7	2 543.4	2 801.0	2 999.2	3 308.6
01-03	**AGRICULTURE, FORESTRY AND FISHING**	8.7	7.4	7.3	8.4	8.4	9.6	10.4	10.4
05-09	**MINING AND QUARRYING**	4.9	6.1	4.7	3.8	1.4	1.5	1.0	2.1
10-33	**MANUFACTURING**	1 246.3	1 230.4	1 161.6	1 251.2	1 430.1	1 539.6	1 726.5	1 866.5
10-12	Food products, beverages and tobacco	16.0	23.4	21.8	24.3	24.1	21.9	22.7	15.9
13-15	Textiles, wearing apparel, leather and related products	20.7	15.5	17.9	18.4	32.2	15.1	22.5	23.8
13	Textiles	14.1	11.2	12.6	14.8	16.4	12.4	20.0	21.8
14	Wearing apparel	5.4	3.5	3.8	2.6	14.4	1.6	1.2	0.7
15	Leather and related products, footwear	1.3	0.9	1.5	1.1	1.3	1.1	1.3	1.3
16-18	Wood and paper products and printing	1.1	1.3	1.2	3.5	5.9	3.1	2.5	3.5
16	Wood and wood products, except furniture	0.4	0.8	1.0	1.3	3.1	0.4	0.8	1.4
17	Paper and paper products	0.2	0.1	0.2	0.2	2.3	2.0	0.9	1.0
18	Printing and reproduction of recorded media	0.5	0.4	0.0	2.0	0.5	0.7	0.8	1.1
19-23	Chemical, rubber, plastic, non-metallic mineral products	219.5	220.3	219.2	226.5	234.2	233.3	255.8	268.4
19	Coke and refined petroleum products	0.8	0.9	0.7	0.8	0.8	0.5	0.5	0.5
20-21	Chemical and pharmaceutical products	138.2	134.7	151.2	147.7	152.9	149.7	150.3	156.8
20	Chemicals and chemical products	55.2	54.3	65.3	70.5	74.1	69.1	80.2	82.2
21	Pharmaceuticals, medicinal, chemical and botanical products	83.0	80.4	85.9	77.2	78.9	80.6	70.0	74.6
22	Rubber and plastic products	46.8	48.6	43.9	49.4	50.9	49.3	60.5	73.7
23	Other non-metallic mineral products	33.6	36.1	23.5	28.6	29.5	33.8	44.5	37.3
24-25	Basic metals, metal products, except machinery and equipment	65.6	69.1	58.8	75.3	78.0	88.8	78.7	100.0
24	Basic metals	32.0	24.7	14.7	17.7	21.6	22.7	16.2	20.7
25	Fabricated metal products, except machinery and equipment	33.6	44.4	44.1	57.6	56.5	66.1	62.6	79.3
26-30	Computer, electronic, optical products; electrical machinery, transport equipment	761.7	772.4	687.7	733.7	855.3	964.9	1 132.4	1 212.2
26	Computer, electronic and optical products	141.8	119.0	95.2	87.3	84.2	89.0	108.4	130.2
27	Electrical equipment	67.1	66.1	77.3	102.7	118.6	148.0	134.0	210.9
28	Machinery and equipment n.e.c.	178.7	177.7	164.4	183.1	214.8	277.6	305.2	291.3
29	Motor vehicles, trailers and semi-trailers	307.0	316.3	256.3	252.5	291.7	331.6	462.8	451.4
30	Other transport equipment	67.2	93.3	94.6	108.1	146.0	118.7	122.1	128.4
31-33	Furniture; repair, installation of machinery and equipment	161.7	128.3	155.0	169.4	200.4	212.7	211.9	242.8
31	Furniture	2.1	1.9	2.7	3.0	5.3	3.8	3.3	2.7
32	Other manufacturing	19.0	20.4	19.0	21.2	26.2	32.6	24.6	24.8
33	Repair and installation of machinery and equipment	140.7	106.0	133.2	145.2	168.9	176.2	184.0	215.3
35-39	**ELECTRICITY, GAS, WATER AND WASTE MANAGEMENT**	10.0	9.8	10.9	11.0	10.3	10.1	13.5	11.5
35-36	Electricity, gas and water	5.1	5.1	3.0	2.2	3.0	3.6	7.0	4.5
37-39	Sewerage, waste management and remediation activities	4.9	4.7	7.9	8.7	7.3	6.5	6.6	7.0
41-43	**CONSTRUCTION**	25.7	25.5	27.2	29.7	26.6	30.4	37.6	46.8
45-99	**TOTAL SERVICES**	923.4	888.9	863.9	935.7	1 066.7	1 209.8	1 210.2	1 371.3
45-82	**Business sector services**	882.0	848.0	818.2	894.3	1 023.6	1 165.9	1 146.7	1 316.2
45-47	**Wholesale and retail trade; motor vehicle and motorcycle repairs**	51.6	63.2	61.5	67.6	68.2	66.3	68.2	62.5
49-53	**Transportation and storage**	0.6	0.4	0.1	0.1	0.4	1.4	1.6	1.6
55-56	**Accommodation and food service activities**	0.0	0.0	0.0	0.0	0.1	0.1	0.0	0.0
58-63	**Information and communication**	246.3	282.9	275.6	300.3	363.2	404.4	417.1	536.2
58-60	Publishing, audiovisual and broadcasting activities	21.5	20.5	15.3	18.1	15.7	17.6	16.4	19.0
58	Publishing activities	21.5	20.5	15.3	18.1	15.6	17.3	16.0	18.6
59-60	Motion picture, video and TV programme production; broadcasting activities	0.0	0.0	0.0	0.0	0.1	0.3	0.4	0.4
59	Motion picture, video and TV programme production; sound and music	0.0	0.0	0.0	0.0	0.1	0.3	0.3	0.4
60	Programming and broadcasting activities	0.0	0.0	0.0	0.0	0.0	0.0	0.1	0.0
61	Telecommunications	34.1	32.4	29.2	38.1	40.2	43.9	42.1	41.9
62-63	IT and other information services	190.8	230.0	231.1	244.2	307.4	342.9	358.5	475.4
62	Computer programming, consultancy and related activities	144.7	173.8	174.3	194.8	224.5	256.9	262.1	365.6
63	Information service activities	46.1	56.3	56.8	49.4	82.8	86.0	96.4	109.8
64-66	**Financial and insurance activities**	133.1	68.1	35.3	36.7	34.4	44.0	54.8	51.3
68-82	**Real estate; professional, scientific and technical; administrative and support**	449.9	433.4	445.6	489.5	557.3	649.6	604.9	664.5
68	Real estate activities	1.4	1.1	2.1	5.6	9.2	22.5	34.1	13.7
69-75x72	Professional, scientific and technical activities, except scientific R&D	81.8	96.3	113.0	132.7	179.0	174.9	146.8	160.2
72	Scientific research and development	366.6	335.0	330.0	350.6	367.8	447.5	416.9	483.8
77-82	Administrative and support service activities	0.0	1.0	0.6	0.7	1.4	4.7	7.1	6.8
84-99	**Community, social and personal services**	41.4	40.9	45.7	41.4	43.1	43.9	63.5	55.2
84-85	Public administration and defence; compulsory social security and education	0.3	0.5	0.3	0.3	1.0	1.9	11.0	8.6
86-88	Human health and social work activities	34.1	30.4	33.3	34.0	35.6	35.6	43.8	38.7
90-93	Arts, entertainment and recreation	4.8	6.8	8.9	5.1	3.5	3.3	3.4	2.9
94-99	Other services; household-employers; extraterritorial bodies	2.3	3.2	3.3	1.9	3.0	3.1	5.3	4.9

Note: Detailed metadata at: http://metalinks.oecd.org/anberd/20170419/301f.
Information on data for Israel: http://oe.cd/israel-disclaimer.
Disclaimer: http://oe.cd/disclaimer

CZECH REPUBLIC

R&D expenditure in industry by product field, current prices
ISIC Rev. 4

Million USD PPP

		2007	2008	2009	2010	2011	2012	2013	2014
	TOTAL BUSINESS ENTERPRISE	2 055.2	2 101.7	2 110.1	2 239.7	2 601.4	2 917.1	3 298.2	3 763.7
01-03	**AGRICULTURE, FORESTRY AND FISHING**	28.7	16.4	16.1	14.0	15.7	15.7	20.1	22.9
05-09	**MINING AND QUARRYING**	3.2	5.9	6.2	6.0	4.6	1.8	2.1	3.3
10-33	**MANUFACTURING**	1 205.1	1 337.2	1 327.0	1 388.2	1 621.0	1 711.1	2 037.5	2 364.1
10-12	Food products, beverages and tobacco	16.2	17.5	21.0	20.5	21.0	27.0	23.3	19.5
13-15	Textiles, wearing apparel, leather and related products	22.3	19.5	20.0	21.3	26.7	17.7	28.2	36.1
13	Textiles	16.3	12.2	14.1	17.2	23.5	15.2	25.1	30.9
14	Wearing apparel	4.5	2.8	3.9	3.0	2.3	1.5	2.6	2.3
15	Leather and related products, footwear	1.5	4.4	2.0	1.2	0.9	1.0	0.6	2.9
16-18	Wood and paper products and printing	1.4	1.2	1.3	4.3	7.6	5.2	3.5	4.0
16	Wood and wood products, except furniture	1.1	0.8	0.7	2.0	4.5	2.6	1.4	2.2
17	Paper and paper products	0.2	0.2	0.3	0.3	2.3	2.4	1.1	1.1
18	Printing and reproduction of recorded media	0.1	0.2	0.4	0.2	0.8	0.2	1.0	0.7
19-23	Chemical, rubber, plastic, non-metallic mineral products	216.4	227.3	229.5	249.4	269.2	239.2	271.9	297.5
19	Coke and refined petroleum products	0.8	1.2	1.3	0.8	1.2	1.7	1.8	4.5
20-21	Chemical and pharmaceutical products	138.7	148.0	161.1	166.2	189.5	143.9	160.3	177.3
20	Chemicals and chemical products	39.4	56.1	44.5	63.7	59.4	51.9	55.8	53.8
21	Pharmaceuticals, medicinal, chemical and botanical products	99.4	92.0	116.6	102.5	130.1	92.0	104.4	123.5
22	Rubber and plastic products	46.9	45.1	42.0	51.8	48.2	55.5	64.0	74.7
23	Other non-metallic mineral products	30.0	32.9	25.2	30.7	30.3	38.0	45.8	41.0
24-25	Basic metals, metal products, except machinery and equipment	58.8	61.3	60.8	67.6	108.7	123.9	123.9	149.3
24	Basic metals	32.7	20.8	16.0	16.4	15.6	14.7	12.8	12.8
25	Fabricated metal products, except machinery and equipment	26.1	40.5	44.7	51.2	93.1	109.1	111.1	136.6
26-30	Computer, electronic, optical products; electrical machinery, transport equipment	620.9	939.3	920.1	949.6	1 084.5	1 236.5	1 497.8	1 755.6
26	Computer, electronic and optical products	118.1	207.9	182.6	196.5	186.0	236.7	267.0	313.3
27	Electrical equipment	74.8	67.1	79.9	106.2	126.8	205.9	124.7	156.2
28	Machinery and equipment n.e.c.	203.1	217.7	224.0	256.1	294.4	250.1	358.1	392.0
29	Motor vehicles, trailers and semi-trailers	101.4	296.9	274.9	238.9	266.7	360.9	556.8	674.5
30	Other transport equipment	123.5	149.7	158.7	151.9	210.6	182.9	191.1	219.5
31-33	Furniture; repair, installation of machinery and equipment	269.1	71.3	74.3	75.5	103.1	61.7	89.0	102.0
31	Furniture	5.0	1.6	3.1	2.1	1.7	4.4	5.0	10.5
32	Other manufacturing	32.7	20.6	19.0	24.8	35.5	29.1	39.9	36.9
33	Repair and installation of machinery and equipment	231.4	49.0	52.2	48.6	65.9	28.3	44.0	54.6
35-39	**ELECTRICITY, GAS, WATER AND WASTE MANAGEMENT**	11.8	10.7	15.9	16.0	21.4	22.9	29.8	28.3
35-36	Electricity, gas and water	7.4	5.4	7.7	7.6	10.7	9.8	10.5	10.6
37-39	Sewerage, waste management and remediation activities	4.4	5.3	8.2	8.3	10.7	13.1	19.3	17.7
41-43	**CONSTRUCTION**	25.6	26.9	28.5	27.4	26.0	28.0	35.1	40.5
45-99	**TOTAL SERVICES**	780.9	704.5	716.4	788.1	912.8	1 137.5	1 173.6	1 304.6
45-82	**Business sector services**	718.7	635.2	645.6	725.5	849.9	1 079.2	1 105.4	1 245.2
45-47	Wholesale and retail trade; motor vehicle and motorcycle repairs	13.1	14.3	13.2	22.8	21.3	1.9	0.0	0.2
49-53	Transportation and storage	3.5	2.0	2.8	9.0	2.1	2.7	4.6	4.4
55-56	Accommodation and food service activities	0.0	0.0	0.0	0.0	0.1	1.2	0.0	0.0
58-63	Information and communication	241.7	241.4	268.3	277.7	384.4	442.5	479.4	644.8
58-60	Publishing, audiovisual and broadcasting activities	106.4	5.1	2.0	1.7	2.0	16.9	0.0	2.4
58	Publishing activities	..	..	..	..	..	12.1	..	..
59-60	Motion picture, video and TV programme production; broadcasting activities	..	..	..	..	..	4.9	..	..
59	Motion picture, video and TV programme production; sound and music	..	..	..	..	..	..	..	..
60	Programming and broadcasting activities	..	..	..	..	..	..	..	..
61	Telecommunications	69.4	33.9	54.2	53.0	47.3	51.8	60.5	70.7
62-63	IT and other information services	66.0	202.4	212.2	223.0	335.1	373.7	418.9	571.8
62	Computer programming, consultancy and related activities	55.0	182.8	192.2	205.0	248.2	265.0	285.8	429.0
63	Information service activities	11.0	19.6	19.9	18.0	86.9	108.7	133.0	142.8
64-66	Financial and insurance activities	122.8	66.0	35.8	40.5	34.1	36.9	48.4	46.9
68-82	Real estate; professional, scientific and technical; administrative and support	337.7	311.5	325.5	375.5	408.0	594.1	573.0	548.9
68	Real estate activities	0.3	0.7	0.9	4.0	4.4	0.2	0.0	0.0
69-75x72	Professional, scientific and technical activities, except scientific R&D	68.9	62.1	88.3	85.8	108.0	29.0	33.1	37.5
72	Scientific research and development	264.1	245.8	236.0	284.7	295.0	564.5	539.3	510.9
77-82	Administrative and support service activities	4.3	2.9	0.3	1.0	0.7	0.4	0.6	0.5
84-99	Community, social and personal services	62.2	69.3	70.9	62.6	62.9	58.3	68.2	59.5
84-85	Public administration and defence; compulsory social security and education	14.6	11.1	12.9	11.1	10.6	10.8	17.0	11.3
86-88	Human health and social work activities	40.7	50.5	47.6	45.8	47.3	45.6	45.9	44.3
90-93	Arts, entertainment and recreation	2.5	6.6	9.0	5.1	3.5	0.2	0.1	0.1
94-99	Other services; household-employers; extraterritorial bodies	4.4	1.1	1.3	0.6	1.5	1.7	5.2	3.8

.. Not available

Note: Detailed metadata at: http://metalinks.oecd.org/anberd/20170419/301f.
Information on data for Israel: http://oe.cd/israel-disclaimer.
Disclaimer: http://oe.cd/disclaimer

CZECH REPUBLIC

R&D expenditure in industry by product field, constant prices
ISIC Rev. 4

2010 USD PPP

		2007	2008	2009	2010	2011	2012	2013	2014
	TOTAL BUSINESS ENTERPRISE	2 219.1	2 168.0	2 075.7	2 239.7	2 543.4	2 801.0	2 999.2	3 308.6
01-03	**AGRICULTURE, FORESTRY AND FISHING**	31.0	17.0	15.8	14.0	15.3	15.1	18.3	20.2
05-09	**MINING AND QUARRYING**	3.5	6.1	6.1	6.0	4.5	1.8	1.9	2.9
10-33	**MANUFACTURING**	1 301.2	1 379.4	1 305.4	1 388.2	1 584.9	1 643.0	1 852.8	2 078.2
10-12	Food products, beverages and tobacco	17.5	18.0	20.7	20.5	20.6	25.9	21.2	17.1
13-15	Textiles, wearing apparel, leather and related products	24.1	20.1	19.6	21.3	26.2	17.0	25.7	31.8
13	Textiles	17.6	12.6	13.9	17.2	23.0	14.6	22.8	27.2
14	Wearing apparel	4.9	2.9	3.8	3.0	2.3	1.4	2.3	2.0
15	Leather and related products, footwear	1.6	4.5	1.9	1.2	0.9	1.0	0.5	2.6
16-18	Wood and paper products and printing	1.5	1.2	1.3	4.3	7.5	5.0	3.2	3.5
16	Wood and wood products, except furniture	1.2	0.8	0.7	2.0	4.4	2.5	1.2	1.9
17	Paper and paper products	0.2	0.2	0.3	0.3	2.2	2.3	1.0	1.0
18	Printing and reproduction of recorded media	0.1	0.2	0.4	2.0	0.8	0.2	0.9	0.7
19-23	Chemical, rubber, plastic, non-metallic mineral products	233.6	234.4	225.8	249.4	263.2	229.7	247.2	261.5
19	Coke and refined petroleum products	0.8	1.2	1.2	0.8	1.2	1.6	1.7	3.9
20-21	Chemical and pharmaceutical products	149.8	152.7	158.5	166.2	185.3	138.2	145.7	155.9
20	Chemicals and chemical products	42.5	57.8	43.8	63.7	58.1	49.9	50.8	47.3
21	Pharmaceuticals, medicinal, chemical and botanical products	107.3	94.9	114.7	102.5	127.2	88.3	95.0	108.6
22	Rubber and plastic products	50.6	46.6	41.3	51.8	47.1	53.3	58.2	65.7
23	Other non-metallic mineral products	32.4	33.9	24.8	30.7	29.6	36.5	41.6	36.0
24-25	Basic metals, metal products, except machinery and equipment	63.5	63.2	59.8	67.6	106.3	118.9	112.6	131.3
24	Basic metals	35.3	21.4	15.8	16.4	15.3	14.2	11.6	11.2
25	Fabricated metal products, except machinery and equipment	28.2	41.8	44.0	51.2	91.0	104.8	101.0	120.0
26-30	Computer, electronic, optical products; electrical machinery, transport equipment	670.5	968.9	905.1	949.6	1 060.3	1 187.3	1 362.0	1 543.3
26	Computer, electronic and optical products	127.5	214.4	179.6	196.5	181.8	227.3	242.8	275.4
27	Electrical equipment	80.8	69.2	78.6	106.2	123.9	197.7	113.4	137.3
28	Machinery and equipment n.e.c.	219.3	224.6	220.4	256.1	287.8	240.2	325.6	344.6
29	Motor vehicles, trailers and semi-trailers	109.5	306.3	270.4	238.9	260.8	346.5	506.4	592.9
30	Other transport equipment	133.3	154.4	156.1	151.9	205.9	175.6	173.8	193.0
31-33	Furniture; repair, installation of machinery and equipment	290.5	73.5	73.1	75.5	100.8	59.3	80.9	89.7
31	Furniture	5.4	1.7	3.0	2.1	1.7	4.2	4.6	9.3
32	Other manufacturing	35.3	21.3	18.7	24.8	34.7	27.9	36.3	32.5
33	Repair and installation of machinery and equipment	249.8	50.5	51.4	48.6	64.4	27.1	40.0	48.0
35-39	**ELECTRICITY, GAS, WATER AND WASTE MANAGEMENT**	12.7	11.1	15.6	16.0	20.9	22.0	27.1	24.9
35-36	Electricity, gas and water	7.9	5.6	7.6	7.6	10.4	9.4	9.5	9.3
37-39	Sewerage, waste management and remediation activities	4.8	5.5	8.1	8.3	10.5	12.6	17.6	15.5
41-43	**CONSTRUCTION**	27.6	27.8	28.0	27.4	25.4	26.9	31.9	35.6
45-99	**TOTAL SERVICES**	843.2	726.7	704.8	788.1	892.4	1 092.2	1 067.2	1 146.9
45-82	**Business sector services**	776.1	655.3	635.1	725.5	830.9	1 036.2	1 005.2	1 094.6
45-47	**Wholesale and retail trade; motor vehicle and motorcycle repairs**	14.2	14.7	13.0	22.8	20.8	1.8	0.0	0.1
49-53	**Transportation and storage**	3.8	2.1	2.7	9.0	2.0	2.6	4.2	3.9
55-56	**Accommodation and food service activities**	0.0	0.0	0.0	0.0	0.1	1.1	0.0	0.0
58-63	**Information and communication**	261.0	249.0	264.0	277.7	375.8	424.8	435.9	566.8
58-60	Publishing, audiovisual and broadcasting activities	114.8	5.2	2.0	1.7	2.0	16.3	0.0	2.1
58	Publishing activities	..	..	..	..	..	11.6	..	..
59-60	Motion picture, video and TV programme production; broadcasting activities	..	..	..	..	..	4.7	..	..
59	Motion picture, video and TV programme production; sound and music	..	..	..	..	..	..	..	..
60	Programming and broadcasting activities	..	..	..	..	..	..	..	..
61	Telecommunications	74.9	35.0	53.3	53.0	46.2	49.8	55.0	62.1
62-63	IT and other information services	71.2	208.8	208.7	223.0	327.6	358.8	380.9	502.7
62	Computer programming, consultancy and related activities	59.4	188.5	189.1	205.0	242.7	254.5	259.9	377.1
63	Information service activities	11.8	20.3	19.6	18.0	85.0	104.3	121.0	125.5
64-66	**Financial and insurance activities**	132.6	68.1	35.2	40.5	33.3	35.4	44.0	41.2
68-82	**Real estate; professional, scientific and technical; administrative and support**	364.6	321.3	320.2	375.5	398.9	570.4	521.1	482.5
68	Real estate activities	0.3	0.7	0.9	4.0	4.3	0.1	0.0	0.0
69-75x72	Professional, scientific and technical activities, except scientific R&D	74.4	64.1	86.9	85.8	105.6	27.9	30.1	32.9
72	Scientific research and development	285.2	253.5	232.1	284.7	288.4	542.0	490.4	449.1
77-82	Administrative and support service activities	4.7	3.0	0.3	1.0	0.7	0.4	0.6	0.5
84-99	**Community, social and personal services**	67.1	71.4	69.7	62.6	61.5	56.0	62.0	52.3
84-85	Public administration and defence; compulsory social security and education	15.7	11.4	12.7	11.1	10.3	10.4	15.5	9.9
86-88	Human health and social work activities	43.9	52.0	46.8	45.8	46.2	43.7	41.7	38.9
90-93	Arts, entertainment and recreation	2.8	6.8	8.9	5.1	3.5	0.2	0.1	0.1
94-99	Other services; household-employers; extraterritorial bodies	4.7	1.2	1.3	0.6	1.4	1.7	4.7	3.3

.. Not available

Note: Detailed metadata at: http://metalinks.oecd.org/anberd/20170419/301f.
Information on data for Israel: http://oe.cd/israel-disclaimer.

Disclaimer: http://oe.cd/disclaimer

DENMARK

R&D expenditure in industry by main activity of the enterprise, current prices
ISIC Rev. 4

Million USD PPP

		2007	2008	2009	2010	2011	2012	2013	2014
	TOTAL BUSINESS ENTERPRISE	..	..	4 754.7	4 673.8	4 859.9	4 897.4	4 941.0	4 952.6
01-03	**AGRICULTURE, FORESTRY AND FISHING**	..	..	3.8	7.0	7.0	5.8	7.1	6.6
05-09	**MINING AND QUARRYING**	..	..	3.6	5.8	5.6	1.9	6.4	11.1
10-33	**MANUFACTURING**	..	..	2 346.3	2 445.8	2 524.4	2 754.5	2 872.8	2 865.0
10-12	Food products, beverages and tobacco	..	..	58.9	49.9	69.0	81.9	64.8	50.0
13-15	Textiles, wearing apparel, leather and related products	..	..	3.4	4.0	2.4	2.7	2.7	2.7
13	Textiles	..	..	3.0	2.5	1.5	1.7	2.3	2.3
14	Wearing apparel	..	..	..	..	..	1.0	0.5	0.4
15	Leather and related products, footwear	..	..	..	..	..	0.0	0.0	0.0
16-18	Wood and paper products and printing	..	..	6.2	6.3	5.9	4.6	46.8	7.8
16	Wood and wood products, except furniture	..	..	1.2	1.1	1.4	1.5	43.4	2.3
17	Paper and paper products	..	..	4.9	3.9	4.2	3.1	3.3	5.6
18	Printing and reproduction of recorded media	..	..	0.1	1.3	0.3	0.0	0.0	0.0
19-23	Chemical, rubber, plastic, non-metallic mineral products	..	..	1 113.1	1 197.2	1 185.8	1 418.6	1 477.9	1 520.4
19	Coke and refined petroleum products	..	..	..	..	..	..	..	..
20-21	Chemical and pharmaceutical products	..	..	..	..	..	..	..	..
20	Chemicals and chemical products	..	..	..	..	..	..	..	..
21	Pharmaceuticals, medicinal, chemical and botanical products	..	..	848.0	932.3	892.2	1 065.8	1 128.2	1 140.6
22	Rubber and plastic products	..	..	54.1	51.1	50.3	53.8	55.1	55.9
23	Other non-metallic mineral products	..	..	10.6	5.5	4.7	22.4	23.5	24.8
24-25	Basic metals, metal products, except machinery and equipment	..	..	22.8	16.0	19.5	19.8	19.8	17.3
24	Basic metals	..	..	2.2	2.8	3.1	3.2	2.9	2.8
25	Fabricated metal products, except machinery and equipment	..	..	20.6	13.1	16.4	16.6	16.9	14.5
26-30	Computer, electronic, optical products; electrical machinery, transport equipment	..	..	1 002.0	1 042.4	1 112.5	1 079.5	1 079.1	1 087.4
26	Computer, electronic and optical products	..	..	338.4	334.9	325.7	373.3	406.6	412.8
27	Electrical equipment	..	..	50.1	70.5	78.6	73.1	69.1	71.0
28	Machinery and equipment n.e.c.	..	..	600.3	621.5	687.7	612.4	581.6	585.2
29	Motor vehicles, trailers and semi-trailers	..	..	10.0	10.5	14.9	15.3	15.7	11.6
30	Other transport equipment	..	..	3.2	5.1	5.5	5.4	6.1	6.8
31-33	Furniture; repair, installation of machinery and equipment	..	..	139.9	129.8	129.3	147.3	181.7	179.4
31	Furniture	..	..	9.2	5.2	6.1	4.5	4.0	5.5
32	Other manufacturing	..	..	129.1	123.9	123.2	141.3	177.7	173.9
33	Repair and installation of machinery and equipment	..	..	1.6	0.7	0.0	1.5	0.0	0.0
35-39	**ELECTRICITY, GAS, WATER AND WASTE MANAGEMENT**	..	..	98.2	31.5	37.3	13.2	12.5	13.5
35-36	Electricity, gas and water	..	..	96.5	30.5	34.2	9.2	10.9	8.9
37-39	Sewerage, waste management and remediation activities	..	..	1.7	0.9	3.1	4.0	1.5	4.6
41-43	**CONSTRUCTION**	..	..	2.1	7.3	5.3	5.9	7.2	5.0
45-99	**TOTAL SERVICES**	..	..	2 300.8	2 176.5	2 280.4	2 116.1	2 035.1	2 051.5
45-82	**Business sector services**	..	..	2 294.7	2 175.9	2 250.4	2 072.9	1 998.0	2 021.4
45-47	**Wholesale and retail trade; motor vehicle and motorcycle repairs**	..	..	167.5	176.3	255.7	236.4	160.9	222.7
49-53	**Transportation and storage**	..	..	27.7	19.4	7.5	15.6	8.9	7.7
55-56	**Accommodation and food service activities**	..	..	0.3	0.5	0.3	0.1	1.9	1.2
58-63	**Information and communication**	..	..	706.5	770.9	749.3	594.8	492.7	471.1
58-60	Publishing, audiovisual and broadcasting activities	..	..	121.1	114.5	89.3	74.3	71.5	86.6
58	Publishing activities	..	..	120.7	105.3	86.9	73.0	67.3	81.5
59-60	Motion picture, video and TV programme production; broadcasting activities	..	..	0.4	9.1	2.5	1.3	4.2	5.1
59	Motion picture, video and TV programme production; sound and music	..	..	0.4	9.1	2.5	1.3	4.2	3.6
60	Programming and broadcasting activities	..	..	0.0	0.0	0.0	0.0	0.0	1.5
61	Telecommunications	..	..	42.3	31.9	52.0	64.0	52.9	30.6
62-63	IT and other information services	..	..	542.9	624.6	607.9	456.5	368.4	353.9
62	Computer programming, consultancy and related activities	..	..	538.6	620.0	595.7	444.5	354.0	341.5
63	Information service activities	..	..	4.3	4.6	12.2	12.0	14.3	12.4
64-66	**Financial and insurance activities**	..	..	467.5	511.0	531.7	541.5	541.9	545.0
68-82	**Real estate; professional, scientific and technical; administrative and support**	..	..	925.3	697.7	705.8	684.1	791.6	773.6
68	Real estate activities	..	..	7.4	0.0	1.3	3.1	6.8	2.0
69-75x72	Professional, scientific and technical activities, except scientific R&D	..	..	246.7	151.5	164.9	161.7	175.1	150.5
72	Scientific research and development	..	..	660.1	538.4	530.1	512.2	605.2	611.3
77-82	Administrative and support service activities	..	..	11.1	7.8	9.5	7.0	4.6	9.8
84-99	**Community, social and personal services**	..	..	6.1	0.6	30.0	43.2	37.1	30.1
84-85	Public administration and defence; compulsory social security and education	..	..	..	..	..	..	..	..
86-88	Human health and social work activities	..	..	..	..	..	..	..	..
90-93	Arts, entertainment and recreation	..	..	3.2	0.3	0.1	6.1	5.2	5.1
94-99	Other services; household-employers; extraterritorial bodies	..	..	0.0	0.1	29.9	29.6	31.5	24.7

.. Not available

Note: Detailed metadata at: http://metalinks.oecd.org/anberd/20170419/301f.
Information on data for Israel: http://oe.cd/israel-disclaimer.
Disclaimer: http://oe.cd/disclaimer

DENMARK

R&D expenditure in industry by main activity of the enterprise, constant prices
ISIC Rev. 4

2010 USD PPP

Code	Activity	2007	2008	2009	2010	2011	2012	2013	2014
	TOTAL BUSINESS ENTERPRISE	..	..	5 001.8	4 673.8	4 758.8	4 745.5	4 610.1	4 569.2
01-03	**AGRICULTURE, FORESTRY AND FISHING**	..	..	4.0	7.0	6.8	5.6	6.7	6.0
05-09	**MINING AND QUARRYING**	..	..	3.8	5.8	5.5	1.8	6.0	10.2
10-33	**MANUFACTURING**	..	..	2 468.2	2 445.8	2 471.9	2 669.0	2 680.4	2 643.3
10-12	Food products, beverages and tobacco	..	..	62.0	49.9	67.6	79.4	60.5	46.1
13-15	Textiles, wearing apparel, leather and related products	..	..	3.5	4.0	2.3	2.6	2.5	2.5
13	Textiles	..	..	3.1	2.5	1.5	1.7	2.1	2.1
14	Wearing apparel	..	..	..	..	..	0.9	0.4	0.4
15	Leather and related products, footwear	..	..	..	..	..	0.0	0.0	0.0
16-18	Wood and paper products and printing	..	..	6.5	6.3	5.7	4.4	43.6	7.2
16	Wood and wood products, except furniture	..	..	1.2	1.1	1.4	1.5	40.5	2.1
17	Paper and paper products	..	..	5.2	3.9	4.1	3.0	3.1	5.2
18	Printing and reproduction of recorded media	..	..	0.1	1.3	0.3	0.0	0.0	0.0
19-23	Chemical, rubber, plastic, non-metallic mineral products	..	..	1 171.0	1 197.2	1 161.1	1 374.6	1 378.9	1 402.7
19	Coke and refined petroleum products	..	..	..	..	..	..	..	..
20-21	Chemical and pharmaceutical products	..	..	..	..	..	..	..	..
20	Chemicals and chemical products	..	..	..	..	..	..	..	..
21	Pharmaceuticals, medicinal, chemical and botanical products	..	..	892.1	932.3	873.6	1 032.8	1 052.6	1 052.4
22	Rubber and plastic products	..	..	56.9	51.1	49.3	52.1	51.4	51.6
23	Other non-metallic mineral products	..	..	11.2	5.5	4.6	21.7	21.9	22.9
24-25	Basic metals, metal products, except machinery and equipment	..	..	24.0	16.0	19.1	19.2	18.5	16.0
24	Basic metals	..	..	2.3	2.8	3.1	3.1	2.7	2.6
25	Fabricated metal products, except machinery and equipment	..	..	21.7	13.1	16.1	16.1	15.7	13.4
26-30	Computer, electronic, optical products; electrical machinery, transport equipment	..	..	1 054.1	1 042.4	1 089.3	1 046.0	1 006.8	1 003.2
26	Computer, electronic and optical products	..	..	356.0	334.9	318.9	361.7	379.4	380.8
27	Electrical equipment	..	..	52.7	70.5	77.0	70.8	64.5	65.5
28	Machinery and equipment n.e.c.	..	..	631.5	621.5	673.4	593.4	542.6	539.9
29	Motor vehicles, trailers and semi-trailers	..	..	10.5	10.5	14.6	14.8	14.6	10.7
30	Other transport equipment	..	..	3.4	5.1	5.4	5.2	5.7	6.2
31-33	Furniture; repair, installation of machinery and equipment	..	..	147.1	129.8	126.6	142.7	169.5	165.5
31	Furniture	..	..	9.7	5.2	6.0	4.3	3.7	5.1
32	Other manufacturing	..	..	135.8	123.9	120.6	136.9	165.8	160.4
33	Repair and installation of machinery and equipment	..	..	1.6	0.7	0.0	1.5	0.0	0.0
35-39	**ELECTRICITY, GAS, WATER AND WASTE MANAGEMENT**	..	..	103.3	31.5	36.5	12.8	11.6	12.4
35-36	Electricity, gas and water	..	..	101.5	30.5	33.5	9.0	10.2	8.2
37-39	Sewerage, waste management and remediation activities	..	..	1.8	0.9	3.1	3.9	1.4	4.3
41-43	**CONSTRUCTION**	..	..	2.2	7.3	5.2	5.7	6.7	4.6
45-99	**TOTAL SERVICES**	..	..	2 420.4	2 176.5	2 232.9	2 050.4	1 898.8	1 892.7
45-82	**Business sector services**	..	..	2 414.0	2 175.9	2 203.5	2 008.6	1 864.2	1 864.9
45-47	Wholesale and retail trade; motor vehicle and motorcycle repairs	..	..	176.2	176.3	250.4	229.5	150.2	205.4
49-53	Transportation and storage	..	..	29.2	19.4	7.4	15.1	8.3	7.1
55-56	Accommodation and food service activities	..	..	0.3	0.5	0.3	0.1	1.7	1.1
58-63	Information and communication	..	..	743.2	770.9	733.7	576.4	459.7	434.7
58-60	Publishing, audiovisual and broadcasting activities	..	..	127.4	114.5	87.5	72.0	66.7	79.9
58	Publishing activities	..	..	127.0	105.3	85.1	70.7	62.8	75.2
59-60	Motion picture, video and TV programme production; broadcasting activities	..	..	0.4	9.1	2.4	1.3	3.9	4.7
59	Motion picture, video and TV programme production; sound and music	..	..	0.4	9.1	2.4	1.3	3.9	3.3
60	Programming and broadcasting activities	..	..	0.0	0.0	0.0	0.0	0.0	1.4
61	Telecommunications	..	..	44.5	31.9	50.9	62.0	49.3	28.2
62-63	IT and other information services	..	..	571.1	624.6	595.3	442.3	343.7	326.5
62	Computer programming, consultancy and related activities	..	..	566.6	620.0	583.3	430.7	330.3	315.1
63	Information service activities	..	..	4.5	4.6	11.9	11.6	13.4	11.4
64-66	Financial and insurance activities	..	..	491.8	511.0	520.6	524.7	505.6	502.8
68-82	Real estate; professional, scientific and technical; administrative and support	..	..	973.4	697.7	691.1	662.8	738.6	713.7
68	Real estate activities	..	..	7.8	0.0	1.2	3.0	6.3	1.9
69-75x72	Professional, scientific and technical activities, except scientific R&D	..	..	259.5	151.5	161.5	156.7	163.4	138.8
72	Scientific research and development	..	..	694.4	538.4	519.1	496.3	564.6	564.0
77-82	Administrative and support service activities	..	..	11.7	7.8	9.3	6.8	4.3	9.1
84-99	**Community, social and personal services**	..	..	6.4	0.6	29.4	41.9	34.6	27.7
84-85	Public administration and defence; compulsory social security and education	..	..	..	..	..	..	..	..
86-88	Human health and social work activities	..	..	..	..	..	..	..	..
90-93	Arts, entertainment and recreation	..	..	3.4	0.3	0.1	5.9	4.9	4.7
94-99	Other services; household-employers; extraterritorial bodies	..	..	0.0	0.1	29.3	28.7	29.4	22.8

.. Not available

Note: Detailed metadata at: http://metalinks.oecd.org/anberd/20170419/301f.
Information on data for Israel: http://oe.cd/israel-disclaimer.
Disclaimer: http://oe.cd/disclaimer

ESTONIA

R&D expenditure in industry by main activity of the enterprise, current prices
ISIC Rev. 4

Million USD PPP

		2007	2008	2009	2010	2011	2012	2013	2014
	TOTAL BUSINESS ENTERPRISE	148.3	164.9	170.8	228.4	474.7	420.3	298.1	237.3
01-03	**AGRICULTURE, FORESTRY AND FISHING**	0.2	0.5	..	..	0.1	..	..	..
05-09	**MINING AND QUARRYING**	..	..	..	..	..	..	..	..
10-33	**MANUFACTURING**	49.7	37.4	35.1	83.9	302.8	182.3	103.0	51.1
10-12	Food products, beverages and tobacco	6.7	3.7	3.9	3.0	2.7	2.6	9.0	6.0
13-15	Textiles, wearing apparel, leather and related products	0.9	1.2	0.7	1.0	1.0	0.9	1.0	1.2
13	Textiles	..	..	..	..	..	..	..	..
14	Wearing apparel	..	..	..	..	..	..	..	..
15	Leather and related products, footwear	..	..	..	..	..	..	..	..
16-18	Wood and paper products and printing	3.7	0.8	0.6	3.9	1.1	0.2	0.6	0.1
16	Wood and wood products, except furniture	3.2	0.8	..	..	..	..	0.6	0.1
17	Paper and paper products	0.4	0.0	0.0	0.0	0.0	0.0	0.0	0.0
18	Printing and reproduction of recorded media	0.0	0.0	..	..	..	..	0.0	0.0
19-23	Chemical, rubber, plastic, non-metallic mineral products	..	..	..	..	..	..	..	..
19	Coke and refined petroleum products	11.2	11.4	4.7	..	263.9	146.3	64.6	9.1
20-21	Chemical and pharmaceutical products	..	..	..	6.9	9.2	8.5	6.7	5.9
20	Chemicals and chemical products	4.5	4.9	5.1	6.4	3.0	6.8	4.8	3.7
21	Pharmaceuticals, medicinal, chemical and botanical products	..	..	..	0.5	6.2	1.7	1.9	2.1
22	Rubber and plastic products	..	0.6	1.6	1.3	1.7	1.6	0.8	7.6
23	Other non-metallic mineral products	0.4	0.4	0.1	..	..	..	..	..
24-25	Basic metals, metal products, except machinery and equipment	0.9	0.2	1.6	..	0.7	0.4	..	..
24	Basic metals	0.0	0.0	0.0	..	0.0	0.0	..	..
25	Fabricated metal products, except machinery and equipment	0.9	0.2	1.6	0.8	0.7	0.4	1.7	1.4
26-30	Computer, electronic, optical products; electrical machinery, transport equipment	16.7	10.9	12.8	13.4	19.2	18.7	16.0	16.7
26	Computer, electronic and optical products	9.0	4.4	5.9	5.6	5.7	4.5	5.0	8.0
27	Electrical equipment	0.8	0.6	2.2	3.2	7.9	8.4	3.5	4.7
28	Machinery and equipment n.e.c.	4.0	4.3	2.8	2.0	1.6	1.4	5.2	1.2
29	Motor vehicles, trailers and semi-trailers	2.9	1.5	1.7	1.8	3.7	4.4	2.3	2.8
30	Other transport equipment	0.0	..	..	..	..	..	..	..
31-33	Furniture; repair, installation of machinery and equipment	..	2.7	3.5	..	3.0	..	2.2	..
31	Furniture	0.9	0.4	0.3	0.5	0.4	0.6	0.4	..
32	Other manufacturing	1.4	1.3	2.8	2.2	2.4	1.6	1.5	1.6
33	Repair and installation of machinery and equipment	..	1.0	0.3	..	0.1	..	0.4	0.2
35-39	**ELECTRICITY, GAS, WATER AND WASTE MANAGEMENT**	3.4	5.4	5.4	4.9	23.7	33.0	9.6	25.3
35-36	Electricity, gas and water	..	..	..	..	..	..	..	..
37-39	Sewerage, waste management and remediation activities	..	..	..	..	..	..	..	..
41-43	**CONSTRUCTION**	..	..	..	..	0.7	5.9	..	..
45-99	**TOTAL SERVICES**	94.5	121.1	129.6	137.7	147.0	198.7	181.2	156.7
45-82	**Business sector services**	94.5	121.1	127.5	137.7	144.5	196.2	179.1	152.8
45-47	Wholesale and retail trade; motor vehicle and motorcycle repairs	5.7	5.8	7.6	2.9	2.9	3.3	2.7	2.7
49-53	Transportation and storage	4.9	4.7	1.3	..	..	..	..	..
55-56	Accommodation and food service activities	0.0	0.0	0.0	0.0	0.0	0.0	0.0	0.0
58-63	Information and communication	52.9	70.3	61.4	57.7	68.9	101.0	85.3	72.5
58-60	Publishing, audiovisual and broadcasting activities	0.0	0.0	..	..	..	..	..	..
58	Publishing activities	..	..	..	..	..	..	..	..
59-60	Motion picture, video and TV programme production; broadcasting activities	..	0.0	0.0	0.0	0.0	0.0	0.0	0.0
59	Motion picture, video and TV programme production; sound and music	0.0	0.0	0.0	0.0	0.0	0.0	0.0	0.0
60	Programming and broadcasting activities	..	0.0	0.0	0.0	0.0	0.0	0.0	0.0
61	Telecommunications	11.0	12.1	..	3.9	11.5	25.0	11.9	10.9
62-63	IT and other information services	41.7	58.2	..	53.7	57.3	75.9	..	..
62	Computer programming, consultancy and related activities	40.3	57.0	49.4	52.8	54.6	73.2	69.7	59.4
63	Information service activities	1.4	..	..	1.0	2.7	2.7	..	..
64-66	Financial and insurance activities	11.3	14.0	19.3	26.0	22.5	22.5	25.4	25.1
68-82	Real estate; professional, scientific and technical; administrative and support	19.5	26.0	37.8	50.6	49.4	69.4	65.4	50.1
68	Real estate activities	0.0	0.0	0.0	0.0	0.0	0.0	0.0	0.0
69-75x72	Professional, scientific and technical activities, except scientific R&D	5.9	6.9	6.8	6.9	7.9	11.2	10.8	9.6
72	Scientific research and development	13.5	18.9	29.1	41.9	40.5	57.5	54.1	40.2
77-82	Administrative and support service activities	..	..	2.0	1.9	..	..	..	..
84-99	Community, social and personal services	..	..	2.1	..	2.6	2.5	2.2	3.9
84-85	Public administration and defence; compulsory social security and education	0.0	0.0	0.0	0.0	0.0	0.0	0.0	0.0
86-88	Human health and social work activities	..	..	2.1	..	2.6	2.5	2.2	3.9
90-93	Arts, entertainment and recreation	0.0	0.0	0.0	0.0	0.0	0.0	0.0	0.0
94-99	Other services; household-employers; extraterritorial bodies	..	0.0	0.0	0.0	0.0	0.0	0.0	0.0

.. Not available

Note: Detailed metadata at: http://metalinks.oecd.org/anberd/20170419/301f.
    Information on data for Israel: http://oe.cd/israel-disclaimer.
Disclaimer: http://oe.cd/disclaimer

ESTONIA

R&D expenditure in industry by main activity of the enterprise, constant prices
ISIC Rev. 4

2010 USD PPP

Code	Activity	2007	2008	2009	2010	2011	2012	2013	2014
	TOTAL BUSINESS ENTERPRISE	175.9	179.7	175.6	228.4	451.4	394.6	269.9	212.9
01-03	**AGRICULTURE, FORESTRY AND FISHING**	0.2	0.5	..	..	0.1	..	..	..
05-09	**MINING AND QUARRYING**	..	..	..	..	..	..	..	..
10-33	**MANUFACTURING**	59.0	40.7	36.1	83.9	287.9	171.1	93.3	45.9
10-12	Food products, beverages and tobacco	8.0	4.1	4.0	3.0	2.6	2.4	8.1	5.4
13-15	Textiles, wearing apparel, leather and related products	1.1	1.3	0.8	1.0	1.0	0.8	0.9	1.1
13	Textiles	..	..	..	..	..	..	..	..
14	Wearing apparel	..	..	..	..	..	..	..	..
15	Leather and related products, footwear	..	..	..	..	..	..	..	..
16-18	Wood and paper products and printing	4.3	0.9	0.6	3.9	1.1	0.2	0.6	0.1
16	Wood and wood products, except furniture	3.8	0.9	..	..	..	..	0.6	0.1
17	Paper and paper products	0.5	0.0	0.0	0.0	0.0	0.0	0.0	0.0
18	Printing and reproduction of recorded media	0.0	0.0	..	..	..	..	0.0	0.0
19-23	Chemical, rubber, plastic, non-metallic mineral products	..	..	..	..	..	..	..	..
19	Coke and refined petroleum products	13.3	12.4	4.9	..	250.9	137.3	58.5	8.2
20-21	Chemical and pharmaceutical products	..	..	..	6.9	8.8	8.0	6.0	5.3
20	Chemicals and chemical products	5.4	5.4	5.3	6.4	2.9	6.4	4.3	3.4
21	Pharmaceuticals, medicinal, chemical and botanical products	..	..	..	0.5	5.9	1.6	1.7	1.9
22	Rubber and plastic products	..	0.7	1.6	1.3	1.7	1.5	0.8	6.8
23	Other non-metallic mineral products	0.5	0.4	0.1	..	..	..	..	..
24-25	Basic metals, metal products, except machinery and equipment	1.1	0.3	1.7	..	0.7	0.4	..	..
24	Basic metals	0.0	0.0	0.0	..	0.0	0.0	..	..
25	Fabricated metal products, except machinery and equipment	1.1	0.3	1.7	0.8	0.7	0.4	1.5	1.2
26-30	Computer, electronic, optical products; electrical machinery, transport equipment	19.8	11.9	13.2	13.4	18.2	17.6	14.5	15.0
26	Computer, electronic and optical products	10.7	4.7	6.1	5.6	5.4	4.2	4.5	7.2
27	Electrical equipment	0.9	0.7	2.3	3.2	7.5	7.9	3.1	4.2
28	Machinery and equipment n.e.c.	4.7	4.7	2.9	2.0	1.5	1.3	4.7	1.1
29	Motor vehicles, trailers and semi-trailers	3.5	1.6	1.8	1.8	3.5	4.2	2.0	2.5
30	Other transport equipment	0.0	..	..	..	..	..	..	..
31-33	Furniture; repair, installation of machinery and equipment	..	3.0	3.6	..	2.8	..	2.0	..
31	Furniture	1.0	0.4	0.3	0.5	0.4	0.5	0.3	..
32	Other manufacturing	1.7	1.5	2.9	2.2	2.3	1.5	1.3	1.4
33	Repair and installation of machinery and equipment	..	1.1	0.3	..	0.1	..	0.3	0.2
35-39	**ELECTRICITY, GAS, WATER AND WASTE MANAGEMENT**	4.0	5.9	5.6	4.9	22.6	31.0	8.7	22.7
35-36	Electricity, gas and water	..	..	..	..	..	..	..	..
37-39	Sewerage, waste management and remediation activities	..	..	..	..	..	..	..	..
41-43	**CONSTRUCTION**	..	..	..	..	0.7	5.6	..	..
45-99	**TOTAL SERVICES**	112.1	131.9	133.2	137.7	139.8	186.5	164.1	140.6
45-82	**Business sector services**	112.1	131.9	131.1	137.7	137.4	184.2	162.1	137.1
45-47	Wholesale and retail trade; motor vehicle and motorcycle repairs	6.8	6.3	7.9	2.9	2.8	3.1	2.5	2.4
49-53	Transportation and storage	5.8	5.2	1.4	..	..	..	..	..
55-56	Accommodation and food service activities	0.0	0.0	0.0	0.0	0.0	0.0	0.0	0.0
58-63	Information and communication	62.7	76.5	63.1	57.7	65.5	94.8	77.2	65.1
58-60	Publishing, audiovisual and broadcasting activities	0.0	0.0	..	..	..	..	..	..
58	Publishing activities	..	..	..	..	..	..	..	..
59-60	Motion picture, video and TV programme production; broadcasting activities	..	0.0	0.0	0.0	0.0	0.0	0.0	0.0
59	Motion picture, video and TV programme production; sound and music	0.0	0.0	0.0	0.0	0.0	0.0	0.0	0.0
60	Programming and broadcasting activities	..	0.0	0.0	0.0	0.0	0.0	0.0	0.0
61	Telecommunications	13.0	13.1	..	3.9	11.0	23.5	10.8	9.7
62-63	IT and other information services	49.5	63.4	..	53.7	54.4	71.3	..	..
62	Computer programming, consultancy and related activities	47.8	62.1	50.8	52.8	51.9	68.7	63.1	53.3
63	Information service activities	1.7	..	..	1.0	2.6	2.6	..	..
64-66	Financial and insurance activities	13.4	15.3	19.9	26.0	21.4	21.1	23.0	22.5
68-82	Real estate; professional, scientific and technical; administrative and support	23.1	28.3	38.9	50.6	46.9	65.1	59.2	45.0
68	Real estate activities	0.0	0.0	0.0	0.0	0.0	0.0	0.0	0.0
69-75x72	Professional, scientific and technical activities, except scientific R&D	6.9	7.5	6.9	6.9	7.5	10.5	9.8	8.7
72	Scientific research and development	16.0	20.6	29.9	41.9	38.5	54.0	49.0	36.1
77-82	Administrative and support service activities	..	..	2.1	1.9	..	..	..	..
84-99	Community, social and personal services	..	..	2.1	..	2.4	2.3	2.0	3.5
84-85	Public administration and defence; compulsory social security and education	0.0	0.0	0.0	0.0	0.0	0.0	0.0	0.0
86-88	Human health and social work activities	..	..	2.1	..	2.4	2.3	2.0	3.5
90-93	Arts, entertainment and recreation	0.0	0.0	0.0	0.0	0.0	0.0	0.0	0.0
94-99	Other services; household-employers; extraterritorial bodies	..	0.0	0.0	0.0	0.0	0.0	0.0	0.0

.. Not available

Note: Detailed metadata at: http://metalinks.oecd.org/anberd/20170419/301f.
Information on data for Israel: http://oe.cd/israel-disclaimer.
Disclaimer: http://oe.cd/disclaimer

FINLAND

R&D expenditure in industry by main activity of the enterprise, current prices
ISIC Rev. 4

Million USD PPP

		2007	2008	2009	2010	2011	2012	2013	2014
	TOTAL BUSINESS ENTERPRISE	4 821.5	5 593.5	5 413.4	5 401.0	5 620.3	5 167.9	5 088.1	4 869.7
01-03	**AGRICULTURE, FORESTRY AND FISHING**	0.3	0.7	1.2	3.9	5.5	2.0	3.2	1.7
05-09	**MINING AND QUARRYING**	6.4	11.1	16.5	9.1	9.3	10.9	9.4	7.0
10-33	**MANUFACTURING**	3 830.7	4 456.0	4 333.3	4 302.6	4 318.3	3 728.4	3 629.5	3 452.7
10-12	Food products, beverages and tobacco	62.2	69.0	63.8	71.8	71.5	65.6	75.7	78.3
13-15	Textiles, wearing apparel, leather and related products	11.4	13.7	19.1	9.6	7.6	5.4	7.0	9.7
13	Textiles	..	..	..	6.5	4.7	3.4	5.3	4.4
14	Wearing apparel	..	..	..	3.0	2.6	1.6	1.3	5.1
15	Leather and related products, footwear	..	..	..	0.2	0.3	0.5	0.3	0.2
16-18	Wood and paper products and printing	111.0	126.2	107.2	129.8	101.1	109.1	105.1	99.9
16	Wood and wood products, except furniture	12.3	11.8	11.4	12.0	10.7	8.5	8.4	8.8
17	Paper and paper products	91.3	105.6	87.6	112.9	84.5	94.3	90.1	85.1
18	Printing and reproduction of recorded media	7.4	8.8	8.2	4.9	5.8	6.4	6.6	6.0
19-23	Chemical, rubber, plastic, non-metallic mineral products	370.8	398.0	358.9	368.2	390.1	385.0	385.8	364.2
19	Coke and refined petroleum products	..	..	..	..	..	..	..	..
20-21	Chemical and pharmaceutical products	285.4	285.3	251.0	253.1	273.6	267.2	274.1	264.8
20	Chemicals and chemical products	..	163.3	128.9	136.0	143.5	117.1	141.5	116.1
21	Pharmaceuticals, medicinal, chemical and botanical products	..	122.0	122.0	117.1	130.1	150.1	132.6	148.8
22	Rubber and plastic products	..	..	..	..	..	..	..	..
23	Other non-metallic mineral products	30.2	30.0	27.0	33.4	33.7	37.3	30.3	32.5
24-25	Basic metals, metal products, except machinery and equipment	86.8	105.1	115.6	116.2	108.3	98.9	93.6	82.3
24	Basic metals	52.6	62.3	63.9	67.0	56.4	51.9	44.8	35.7
25	Fabricated metal products, except machinery and equipment	34.2	42.8	51.7	49.3	51.9	47.0	48.9	46.6
26-30	Computer, electronic, optical products; electrical machinery, transport equipment	3 139.7	3 705.1	3 633.9	3 572.5	3 604.0	3 023.4	2 929.2	2 788.6
26	Computer, electronic and optical products	2 526.3	2 988.6	2 943.3	2 875.7	2 794.6	2 097.5	1 968.6	1 920.0
27	Electrical equipment	159.9	230.7	236.8	258.7	289.4	318.4	332.0	335.1
28	Machinery and equipment n.e.c.	405.9	439.0	389.4	385.5	444.2	518.7	557.6	488.7
29	Motor vehicles, trailers and semi-trailers	21.7	21.4	25.7	21.5	22.9	23.2	27.9	28.4
30	Other transport equipment	25.8	25.5	38.8	31.0	52.9	65.5	43.1	16.5
31-33	Furniture; repair, installation of machinery and equipment	48.7	39.0	34.8	34.5	35.8	40.9	33.0	29.7
31	Furniture	..	..	..	..	..	..	..	..
32	Other manufacturing	..	20.7	16.7	16.2	15.4	20.3	14.7	15.4
33	Repair and installation of machinery and equipment	..	..	..	..	..	..	..	..
35-39	**ELECTRICITY, GAS, WATER AND WASTE MANAGEMENT**	34.9	37.4	43.3	45.7	57.4	62.4	53.5	40.6
35-36	Electricity, gas and water	..	12.0	15.8	23.6	26.0	33.7	27.7	21.1
37-39	Sewerage, waste management and remediation activities	..	25.3	27.6	22.1	31.4	28.7	25.8	19.7
41-43	**CONSTRUCTION**	35.4	36.0	48.9	64.3	55.3	56.5	50.4	88.0
45-99	**TOTAL SERVICES**	913.7	1 052.2	970.2	975.4	1 174.5	1 307.7	1 342.1	1 279.7
45-82	Business sector services	904.6	1 042.1	957.9	955.2	1 153.6	1 278.5	1 316.8	1 250.7
45-47	Wholesale and retail trade; motor vehicle and motorcycle repairs	66.1	76.7	82.1	80.3	101.7	129.0	93.5	79.5
49-53	Transportation and storage	..	22.1	20.0	11.7	17.3	19.6	17.2	16.1
55-56	Accommodation and food service activities	..	..	..	0.7	0.7	1.1	0.5	0.1
58-63	Information and communication	..	468.8	418.4	460.8	500.5	514.4	603.2	564.4
58-60	Publishing, audiovisual and broadcasting activities	..	15.0	11.5	57.8	64.4	64.0	75.3	90.3
58	Publishing activities	..	12.3	9.3	55.7	61.3	62.2	74.2	86.8
59-60	Motion picture, video and TV programme production; broadcasting activities	..	2.7	2.2	2.2	3.1	1.8	1.1	3.5
59	Motion picture, video and TV programme production; sound and music	..	..	..	2.1	..	..	..	..
60	Programming and broadcasting activities	..	..	..	0.1	..	..	..	..
61	Telecommunications	..	60.5	50.6	48.8	42.3	27.4	38.8	40.1
62-63	IT and other information services	373.0	393.2	356.3	354.2	393.8	423.0	489.1	434.1
62	Computer programming, consultancy and related activities	..	377.1	342.1	337.4	383.3	416.9	473.8	410.7
63	Information service activities	..	16.2	14.2	16.7	10.5	6.1	15.3	23.4
64-66	Financial and insurance activities	37.8	83.5	77.1	76.3	79.3	94.8	75.6	103.9
68-82	Real estate; professional, scientific and technical; administrative and support	335.8	390.9	360.3	325.4	454.1	519.6	526.8	486.6
68	Real estate activities	..	..	..	2.6	3.1	3.2	1.4	0.2
69-75x72	Professional, scientific and technical activities, except scientific R&D	..	214.7	188.3	190.7	170.0	192.3	154.2	140.7
72	Scientific research and development	180.9	176.3	172.0	128.8	276.4	318.8	367.5	338.7
77-82	Administrative and support service activities	..	..	..	3.3	4.5	5.3	3.5	6.8
84-99	Community, social and personal services	9.1	10.2	12.3	20.2	21.0	29.2	25.3	29.0
84-85	Public administration and defence; compulsory social security and education	..	..	..	0.0	1.4	3.3	1.4	1.9
86-88	Human health and social work activities	..	..	..	2.8	3.0	4.0	5.3	2.2
90-93	Arts, entertainment and recreation	..	..	..	14.5	13.2	16.8	16.7	22.5
94-99	Other services; household-employers; extraterritorial bodies	..	..	..	2.9	3.4	5.1	1.9	2.4

.. Not available

Note: Detailed metadata at: http://metalinks.oecd.org/anberd/20170419/301f.
Information on data for Israel: http://oe.cd/israel-disclaimer.
Disclaimer: http://oe.cd/disclaimer

FINLAND

R&D expenditure in industry by main activity of the enterprise, constant prices
ISIC Rev. 4

2010 USD PPP

ISIC	Activity	2007	2008	2009	2010	2011	2012	2013	2014
	TOTAL BUSINESS ENTERPRISE	5 291.7	5 803.2	5 411.8	5 401.0	5 474.2	4 945.9	4 727.7	4 453.1
01-03	**AGRICULTURE, FORESTRY AND FISHING**	0.4	0.7	1.2	3.9	5.4	1.9	3.0	1.5
05-09	**MINING AND QUARRYING**	7.1	11.6	16.5	9.1	9.0	10.4	8.7	6.4
10-33	**MANUFACTURING**	4 204.3	4 623.1	4 332.0	4 302.6	4 206.0	3 568.2	3 372.4	3 157.3
10-12	Food products, beverages and tobacco	68.2	71.5	63.8	71.8	69.6	62.8	70.4	71.6
13-15	Textiles, wearing apparel, leather and related products	12.5	14.2	19.1	9.6	7.4	5.2	6.5	8.9
13	Textiles	..	..	..	6.5	4.5	3.2	4.9	4.0
14	Wearing apparel	..	..	..	3.0	2.5	1.6	1.3	4.7
15	Leather and related products, footwear	..	..	..	0.2	0.3	0.4	0.3	0.2
16-18	Wood and paper products and printing	121.9	130.9	107.2	129.8	98.4	104.5	97.7	91.4
16	Wood and wood products, except furniture	13.5	12.2	11.4	12.0	10.4	8.1	7.8	8.1
17	Paper and paper products	100.2	109.5	87.6	112.9	82.3	90.2	83.7	77.9
18	Printing and reproduction of recorded media	8.2	9.2	8.2	4.9	5.7	6.1	6.2	5.5
19-23	Chemical, rubber, plastic, non-metallic mineral products	407.0	413.0	358.8	368.2	379.9	368.5	358.5	333.0
19	Coke and refined petroleum products	..	..	..	..	..	..	..	..
20-21	Chemical and pharmaceutical products	313.2	296.0	250.9	253.1	266.5	255.8	254.7	242.2
20	Chemicals and chemical products	..	169.5	128.9	136.0	139.8	112.1	131.5	106.1
21	Pharmaceuticals, medicinal, chemical and botanical products	..	126.6	122.0	117.1	126.7	143.7	123.2	136.0
22	Rubber and plastic products	..	..	..	..	..	..	..	..
23	Other non-metallic mineral products	33.2	31.1	27.0	33.4	32.8	35.7	28.1	29.7
24-25	Basic metals, metal products, except machinery and equipment	95.3	109.0	115.5	116.2	105.5	94.7	87.0	75.2
24	Basic metals	57.7	64.6	63.8	67.0	54.9	49.7	41.6	32.6
25	Fabricated metal products, except machinery and equipment	37.6	44.4	51.7	49.3	50.5	45.0	45.4	42.6
26-30	Computer, electronic, optical products; electrical machinery, transport equipment	3 445.8	3 844.0	3 632.9	3 572.5	3 510.3	2 893.5	2 721.7	2 550.1
26	Computer, electronic and optical products	2 772.7	3 100.7	2 942.4	2 875.7	2 722.0	2 007.4	1 829.2	1 755.8
27	Electrical equipment	175.5	239.3	236.7	258.7	281.8	304.7	308.5	306.4
28	Machinery and equipment n.e.c.	445.5	455.5	389.3	385.5	432.6	496.5	518.1	446.9
29	Motor vehicles, trailers and semi-trailers	23.8	22.2	25.7	21.5	22.3	22.2	25.9	26.0
30	Other transport equipment	28.4	26.4	38.8	31.0	51.6	62.7	40.1	15.0
31-33	Furniture; repair, installation of machinery and equipment	53.5	40.5	34.7	34.5	34.8	39.2	30.6	27.1
31	Furniture	..	..	..	..	..	..	..	..
32	Other manufacturing	..	21.5	16.7	16.2	15.0	19.4	13.7	14.0
33	Repair and installation of machinery and equipment	..	..	..	..	..	..	..	..
35-39	**ELECTRICITY, GAS, WATER AND WASTE MANAGEMENT**	38.3	38.8	43.3	45.7	55.9	59.7	49.7	37.2
35-36	Electricity, gas and water	..	12.5	15.8	23.6	25.3	32.3	25.8	19.3
37-39	Sewerage, waste management and remediation activities	..	26.3	27.6	22.1	30.6	27.4	23.9	18.0
41-43	**CONSTRUCTION**	38.9	37.4	48.9	64.3	53.9	54.1	46.8	80.5
45-99	**TOTAL SERVICES**	1 002.8	1 091.7	969.9	975.4	1 144.0	1 251.6	1 247.1	1 170.3
45-82	**Business sector services**	992.8	1 081.1	957.6	955.2	1 123.6	1 223.6	1 223.5	1 143.7
45-47	Wholesale and retail trade; motor vehicle and motorcycle repairs	72.6	79.6	82.0	80.3	99.0	123.5	86.9	72.7
49-53	Transportation and storage	..	22.9	20.0	11.7	16.9	18.7	16.0	14.7
55-56	Accommodation and food service activities	..	..	..	0.7	0.7	1.0	0.4	0.1
58-63	Information and communication	..	486.4	418.3	460.8	487.5	492.3	560.5	516.2
58-60	Publishing, audiovisual and broadcasting activities	..	15.6	11.5	57.8	62.7	61.3	70.0	82.6
58	Publishing activities	..	12.8	9.3	55.7	59.7	59.6	68.9	79.4
59-60	Motion picture, video and TV programme production; broadcasting activities	..	2.8	2.2	2.2	3.0	1.7	1.0	3.2
59	Motion picture, video and TV programme production; sound and music	..	..	..	2.1	..	..	..	..
60	Programming and broadcasting activities	..	..	..	0.1	..	..	..	..
61	Telecommunications	..	62.8	50.6	48.8	41.2	26.2	36.1	36.7
62-63	IT and other information services	409.4	408.0	356.2	354.2	383.6	404.8	454.4	397.0
62	Computer programming, consultancy and related activities	..	391.2	342.0	337.4	373.4	399.0	440.3	375.6
63	Information service activities	..	16.8	14.2	16.7	10.2	5.8	14.2	21.4
64-66	Financial and insurance activities	41.4	86.7	77.1	76.3	77.3	90.8	70.3	95.0
68-82	Real estate; professional, scientific and technical; administrative and support	368.6	405.6	360.2	325.4	442.3	497.3	489.4	445.0
68	Real estate activities	..	..	..	2.6	3.0	3.1	1.3	0.2
69-75x72	Professional, scientific and technical activities, except scientific R&D	..	222.7	188.2	190.7	165.6	184.0	143.3	128.7
72	Scientific research and development	198.5	182.9	172.0	128.8	269.2	305.1	341.5	309.7
77-82	Administrative and support service activities	..	..	..	3.3	4.4	5.1	3.3	6.3
84-99	Community, social and personal services	9.9	10.6	12.3	20.2	20.4	27.9	23.5	26.6
84-85	Public administration and defence; compulsory social security and education	..	..	..	0.0	1.3	3.1	1.3	1.7
86-88	Human health and social work activities	..	..	..	2.8	3.0	3.8	4.9	2.0
90-93	Arts, entertainment and recreation	..	..	..	14.5	12.8	16.1	15.5	20.6
94-99	Other services; household-employers; extraterritorial bodies	..	..	..	2.9	3.3	4.9	1.7	2.2

.. Not available

Note: Detailed metadata at: http://metalinks.oecd.org/anberd/20170419/301f.
Information on data for Israel: http://oe.cd/israel-disclaimer.
Disclaimer: http://oe.cd/disclaimer

FINLAND

R&D expenditure in industry by product field, current prices
ISIC Rev. 4

Million USD PPP

		2007	2008	2009	2010	2011	2012	2013	2014
	TOTAL BUSINESS ENTERPRISE	..	..	..	5 401.0	5 620.3	5 167.9	5 088.1	4 869.7
01-03	**AGRICULTURE, FORESTRY AND FISHING**	..	..	..	13.3	22.3	21.0	13.8	12.2
05-09	**MINING AND QUARRYING**	..	..	..	41.8	40.8	18.4	15.5	15.7
10-33	**MANUFACTURING**	..	..	..	4 414.7	4 500.8	3 916.0	3 803.6	3 671.7
10-12	Food products, beverages and tobacco	..	..	..	74.3	71.0	81.2	82.1	86.9
13-15	Textiles, wearing apparel, leather and related products	..	..	..	13.6	14.1	9.4	10.2	11.3
13	Textiles	..	..	..	9.2	8.7	5.8	7.8	5.1
14	Wearing apparel	..	..	..	4.2	4.8	2.8	2.0	5.9
15	Leather and related products, footwear	..	..	..	0.3	0.6	0.8	0.4	0.2
16-18	Wood and paper products and printing	..	..	..	124.0	95.4	109.5	108.2	99.8
16	Wood and wood products, except furniture	..	..	..	9.1	7.8	7.2	8.6	8.1
17	Paper and paper products	..	..	..	112.3	82.0	95.3	92.1	85.2
18	Printing and reproduction of recorded media	..	..	..	2.7	5.6	6.0	7.5	6.6
19-23	Chemical, rubber, plastic, non-metallic mineral products	..	..	..	416.4	432.9	406.1	403.0	369.0
19	Coke and refined petroleum products	..	..	..	45.9	47.9	49.1	51.1	33.8
20-21	Chemical and pharmaceutical products	..	..	..	313.1	326.0	297.1	292.9	280.1
20	Chemicals and chemical products	..	..	..	130.8	134.6	100.8	125.8	94.7
21	Pharmaceuticals, medicinal, chemical and botanical products	..	..	..	182.2	191.4	196.3	167.0	185.4
22	Rubber and plastic products	..	..	..	36.9	41.6	43.0	48.3	40.8
23	Other non-metallic mineral products	..	..	..	20.5	17.5	16.9	10.7	14.3
24-25	Basic metals, metal products, except machinery and equipment	..	..	..	214.5	150.9	94.4	145.4	158.2
24	Basic metals	..	..	..	41.6	37.4	35.1	31.1	42.4
25	Fabricated metal products, except machinery and equipment	..	..	..	172.9	113.5	59.3	114.3	115.8
26-30	Computer, electronic, optical products; electrical machinery, transport equipment	..	..	..	3 495.5	3 658.3	3 133.7	2 971.2	2 859.6
26	Computer, electronic and optical products	..	..	..	2 956.0	2 937.1	2 256.8	2 118.9	2 060.8
27	Electrical equipment	..	..	..	241.4	278.5	314.7	320.5	331.1
28	Machinery and equipment n.e.c.	..	..	..	239.7	348.6	457.9	452.7	416.1
29	Motor vehicles, trailers and semi-trailers	..	..	..	16.8	18.7	5.9	11.7	8.5
30	Other transport equipment	..	..	..	41.6	75.4	98.5	67.4	43.0
31-33	Furniture; repair, installation of machinery and equipment	..	..	..	76.3	78.2	81.8	83.5	87.0
31	Furniture	..	..	..	4.6	6.3	7.6	6.1	7.0
32	Other manufacturing	..	..	..	55.4	60.5	61.9	66.9	73.3
33	Repair and installation of machinery and equipment	..	..	..	16.4	11.4	12.3	10.5	6.6
35-39	**ELECTRICITY, GAS, WATER AND WASTE MANAGEMENT**	..	..	..	45.5	41.7	32.6	28.0	22.1
35-36	Electricity, gas and water	..	..	..	38.7	30.1	27.7	20.9	17.3
37-39	Sewerage, waste management and remediation activities	..	..	..	6.7	11.6	4.9	7.1	4.9
41-43	**CONSTRUCTION**	..	..	..	65.0	74.0	72.4	62.4	26.3
45-99	**TOTAL SERVICES**	..	..	..	820.8	940.7	1 107.5	1 165.0	1 122.1
45-82	**Business sector services**	..	..	..	779.8	900.8	1 034.6	1 098.9	1 046.6
45-47	Wholesale and retail trade; motor vehicle and motorcycle repairs	..	..	..	6.4	15.7	3.4	7.8	7.0
49-53	Transportation and storage	..	..	..	12.4	17.4	18.3	14.8	17.1
55-56	Accommodation and food service activities	..	..	..	1.3	8.2	1.1	0.4	0.2
58-63	Information and communication	..	..	..	518.0	644.7	760.1	806.2	725.2
58-60	Publishing, audiovisual and broadcasting activities	..	..	..	9.0	11.6	15.3	19.9	15.1
58	Publishing activities	..	..	..	7.0	9.1	13.1	17.8	12.7
59-60	Motion picture, video and TV programme production; broadcasting activities	..	..	..	2.1	2.5	2.3	2.1	2.4
59	Motion picture, video and TV programme production; sound and music	..	..	..	0.7	1.0	1.1	0.2	0.9
60	Programming and broadcasting activities	..	..	..	1.3	1.5	1.2	1.9	1.5
61	Telecommunications	..	..	..	90.3	227.9	290.3	273.2	218.4
62-63	IT and other information services	..	..	..	418.7	405.1	454.4	513.1	491.7
62	Computer programming, consultancy and related activities	..	..	..	293.2	279.4	327.9	366.6	361.1
63	Information service activities	..	..	..	125.5	125.8	126.6	146.5	130.6
64-66	Financial and insurance activities	..	..	..	73.1	75.2	92.6	71.9	102.4
68-82	Real estate; professional, scientific and technical; administrative and support	..	..	..	168.6	139.6	159.0	197.8	194.6
68	Real estate activities	..	..	..	10.0	2.7	5.7	4.5	3.6
69-75x72	Professional, scientific and technical activities, except scientific R&D	..	..	..	41.4	21.8	22.9	22.8	31.6
72	Scientific research and development	..	..	..	110.3	107.1	126.9	164.7	154.9
77-82	Administrative and support service activities	..	..	..	6.9	8.0	3.6	5.7	4.6
84-99	Community, social and personal services	..	..	..	41.0	39.9	72.9	66.1	75.5
84-85	Public administration and defence; compulsory social security and education	..	..	..	1.2	1.8	4.4	1.7	3.4
86-88	Human health and social work activities	..	..	..	7.2	4.2	7.4	11.3	8.2
90-93	Arts, entertainment and recreation	..	..	..	10.1	10.1	10.2	11.8	11.7
94-99	Other services; household-employers; extraterritorial bodies	..	..	..	22.6	23.8	51.0	41.3	52.2

.. Not available

Note: Detailed metadata at: http://metalinks.oecd.org/anberd/20170419/301f.
    Information on data for Israel: http://oe.cd/israel-disclaimer.
Disclaimer: http://oe.cd/disclaimer

FINLAND

R&D expenditure in industry by product field, constant prices
ISIC Rev. 4

2010 USD PPP

		2007	2008	2009	2010	2011	2012	2013	2014
	TOTAL BUSINESS ENTERPRISE	..	..	..	5 401.0	5 474.2	4 945.9	4 727.7	4 453.1
01-03	**AGRICULTURE, FORESTRY AND FISHING**	..	..	..	13.3	21.7	20.1	12.8	11.1
05-09	**MINING AND QUARRYING**	..	..	..	41.8	39.7	17.6	14.4	14.4
10-33	**MANUFACTURING**	..	..	..	4 414.7	4 383.8	3 747.8	3 534.2	3 357.6
10-12	Food products, beverages and tobacco	..	..	..	74.3	69.2	77.7	76.3	79.5
13-15	Textiles, wearing apparel, leather and related products	..	..	..	13.6	13.7	9.0	9.5	10.3
13	Textiles	..	..	..	9.2	8.4	5.6	7.3	4.6
14	Wearing apparel	..	..	..	4.2	4.7	2.7	1.8	5.4
15	Leather and related products, footwear	..	..	..	0.3	0.6	0.8	0.4	0.2
16-18	Wood and paper products and printing	..	..	..	124.0	92.9	104.8	100.6	91.3
16	Wood and wood products, except furniture	..	..	..	9.1	7.6	6.9	8.0	7.4
17	Paper and paper products	..	..	..	112.3	79.8	91.2	85.6	77.9
18	Printing and reproduction of recorded media	..	..	..	2.7	5.5	5.7	7.0	6.1
19-23	Chemical, rubber, plastic, non-metallic mineral products	..	..	..	416.4	421.7	388.6	374.4	337.4
19	Coke and refined petroleum products	..	..	..	45.9	46.6	47.0	47.5	30.9
20-21	Chemical and pharmaceutical products	..	..	..	313.1	317.5	284.3	272.1	256.1
20	Chemicals and chemical products	..	..	..	130.8	131.1	96.5	116.9	86.6
21	Pharmaceuticals, medicinal, chemical and botanical products	..	..	..	182.2	186.4	187.8	155.2	169.5
22	Rubber and plastic products	..	..	..	36.9	40.5	41.2	44.9	37.3
23	Other non-metallic mineral products	..	..	..	20.5	17.0	16.2	10.0	13.0
24-25	Basic metals, metal products, except machinery and equipment	..	..	..	214.5	147.0	90.3	135.1	144.6
24	Basic metals	..	..	..	41.6	36.4	33.6	28.9	38.8
25	Fabricated metal products, except machinery and equipment	..	..	..	172.9	110.6	56.7	106.2	105.9
26-30	Computer, electronic, optical products; electrical machinery, transport equipment	..	..	..	3 495.5	3 563.2	2 999.1	2 760.8	2 615.0
26	Computer, electronic and optical products	..	..	..	2 956.0	2 860.8	2 159.8	1 968.8	1 884.6
27	Electrical equipment	..	..	..	241.4	271.3	301.1	297.8	302.8
28	Machinery and equipment n.e.c.	..	..	..	239.7	339.5	438.2	420.7	380.5
29	Motor vehicles, trailers and semi-trailers	..	..	..	16.8	18.2	5.7	10.9	7.8
30	Other transport equipment	..	..	..	41.6	73.4	94.2	62.7	39.3
31-33	Furniture; repair, installation of machinery and equipment	..	..	..	76.3	76.2	78.2	77.6	79.5
31	Furniture	..	..	..	4.6	6.2	7.2	5.6	6.4
32	Other manufacturing	..	..	..	55.4	58.9	59.2	62.1	67.1
33	Repair and installation of machinery and equipment	..	..	..	16.4	11.1	11.8	9.8	6.1
35-39	**ELECTRICITY, GAS, WATER AND WASTE MANAGEMENT**	..	..	..	45.5	40.6	31.2	26.0	20.2
35-36	Electricity, gas and water	..	..	..	38.7	29.3	26.5	19.4	15.8
37-39	Sewerage, waste management and remediation activities	..	..	..	6.7	11.3	4.7	6.6	4.5
41-43	**CONSTRUCTION**	..	..	..	65.0	72.0	69.3	57.9	24.0
45-99	**TOTAL SERVICES**	..	..	..	820.8	916.3	1 059.9	1 082.5	1 026.1
45-82	**Business sector services**	..	..	..	779.8	877.4	990.2	1 021.1	957.1
45-47	**Wholesale and retail trade; motor vehicle and motorcycle repairs**	..	..	..	6.4	15.2	3.3	7.3	6.4
49-53	**Transportation and storage**	..	..	..	12.4	17.0	17.6	13.8	15.7
55-56	**Accommodation and food service activities**	..	..	..	1.3	7.9	1.0	0.4	0.2
58-63	**Information and communication**	..	..	..	518.0	628.0	727.5	749.1	663.2
58-60	Publishing, audiovisual and broadcasting activities	..	..	..	9.0	11.3	14.7	18.5	13.8
58	Publishing activities	..	..	..	7.0	8.9	12.5	16.5	11.6
59-60	Motion picture, video and TV programme production; broadcasting activities	..	..	..	2.1	2.5	2.2	2.0	2.2
59	Motion picture, video and TV programme production; sound and music	..	..	..	0.7	1.0	1.1	0.2	0.8
60	Programming and broadcasting activities	..	..	..	1.3	1.5	1.1	1.7	1.4
61	Telecommunications	..	..	..	90.3	222.0	277.9	253.8	199.7
62-63	IT and other information services	..	..	..	418.7	394.6	434.9	476.7	449.7
62	Computer programming, consultancy and related activities	..	..	..	293.2	272.1	313.8	340.6	330.2
63	Information service activities	..	..	..	125.5	122.5	121.1	136.1	119.5
64-66	**Financial and insurance activities**	..	..	..	73.1	73.3	88.6	66.8	93.7
68-82	**Real estate; professional, scientific and technical; administrative and support**	..	..	..	168.6	136.0	152.2	183.8	178.0
68	Real estate activities	..	..	..	10.0	2.7	5.4	4.2	3.3
69-75x72	Professional, scientific and technical activities, except scientific R&D	..	..	..	41.4	21.3	21.9	21.2	28.9
72	Scientific research and development	..	..	..	110.3	104.3	121.4	153.1	141.6
77-82	Administrative and support service activities	..	..	..	6.9	7.8	3.4	5.3	4.2
84-99	**Community, social and personal services**	..	..	..	41.0	38.9	69.7	61.4	69.0
84-85	Public administration and defence; compulsory social security and education	..	..	..	1.2	1.8	4.2	1.5	3.1
86-88	Human health and social work activities	..	..	..	7.2	4.1	7.1	10.5	7.5
90-93	Arts, entertainment and recreation	..	..	..	10.1	9.8	9.7	11.0	10.7
94-99	Other services; household-employers; extraterritorial bodies	..	..	..	22.6	23.1	48.8	38.4	47.8

.. Not available

Note: Detailed metadata at: http://metalinks.oecd.org/anberd/20170419/301f.
Information on data for Israel: http://oe.cd/israel-disclaimer.

Disclaimer: http://oe.cd/disclaimer

FRANCE

R&D expenditure in industry by main activity of the enterprise, current prices
ISIC Rev. 4

Million USD PPP

		2007	2008	2009	2010	2011	2012	2013	2014
	TOTAL BUSINESS ENTERPRISE	27 812.6	29 211.9	30 659.8	32 184.0	34 290.4	35 581.4	37 868.7	..
01-03	**AGRICULTURE, FORESTRY AND FISHING**	134.8	117.1	146.7	159.4	179.9	185.4	219.4	..
05-09	**MINING AND QUARRYING**	5.0	6.5	17.5	17.6	14.1	17.5	18.5	..
10-33	**MANUFACTURING**	16 312.7	16 890.8	16 340.9	16 206.4	17 057.9	17 866.7	19 226.1	..
10-12	Food products, beverages and tobacco	281.1	336.9	366.8	443.6	396.1	414.1	445.5	..
13-15	Textiles, wearing apparel, leather and related products	162.2	214.9	157.7	165.3	134.5	134.9	154.6	..
13	Textiles	105.8	130.4	113.1	102.7	89.8	88.1	98.3	..
14	Wearing apparel	50.4	74.6	36.4	51.1	37.4	39.9	50.1	..
15	Leather and related products, footwear	5.9	9.9	8.1	11.5	7.2	7.0	6.3	..
16-18	Wood and paper products and printing	78.1	81.9	80.7	66.5	78.0	87.8	92.6	..
16	Wood and wood products, except furniture	17.8	16.3	19.8	17.8	17.1	22.6	22.8	..
17	Paper and paper products	35.2	42.1	28.0	31.8	48.5	47.3	52.4	..
18	Printing and reproduction of recorded media	25.2	23.5	32.8	16.9	12.5	17.9	17.4	..
19-23	Chemical, rubber, plastic, non-metallic mineral products	3 599.6	3 550.8	3 306.0	3 347.4	3 166.3	3 285.7	3 453.2	..
19	Coke and refined petroleum products	103.0	100.8	106.3	127.0	127.8	91.8	124.1	..
20-21	Chemical and pharmaceutical products	2 497.5	2 481.1	2 187.2	2 243.1	1 988.2	2 031.0	2 157.3	..
20	Chemicals and chemical products	1 262.4	1 288.1	1 196.2	1 266.4	990.5	1 074.4	1 164.6	..
21	Pharmaceuticals, medicinal, chemical and botanical products	1 235.1	1 192.9	991.0	976.7	997.7	956.6	992.7	..
22	Rubber and plastic products	804.8	761.6	782.7	784.3	832.8	943.3	936.2	..
23	Other non-metallic mineral products	194.3	207.3	229.8	193.0	217.5	219.6	235.5	..
24-25	Basic metals, metal products, except machinery and equipment	652.8	703.4	1 031.7	880.6	1 074.2	1 105.3	1 167.0	..
24	Basic metals	328.8	362.0	325.9	143.0	289.7	290.5	305.8	..
25	Fabricated metal products, except machinery and equipment	324.0	341.4	705.8	737.7	784.5	814.8	861.1	..
26-30	Computer, electronic, optical products; electrical machinery, transport equipment	11 165.4	11 513.5	10 790.1	10 792.9	11 540.5	12 107.4	13 147.3	..
26	Computer, electronic and optical products	4 037.3	3 727.9	3 913.6	3 622.9	3 795.6	4 007.9	4 524.1	..
27	Electrical equipment	864.0	806.0	972.7	743.4	771.2	790.5	814.1	..
28	Machinery and equipment n.e.c.	853.2	909.5	1 081.7	1 117.6	1 219.0	1 293.3	1 276.5	..
29	Motor vehicles, trailers and semi-trailers	2 123.8	2 587.7	1 923.5	2 115.8	2 280.0	2 251.7	2 352.3	..
30	Other transport equipment	3 287.1	3 482.3	2 898.7	3 193.3	3 474.7	3 763.9	4 180.4	..
31-33	Furniture; repair, installation of machinery and equipment	373.4	489.4	607.8	510.1	668.3	731.5	765.8	..
31	Furniture	9.7	6.9	22.1	21.4	20.8	20.7	22.7	..
32	Other manufacturing	232.6	254.0	252.9	261.6	328.3	345.5	378.0	..
33	Repair and installation of machinery and equipment	131.0	228.6	332.8	227.1	319.2	365.3	365.1	..
35-39	**ELECTRICITY, GAS, WATER AND WASTE MANAGEMENT**	440.2	456.7	552.5	588.4	643.7	647.8	708.8	..
35-36	Electricity, gas and water	422.1	437.1	527.9	534.1	611.8	621.1	670.0	..
37-39	Sewerage, waste management and remediation activities	18.1	19.6	24.6	54.3	31.9	26.8	38.8	..
41-43	**CONSTRUCTION**	91.8	100.0	184.2	193.8	153.5	173.2	180.9	..
45-99	**TOTAL SERVICES**	10 828.2	11 640.7	13 418.1	15 018.3	16 241.2	16 690.9	17 514.8	..
45-82	**Business sector services**	10 783.3	11 597.8	13 366.1	14 962.6	16 177.5	16 625.1	17 434.9	..
45-47	Wholesale and retail trade; motor vehicle and motorcycle repairs	729.0	683.8	1 168.3	1 430.4	1 757.4	1 819.0	2 024.4	..
49-53	Transportation and storage	49.9	53.7	85.3	41.4	57.6	55.5	56.7	..
55-56	Accommodation and food service activities	0.1	0.1	3.3	3.8	0.4	4.1	5.2	..
58-63	Information and communication	2 421.9	2 713.1	3 028.3	3 484.3	3 581.2	3 935.3	4 482.7	..
58-60	Publishing, audiovisual and broadcasting activities	755.4	870.0	831.8	954.4	939.2	1 067.4	1 220.4	..
58	Publishing activities	707.6	831.8	786.6	840.4	870.4	983.2	1 152.3	..
59-60	Motion picture, video and TV programme production; broadcasting activities	47.8	38.1	45.2	114.0	68.8	84.2	68.1	..
59	Motion picture, video and TV programme production; sound and music	..	..	41.5	99.9	58.9	74.9	61.2	..
60	Programming and broadcasting activities	..	..	3.7	14.0	10.0	9.4	7.0	..
61	Telecommunications	834.9	815.9	799.2	775.6	708.4	853.8	1 035.6	..
62-63	IT and other information services	831.6	1 027.2	1 397.3	1 754.3	1 933.6	2 014.1	2 226.8	..
62	Computer programming, consultancy and related activities	777.2	955.1	1 279.7	1 611.0	1 797.5	1 892.7	2 089.1	..
63	Information service activities	54.4	72.2	117.6	143.3	136.1	121.4	137.6	..
64-66	Financial and insurance activities	125.8	178.3	188.1	259.3	311.0	302.9	312.5	..
68-82	Real estate; professional, scientific and technical; administrative and support	7 456.7	7 968.8	8 892.9	9 746.0	10 469.8	10 508.2	10 553.3	..
68	Real estate activities	0.0	1.0	1.1	2.5	4.3	2.1	2.7	..
69-75x72	Professional, scientific and technical activities, except scientific R&D	3 682.6	3 985.2	4 406.7	5 299.2	5 970.7	5 926.6	5 868.0	..
72	Scientific research and development	3 688.8	3 936.4	4 038.7	4 316.0	4 332.2	4 388.8	4 437.2	..
77-82	Administrative and support service activities	85.3	46.2	446.4	128.2	162.6	190.7	245.5	..
84-99	Community, social and personal services	44.9	42.9	52.0	55.7	63.7	65.7	79.9	..
84-85	Public administration and defence; compulsory social security and education	7.0	9.2	7.9	5.5	4.6	4.5	5.8	..
86-88	Human health and social work activities	4.5	2.6	5.8	12.1	16.9	18.0	24.8	..
90-93	Arts, entertainment and recreation	0.2	4.1	2.3	1.4	4.1	6.9	8.1	..
94-99	Other services; household-employers; extraterritorial bodies	33.2	27.0	36.0	36.7	38.2	36.4	41.2	..

.. Not available

Note: Detailed metadata at: http://metalinks.oecd.org/anberd/20170419/301f.
   Information on data for Israel: http://oe.cd/israel-disclaimer.
Disclaimer: http://oe.cd/disclaimer

FRANCE

R&D expenditure in industry by main activity of the enterprise, constant prices
ISIC Rev. 4

2010 USD PPP

		2007	2008	2009	2010	2011	2012	2013	2014
	TOTAL BUSINESS ENTERPRISE	30 056.8	30 554.5	31 312.7	32 184.0	33 504.3	34 488.0	34 981.6	..
01-03	**AGRICULTURE, FORESTRY AND FISHING**	145.7	122.5	149.8	159.4	175.8	179.7	202.7	..
05-09	**MINING AND QUARRYING**	5.4	6.8	17.8	17.6	13.8	17.0	17.1	..
10-33	**MANUFACTURING**	17 628.9	17 667.1	16 688.8	16 206.4	16 666.9	17 317.7	17 760.3	..
10-12	Food products, beverages and tobacco	303.8	352.4	374.6	443.6	387.0	401.3	411.6	..
13-15	Textiles, wearing apparel, leather and related products	175.2	224.8	161.1	165.3	131.4	130.8	142.9	..
13	Textiles	114.3	136.4	115.6	102.7	87.8	85.4	90.8	..
14	Wearing apparel	54.5	78.0	37.2	51.1	36.6	38.7	46.3	..
15	Leather and related products, footwear	6.4	10.4	8.3	11.5	7.1	6.8	5.8	..
16-18	Wood and paper products and printing	84.5	85.7	82.4	66.5	76.2	85.1	85.6	..
16	Wood and wood products, except furniture	19.2	17.1	20.2	17.8	16.7	21.9	21.1	..
17	Paper and paper products	38.0	44.0	28.6	31.8	47.4	45.8	48.4	..
18	Printing and reproduction of recorded media	27.2	24.6	33.5	16.9	12.2	17.3	16.1	..
19-23	Chemical, rubber, plastic, non-metallic mineral products	3 890.1	3 714.0	3 376.4	3 347.4	3 093.7	3 184.7	3 189.9	..
19	Coke and refined petroleum products	111.3	105.5	108.5	127.0	124.9	89.0	114.6	..
20-21	Chemical and pharmaceutical products	2 699.0	2 595.1	2 233.7	2 243.1	1 942.6	1 968.6	1 992.9	..
20	Chemicals and chemical products	1 364.3	1 347.3	1 221.7	1 266.4	967.8	1 041.4	1 075.8	..
21	Pharmaceuticals, medicinal, chemical and botanical products	1 334.7	1 247.8	1 012.1	976.7	974.8	927.3	917.0	..
22	Rubber and plastic products	869.7	796.6	799.4	784.3	813.7	914.3	864.9	..
23	Other non-metallic mineral products	210.0	216.8	234.7	193.0	212.5	212.8	217.6	..
24-25	Basic metals, metal products, except machinery and equipment	705.5	735.7	1 053.7	880.6	1 049.5	1 071.3	1 078.0	..
24	Basic metals	355.4	378.6	332.9	143.0	283.0	281.6	282.5	..
25	Fabricated metal products, except machinery and equipment	350.1	357.1	720.8	737.7	766.5	789.7	795.5	..
26-30	Computer, electronic, optical products; electrical machinery, transport equipment	12 066.3	12 042.7	11 019.9	10 792.9	11 276.0	11 735.4	12 145.0	..
26	Computer, electronic and optical products	4 363.1	3 899.3	3 997.0	3 622.9	3 708.6	3 884.8	4 179.2	..
27	Electrical equipment	933.7	843.0	993.4	743.4	753.5	766.2	752.1	..
28	Machinery and equipment n.e.c.	922.0	951.4	1 104.7	1 117.6	1 191.1	1 253.5	1 179.2	..
29	Motor vehicles, trailers and semi-trailers	2 295.2	2 706.6	1 964.4	2 115.8	2 227.8	2 182.5	2 173.0	..
30	Other transport equipment	3 552.3	3 642.4	2 960.4	3 193.3	3 395.0	3 648.3	3 861.7	..
31-33	Furniture; repair, installation of machinery and equipment	403.5	511.9	620.8	510.1	653.0	709.0	707.4	..
31	Furniture	10.5	7.2	22.6	21.4	20.3	20.1	21.0	..
32	Other manufacturing	251.4	265.7	258.3	261.6	320.8	334.9	349.2	..
33	Repair and installation of machinery and equipment	141.6	239.1	339.8	227.1	311.8	354.0	337.3	..
35-39	**ELECTRICITY, GAS, WATER AND WASTE MANAGEMENT**	475.7	477.7	564.2	588.4	628.9	627.8	654.8	..
35-36	Electricity, gas and water	456.1	457.2	539.1	534.1	597.7	602.0	618.9	..
37-39	Sewerage, waste management and remediation activities	19.5	20.5	25.2	54.3	31.2	25.9	35.9	..
41-43	**CONSTRUCTION**	99.2	104.6	188.1	193.8	150.0	167.8	167.1	..
45-99	**TOTAL SERVICES**	11 702.0	12 175.8	13 703.8	15 018.3	15 868.9	16 177.9	16 179.5	..
45-82	**Business sector services**	11 653.4	12 130.9	13 650.7	14 962.6	15 806.6	16 114.2	16 105.7	..
45-47	**Wholesale and retail trade; motor vehicle and motorcycle repairs**	787.9	715.2	1 193.1	1 430.4	1 717.1	1 763.1	1 870.1	..
49-53	**Transportation and storage**	53.9	56.2	87.1	41.4	56.3	53.8	52.4	..
55-56	**Accommodation and food service activities**	0.1	0.1	3.3	3.8	0.4	4.0	4.8	..
58-63	**Information and communication**	2 617.3	2 837.8	3 092.8	3 484.3	3 499.1	3 814.4	4 141.0	..
58-60	Publishing, audiovisual and broadcasting activities	816.3	910.0	849.5	954.4	917.7	1 034.6	1 127.3	..
58	Publishing activities	764.7	870.1	803.3	840.4	850.5	953.0	1 064.4	..
59-60	Motion picture, video and TV programme production; broadcasting activities	51.6	39.9	46.2	114.0	67.2	81.6	62.9	..
59	Motion picture, video and TV programme production; sound and music	..	..	42.4	99.9	57.5	72.6	56.5	..
60	Programming and broadcasting activities	..	..	3.8	14.0	9.7	9.1	6.5	..
61	Telecommunications	902.2	853.4	816.2	775.6	692.1	827.6	956.7	..
62-63	IT and other information services	898.7	1 074.5	1 427.0	1 754.3	1 889.3	1 952.2	2 057.0	..
62	Computer programming, consultancy and related activities	839.9	999.0	1 306.9	1 611.0	1 756.3	1 834.5	1 929.9	..
63	Information service activities	58.8	75.5	120.1	143.3	133.0	117.7	127.1	..
64-66	**Financial and insurance activities**	135.9	186.5	192.1	259.3	303.8	293.5	288.7	..
68-82	**Real estate; professional, scientific and technical; administrative and support**	8 058.3	8 335.0	9 082.2	9 746.0	10 229.8	10 185.3	9 748.7	..
68	Real estate activities	0.0	1.1	1.1	2.5	4.2	2.1	2.5	..
69-75x72	Professional, scientific and technical activities, except scientific R&D	3 979.7	4 168.4	4 500.5	5 299.2	5 833.9	5 744.4	5 420.6	..
72	Scientific research and development	3 986.4	4 117.3	4 124.7	4 316.0	4 232.9	4 254.0	4 099.0	..
77-82	Administrative and support service activities	92.1	48.3	455.9	128.2	158.9	184.8	226.6	..
84-99	**Community, social and personal services**	48.6	44.9	53.1	55.7	62.3	63.7	73.8	..
84-85	Public administration and defence; compulsory social security and education	7.6	9.6	8.1	5.5	4.5	4.4	5.4	..
86-88	Human health and social work activities	4.8	2.7	5.9	12.1	16.5	17.4	22.9	..
90-93	Arts, entertainment and recreation	0.2	4.3	2.4	1.4	4.0	6.7	7.5	..
94-99	Other services; household-employers; extraterritorial bodies	35.9	28.3	36.8	36.7	37.3	35.2	38.0	..

.. Not available

Note: Detailed metadata at: http://metalinks.oecd.org/anberd/20170419/301f.
    Information on data for Israel: http://oe.cd/israel-disclaimer.
Disclaimer: http://oe.cd/disclaimer

FRANCE

R&D expenditure in industry by product field, current prices
ISIC Rev. 4

Million USD PPP

		2007	2008	2009	2010	2011	2012	2013	2014
	TOTAL BUSINESS ENTERPRISE	27 812.6	29 211.9	30 659.8	32 184.0	34 290.4	35 581.4	37 868.7	..
01-03	**AGRICULTURE, FORESTRY AND FISHING**	392.6	416.9	459.4	477.1	496.5	532.2	625.0	..
05-09	**MINING AND QUARRYING**	195.4	190.9	266.3	270.6	281.2	295.3	298.1	..
10-33	**MANUFACTURING**	23 152.6	23 887.7	24 301.9	24 663.6	26 216.5	26 762.7	27 943.7	..
10-12	Food products, beverages and tobacco	596.8	629.1	666.2	726.4	721.6	734.8	812.7	..
13-15	Textiles, wearing apparel, leather and related products	189.6	200.3	162.8	194.4	166.2	149.4	173.0	..
13	Textiles	131.0	106.4	91.6	103.8	92.9	80.1	88.9	..
14	Wearing apparel	50.3	78.8	57.7	74.7	66.3	61.7	74.4	..
15	Leather and related products, footwear	8.3	15.1	13.5	15.9	7.0	7.6	9.7	..
16-18	Wood and paper products and printing	108.6	102.4	95.9	92.3	116.8	123.2	125.2	..
16	Wood and wood products, except furniture	31.8	25.7	34.9	32.6	34.3	35.4	34.4	..
17	Paper and paper products	58.5	67.7	53.2	53.7	73.7	75.3	78.6	..
18	Printing and reproduction of recorded media	18.3	9.0	7.9	6.0	8.8	12.3	12.2	..
19-23	Chemical, rubber, plastic, non-metallic mineral products	6 894.0	6 955.8	7 013.1	6 958.7	7 076.0	7 239.4	7 717.4	..
19	Coke and refined petroleum products	245.4	233.0	249.7	261.0	255.9	238.4	277.3	..
20-21	Chemical and pharmaceutical products	5 550.5	5 596.6	5 618.3	5 530.7	5 565.1	5 649.9	6 025.7	..
20	Chemicals and chemical products	1 625.6	1 638.6	1 684.0	1 753.8	1 831.9	1 940.2	2 187.4	..
21	Pharmaceuticals, medicinal, chemical and botanical products	3 925.0	3 958.0	3 934.3	3 776.9	3 733.2	3 709.7	3 838.3	..
22	Rubber and plastic products	778.8	783.2	768.5	814.9	887.7	979.6	993.6	..
23	Other non-metallic mineral products	319.2	343.0	376.5	352.2	367.3	371.4	420.8	..
24-25	Basic metals, metal products, except machinery and equipment	999.5	1 051.4	1 090.7	1 216.3	1 295.3	1 295.2	1 349.1	..
24	Basic metals	403.5	450.1	413.4	468.2	503.5	462.0	484.6	..
25	Fabricated metal products, except machinery and equipment	596.0	601.3	677.3	748.1	791.9	833.1	864.5	..
26-30	Computer, electronic, optical products; electrical machinery, transport equipment	14 025.7	14 600.0	14 843.9	15 031.0	16 321.0	16 722.7	17 254.6	..
26	Computer, electronic and optical products	4 536.6	4 335.2	4 582.5	4 558.4	4 586.2	4 781.8	5 067.4	..
27	Electrical equipment	912.4	853.2	1 008.1	1 036.0	1 141.1	1 179.5	1 257.5	..
28	Machinery and equipment n.e.c.	951.9	1 047.4	1 063.0	1 112.0	1 214.9	1 302.3	1 365.1	..
29	Motor vehicles, trailers and semi-trailers	4 446.2	4 945.0	4 964.7	4 944.9	5 592.0	5 324.8	4 881.6	..
30	Other transport equipment	3 178.6	3 419.2	3 225.6	3 379.7	3 786.8	4 134.8	4 683.1	..
31-33	Furniture; repair, installation of machinery and equipment	338.5	348.8	429.3	444.4	519.7	498.2	511.5	..
31	Furniture	..	..	..	19.8	28.2	23.1	27.5	..
32	Other manufacturing	327.3	335.4	361.8	424.6	491.5	475.1	484.0	..
33	Repair and installation of machinery and equipment	..	..	..	0.0	0.0	0.0	0.0	..
35-39	**ELECTRICITY, GAS, WATER AND WASTE MANAGEMENT**	534.7	537.0	619.2	613.8	697.5	710.4	770.2	..
35-36	Electricity, gas and water	459.0	479.3	555.0	575.3	652.6	664.2	717.5	..
37-39	Sewerage, waste management and remediation activities	75.6	57.7	64.2	38.6	44.9	46.2	52.8	..
41-43	**CONSTRUCTION**	110.2	90.3	108.7	103.6	128.3	138.2	128.4	..
45-99	**TOTAL SERVICES**	3 427.2	4 089.0	4 904.3	6 055.2	6 470.4	7 142.6	8 090.2	..
45-82	**Business sector services**	3 409.5	4 061.3	4 882.5	6 028.8	6 434.9	7 084.8	8 015.6	..
45-47	Wholesale and retail trade; motor vehicle and motorcycle repairs	0.0	0.0	0.0	0.0	0.0	0.0	0.0	..
49-53	Transportation and storage	39.8	35.4	49.5	52.6	72.4	63.8	62.3	..
55-56	Accommodation and food service activities	0.0	0.0	0.0	0.0	0.0	0.0	0.0	..
58-63	Information and communication	2 366.8	3 038.3	3 479.7	4 085.6	4 233.4	4 523.6	5 019.7	..
58-60	Publishing, audiovisual and broadcasting activities	490.2	702.3	862.7	1 057.0	1 063.4	1 132.3	1 303.2	..
58	Publishing activities	458.5	643.5	776.6	899.1	956.2	1 007.5	1 202.8	..
59-60	Motion picture, video and TV programme production; broadcasting activities	31.7	58.8	86.1	157.8	107.2	125.0	100.4	..
59	Motion picture, video and TV programme production; sound and music	..	36.7	35.4	94.7	53.9	67.6	51.5	..
60	Programming and broadcasting activities	..	22.1	50.8	63.2	53.3	57.3	48.7	..
61	Telecommunications	902.0	963.6	929.0	945.5	959.7	1 097.4	1 216.4	..
62-63	IT and other information services	974.6	1 372.4	1 688.0	2 083.1	2 210.3	2 294.0	2 500.0	..
62	Computer programming, consultancy and related activities	933.9	1 338.3	1 570.6	1 928.0	2 020.0	2 133.1	2 326.5	..
63	Information service activities	40.7	34.1	117.4	155.1	190.3	160.8	173.5	..
64-66	Financial and insurance activities	74.9	156.2	195.5	202.2	231.9	235.8	246.5	..
68-82	Real estate; professional, scientific and technical; administrative and support	927.7	831.2	1 157.8	1 688.5	1 897.2	2 261.4	2 687.1	..
68	Real estate activities	0.0	0.0	0.0	0.0	0.0	0.0	0.0	..
69-75x72	Professional, scientific and technical activities, except scientific R&D	796.4	578.6	786.9	1 162.7	1 275.4	1 486.6	1 819.1	..
72	Scientific research and development	68.2	184.3	298.2	406.8	501.8	621.6	699.7	..
77-82	Administrative and support service activities	63.1	68.3	72.7	118.9	119.9	153.3	168.3	..
84-99	Community, social and personal services	17.6	27.7	21.8	26.4	35.5	57.8	74.6	..
84-85	Public administration and defence; compulsory social security and education	..	2.1	3.8	1.2	3.1	4.3	4.1	..
86-88	Human health and social work activities	9.6	21.8	15.4	20.7	23.1	30.1	37.0	..
90-93	Arts, entertainment and recreation	..	3.8	0.8	1.2	2.5	3.6	7.3	..
94-99	Other services; household-employers; extraterritorial bodies	0.0	0.1	1.9	3.2	6.8	19.8	26.3	..

.. Not available

Note: Detailed metadata at: http://metalinks.oecd.org/anberd/20170419/301f.
    Information on data for Israel: http://oe.cd/israel-disclaimer.
Disclaimer: http://oe.cd/disclaimer

FRANCE

R&D expenditure in industry by product field, constant prices
ISIC Rev. 4

2010 USD PPP

		2007	2008	2009	2010	2011	2012	2013	2014
	TOTAL BUSINESS ENTERPRISE	30 056.8	30 554.5	31 312.7	32 184.0	33 504.3	34 488.0	34 981.6	..
01-03	**AGRICULTURE, FORESTRY AND FISHING**	424.2	436.0	469.2	477.1	485.1	515.8	577.3	..
05-09	**MINING AND QUARRYING**	211.2	199.7	271.9	270.6	274.7	286.2	275.3	..
10-33	**MANUFACTURING**	25 020.8	24 985.7	24 819.4	24 663.6	25 615.5	25 940.3	25 813.3	..
10-12	Food products, beverages and tobacco	644.9	658.0	680.4	726.4	705.0	712.2	750.7	..
13-15	Textiles, wearing apparel, leather and related products	204.9	209.5	166.2	194.4	162.3	144.8	159.8	..
13	Textiles	141.6	111.3	93.5	103.8	90.8	77.6	82.1	..
14	Wearing apparel	54.3	82.4	58.9	74.7	64.8	59.8	68.7	..
15	Leather and related products, footwear	9.0	15.8	13.8	15.9	6.8	7.3	9.0	..
16-18	Wood and paper products and printing	117.4	107.1	97.9	92.3	114.1	119.4	115.6	..
16	Wood and wood products, except furniture	34.4	26.9	35.6	32.6	33.5	34.3	31.8	..
17	Paper and paper products	63.2	70.8	54.3	53.7	72.0	73.0	72.6	..
18	Printing and reproduction of recorded media	19.8	9.4	8.0	6.0	8.6	11.9	11.3	..
19-23	Chemical, rubber, plastic, non-metallic mineral products	7 450.2	7 275.5	7 162.4	6 958.7	6 913.8	7 016.9	7 129.0	..
19	Coke and refined petroleum products	265.3	243.7	255.0	261.0	250.2	231.1	256.2	..
20-21	Chemical and pharmaceutical products	5 998.4	5 853.8	5 738.0	5 530.7	5 437.5	5 476.3	5 566.3	..
20	Chemicals and chemical products	1 756.7	1 713.9	1 719.8	1 753.8	1 789.9	1 880.6	2 020.7	..
21	Pharmaceuticals, medicinal, chemical and botanical products	4 241.7	4 139.9	4 018.1	3 776.9	3 647.6	3 595.7	3 545.7	..
22	Rubber and plastic products	841.6	819.2	784.9	814.9	867.4	949.5	917.8	..
23	Other non-metallic mineral products	345.0	358.8	384.6	352.2	358.9	360.0	388.7	..
24-25	Basic metals, metal products, except machinery and equipment	1 080.2	1 099.7	1 114.0	1 216.3	1 265.6	1 255.4	1 246.2	..
24	Basic metals	436.1	470.8	422.2	468.2	491.9	447.8	447.7	..
25	Fabricated metal products, except machinery and equipment	644.1	628.9	691.7	748.1	773.7	807.5	798.6	..
26-30	Computer, electronic, optical products; electrical machinery, transport equipment	15 157.4	15 271.1	15 159.9	15 031.0	15 946.9	16 208.8	15 939.1	..
26	Computer, electronic and optical products	4 902.7	4 534.4	4 680.1	4 558.4	4 481.1	4 634.9	4 681.1	..
27	Electrical equipment	986.0	892.4	1 029.5	1 036.0	1 114.9	1 142.8	1 161.6	..
28	Machinery and equipment n.e.c.	1 028.7	1 095.6	1 085.6	1 112.0	1 187.1	1 262.2	1 261.1	..
29	Motor vehicles, trailers and semi-trailers	4 805.0	5 172.3	5 070.4	4 944.9	5 463.8	5 161.1	4 509.4	..
30	Other transport equipment	3 435.0	3 576.4	3 294.3	3 379.7	3 700.0	4 007.7	4 326.1	..
31-33	Furniture; repair, installation of machinery and equipment	365.8	364.1	438.5	444.4	507.8	482.9	472.5	..
31	Furniture	..	..	..	19.8	27.6	22.4	25.4	..
32	Other manufacturing	353.7	350.9	369.5	424.6	480.2	460.5	447.1	..
33	Repair and installation of machinery and equipment	..	..	..	0.0	0.0	0.0	0.0	..
35-39	**ELECTRICITY, GAS, WATER AND WASTE MANAGEMENT**	577.8	561.7	632.4	613.8	681.5	688.6	711.5	..
35-36	Electricity, gas and water	496.1	501.3	566.8	575.3	637.6	643.8	662.8	..
37-39	Sewerage, waste management and remediation activities	81.7	60.4	65.6	38.6	43.9	44.8	48.8	..
41-43	**CONSTRUCTION**	119.1	94.4	111.0	103.6	125.3	134.0	118.6	..
45-99	**TOTAL SERVICES**	3 703.7	4 277.0	5 008.7	6 055.2	6 322.1	6 923.1	7 473.4	..
45-82	**Business sector services**	3 684.7	4 248.0	4 986.4	6 028.8	6 287.4	6 867.1	7 404.5	..
45-47	Wholesale and retail trade; motor vehicle and motorcycle repairs	0.0	0.0	0.0	0.0	0.0	0.0	0.0	..
49-53	Transportation and storage	43.0	37.1	50.6	52.6	70.7	61.9	57.5	..
55-56	Accommodation and food service activities	0.0	0.0	0.0	0.0	0.0	0.0	0.0	..
58-63	Information and communication	2 557.8	3 177.9	3 553.8	4 085.6	4 136.4	4 384.6	4 637.0	..
58-60	Publishing, audiovisual and broadcasting activities	529.8	734.6	881.1	1 057.0	1 039.0	1 097.5	1 203.9	..
58	Publishing activities	495.5	673.1	793.1	899.1	934.3	976.5	1 111.1	..
59-60	Motion picture, video and TV programme production; broadcasting activities	34.3	61.5	88.0	157.8	104.7	121.1	92.7	..
59	Motion picture, video and TV programme production; sound and music	..	38.4	36.1	94.7	52.6	65.6	47.6	..
60	Programming and broadcasting activities	..	23.1	51.9	63.2	52.1	55.6	45.0	..
61	Telecommunications	974.8	1 007.9	948.7	945.5	937.7	1 063.6	1 123.7	..
62-63	IT and other information services	1 053.2	1 435.5	1 724.0	2 083.1	2 159.6	2 223.5	2 309.4	..
62	Computer programming, consultancy and related activities	1 009.3	1 399.8	1 604.1	1 928.0	1 973.7	2 067.6	2 149.2	..
63	Information service activities	43.9	35.6	119.9	155.1	186.0	155.9	160.3	..
64-66	Financial and insurance activities	81.0	163.4	199.6	202.2	226.6	228.5	227.7	..
68-82	Real estate; professional, scientific and technical; administrative and support	1 002.6	869.4	1 182.4	1 688.5	1 853.7	2 191.9	2 482.2	..
68	Real estate activities	0.0	0.0	0.0	0.0	0.0	0.0	0.0	..
69-75x72	Professional, scientific and technical activities, except scientific R&D	860.6	605.2	803.6	1 162.7	1 246.2	1 440.9	1 680.4	..
72	Scientific research and development	73.8	192.8	304.6	406.8	490.3	602.5	646.4	..
77-82	Administrative and support service activities	68.2	71.4	74.2	118.9	117.2	148.6	155.5	..
84-99	Community, social and personal services	19.1	29.0	22.3	26.4	34.7	56.0	68.9	..
84-85	Public administration and defence; compulsory social security and education	..	2.2	3.9	1.2	3.0	4.2	3.8	..
86-88	Human health and social work activities	10.4	22.8	15.7	20.7	22.5	29.2	34.2	..
90-93	Arts, entertainment and recreation	..	3.9	0.8	1.2	2.5	3.4	6.7	..
94-99	Other services; household-employers; extraterritorial bodies	0.0	0.1	1.9	3.2	6.7	19.2	24.3	..

.. Not available
Note: Detailed metadata at: http://metalinks.oecd.org/anberd/20170419/301f.
     Information on data for Israel: http://oe.cd/israel-disclaimer.
Disclaimer: http://oe.cd/disclaimer

GERMANY

R&D expenditure in industry by main activity of the enterprise, current prices
ISIC Rev. 4

Million USD PPP

ISIC	Activity	2007	2008	2009	2010	2011	2012	2013	2014
	TOTAL BUSINESS ENTERPRISE	51 326.1	56 159.1	55 887.4	58 402.0	64 758.0	68 327.0	69 199.4	74 351.7
01-03	**AGRICULTURE, FORESTRY AND FISHING**	112.4	120.7	162.0	177.1	159.9	175.7	185.8	178.6
05-09	**MINING AND QUARRYING**	33.3	34.3	16.7	15.3	12.7	13.6	19.9	16.2
10-33	**MANUFACTURING**	45 243.8	49 704.4	47 785.3	50 078.6	55 447.2	58 854.9	59 488.0	64 549.6
10-12	Food products, beverages and tobacco	378.6	335.0	392.5	408.9	390.5	400.0	406.5	415.4
13-15	Textiles, wearing apparel, leather and related products	158.4	163.6	155.9	154.3	151.1	155.4	146.0	150.0
13	Textiles	112.8	116.4	87.3	84.6	78.7	81.8	72.6	72.3
14	Wearing apparel	39.1	40.5	61.7	62.7	65.4	66.3	66.1	70.3
15	Leather and related products, footwear	6.4	6.7	6.9	7.1	7.0	7.2	7.2	7.4
16-18	Wood and paper products and printing	215.5	221.2	217.4	258.9	231.6	218.4	293.2	291.9
16	Wood and wood products, except furniture	24.2	24.7	24.8	28.5	28.7	25.2	25.7	25.4
17	Paper and paper products	72.5	74.6	79.0	92.1	77.7	73.8	130.3	134.1
18	Printing and reproduction of recorded media	118.8	121.9	113.6	138.3	125.3	119.4	137.2	132.4
19-23	Chemical, rubber, plastic, non-metallic mineral products	9 136.7	9 604.6	10 272.0	10 040.9	11 011.9	11 337.5	11 338.6	11 868.2
19	Coke and refined petroleum products	104.7	107.3	114.8	110.9	119.6	121.9	121.0	155.1
20-21	Chemical and pharmaceutical products	7 698.3	8 093.8	8 756.6	8 538.1	9 339.5	9 638.4	9 587.5	9 996.7
20	Chemicals and chemical products	3 748.5	3 932.1	3 947.4	3 887.7	4 179.7	4 440.5	4 323.3	4 733.6
21	Pharmaceuticals, medicinal, chemical and botanical products	3 949.8	4 161.7	4 809.2	4 650.4	5 159.8	5 197.9	5 264.2	5 263.1
22	Rubber and plastic products	1 035.3	1 079.1	1 045.7	1 036.9	1 196.1	1 214.4	1 253.0	1 322.2
23	Other non-metallic mineral products	298.4	324.4	355.0	355.0	356.8	362.8	377.1	394.1
24-25	Basic metals, metal products, except machinery and equipment	1 288.9	1 389.4	1 489.3	1 500.2	1 574.8	1 644.5	1 644.9	1 675.8
24	Basic metals	446.5	485.3	610.9	613.5	654.5	688.1	684.6	697.5
25	Fabricated metal products, except machinery and equipment	842.4	904.2	878.4	886.7	920.3	956.4	960.4	978.2
26-30	Computer, electronic, optical products; electrical machinery, transport equipment	32 987.0	36 882.0	33 976.1	36 416.5	40 548.1	43 633.5	44 007.0	48 364.8
26	Computer, electronic and optical products	7 250.7	7 892.1	7 178.5	7 460.4	8 321.4	9 389.4	9 484.6	9 792.5
27	Electrical equipment	1 676.2	1 822.9	1 645.9	1 673.4	2 030.7	2 200.5	2 751.8	2 833.0
28	Machinery and equipment n.e.c.	5 263.9	5 693.3	5 552.9	5 721.0	6 215.6	6 583.2	6 960.7	7 371.2
29	Motor vehicles, trailers and semi-trailers	16 308.0	18 629.7	17 060.2	18 432.8	20 681.6	22 052.6	22 203.0	25 656.6
30	Other transport equipment	2 488.2	2 844.2	2 538.4	3 128.9	3 298.8	3 408.0	2 606.8	2 698.4
31-33	Furniture; repair, installation of machinery and equipment	1 078.7	1 108.6	1 282.0	1 298.9	1 539.2	1 465.7	1 651.8	1 783.5
31	Furniture	147.9	119.1	63.1	65.2	52.9	50.7	48.3	50.9
32	Other manufacturing	448.7	466.0	539.8	548.6	697.3	667.3	786.7	843.5
33	Repair and installation of machinery and equipment	482.1	523.5	679.2	685.1	789.0	747.8	816.7	889.1
35-39	**ELECTRICITY, GAS, WATER AND WASTE MANAGEMENT**	148.1	156.6	267.1	244.4	250.3	236.4	269.4	255.0
35-36	Electricity, gas and water	140.5	149.3	258.0	235.8	235.4	224.3	251.8	238.1
37-39	Sewerage, waste management and remediation activities	7.6	7.3	9.1	8.6	14.8	12.1	17.6	17.0
41-43	**CONSTRUCTION**	68.9	67.8	85.2	95.2	83.4	89.7	103.3	104.4
45-99	**TOTAL SERVICES**	5 719.7	6 075.4	7 571.2	7 791.4	8 804.6	8 956.7	9 133.1	9 248.0
45-82	**Business sector services**	..	6 074.8	7 549.7	7 771.4	8 773.6	8 925.3	9 095.8	9 211.3
45-47	Wholesale and retail trade; motor vehicle and motorcycle repairs	189.5	201.1	251.6	278.9	331.7	360.2	333.9	334.9
49-53	Transportation and storage	..	75.1	71.3	79.0	137.7	156.0	118.3	124.1
55-56	Accommodation and food service activities	0.4	0.4	0.4	0.5	0.5	0.5	0.3	0.3
58-63	Information and communication	2 202.2	2 335.6	3 165.5	3 300.0	3 790.4	4 033.4	4 095.7	4 212.3
58-60	Publishing, audiovisual and broadcasting activities	22.2	22.9	47.2	46.9	53.5	53.4	34.5	35.2
58	Publishing activities	..	..	..	..	..	..	..	..
59-60	Motion picture, video and TV programme production; broadcasting activities	..	..	..	..	..	..	..	..
59	Motion picture, video and TV programme production; sound and music	..	..	..	..	..	..	..	..
60	Programming and broadcasting activities	..	..	..	..	..	..	..	..
61	Telecommunications	228.5	233.4	703.2	750.0	723.8	789.0	483.2	497.1
62-63	IT and other information services	1 951.5	2 079.2	2 415.1	2 503.0	3 013.0	3 189.7	3 578.0	3 680.0
62	Computer programming, consultancy and related services	1 874.3	1 996.0	2 347.0	2 436.1	2 893.6	3 065.2	3 452.1	3 551.2
63	Information service activities	77.2	83.3	68.1	67.0	119.4	124.5	126.0	128.8
64-66	Financial and insurance activities	249.9	268.2	413.0	289.3	330.8	336.9	375.0	414.3
68-82	Real estate; professional, scientific and technical; administrative and support	3 004.4	3 194.5	3 647.9	3 823.4	4 182.6	4 038.3	4 172.5	4 125.5
68	Real estate activities	0.0	0.0	0.7	0.6	1.0	1.0	0.9	0.9
69-75x72	Professional, scientific and technical activities, except scientific R&D	1 075.8	1 142.7	1 635.3	1 702.1	1 967.2	1 837.5	1 958.3	1 813.5
72	Scientific research and development	1 685.5	1 795.6	1 970.0	2 074.8	2 168.8	2 150.7	2 176.6	2 274.4
77-82	Administrative and support service activities	243.1	256.2	41.8	45.9	45.6	49.0	36.7	36.7
84-99	Community, social and personal services	..	0.6	21.5	20.0	30.9	31.4	37.3	36.7
84-85	Public administration and defence; compulsory social security and education	..	..	..	..	2.8	2.8	3.5	3.3
86-88	Human health and social work activities	..	..	..	..	4.6	4.7	8.1	8.2
90-93	Arts, entertainment and recreation	..	..	..	..	1.6	1.7	4.5	4.4
94-99	Other services; household-employers; extraterritorial bodies	..	..	..	..	21.9	22.2	21.2	20.7

.. Not available

Note: Detailed metadata at: http://metalinks.oecd.org/anberd/20170419/301f.
  Information on data for Israel: http://oe.cd/israel-disclaimer.
Disclaimer: http://oe.cd/disclaimer

GERMANY

R&D expenditure in industry by main activity of the enterprise, constant prices
ISIC Rev. 4

2010 USD PPP

		2007	2008	2009	2010	2011	2012	2013	2014
	TOTAL BUSINESS ENTERPRISE	55 369.2	58 786.2	56 770.6	58 402.0	62 891.1	65 226.8	63 703.3	66 563.3
01-03	**AGRICULTURE, FORESTRY AND FISHING**	121.2	126.3	164.5	177.1	155.3	167.7	171.0	159.9
05-09	**MINING AND QUARRYING**	35.9	35.9	16.9	15.3	12.3	13.0	18.3	14.5
10-33	**MANUFACTURING**	48 807.7	52 029.5	48 540.4	50 078.6	53 848.7	56 184.6	54 763.1	57 788.0
10-12	Food products, beverages and tobacco	408.4	350.6	398.7	408.9	379.2	381.9	374.3	371.8
13-15	Textiles, wearing apparel, leather and related products	170.9	171.2	158.4	154.3	146.8	148.3	134.4	134.3
13	Textiles	121.7	121.9	88.7	84.6	76.5	78.1	66.8	64.7
14	Wearing apparel	42.2	42.4	62.7	62.7	63.5	63.3	60.9	62.9
15	Leather and related products, footwear	6.9	7.0	7.0	7.1	6.8	6.9	6.7	6.7
16-18	Wood and paper products and printing	232.5	231.6	220.8	258.9	225.0	208.4	270.0	261.4
16	Wood and wood products, except furniture	26.1	25.9	25.2	28.5	27.8	24.0	23.7	22.8
17	Paper and paper products	78.2	78.1	80.2	92.1	75.5	70.5	120.0	120.1
18	Printing and reproduction of recorded media	128.1	127.6	115.4	138.3	121.7	114.0	126.3	118.5
19-23	Chemical, rubber, plastic, non-metallic mineral products	9 856.4	10 053.9	10 434.4	10 040.9	10 694.4	10 823.1	10 438.0	10 625.0
19	Coke and refined petroleum products	113.0	112.3	116.6	110.9	116.1	116.4	111.4	138.9
20-21	Chemical and pharmaceutical products	8 304.7	8 472.5	8 895.0	8 538.1	9 070.2	9 201.1	8 826.0	8 949.6
20	Chemicals and chemical products	4 043.8	4 116.0	4 009.7	3 887.7	4 059.2	4 239.1	3 979.9	4 237.8
21	Pharmaceuticals, medicinal, chemical and botanical products	4 261.0	4 356.4	4 885.2	4 650.4	5 011.0	4 962.0	4 846.1	4 711.8
22	Rubber and plastic products	1 116.8	1 129.6	1 062.2	1 036.9	1 161.6	1 159.3	1 153.4	1 183.7
23	Other non-metallic mineral products	321.9	339.5	360.6	355.0	346.5	346.3	347.1	352.8
24-25	Basic metals, metal products, except machinery and equipment	1 390.5	1 454.4	1 512.8	1 500.2	1 529.4	1 569.9	1 514.3	1 500.2
24	Basic metals	481.7	508.0	620.6	613.5	635.6	656.9	630.2	624.4
25	Fabricated metal products, except machinery and equipment	908.8	946.5	892.3	886.7	893.8	913.0	884.1	875.8
26-30	Computer, electronic, optical products; electrical machinery, transport equipment	35 585.5	38 607.3	34 513.0	36 416.5	39 379.2	41 653.8	40 511.7	43 298.6
26	Computer, electronic and optical products	7 821.9	8 261.3	7 292.0	7 460.4	8 081.5	8 963.4	8 731.3	8 766.7
27	Electrical equipment	1 808.2	1 908.2	1 672.0	1 673.4	1 972.2	2 100.6	2 533.2	2 536.2
28	Machinery and equipment n.e.c.	5 678.6	5 959.6	5 640.7	5 721.0	6 036.4	6 284.5	6 407.9	6 599.0
29	Motor vehicles, trailers and semi-trailers	17 592.6	19 501.2	17 329.8	18 432.8	20 085.4	21 052.0	20 439.5	22 969.0
30	Other transport equipment	2 684.2	2 977.3	2 578.5	3 128.9	3 203.7	3 253.3	2 399.8	2 415.7
31-33	Furniture; repair, installation of machinery and equipment	1 163.6	1 160.5	1 302.3	1 298.9	1 494.8	1 399.2	1 520.6	1 596.7
31	Furniture	159.5	124.7	64.1	65.2	51.3	48.4	44.5	45.5
32	Other manufacturing	484.0	487.8	548.3	548.6	677.2	637.0	724.2	755.1
33	Repair and installation of machinery and equipment	520.1	548.0	689.9	685.1	766.2	713.9	751.8	796.0
35-39	**ELECTRICITY, GAS, WATER AND WASTE MANAGEMENT**	159.8	164.0	271.3	244.4	243.1	225.7	248.0	228.3
35-36	Electricity, gas and water	151.6	156.3	262.1	235.8	228.7	214.1	231.8	213.1
37-39	Sewerage, waste management and remediation activities	8.2	7.7	9.3	8.6	14.4	11.5	16.2	15.2
41-43	**CONSTRUCTION**	74.4	70.9	86.5	95.2	81.0	85.6	95.1	93.4
45-99	**TOTAL SERVICES**	6 170.2	6 359.6	7 690.8	7 791.4	8 550.7	8 550.3	8 407.7	8 279.2
45-82	**Business sector services**	..	6 359.0	7 669.0	7 771.4	8 520.7	8 520.3	8 373.3	8 246.4
45-47	Wholesale and retail trade; motor vehicle and motorcycle repairs	204.4	210.5	255.5	278.9	322.1	343.9	307.4	299.8
49-53	Transportation and storage	..	78.6	72.5	79.0	133.7	148.9	108.9	111.1
55-56	Accommodation and food service activities	0.4	0.4	0.4	0.5	0.5	0.5	0.2	0.2
58-63	Information and communication	2 375.6	2 444.8	3 215.5	3 300.0	3 681.1	3 850.4	3 770.4	3 771.1
58-60	Publishing, audiovisual and broadcasting activities	23.9	24.0	47.9	46.9	52.0	50.9	31.8	31.5
58	Publishing activities	..	..	..	..	..	..	..	..
59-60	Motion picture, video and TV programme production; broadcasting activities	..	..	..	..	..	..	..	..
59	Motion picture, video and TV programme production; sound and music	..	..	..	..	..	..	..	..
60	Programming and broadcasting activities	..	..	..	..	..	..	..	..
61	Telecommunications	246.5	244.3	714.3	750.0	702.9	753.2	444.8	445.1
62-63	IT and other information services	2 105.2	2 176.5	2 453.3	2 503.0	2 926.2	3 045.0	3 293.8	3 294.5
62	Computer programming, consultancy and related activities	2 022.0	2 089.3	2 384.1	2 436.1	2 810.2	2 926.2	3 177.9	3 179.2
63	Information service activities	83.2	87.1	69.2	67.0	116.0	118.8	116.0	115.3
64-66	Financial and insurance activities	269.6	280.7	419.6	289.3	321.2	321.6	345.2	370.9
68-82	Real estate; professional, scientific and technical; administrative and support	3 241.0	3 344.0	3 705.5	3 823.4	4 062.0	3 855.0	3 841.1	3 693.3
68	Real estate activities	0.0	0.0	0.8	0.6	1.0	1.0	0.8	0.8
69-75x72	Professional, scientific and technical activities, except scientific R&D	1 160.5	1 196.2	1 661.2	1 702.1	1 910.5	1 754.2	1 802.8	1 623.5
72	Scientific research and development	1 818.3	1 879.6	2 001.1	2 074.8	2 106.3	2 053.1	2 003.8	2 036.1
77-82	Administrative and support service activities	262.2	268.2	42.5	45.9	44.3	46.8	33.8	32.8
84-99	Community, social and personal services	..	0.6	21.8	20.0	30.0	30.0	34.4	32.8
84-85	Public administration and defence; compulsory social security and education	..	..	..	..	2.7	2.7	3.2	2.9
86-88	Human health and social work activities	..	..	..	..	4.4	4.5	7.5	7.4
90-93	Arts, entertainment and recreation	..	..	..	..	1.6	1.6	4.2	4.0
94-99	Other services; household-employers; extraterritorial bodies	..	..	..	..	21.3	21.2	19.5	18.6

.. Not available

Note: Detailed metadata at: http://metalinks.oecd.org/anberd/20170419/301f.
Information on data for Israel: http://oe.cd/israel-disclaimer.

Disclaimer: http://oe.cd/disclaimer

HUNGARY

R&D expenditure in industry by main activity of the enterprise, current prices
ISIC Rev. 4

Million USD PPP

		2007	2008	2009	2010	2011	2012	2013	2014
	TOTAL BUSINESS ENTERPRISE	921.2	1 069.0	1 342.6	1 470.5	1 690.4	1 899.9	2 335.9	2 451.5
01-03	AGRICULTURE, FORESTRY AND FISHING	18.5	19.4	25.0	28.8	32.0	43.5	52.5	55.9
05-09	MINING AND QUARRYING	0.0	0.0	0.0	0.0	0.0	2.3	1.1	1.5
10-33	MANUFACTURING	675.8	781.6	913.7	956.0	1 049.8	1 191.6	1 325.0	1 262.0
10-12	Food products, beverages and tobacco	13.6	12.9	23.1	29.6	36.2	36.5	42.7	25.4
13-15	Textiles, wearing apparel, leather and related products	0.8	0.4	0.5	0.3	0.2	0.6	7.5	4.6
13	Textiles	..	..	..	..	..	..	2.4	..
14	Wearing apparel	..	..	..	..	..	..	0.8	0.7
15	Leather and related products, footwear	..	..	..	..	..	..	4.2	..
16-18	Wood and paper products and printing	4.8	5.6	9.1	8.6	9.5	12.2	31.3	29.3
16	Wood and wood products, except furniture	0.2	0.7	1.4	1.0	2.0	0.5	4.6	2.0
17	Paper and paper products	1.1	0.5	0.6	2.7	4.6	5.5	22.1	3.5
18	Printing and reproduction of recorded media	3.5	4.4	7.1	4.9	2.9	6.1	4.7	23.8
19-23	Chemical, rubber, plastic, non-metallic mineral products	361.5	440.3	490.5	497.3	498.2	561.2	552.5	567.3
19	Coke and refined petroleum products	17.9	24.6	26.1	12.1	13.7	14.5	11.2	10.9
20-21	Chemical and pharmaceutical products	331.4	403.4	443.0	466.9	460.3	511.6	513.4	524.2
20	Chemicals and chemical products	19.9	23.1	28.6	24.4	26.2	18.2	32.8	18.0
21	Pharmaceuticals, medicinal, chemical and botanical products	311.4	380.3	414.4	442.5	434.1	493.4	480.6	506.2
22	Rubber and plastic products	9.5	9.6	18.2	12.2	17.3	19.0	20.8	25.3
23	Other non-metallic mineral products	2.7	2.7	3.1	6.2	6.8	16.2	7.1	6.9
24-25	Basic metals, metal products, except machinery and equipment	8.3	10.9	16.8	16.1	20.3	51.0	47.4	57.3
24	Basic metals	3.9	5.5	7.3	8.0	4.9	6.2	9.2	14.1
25	Fabricated metal products, except machinery and equipment	4.5	5.3	9.6	8.1	15.4	44.8	38.2	43.3
26-30	Computer, electronic, optical products; electrical machinery, transport equipment	283.1	293.3	345.8	367.5	445.4	478.1	570.1	515.8
26	Computer, electronic and optical products	99.3	78.1	123.8	116.1	149.2	129.4	129.8	51.2
27	Electrical equipment	37.5	42.0	46.7	41.9	48.8	45.7	66.1	65.5
28	Machinery and equipment n.e.c.	39.4	37.7	30.9	65.1	88.4	113.3	127.3	131.3
29	Motor vehicles, trailers and semi-trailers	105.8	134.1	133.7	142.5	157.2	187.6	244.8	255.2
30	Other transport equipment	1.0	1.4	10.7	1.9	1.7	2.1	2.0	12.6
31-33	Furniture; repair, installation of machinery and equipment	3.6	18.3	27.9	36.5	40.1	52.0	73.6	62.3
31	Furniture	0.4	0.2	0.6	1.1	3.3	3.4	13.5	5.3
32	Other manufacturing	0.4	10.1	11.8	18.9	24.2	28.0	28.8	40.9
33	Repair and installation of machinery and equipment	2.9	8.0	15.5	16.5	12.6	20.5	31.3	16.2
35-39	ELECTRICITY, GAS, WATER AND WASTE MANAGEMENT	5.9	7.3	9.9	7.9	6.5	4.9	18.2	12.5
35-36	Electricity, gas and water	2.5	1.7	2.2	3.5	2.9	2.7	3.8	6.2
37-39	Sewerage, waste management and remediation activities	3.4	5.6	7.7	4.4	3.6	2.2	14.4	6.3
41-43	CONSTRUCTION	1.7	3.0	9.9	5.9	8.2	8.5	23.5	21.4
45-99	TOTAL SERVICES	219.3	257.7	383.9	472.0	593.8	649.2	915.6	1 098.2
45-82	Business sector services	205.6	235.3	355.1	434.4	553.1	598.2	868.9	1 043.6
45-47	Wholesale and retail trade; motor vehicle and motorcycle repairs	114.7	78.3	89.7	189.4	268.2	223.8	307.3	361.9
49-53	Transportation and storage	1.5	1.7	1.8	0.2	1.8	4.3	11.8	9.2
55-56	Accommodation and food service activities	0.1	0.3	0.2	0.0	..	..	..	2.0
58-63	Information and communication	32.7	76.2	148.8	109.8	134.6	255.7	368.7	502.4
58-60	Publishing, audiovisual and broadcasting activities	5.6	3.9	8.9	11.9	13.8	20.6	30.2	30.2
58	Publishing activities	5.6	3.5	8.2	9.9	13.0	20.6	..	..
59-60	Motion picture, video and TV programme production; broadcasting activities	0.0	0.4	0.7	2.0	0.8	0.0	..	..
59	Motion picture, video and TV programme production; sound and music	..	..	..	..	..	..	..	..
60	Programming and broadcasting activities	..	..	..	..	..	..	..	..
61	Telecommunications	2.8	3.0	3.7	1.6	3.6	4.3	10.9	91.8
62-63	IT and other information services	24.3	69.4	136.2	96.3	117.2	230.8	327.6	380.4
62	Computer programming, consultancy and related activities	23.3	68.6	131.5	93.3	113.8	220.1	303.7	354.4
63	Information service activities	1.0	0.8	4.7	3.1	3.4	10.7	23.9	25.9
64-66	Financial and insurance activities	1.9	2.4	0.9	2.7	..	..	..	2.2
68-82	Real estate; professional, scientific and technical; administrative and support	54.7	76.5	113.7	132.3	143.9	109.5	178.3	165.9
68	Real estate activities	1.5	3.1	6.6	2.9	5.4	3.8	10.1	15.2
69-75x72	Professional, scientific and technical activities, except scientific R&D	35.2	66.7	101.1	106.4	129.4	99.1	139.9	122.7
72	Scientific research and development	10.9	3.7	2.0	18.3	3.1	1.7	18.7	8.2
77-82	Administrative and support service activities	7.1	3.0	4.0	4.6	6.1	4.9	9.7	19.9
84-99	Community, social and personal services	13.8	22.3	28.8	37.6	40.7	51.0	46.7	54.6
84-85	Public administration and defence; compulsory social security and education	1.4	0.9	1.2	1.2	0.7	7.2	5.0	7.8
86-88	Human health and social work activities	11.0	18.5	22.7	29.8	31.1	37.1	29.3	36.3
90-93	Arts, entertainment and recreation	0.3	0.8	0.6	0.6	1.2	1.6	2.2	2.4
94-99	Other services; household-employers; extraterritorial bodies	1.0	2.2	4.4	5.9	7.6	5.0	10.3	8.0

.. Not available

Note: Detailed metadata at: http://metalinks.oecd.org/anberd/20170419/301f.
Information on data for Israel: http://oe.cd/israel-disclaimer.
Disclaimer: http://oe.cd/disclaimer

HUNGARY

R&D expenditure in industry by main activity of the enterprise, constant prices
ISIC Rev. 4

2010 USD PPP

		2007	2008	2009	2010	2011	2012	2013	2014
	TOTAL BUSINESS ENTERPRISE	1 094.4	1 180.5	1 388.3	1 470.5	1 628.9	1 789.6	2 124.6	2 223.4
01-03	**AGRICULTURE, FORESTRY AND FISHING**	21.9	21.4	25.9	28.8	30.9	40.9	47.8	50.7
05-09	**MINING AND QUARRYING**	0.0	0.0	0.0	0.0	0.0	2.2	1.0	1.4
10-33	**MANUFACTURING**	802.9	863.1	944.9	956.0	1 011.6	1 122.4	1 205.1	1 144.6
10-12	Food products, beverages and tobacco	16.1	14.2	23.9	29.6	34.9	34.4	38.9	23.1
13-15	Textiles, wearing apparel, leather and related products	1.0	0.4	0.5	0.3	0.2	0.6	6.8	4.2
13	Textiles	..	..	..	..	..	..	2.2	..
14	Wearing apparel	..	..	..	..	..	..	0.7	0.6
15	Leather and related products, footwear	..	..	..	..	..	..	3.8	..
16-18	Wood and paper products and printing	5.8	6.2	9.4	8.6	9.2	11.5	28.5	26.6
16	Wood and wood products, except furniture	0.3	0.8	1.4	1.0	1.9	0.5	4.2	1.8
17	Paper and paper products	1.3	0.6	0.7	2.7	4.4	5.2	20.1	3.1
18	Printing and reproduction of recorded media	4.2	4.8	7.4	4.9	2.8	5.8	4.2	21.6
19-23	Chemical, rubber, plastic, non-metallic mineral products	429.5	486.2	507.2	497.3	480.0	528.6	502.5	514.5
19	Coke and refined petroleum products	21.3	27.2	27.0	12.1	13.2	13.6	10.2	9.9
20-21	Chemical and pharmaceutical products	393.7	445.4	458.1	466.9	443.6	481.9	467.0	475.4
20	Chemicals and chemical products	23.7	25.5	29.6	24.4	25.3	17.1	29.9	16.3
21	Pharmaceuticals, medicinal, chemical and botanical products	370.0	419.9	428.6	442.5	418.3	464.8	437.1	459.1
22	Rubber and plastic products	11.3	10.6	18.8	12.2	16.7	17.9	18.9	22.9
23	Other non-metallic mineral products	3.2	3.0	3.2	6.2	6.6	15.2	6.5	6.3
24-25	Basic metals, metal products, except machinery and equipment	9.9	12.0	17.4	16.1	19.6	48.1	43.1	52.0
24	Basic metals	4.6	6.1	7.5	8.0	4.8	5.8	8.3	12.8
25	Fabricated metal products, except machinery and equipment	5.3	5.9	9.9	8.1	14.8	42.2	34.8	39.2
26-30	Computer, electronic, optical products; electrical machinery, transport equipment	336.3	323.9	357.6	367.5	429.2	450.3	518.5	467.8
26	Computer, electronic and optical products	118.0	86.2	128.0	116.1	143.8	121.8	118.1	46.5
27	Electrical equipment	44.5	46.4	48.3	41.9	47.0	43.1	60.1	59.4
28	Machinery and equipment n.e.c.	46.8	41.7	32.0	65.1	85.2	106.7	115.8	119.1
29	Motor vehicles, trailers and semi-trailers	125.7	148.1	138.2	142.5	151.5	176.7	222.7	231.4
30	Other transport equipment	1.2	1.5	11.1	1.9	1.7	2.0	1.8	11.4
31-33	Furniture; repair, installation of machinery and equipment	4.3	20.2	28.9	36.5	38.6	49.0	66.9	56.5
31	Furniture	0.5	0.3	0.6	1.1	3.2	3.2	12.3	4.8
32	Other manufacturing	0.5	11.1	12.2	18.9	23.3	26.4	26.2	37.1
33	Repair and installation of machinery and equipment	3.4	8.8	16.0	16.5	12.1	19.3	28.5	14.7
35-39	**ELECTRICITY, GAS, WATER AND WASTE MANAGEMENT**	7.0	8.0	10.2	7.9	6.3	4.6	16.6	11.3
35-36	Electricity, gas and water	3.0	1.8	2.3	3.5	2.8	2.5	3.5	5.6
37-39	Sewerage, waste management and remediation activities	4.0	6.2	7.9	4.4	3.5	2.1	13.1	5.7
41-43	**CONSTRUCTION**	2.0	3.3	10.2	5.9	7.9	8.0	21.4	19.4
45-99	**TOTAL SERVICES**	260.6	284.5	397.0	472.0	572.2	611.5	832.8	996.0
45-82	**Business sector services**	244.2	259.9	367.2	434.4	533.0	563.5	790.3	946.5
45-47	**Wholesale and retail trade; motor vehicle and motorcycle repairs**	136.2	86.5	92.8	189.4	258.5	210.8	279.5	328.2
49-53	**Transportation and storage**	1.8	1.8	1.9	0.2	1.7	4.0	10.8	8.3
55-56	**Accommodation and food service activities**	0.1	0.3	0.2	0.0	..	..	..	1.8
58-63	**Information and communication**	38.8	84.2	153.9	109.8	129.7	240.9	335.3	455.6
58-60	Publishing, audiovisual and broadcasting activities	6.6	4.3	9.2	11.9	13.3	19.4	27.5	27.4
58	Publishing activities	6.6	3.8	8.5	9.9	12.5	19.4	..	..
59-60	Motion picture, video and TV programme production; broadcasting activities	0.0	0.5	0.7	2.0	0.8	0.0	..	..
59	Motion picture, video and TV programme production; sound and music	..	..	..	..	..	..	..	..
60	Programming and broadcasting activities	..	..	..	..	..	..	..	..
61	Telecommunications	3.3	3.3	3.8	1.6	3.5	4.1	10.0	83.2
62-63	IT and other information services	28.9	76.6	140.9	96.3	113.0	217.4	297.9	345.0
62	Computer programming, consultancy and related activities	27.6	75.8	136.0	93.3	109.7	207.4	276.2	321.5
63	Information service activities	1.2	0.9	4.9	3.1	3.3	10.1	21.7	23.5
64-66	**Financial and insurance activities**	2.3	2.6	0.9	2.7	..	..	..	2.0
68-82	**Real estate; professional, scientific and technical; administrative and support**	65.0	84.5	117.6	132.3	138.7	103.1	162.2	150.5
68	Real estate activities	1.7	3.4	6.8	2.9	5.2	3.5	9.1	13.7
69-75x72	Professional, scientific and technical activities, except scientific R&D	41.9	73.7	104.5	106.4	124.6	93.3	127.2	111.3
72	Scientific research and development	12.9	4.0	2.0	18.3	3.0	1.6	17.0	7.4
77-82	Administrative and support service activities	8.4	3.3	4.2	4.6	5.9	4.7	8.8	18.1
84-99	**Community, social and personal services**	16.4	24.6	29.8	37.6	39.2	48.0	42.5	49.5
84-85	Public administration and defence; compulsory social security and education	1.7	0.9	1.2	1.2	0.7	6.8	4.5	7.1
86-88	Human health and social work activities	13.1	20.4	23.4	29.8	30.0	34.9	26.6	33.0
90-93	Arts, entertainment and recreation	0.4	0.9	0.6	0.6	1.1	1.5	2.0	2.2
94-99	Other services; household-employers; extraterritorial bodies	1.2	2.4	4.5	5.9	7.4	4.7	9.4	7.3

.. Not available

Note: Detailed metadata at: http://metalinks.oecd.org/anberd/20170419/301f.
Information on data for Israel: http://oe.cd/israel-disclaimer.

Disclaimer: http://oe.cd/disclaimer

ISRAEL

R&D expenditure in industry by main activity of the enterprise, current prices
ISIC Rev. 4

Million USD PPP

		2007	2008	2009	2010	2011	2012	2013	2014
	TOTAL BUSINESS ENTERPRISE	7 203.5	7 109.3	6 910.2	7 194.0	7 979.6	8 788.5	9 643.0	10 395.0
01-03	**AGRICULTURE, FORESTRY AND FISHING**	..	..	..	..	..	..	..	..
05-09	**MINING AND QUARRYING**	..	..	..	3.5	3.3	5.8	6.5	6.6
10-33	**MANUFACTURING**	2 491.4	2 201.1	1 989.5	2 171.1	2 396.1	2 372.1	2 581.5	2 512.0
10-12	Food products, beverages and tobacco	5.2	19.8	11.2	15.1	20.0	24.1	18.4	16.9
13-15	Textiles, wearing apparel, leather and related products	33.5	24.9	26.0	17.1	22.0	22.8	20.5	21.3
13	Textiles	..	..	..	..	..	..	..	..
14	Wearing apparel	..	..	..	..	..	..	..	..
15	Leather and related products, footwear	..	..	..	..	..	..	..	..
16-18	Wood and paper products and printing	..	..	..	5.0	3.4	3.5	3.2	1.3
16	Wood and wood products, except furniture	..	..	..	..	..	..	..	..
17	Paper and paper products	..	..	..	..	..	..	..	..
18	Printing and reproduction of recorded media	..	..	..	..	..	..	..	..
19-23	Chemical, rubber, plastic, non-metallic mineral products	414.3	382.4	422.9	416.3	375.6	401.0	495.1	410.0
19	Coke and refined petroleum products	..	..	..	64.2	45.9	66.0	64.9	77.2
20-21	Chemical and pharmaceutical products	..	..	..	..	..	..	..	..
20	Chemicals and chemical products	..	..	..	..	..	..	..	..
21	Pharmaceuticals, medicinal, chemical and botanical products	..	..	..	313.9	283.2	286.2	382.4	285.8
22	Rubber and plastic products	..	..	..	..	..	..	..	..
23	Other non-metallic mineral products	..	..	..	..	..	..	..	..
24-25	Basic metals, metal products, except machinery and equipment	67.9	51.2	62.4	42.7	89.5	53.9	53.9	52.6
24	Basic metals	..	..	..	..	..	..	..	..
25	Fabricated metal products, except machinery and equipment	..	..	..	..	..	..	..	..
26-30	Computer, electronic, optical products; electrical machinery, transport equipment	1 970.5	1 722.9	1 467.0	1 654.9	1 861.1	1 839.0	1 960.7	1 983.7
26	Computer, electronic and optical products	1 718.8	1 404.0	1 239.3	1 408.4	1 559.4	1 497.9	1 596.0	1 628.2
27	Electrical equipment	..	..	..	..	..	..	206.7	204.8
28	Machinery and equipment n.e.c.	..	..	..	..	..	..	0.6	0.6
29	Motor vehicles, trailers and semi-trailers	..	..	..	..	..	..	..	..
30	Other transport equipment	..	..	..	..	..	..	..	..
31-33	Furniture; repair, installation of machinery and equipment	..	..	..	..	..	..	..	..
31	Furniture	..	..	..	..	..	..	..	..
32	Other manufacturing	..	..	..	20.0	24.5	27.7	29.7	26.3
33	Repair and installation of machinery and equipment	..	..	..	..	..	..	..	..
35-39	**ELECTRICITY, GAS, WATER AND WASTE MANAGEMENT**	84.2	116.6	67.3	34.3	74.2	70.2	1.1	0.8
35-36	Electricity, gas and water	..	..	..	..	..	..	0.7	0.5
37-39	Sewerage, waste management and remediation activities	..	..	..	..	..	..	0.5	0.3
41-43	**CONSTRUCTION**	..	..	..	..	..	..	4.1	2.5
45-99	**TOTAL SERVICES**	4 627.8	4 791.6	4 853.5	4 985.1	5 506.0	6 340.3	7 049.7	7 873.3
45-82	**Business sector services**	..	..	..	4 823.8	5 331.7	6 151.5	6 843.5	7 657.3
45-47	Wholesale and retail trade; motor vehicle and motorcycle repairs	..	..	..	..	..	..	5.7	3.4
49-53	Transportation and storage	..	..	..	0.0	0.0	0.0	0.0	0.0
55-56	Accommodation and food service activities	..	..	..	0.0	0.0	0.0	0.0	0.0
58-63	Information and communication	2 026.4	2 073.3	2 203.9	2 051.9	2 415.9	2 983.6	3 445.4	3 901.2
58-60	Publishing, audiovisual and broadcasting activities	..	..	..	21.3	25.1	31.0	35.8	44.8
58	Publishing activities	..	..	..	..	..	..	..	..
59-60	Motion picture, video and TV programme production; broadcasting activities	..	..	..	..	..	..	..	..
59	Motion picture, video and TV programme production; sound and music	..	..	..	..	..	..	..	..
60	Programming and broadcasting activities	..	..	..	..	..	..	..	..
61	Telecommunications	..	..	..	..	..	..	..	..
62-63	IT and other information services	..	..	..	..	..	..	..	..
62	Computer programming, consultancy and related activities	..	..	..	..	..	..	..	..
63	Information service activities	..	..	..	6.8	8.1	10.0	11.5	12.3
64-66	Financial and insurance activities	..	..	..	3.0	6.4	5.1	23.5	17.7
68-82	Real estate; professional, scientific and technical; administrative and support	..	..	..	2 768.9	2 909.4	3 162.7	3 369.0	3 735.0
68	Real estate activities	..	..	..	0.0	0.0	0.0	0.0	0.0
69-75x72	Professional, scientific and technical activities, except scientific R&D	..	..	..	..	..	..	..	..
72	Scientific research and development	2 553.5	2 701.2	2 643.9	2 768.9	2 909.4	3 162.7	3 359.7	3 724.4
77-82	Administrative and support service activities	..	..	..	..	..	..	..	..
84-99	Community, social and personal services	..	..	..	161.3	174.3	188.9	206.2	216.0
84-85	Public administration and defence; compulsory social security and education	..	..	..	..	..	..	..	..
86-88	Human health and social work activities	..	..	..	..	..	..	..	..
90-93	Arts, entertainment and recreation	..	..	..	..	..	..	..	..
94-99	Other services; household-employers; extraterritorial bodies	..	..	..	..	..	..	..	..

.. Not available

Note: Detailed metadata at: http://metalinks.oecd.org/anberd/20170419/301f.
  Information on data for Israel: http://oe.cd/israel-disclaimer.
Disclaimer: http://oe.cd/disclaimer

ISRAEL

R&D expenditure in industry by main activity of the enterprise, constant prices
ISIC Rev. 4

2010 USD PPP

		2007	2008	2009	2010	2011	2012	2013	2014
	TOTAL BUSINESS ENTERPRISE	7 273.9	7 287.2	6 994.6	7 194.0	7 779.1	8 279.9	8 626.5	9 222.4
01-03	AGRICULTURE, FORESTRY AND FISHING	..	..	..	..	..	..	..	..
05-09	MINING AND QUARRYING	..	..	..	3.5	3.2	5.5	5.8	5.8
10-33	MANUFACTURING	2 515.7	2 256.2	2 013.8	2 171.1	2 335.9	2 234.8	2 309.4	2 228.6
10-12	Food products, beverages and tobacco	5.2	20.3	11.3	15.1	19.5	22.7	16.5	15.0
13-15	Textiles, wearing apparel, leather and related products	33.7	25.5	26.3	17.1	21.4	21.5	18.3	18.9
13	Textiles	..	..	..	..	..	..	..	..
14	Wearing apparel	..	..	..	..	..	..	..	..
15	Leather and related products, footwear	..	..	..	..	..	..	..	..
16-18	Wood and paper products and printing	..	..	..	5.0	3.3	3.3	2.8	1.1
16	Wood and wood products, except furniture	..	..	..	..	..	..	..	..
17	Paper and paper products	..	..	..	..	..	..	..	..
18	Printing and reproduction of recorded media	..	..	..	..	..	..	..	..
19-23	Chemical, rubber, plastic, non-metallic mineral products	418.3	391.9	428.0	416.3	366.2	377.8	442.9	363.7
19	Coke and refined petroleum products	..	..	..	64.2	44.7	62.1	58.0	68.5
20-21	Chemical and pharmaceutical products	..	..	..	..	..	..	..	..
20	Chemicals and chemical products	..	..	..	..	..	..	..	..
21	Pharmaceuticals, medicinal, chemical and botanical products	..	..	..	313.9	276.1	269.7	342.1	253.5
22	Rubber and plastic products	..	..	..	..	..	..	..	..
23	Other non-metallic mineral products	..	..	..	..	..	..	..	..
24-25	Basic metals, metal products, except machinery and equipment	68.6	52.4	63.2	42.7	87.2	50.8	48.2	46.7
24	Basic metals	..	..	..	..	..	..	..	..
25	Fabricated metal products, except machinery and equipment	..	..	..	..	..	..	..	..
26-30	Computer, electronic, optical products; electrical machinery, transport equipment	1 989.8	1 766.0	1 484.9	1 654.9	1 814.3	1 732.6	1 754.1	1 759.9
26	Computer, electronic and optical products	1 735.6	1 439.2	1 254.5	1 408.4	1 520.2	1 411.2	1 427.7	1 444.5
27	Electrical equipment	..	..	..	..	..	..	184.9	181.7
28	Machinery and equipment n.e.c.	..	..	..	..	..	..	0.6	0.6
29	Motor vehicles, trailers and semi-trailers	..	..	..	..	..	..	..	..
30	Other transport equipment	..	..	..	..	..	..	..	..
31-33	Furniture; repair, installation of machinery and equipment	..	..	..	..	..	..	..	..
31	Furniture	..	..	..	..	..	..	..	..
32	Other manufacturing	..	..	..	20.0	23.9	26.1	26.5	23.3
33	Repair and installation of machinery and equipment	..	..	..	..	..	..	..	..
35-39	ELECTRICITY, GAS, WATER AND WASTE MANAGEMENT	84.8	119.5	68.1	34.3	72.3	66.0	1.0	0.7
35-36	Electricity, gas and water	..	..	..	..	..	..	0.6	0.5
37-39	Sewerage, waste management and remediation activities	..	..	..	..	..	..	0.4	0.2
41-43	CONSTRUCTION	..	..	..	..	..	..	3.7	2.2
45-99	TOTAL SERVICES	4 673.0	4 911.5	4 912.7	4 985.1	5 367.7	5 973.4	6 306.6	6 985.1
45-82	Business sector services	..	..	..	4 823.8	5 197.8	5 795.5	6 122.2	6 793.5
45-47	Wholesale and retail trade; motor vehicle and motorcycle repairs	..	..	..	..	..	..	5.1	3.0
49-53	Transportation and storage	..	..	..	0.0	0.0	0.0	0.0	0.0
55-56	Accommodation and food service activities	..	..	..	0.0	0.0	0.0	0.0	0.0
58-63	Information and communication	2 046.2	2 125.2	2 230.8	2 051.9	2 355.2	2 811.0	3 082.2	3 461.1
58-60	Publishing, audiovisual and broadcasting activities	..	..	..	21.3	24.5	29.2	32.0	39.8
58	Publishing activities	..	..	..	..	..	..	..	..
59-60	Motion picture, video and TV programme production; broadcasting activities	..	..	..	..	..	..	..	..
59	Motion picture, video and TV programme production; sound and music	..	..	..	..	..	..	..	..
60	Programming and broadcasting activities	..	..	..	..	..	..	..	..
61	Telecommunications	..	..	..	..	..	..	..	..
62-63	IT and other information services	..	..	..	..	..	..	..	..
62	Computer programming, consultancy and related activities	..	..	..	..	..	..	..	..
63	Information service activities	..	..	..	6.8	7.9	9.4	10.3	10.9
64-66	Financial and insurance activities	..	..	..	3.0	6.3	4.8	21.0	15.7
68-82	Real estate; professional, scientific and technical; administrative and support	..	..	..	2 768.9	2 836.3	2 979.7	3 013.9	3 313.7
68	Real estate activities	..	..	..	0.0	0.0	0.0	0.0	0.0
69-75x72	Professional, scientific and technical activities, except scientific R&D	..	..	..	..	..	..	..	..
72	Scientific research and development	2 578.5	2 768.8	2 676.2	2 768.9	2 836.3	2 979.7	3 005.6	3 304.3
77-82	Administrative and support service activities	..	..	..	..	..	..	..	..
84-99	Community, social and personal services	..	..	..	161.3	169.9	178.0	184.5	191.6
84-85	Public administration and defence; compulsory social security and education	..	..	..	..	..	..	..	..
86-88	Human health and social work activities	..	..	..	..	..	..	..	..
90-93	Arts, entertainment and recreation	..	..	..	..	..	..	..	..
94-99	Other services; household-employers; extraterritorial bodies	..	..	..	..	..	..	..	..

.. Not available

Note: Detailed metadata at: http://metalinks.oecd.org/anberd/20170419/301f.
   Information on data for Israel: http://oe.cd/israel-disclaimer.
Disclaimer: http://oe.cd/disclaimer

ITALY

R&D expenditure in industry by main activity of the enterprise, current prices
ISIC Rev. 4

Million USD PPP

		2007	2008	2009	2010	2011	2012	2013	2014
	TOTAL BUSINESS ENTERPRISE	11 665.5	12 981.2	13 289.7	13 709.0	14 268.5	14 854.5	15 585.0	16 807.0
01-03	AGRICULTURE, FORESTRY AND FISHING	0.2	2.2	2.3	4.5	4.3	4.5	6.0	9.5
05-09	MINING AND QUARRYING	161.3	224.2	214.2	97.1	82.6	83.3	80.0	72.5
10-33	MANUFACTURING	8 114.3	9 236.1	9 256.8	9 820.0	10 501.7	11 035.4	11 239.1	11 894.6
10-12	Food products, beverages and tobacco	167.1	200.5	202.8	212.8	198.1	229.5	255.6	272.0
13-15	Textiles, wearing apparel, leather and related products	304.5	428.0	474.4	549.3	572.6	611.2	652.4	697.6
13	Textiles	103.9	95.2	117.6	149.7	131.9	137.3	150.3	172.4
14	Wearing apparel	142.9	243.0	252.5	269.5	281.5	301.4	304.8	308.3
15	Leather and related products, footwear	57.7	89.8	104.4	130.1	159.1	172.4	197.4	216.9
16-18	Wood and paper products and printing	67.5	82.3	96.2	89.9	95.3	87.1	101.7	106.8
16	Wood and wood products, except furniture	11.1	18.1	21.2	18.1	17.9	18.3	18.5	18.5
17	Paper and paper products	45.7	48.0	57.8	57.5	63.7	56.7	69.5	70.2
18	Printing and reproduction of recorded media	10.7	16.2	17.3	14.3	13.7	12.0	13.7	18.2
19-23	Chemical, rubber, plastic, non-metallic mineral products	1 304.5	1 510.5	1 531.8	1 635.2	1 640.7	1 765.1	1 753.5	1 840.2
19	Coke and refined petroleum products	14.2	16.3	6.9	11.9	16.6	16.4	18.3	23.6
20-21	Chemical and pharmaceutical products	922.5	1 066.6	1 131.3	1 192.8	1 208.9	1 244.3	1 233.6	1 221.6
20	Chemicals and chemical products	402.5	454.0	438.7	470.8	446.6	472.8	494.7	525.0
21	Pharmaceuticals, medicinal, chemical and botanical products	520.1	612.6	692.5	722.0	762.4	771.5	738.9	696.6
22	Rubber and plastic products	270.5	300.1	271.4	307.9	309.6	375.5	370.5	446.9
23	Other non-metallic mineral products	97.3	127.5	122.3	122.6	105.6	128.8	131.1	148.0
24-25	Basic metals, metal products, except machinery and equipment	304.8	523.5	453.5	471.6	494.1	507.3	568.5	538.7
24	Basic metals	113.5	139.2	124.2	124.9	138.9	134.4	125.7	110.3
25	Fabricated metal products, except machinery and equipment	191.2	384.3	329.3	346.6	355.2	372.9	442.8	428.4
26-30	Computer, electronic, optical products; electrical machinery, transport equipment	5 749.3	6 241.7	6 233.3	6 592.0	7 244.2	7 533.5	7 608.5	8 106.6
26	Computer, electronic and optical products	1 558.3	1 528.5	1 651.5	1 787.0	1 902.8	1 828.9	1 758.9	1 783.8
27	Electrical equipment	352.5	484.1	494.6	562.8	607.1	631.0	655.7	635.9
28	Machinery and equipment n.e.c.	1 099.6	1 355.6	1 402.6	1 377.9	1 539.2	1 731.5	1 862.1	1 990.4
29	Motor vehicles, trailers and semi-trailers	1 290.8	1 478.8	1 289.2	1 393.7	1 710.5	1 844.0	1 973.0	2 378.6
30	Other transport equipment	1 448.0	1 394.7	1 395.4	1 470.7	1 484.8	1 498.0	1 359.0	1 317.9
31-33	Furniture; repair, installation of machinery and equipment	216.7	249.6	264.7	269.3	256.6	301.8	298.4	332.6
31	Furniture	49.6	75.4	73.9	65.3	69.2	75.4	77.1	91.2
32	Other manufacturing	91.6	95.6	98.9	116.8	118.9	146.3	129.2	147.7
33	Repair and installation of machinery and equipment	75.5	78.6	91.9	87.2	68.5	80.1	92.0	93.6
35-39	ELECTRICITY, GAS, WATER AND WASTE MANAGEMENT	55.9	103.5	25.7	22.7	28.1	37.2	43.8	213.7
35-36	Electricity, gas and water	50.0	96.0	15.4	15.2	20.6	28.0	36.4	195.7
37-39	Sewerage, waste management and remediation activities	5.9	7.5	10.3	7.5	7.5	9.2	7.5	18.0
41-43	CONSTRUCTION	37.8	53.6	61.9	54.2	42.0	48.7	57.2	51.2
45-99	TOTAL SERVICES	3 296.1	3 361.6	3 728.8	3 710.5	3 609.7	3 645.4	4 158.9	4 565.4
45-82	Business sector services	3 240.0	3 293.8	3 635.8	3 620.5	3 500.0	3 477.1	3 917.1	4 306.5
45-47	Wholesale and retail trade; motor vehicle and motorcycle repairs	312.4	361.1	372.8	395.1	336.9	365.2	434.8	484.2
49-53	Transportation and storage	42.9	72.5	42.1	41.1	36.6	23.9	55.1	51.5
55-56	Accommodation and food service activities	1.9	2.2	2.9	4.4	3.8	3.2	2.4	3.0
58-63	Information and communication	1 124.1	1 408.5	1 673.1	1 612.0	1 489.9	1 515.3	1 766.3	1 676.0
58-60	Publishing, audiovisual and broadcasting activities	76.9	17.4	18.2	17.0	16.3	23.7	21.3	26.6
58	Publishing activities	66.5	4.3	5.2	6.0	5.9	15.1	12.2	17.7
59-60	Motion picture, video and TV programme production; broadcasting activities	10.4	13.0	13.0	11.0	10.4	8.6	9.0	8.9
59	Motion picture, video and TV programme production; sound and music	..	..	..	..	..	..	..	..
60	Programming and broadcasting activities								
61	Telecommunications	570.0	1 107.3	1 295.0	1 238.3	1 090.8	1 088.2	578.4	424.8
62-63	IT and other information services	477.2	283.8	360.0	356.7	382.8	403.4	1 166.4	1 224.6
62	Computer programming, consultancy and related activities	464.4	268.1	332.0	328.8	346.8	362.2	662.5	1 170.8
63	Information service activities	12.8	15.7	27.9	28.0	36.0	41.2	503.9	53.8
64-66	Financial and insurance activities	170.0	204.0	240.3	253.1	188.4	229.4	253.5	305.7
68-82	Real estate; professional, scientific and technical; administrative and support	1 588.7	1 245.5	1 304.7	1 314.8	1 444.3	1 340.1	1 405.0	1 786.0
68	Real estate activities	2.5	3.7	30.2	13.3	7.0	10.3	3.0	4.0
69-75x72	Professional, scientific and technical activities, except scientific R&D	654.1	257.1	402.5	423.2	495.2	431.8	461.0	491.1
72	Scientific research and development	912.3	965.7	858.4	866.1	930.2	879.3	930.2	1 251.1
77-82	Administrative and support service activities	19.9	19.0	13.5	12.1	12.0	18.6	10.9	39.8
84-99	Community, social and personal services	56.0	67.9	93.1	90.1	109.7	168.4	241.8	259.0
84-85	Public administration and defence; compulsory social security and education	5.9	1.9	1.8	3.1	2.9	1.9	2.3	2.2
86-88	Human health and social work activities	48.0	61.8	82.0	76.3	94.4	155.1	216.9	225.3
90-93	Arts, entertainment and recreation	1.1	1.0	1.2	2.2	2.0	1.3	10.5	19.6
94-99	Other services; household-employers; extraterritorial bodies	1.0	3.2	8.0	8.4	10.4	10.0	12.1	11.8

.. Not available

Note: Detailed metadata at: http://metalinks.oecd.org/anberd/20170419/301f.
Information on data for Israel: http://oe.cd/israel-disclaimer.
Disclaimer: http://oe.cd/disclaimer

ITALY

R&D expenditure in industry by main activity of the enterprise, constant prices
ISIC Rev. 4

2010 USD PPP

Code	Industry	2007	2008	2009	2010	2011	2012	2013	2014
	TOTAL BUSINESS ENTERPRISE	12 842.4	13 484.0	13 309.4	13 709.0	13 824.9	13 991.8	14 288.7	15 227.7
01-03	**AGRICULTURE, FORESTRY AND FISHING**	0.3	2.3	2.3	4.5	4.2	4.3	5.5	8.6
05-09	**MINING AND QUARRYING**	177.5	232.9	214.5	97.1	80.1	78.5	73.3	65.7
10-33	**MANUFACTURING**	8 932.9	9 593.9	9 270.4	9 820.0	10 175.2	10 394.5	10 304.3	10 776.9
10-12	Food products, beverages and tobacco	183.9	208.2	203.1	212.8	191.9	216.2	234.4	246.5
13-15	Textiles, wearing apparel, leather and related products	335.2	444.6	475.1	549.3	554.8	575.7	598.2	632.1
13	Textiles	114.4	98.9	117.8	149.7	127.8	129.4	137.8	156.2
14	Wearing apparel	157.3	252.4	252.8	269.5	272.8	283.9	279.4	279.4
15	Leather and related products, footwear	63.6	93.3	104.5	130.1	154.1	162.4	181.0	196.5
16-18	Wood and paper products and printing	74.3	85.5	96.3	89.9	92.3	82.0	93.2	96.8
16	Wood and wood products, except furniture	12.2	18.8	21.2	18.1	17.4	17.3	16.9	16.7
17	Paper and paper products	50.3	49.8	57.8	57.5	61.7	53.4	63.7	63.6
18	Printing and reproduction of recorded media	11.8	16.8	17.3	14.3	13.3	11.3	12.6	16.4
19-23	Chemical, rubber, plastic, non-metallic mineral products	1 436.1	1 569.0	1 534.1	1 635.2	1 589.7	1 662.6	1 607.7	1 667.2
19	Coke and refined petroleum products	15.6	17.0	6.9	11.9	16.1	15.5	16.8	21.4
20-21	Chemical and pharmaceutical products	1 015.6	1 107.9	1 132.9	1 192.8	1 171.3	1 172.0	1 131.0	1 106.8
20	Chemicals and chemical products	443.1	471.6	439.4	470.8	432.7	445.3	453.5	475.7
21	Pharmaceuticals, medicinal, chemical and botanical products	572.5	636.3	693.5	722.0	738.7	726.7	677.4	631.2
22	Rubber and plastic products	297.7	311.7	271.8	307.9	300.0	353.7	339.7	404.9
23	Other non-metallic mineral products	107.2	132.4	122.5	122.6	102.3	121.3	120.2	134.1
24-25	Basic metals, metal products, except machinery and equipment	335.5	543.8	454.2	471.6	478.8	477.8	521.2	488.1
24	Basic metals	125.0	144.6	124.4	124.9	134.6	126.6	115.3	100.0
25	Fabricated metal products, except machinery and equipment	210.5	399.2	329.8	346.6	344.2	351.2	406.0	388.1
26-30	Computer, electronic, optical products; electrical machinery, transport equipment	6 329.3	6 483.5	6 242.5	6 592.0	7 019.0	7 095.9	6 975.7	7 344.8
26	Computer, electronic and optical products	1 715.5	1 587.7	1 654.0	1 787.0	1 843.6	1 722.6	1 612.7	1 616.1
27	Electrical equipment	388.1	502.9	495.3	562.8	588.2	594.3	601.2	576.2
28	Machinery and equipment n.e.c.	1 210.5	1 408.1	1 404.6	1 377.9	1 491.4	1 630.9	1 707.2	1 803.4
29	Motor vehicles, trailers and semi-trailers	1 421.1	1 536.0	1 291.1	1 393.7	1 657.3	1 736.9	1 808.9	2 155.1
30	Other transport equipment	1 594.1	1 448.7	1 397.5	1 470.7	1 438.6	1 411.0	1 246.0	1 194.0
31-33	Furniture; repair, installation of machinery and equipment	238.5	259.3	265.1	269.3	248.6	284.3	273.6	301.4
31	Furniture	54.6	78.3	74.0	65.3	67.0	71.0	70.7	82.7
32	Other manufacturing	100.8	99.3	99.1	116.8	115.2	137.8	118.5	133.9
33	Repair and installation of machinery and equipment	83.1	81.6	92.0	87.2	66.4	75.5	84.4	84.8
35-39	**ELECTRICITY, GAS, WATER AND WASTE MANAGEMENT**	61.5	107.5	25.7	22.7	27.2	35.0	40.2	193.6
35-36	Electricity, gas and water	55.0	99.7	15.5	15.2	19.9	26.3	33.4	177.3
37-39	Sewerage, waste management and remediation activities	6.5	7.8	10.3	7.5	7.3	8.7	6.8	16.3
41-43	**CONSTRUCTION**	41.6	55.7	62.0	54.2	40.7	45.9	52.4	46.4
45-99	**TOTAL SERVICES**	3 628.6	3 491.9	3 734.3	3 710.5	3 497.4	3 433.7	3 813.0	4 136.4
45-82	**Business sector services**	3 566.9	3 421.3	3 641.1	3 620.5	3 391.2	3 275.1	3 591.4	3 901.8
45-47	**Wholesale and retail trade; motor vehicle and motorcycle repairs**	343.9	375.1	373.4	395.1	326.4	344.0	398.7	438.7
49-53	**Transportation and storage**	47.3	75.3	42.1	41.1	35.5	22.5	50.5	46.7
55-56	**Accommodation and food service activities**	2.0	2.3	2.9	4.4	3.7	3.0	2.2	2.8
58-63	**Information and communication**	1 237.6	1 463.0	1 675.5	1 612.0	1 443.6	1 427.2	1 619.4	1 518.5
58-60	Publishing, audiovisual and broadcasting activities	84.6	18.0	18.2	17.0	15.8	22.3	19.5	24.1
58	Publishing activities	73.2	4.5	5.2	6.0	5.7	14.2	11.2	16.0
59-60	Motion picture, video and TV programme production; broadcasting activities	11.4	13.5	13.0	11.0	10.1	8.1	8.2	8.1
59	Motion picture, video and TV programme production; sound and music	..	..	..	..	..	..	..	..
60	Programming and broadcasting activities	..	..	..	..	..	..	..	..
61	Telecommunications	627.5	1 150.2	1 296.9	1 238.3	1 056.9	1 025.0	530.3	384.9
62-63	IT and other information services	525.4	294.8	360.5	356.7	370.9	379.9	1 069.4	1 109.5
62	Computer programming, consultancy and related activities	511.3	278.5	332.5	328.8	336.0	341.1	607.4	1 060.8
63	Information service activities	14.1	16.3	27.9	28.0	34.9	38.8	462.0	48.7
64-66	**Financial and insurance activities**	187.2	211.9	240.6	253.1	182.5	216.0	232.4	276.9
68-82	**Real estate; professional, scientific and technical; administrative and support**	1 749.0	1 293.8	1 306.6	1 314.8	1 399.4	1 262.2	1 288.2	1 618.2
68	Real estate activities	2.7	3.8	30.3	13.3	6.8	9.7	2.7	3.6
69-75x72	Professional, scientific and technical activities, except scientific R&D	720.0	267.1	403.1	423.2	479.8	406.8	422.7	445.0
72	Scientific research and development	1 004.3	1 003.1	859.7	866.1	901.2	828.3	852.8	1 133.6
77-82	Administrative and support service activities	21.9	19.7	13.5	12.1	11.6	17.5	10.0	36.0
84-99	**Community, social and personal services**	61.7	70.5	93.2	90.1	106.3	158.6	221.7	234.6
84-85	Public administration and defence; compulsory social security and education	6.5	2.0	1.8	3.1	2.8	1.8	2.1	2.0
86-88	Human health and social work activities	52.8	64.2	82.2	76.3	91.4	146.1	198.9	204.1
90-93	Arts, entertainment and recreation	1.2	1.1	1.2	2.2	1.9	1.3	9.6	17.8
94-99	Other services; household-employers; extraterritorial bodies	1.1	3.3	8.1	8.4	10.1	9.4	11.1	10.7

.. Not available

Note: Detailed metadata at: http://metalinks.oecd.org/anberd/20170419/301f.
Information on data for Israel: http://oe.cd/israel-disclaimer.
Disclaimer: http://oe.cd/disclaimer

ITALY

R&D expenditure in industry by product field, current prices
ISIC Rev. 4

Million USD PPP

		2007	2008	2009	2010	2011	2012	2013	2014
	TOTAL BUSINESS ENTERPRISE	..	12 981.2	13 289.7	13 709.0	14 268.5	14 854.5	15 585.0	16 807.0
01-03	**AGRICULTURE, FORESTRY AND FISHING**	..	151.7	106.6	86.6	119.3	130.4	130.9	156.9
05-09	**MINING AND QUARRYING**	..	262.3	228.6	54.6	47.3	50.2	82.7	53.4
10-33	**MANUFACTURING**	..	10 285.5	10 188.4	10 907.0	11 511.1	11 772.1	12 192.1	12 688.8
10-12	Food products, beverages and tobacco	..	462.2	295.8	328.1	278.6	324.6	385.8	408.2
13-15	Textiles, wearing apparel, leather and related products	..	585.0	591.5	701.6	736.0	785.0	940.0	1 407.5
13	Textiles	..	210.9	232.7	283.9	269.5	296.1	354.0	690.3
14	Wearing apparel	..	285.2	251.6	275.4	295.4	310.7	328.5	457.4
15	Leather and related products, footwear	..	88.9	107.2	142.3	171.1	178.3	257.4	259.9
16-18	Wood and paper products and printing	..	184.1	173.9	164.8	171.3	171.2	209.7	316.8
16	Wood and wood products, except furniture	..	67.5	59.8	47.6	46.0	53.6	64.6	75.5
17	Paper and paper products	..	84.6	87.2	89.0	95.8	94.3	99.1	195.1
18	Printing and reproduction of recorded media	..	32.0	26.9	28.2	29.5	23.3	46.0	46.1
19-23	Chemical, rubber, plastic, non-metallic mineral products	..	1 926.4	2 049.3	2 235.5	2 291.9	2 281.3	2 229.7	2 337.2
19	Coke and refined petroleum products	..	19.8	94.1	126.1	130.2	115.5	128.6	56.9
20-21	Chemical and pharmaceutical products	..	1 385.6	1 492.3	1 601.0	1 609.5	1 551.2	1 505.5	1 517.7
20	Chemicals and chemical products	..	396.8	455.8	492.8	439.0	455.2	534.5	545.1
21	Pharmaceuticals, medicinal, chemical and botanical products	..	988.8	1 036.5	1 108.2	1 170.4	1 096.0	971.0	972.6
22	Rubber and plastic products	..	360.5	321.4	362.3	419.8	455.0	429.7	596.7
23	Other non-metallic mineral products	..	160.5	141.5	146.0	132.3	159.5	166.0	165.9
24-25	Basic metals, metal products, except machinery and equipment	..	720.2	697.7	602.8	622.0	682.1	821.7	715.7
24	Basic metals	..	247.7	251.2	265.6	280.5	321.9	424.8	323.8
25	Fabricated metal products, except machinery and equipment	..	472.5	446.5	337.2	341.5	360.2	396.9	391.9
26-30	Computer, electronic, optical products; electrical machinery, transport equipment	..	6 237.0	6 236.7	6 723.0	7 262.2	7 371.9	7 439.2	7 298.9
26	Computer, electronic and optical products	..	1 797.5	1 870.8	1 969.4	2 031.3	1 983.3	1 966.2	2 001.3
27	Electrical equipment	..	289.4	352.3	415.8	486.8	504.7	535.7	424.5
28	Machinery and equipment n.e.c.	..	904.9	1 005.6	952.4	1 069.6	1 172.6	1 225.7	1 350.0
29	Motor vehicles, trailers and semi-trailers	..	1 699.1	1 674.1	1 929.4	2 140.7	2 246.7	2 235.4	2 566.2
30	Other transport equipment	..	1 546.0	1 333.9	1 455.9	1 534.0	1 464.3	1 476.2	957.0
31-33	Furniture; repair, installation of machinery and equipment	..	170.6	143.4	151.2	149.1	156.1	165.9	204.4
31	Furniture	..	45.7	40.6	43.5	46.8	43.7	45.6	55.1
32	Other manufacturing	..	74.8	82.2	88.8	91.1	93.5	93.9	121.4
33	Repair and installation of machinery and equipment	..	50.1	20.6	18.9	11.2	18.9	26.3	27.9
35-39	**ELECTRICITY, GAS, WATER AND WASTE MANAGEMENT**	..	233.9	329.1	319.2	328.6	303.1	305.7	432.8
35-36	Electricity, gas and water	..	196.1	289.9	268.1	277.7	258.6	264.9	382.7
37-39	Sewerage, waste management and remediation activities	..	37.8	39.2	51.1	50.9	44.4	40.9	50.1
41-43	**CONSTRUCTION**	..	50.7	128.2	69.8	64.6	145.2	70.6	78.4
45-99	**TOTAL SERVICES**	..	1 997.1	2 308.9	2 271.9	2 197.6	2 453.6	2 803.0	3 396.7
45-82	**Business sector services**	..	1 244.0	1 427.6	1 479.1	2 021.4	2 209.9	2 524.3	3 145.3
45-47	Wholesale and retail trade; motor vehicle and motorcycle repairs	..	80.6	71.8	47.8	42.6	72.2	169.7	393.2
49-53	Transportation and storage	..	101.3	92.9	68.8	66.4	75.2	70.6	78.3
55-56	Accommodation and food service activities	..	6.1	9.2	10.9	10.4	16.7	8.3	15.4
58-63	Information and communication	..	711.1	835.8	931.6	1 494.0	1 539.6	1 626.2	1 847.4
58-60	Publishing, audiovisual and broadcasting activities	..	15.4	13.6	9.2	12.0	14.0	17.1	24.0
58	Publishing activities	..	0.0	0.0	0.0	0.0	0.0	0.0	0.0
59-60	Motion picture, video and TV programme production; broadcasting activities	..	15.4	13.6	9.2	12.0	14.0	17.1	24.0
59	Motion picture, video and TV programme production; sound and music	..	15.4	13.6	9.2	12.0	14.0	17.1	24.0
60	Programming and broadcasting activities	..	0.0	0.0	0.0	0.0	0.0	0.0	0.0
61	Telecommunications	..	297.7	416.7	523.7	1 050.9	1 084.5	1 010.7	1 135.0
62-63	IT and other information services	..	398.0	405.5	398.7	431.0	441.1	598.4	688.4
62	Computer programming, consultancy and related activities	..	372.7	382.2	372.6	406.9	414.9	554.0	616.4
63	Information service activities	..	25.3	23.4	26.2	24.1	26.2	44.4	72.0
64-66	Financial and insurance activities	..	213.5	253.8	273.7	216.4	271.2	315.8	364.3
68-82	Real estate; professional, scientific and technical; administrative and support	..	131.3	164.1	146.3	191.5	235.0	333.8	446.7
68	Real estate activities	..	0.4	2.9	0.8	0.1	0.1	1.0	1.0
69-75x72	Professional, scientific and technical activities, except scientific R&D	..	125.7	158.8	142.3	188.6	231.5	329.2	441.9
72	Scientific research and development	..	0.0	0.0	0.0	0.0	0.0	0.0	0.0
77-82	Administrative and support service activities	..	5.2	2.5	3.2	2.8	3.3	3.7	3.8
84-99	Community, social and personal services	..	753.1	881.3	792.8	176.2	243.7	278.7	251.4
84-85	Public administration and defence; compulsory social security and education	..	27.6	32.8	42.6	44.6	51.8	51.7	42.0
86-88	Human health and social work activities	..	59.6	80.2	82.9	114.4	176.3	216.8	187.7
90-93	Arts, entertainment and recreation	..	0.6	2.7	3.1	0.5	3.7	1.9	5.6
94-99	Other services; household-employers; extraterritorial bodies	..	665.3	765.5	664.1	16.7	11.9	8.3	16.2

.. Not available

Note: Detailed metadata at: http://metalinks.oecd.org/anberd/20170419/301f.
Information on data for Israel: http://oe.cd/israel-disclaimer.
Disclaimer: http://oe.cd/disclaimer

ITALY

R&D expenditure in industry by product field, constant prices
ISIC Rev. 4

2010 USD PPP

		2007	2008	2009	2010	2011	2012	2013	2014
	TOTAL BUSINESS ENTERPRISE	..	13 484.0	13 309.4	13 709.0	13 824.9	13 991.8	14 288.7	15 227.7
01-03	**AGRICULTURE, FORESTRY AND FISHING**	..	157.6	106.7	86.6	115.6	122.8	120.0	142.1
05-09	**MINING AND QUARRYING**	..	272.5	228.9	54.6	45.8	47.2	75.8	48.4
10-33	**MANUFACTURING**	..	10 683.9	10 203.4	10 907.0	11 153.2	11 088.4	11 178.1	11 496.5
10-12	Food products, beverages and tobacco	..	480.1	296.3	328.1	270.0	305.7	353.7	369.9
13-15	Textiles, wearing apparel, leather and related products	..	607.7	592.4	701.6	713.1	739.4	861.8	1 275.3
13	Textiles	..	219.1	233.1	283.9	261.2	278.9	324.6	625.4
14	Wearing apparel	..	296.2	251.9	275.4	286.2	292.6	301.2	414.4
15	Leather and related products, footwear	..	92.4	107.4	142.3	165.8	167.9	236.0	235.5
16-18	Wood and paper products and printing	..	191.3	174.2	164.8	166.0	161.2	192.3	287.0
16	Wood and wood products, except furniture	..	70.1	59.9	47.6	44.6	50.5	59.2	68.5
17	Paper and paper products	..	87.9	87.4	89.0	92.8	88.8	90.9	176.7
18	Printing and reproduction of recorded media	..	33.3	26.9	28.2	28.6	21.9	42.2	41.8
19-23	Chemical, rubber, plastic, non-metallic mineral products	..	2 001.0	2 052.3	2 235.5	2 220.6	2 148.8	2 044.3	2 117.6
19	Coke and refined petroleum products	..	20.5	94.2	126.1	126.2	108.8	117.9	51.5
20-21	Chemical and pharmaceutical products	..	1 439.3	1 494.5	1 601.0	1 559.5	1 461.1	1 380.3	1 375.1
20	Chemicals and chemical products	..	412.2	456.4	492.8	425.4	428.8	490.0	493.9
21	Pharmaceuticals, medicinal, chemical and botanical products	..	1 027.1	1 038.0	1 108.2	1 134.1	1 032.3	890.3	881.2
22	Rubber and plastic products	..	374.4	321.9	362.3	406.8	428.6	393.9	540.6
23	Other non-metallic mineral products	..	166.7	141.7	146.0	128.2	150.3	152.2	150.3
24-25	Basic metals, metal products, except machinery and equipment	..	748.1	698.7	602.8	602.7	642.4	753.4	648.5
24	Basic metals	..	257.3	251.5	265.6	271.8	303.2	389.4	293.4
25	Fabricated metal products, except machinery and equipment	..	490.8	447.2	337.2	330.9	339.2	363.9	355.1
26-30	Computer, electronic, optical products; electrical machinery, transport equipment	..	6 478.6	6 245.9	6 723.0	7 036.4	6 943.7	6 820.5	6 613.1
26	Computer, electronic and optical products	..	1 867.1	1 873.5	1 969.4	1 968.1	1 868.1	1 802.7	1 813.2
27	Electrical equipment	..	300.6	352.8	415.8	471.6	475.4	491.1	384.6
28	Machinery and equipment n.e.c.	..	940.0	1 007.1	952.4	1 036.4	1 104.5	1 123.8	1 223.1
29	Motor vehicles, trailers and semi-trailers	..	1 764.9	1 676.6	1 929.4	2 074.1	2 116.2	2 049.5	2 325.1
30	Other transport equipment	..	1 605.9	1 335.9	1 455.9	1 486.3	1 379.3	1 353.4	867.0
31-33	Furniture; repair, installation of machinery and equipment	..	177.2	143.6	151.2	144.4	147.0	152.1	185.2
31	Furniture	..	47.5	40.7	43.5	45.3	41.2	41.8	49.9
32	Other manufacturing	..	77.7	82.3	88.8	88.2	88.1	86.1	110.0
33	Repair and installation of machinery and equipment	..	52.1	20.7	18.9	10.9	17.8	24.1	25.3
35-39	**ELECTRICITY, GAS, WATER AND WASTE MANAGEMENT**	..	243.0	329.5	319.2	318.4	285.4	280.3	392.2
35-36	Electricity, gas and water	..	203.7	290.3	268.1	269.1	243.6	242.8	346.8
37-39	Sewerage, waste management and remediation activities	..	39.2	39.3	51.1	49.3	41.8	37.5	45.4
41-43	**CONSTRUCTION**	..	52.6	128.4	69.8	62.6	136.8	64.7	71.0
45-99	**TOTAL SERVICES**	..	2 074.4	2 312.3	2 271.9	2 129.3	2 311.1	2 569.9	3 077.5
45-82	**Business sector services**	..	1 292.2	1 429.7	1 479.1	1 958.5	2 081.5	2 314.4	2 849.7
45-47	Wholesale and retail trade; motor vehicle and motorcycle repairs	..	83.8	71.9	47.8	41.3	68.0	155.6	356.3
49-53	Transportation and storage	..	105.2	93.1	68.8	64.4	70.8	64.7	71.0
55-56	Accommodation and food service activities	..	6.4	9.2	10.9	10.1	15.7	7.6	13.9
58-63	Information and communication	..	738.7	837.1	931.6	1 447.6	1 450.2	1 490.9	1 673.8
58-60	Publishing, audiovisual and broadcasting activities	..	16.0	13.6	9.2	11.6	13.2	15.7	21.7
58	Publishing activities	..	0.0	0.0	0.0	0.0	0.0	0.0	0.0
59-60	Motion picture, video and TV programme production; broadcasting activities	..	16.0	13.6	9.2	11.6	13.2	15.7	21.7
59	Motion picture, video and TV programme production; sound and music	..	16.0	13.6	9.2	11.6	13.2	15.7	21.7
60	Programming and broadcasting activities	..	0.0	0.0	0.0	0.0	0.0	0.0	0.0
61	Telecommunications	..	309.2	417.3	523.7	1 018.2	1 021.5	926.6	1 028.4
62-63	IT and other information services	..	413.4	406.1	398.7	417.6	415.5	548.6	623.7
62	Computer programming, consultancy and related activities	..	387.2	382.7	372.6	394.2	390.8	507.9	558.5
63	Information service activities	..	26.2	23.4	26.2	23.4	24.7	40.7	65.2
64-66	Financial and insurance activities	..	221.7	254.1	273.7	209.7	255.5	289.5	330.1
68-82	Real estate; professional, scientific and technical; administrative and support	..	136.4	164.3	146.3	185.6	221.3	306.1	404.7
68	Real estate activities	..	0.4	2.9	0.8	0.1	0.1	0.9	0.9
69-75x72	Professional, scientific and technical activities, except scientific R&D	..	130.6	159.0	142.3	182.8	218.1	301.8	400.4
72	Scientific research and development	..	0.0	0.0	0.0	0.0	0.0	0.0	0.0
77-82	Administrative and support service activities	..	5.4	2.5	3.2	2.7	3.1	3.4	3.4
84-99	**Community, social and personal services**	..	782.3	882.6	792.8	170.7	229.5	255.5	227.8
84-85	Public administration and defence; compulsory social security and education	..	28.6	32.9	42.6	43.2	48.8	47.4	38.0
86-88	Human health and social work activities	..	61.9	80.3	82.9	110.9	166.0	198.8	170.0
90-93	Arts, entertainment and recreation	..	0.7	2.7	3.1	0.5	3.5	1.7	5.1
94-99	Other services; household-employers; extraterritorial bodies	..	691.1	766.6	664.1	16.2	11.2	7.6	14.7

.. Not available

Note: Detailed metadata at: http://metalinks.oecd.org/anberd/20170419/301f.
Information on data for Israel: http://oe.cd/israel-disclaimer.

Disclaimer: http://oe.cd/disclaimer

JAPAN

R&D expenditure in industry by main activity of the enterprise, current prices
ISIC Rev. 4

Million USD PPP

		2007	2008	2009	2010	2011	2012	2013	2014
	TOTAL BUSINESS ENTERPRISE	114 968.2	116 687.8	103 760.1	107 581.3	114 204.6	116 716.3	125 340.2	132 644.8
01-03	**AGRICULTURE, FORESTRY AND FISHING**	73.7	28.8	27.1	41.1	27.6	17.8	21.2	18.5
05-09	**MINING AND QUARRYING**	191.5	109.0	136.0	89.6	30.3	29.0	43.1	36.8
10-33	**MANUFACTURING**	101 245.2	101 699.3	90 381.0	93 748.1	100 352.8	102 653.6	111 213.5	114 766.1
10-12	Food products, beverages and tobacco	2 326.1	2 285.0	2 095.7	2 127.5	2 085.7	2 113.7	2 307.7	2 046.9
13-15	Textiles, wearing apparel, leather and related products	1 108.0	1 233.9	1 043.6	1 125.4	1 266.2	1 305.1	1 366.8	1 328.1
13	Textiles	1 022.9	1 154.9	977.6	1 050.5	1 191.3	1 240.0	1 298.0	1 251.9
14	Wearing apparel	35.5	36.9	28.4	30.4	40.9	29.6	30.8	41.2
15	Leather and related products, footwear	49.6	42.0	37.6	44.4	34.0	35.4	38.1	35.0
16-18	Wood and paper products and printing	859.6	831.8	728.6	772.3	734.3	677.2	579.9	593.9
16	Wood and wood products, except furniture	104.4	85.5	67.0	81.8	86.0	101.3	91.6	83.8
17	Paper and paper products	380.4	374.3	335.7	377.6	319.8	240.5	203.4	283.7
18	Printing and reproduction of recorded media	374.8	372.0	325.9	312.9	328.5	335.4	284.9	226.4
19-23	Chemical, rubber, plastic, non-metallic mineral products	21 522.6	22 673.0	20 922.1	22 250.0	22 802.7	24 183.4	26 456.1	27 153.6
19	Coke and refined petroleum products	479.0	510.7	440.8	468.1	447.7	440.0	462.6	410.9
20-21	Chemical and pharmaceutical products	17 255.0	18 156.8	16 873.9	18 093.4	18 371.2	19 688.5	21 617.6	21 954.7
20	Chemicals and chemical products	6 833.1	7 068.8	6 538.9	6 663.4	6 925.1	7 162.5	7 425.8	7 355.6
21	Pharmaceuticals, medicinal, chemical and botanical products	10 421.9	11 088.0	10 335.1	11 430.0	11 446.1	12 526.0	14 191.7	14 599.1
22	Rubber and plastic products	2 547.0	2 539.5	2 377.6	2 421.2	2 594.7	2 638.7	2 917.8	3 301.9
23	Other non-metallic mineral products	1 241.6	1 466.0	1 229.7	1 267.3	1 389.0	1 416.3	1 458.2	1 486.2
24-25	Basic metals, metal products, except machinery and equipment	2 840.8	2 679.0	2 473.5	2 649.2	2 865.7	2 658.2	2 748.6	2 993.1
24	Basic metals	2 077.6	2 238.6	2 027.2	2 155.4	2 360.2	2 166.9	2 257.8	2 474.5
25	Fabricated metal products, except machinery and equipment	763.2	440.4	446.3	493.8	505.5	491.4	490.7	518.6
26-30	Computer, electronic, optical products; electrical machinery, transport equipment	71 009.3	70 117.9	61 365.8	62 846.2	68 596.4	69 587.1	75 322.9	78 417.1
26	Computer, electronic and optical products	32 713.9	32 229.4	27 327.2	26 265.9	29 244.8	28 387.1	28 762.9	28 188.8
27	Electrical equipment	3 548.4	3 428.5	2 967.4	3 410.2	3 221.7	3 267.6	3 469.0	3 449.3
28	Machinery and equipment n.e.c.	9 725.3	9 766.2	9 457.7	9 537.0	10 211.0	10 414.6	12 320.2	12 516.8
29	Motor vehicles, trailers and semi-trailers	24 622.8	24 255.9	21 261.7	23 156.3	25 408.9	26 930.1	30 007.7	33 387.1
30	Other transport equipment	399.0	438.0	351.9	476.9	510.1	587.7	763.1	875.2
31-33	Furniture; repair, installation of machinery and equipment	1 578.8	1 878.6	1 751.6	1 977.6	2 002.0	2 128.9	2 431.4	2 233.2
31	Furniture	140.8	180.6	115.6	93.4	106.8	98.0	97.4	109.5
32	Other manufacturing	1 438.0	1 698.0	1 636.1	1 884.2	1 895.2	2 030.9	2 334.0	2 123.7
33	Repair and installation of machinery and equipment	..	..	..	..	..	..	..	..
35-39	**ELECTRICITY, GAS, WATER AND WASTE MANAGEMENT**	622.7	617.5	550.0	595.6	505.6	503.7	512.6	467.2
35-36	Electricity, gas and water	..	..	..	..	..	..	..	..
37-39	Sewerage, waste management and remediation activities	..	..	..	..	..	..	..	..
41-43	**CONSTRUCTION**	983.9	1 026.0	1 001.7	1 023.1	1 024.1	1 066.6	1 061.8	956.9
45-99	**TOTAL SERVICES**	11 851.2	13 207.1	11 664.4	12 083.8	12 264.2	12 445.6	12 488.0	16 399.4
45-82	**Business sector services**	11 851.2	13 207.1	11 664.4	12 083.8	12 264.2	12 445.6	12 488.0	16 399.4
45-47	Wholesale and retail trade; motor vehicle and motorcycle repairs	269.1	361.3	385.1	360.6	313.1	463.2	489.2	645.1
49-53	Transportation and storage	278.0	337.4	326.9	306.4	326.9	425.8	519.5	564.9
55-56	Accommodation and food service activities	..	..	..	..	..	..	..	..
58-63	Information and communication	4 096.8	5 096.9	4 598.5	4 838.4	5 237.9	5 181.1	4 589.8	6 721.0
58-60	Publishing, audiovisual and broadcasting activities	115.8	126.4	110.2	102.9	8.7	9.5	18.9	16.4
58	Publishing activities	13.7	22.2	8.5	6.7	4.6	6.3	8.6	9.4
59-60	Motion picture, video and TV programme production; broadcasting activities	102.1	104.1	101.7	96.2	4.1	3.2	10.3	7.0
59	Motion picture, video and TV programme production; sound and music	2.7	4.2	2.0	0.4	0.7	0.7	1.8	1.9
60	Programming and broadcasting activities	99.4	99.9	99.7	95.8	3.5	2.5	8.5	5.0
61	Telecommunications	2 059.4	2 800.8	2 283.3	2 277.2	2 779.8	2 832.9	2 766.0	3 708.6
62-63	IT and other information services	1 921.5	2 169.8	2 205.0	2 458.2	2 449.5	2 338.7	1 804.8	2 996.1
62	Computer programming, consultancy and related activities	1 564.2	1 893.5	1 921.5	2 179.3	2 142.3	2 093.0	1 592.9	2 701.7
63	Information service activities	357.3	276.2	283.6	278.9	307.1	245.7	211.8	294.4
64-66	Financial and insurance activities	14.6	21.0	19.5	22.8	30.5	17.6	21.6	32.0
68-82	Real estate; professional, scientific and technical; administrative and support	7 192.7	7 390.5	6 334.3	6 555.7	6 355.8	6 357.8	6 867.9	8 436.4
68	Real estate activities	..	..	..	..	..	..	..	..
69-75x72	Professional, scientific and technical activities, except scientific R&D	420.7	407.7	427.4	387.8	342.0	588.2	711.3	730.0
72	Scientific research and development	6 725.1	6 926.5	5 850.3	6 107.3	5 958.0	5 713.5	6 103.9	7 648.4
77-82	Administrative and support service activities	46.9	56.3	56.7	60.6	55.7	56.1	52.7	58.1
84-99	Community, social and personal services	..	..	..	..	..	..	..	..
84-85	Public administration and defence; compulsory social security and education	..	..	..	..	..	..	..	..
86-88	Human health and social work activities	..	..	..	..	..	..	..	..
90-93	Arts, entertainment and recreation	..	..	..	..	..	..	..	..
94-99	Other services; household-employers; extraterritorial bodies	..	..	..	..	..	..	..	..

.. Not available

Note: Detailed metadata at: http://metalinks.oecd.org/anberd/20170419/301f.
    Information on data for Israel: http://oe.cd/israel-disclaimer.
Disclaimer: http://oe.cd/disclaimer

JAPAN

R&D expenditure in industry by main activity of the enterprise, constant prices
ISIC Rev. 4

2010 USD PPP

		2007	2008	2009	2010	2011	2012	2013	2014
	TOTAL BUSINESS ENTERPRISE	119 078.7	118 895.9	105 027.4	107 581.3	112 001.8	112 120.1	117 582.4	123 799.1
01-03	**AGRICULTURE, FORESTRY AND FISHING**	76.4	29.4	27.4	41.1	27.1	17.1	19.9	17.3
05-09	**MINING AND QUARRYING**	198.4	111.1	137.7	89.6	29.7	27.8	40.4	34.3
10-33	**MANUFACTURING**	104 865.1	103 623.7	91 484.8	93 748.1	98 417.2	98 611.2	104 330.1	107 112.7
10-12	Food products, beverages and tobacco	2 409.3	2 328.3	2 121.3	2 127.5	2 045.4	2 030.4	2 164.9	1 910.4
13-15	Textiles, wearing apparel, leather and related products	1 147.6	1 257.2	1 056.3	1 125.4	1 241.8	1 253.7	1 282.2	1 239.5
13	Textiles	1 059.4	1 176.8	989.5	1 050.5	1 168.3	1 191.2	1 217.6	1 168.4
14	Wearing apparel	36.8	37.6	28.7	30.4	40.1	28.5	28.9	38.5
15	Leather and related products, footwear	51.4	42.8	38.1	44.4	33.3	34.0	35.7	32.7
16-18	Wood and paper products and printing	890.4	847.6	737.5	772.3	720.1	650.5	544.0	554.3
16	Wood and wood products, except furniture	108.1	87.1	67.8	81.8	84.3	97.3	85.9	78.2
17	Paper and paper products	394.0	381.4	339.8	377.6	313.6	231.0	190.8	264.8
18	Printing and reproduction of recorded media	388.2	379.1	329.9	312.9	322.2	322.2	267.3	211.3
19-23	Chemical, rubber, plastic, non-metallic mineral products	22 292.1	23 102.1	21 177.7	22 250.0	22 362.8	23 231.1	24 818.7	25 342.8
19	Coke and refined petroleum products	496.2	520.3	446.2	468.1	439.1	422.6	434.0	383.5
20-21	Chemical and pharmaceutical products	17 872.0	18 500.4	17 080.0	18 093.4	18 016.9	18 913.2	20 279.6	20 490.6
20	Chemicals and chemical products	7 077.4	7 202.6	6 618.7	6 663.4	6 791.5	6 880.4	6 966.2	6 865.0
21	Pharmaceuticals, medicinal, chemical and botanical products	10 794.5	11 297.9	10 461.3	11 430.0	11 225.3	12 032.7	13 313.4	13 625.5
22	Rubber and plastic products	2 638.0	2 587.6	2 406.7	2 421.2	2 544.7	2 534.8	2 737.2	3 081.7
23	Other non-metallic mineral products	1 286.0	1 493.8	1 244.8	1 267.3	1 362.2	1 360.5	1 367.9	1 387.0
24-25	Basic metals, metal products, except machinery and equipment	2 942.3	2 729.7	2 503.7	2 649.2	2 810.4	2 553.6	2 578.5	2 793.5
24	Basic metals	2 151.8	2 281.0	2 052.0	2 155.4	2 314.7	2 081.6	2 118.1	2 309.5
25	Fabricated metal products, except machinery and equipment	790.5	448.7	451.7	493.8	495.7	472.0	460.4	484.0
26-30	Computer, electronic, optical products; electrical machinery, transport equipment	73 548.2	71 444.8	62 115.3	62 846.2	67 273.3	66 846.8	70 660.9	73 187.7
26	Computer, electronic and optical products	33 883.5	32 839.3	27 660.9	26 265.9	28 680.7	27 269.2	26 982.7	26 309.0
27	Electrical equipment	3 675.2	3 493.4	3 003.6	3 410.2	3 159.6	3 138.9	3 254.3	3 219.2
28	Machinery and equipment n.e.c.	10 073.0	9 951.0	9 573.2	9 537.0	10 014.0	10 004.5	11 557.7	11 682.1
29	Motor vehicles, trailers and semi-trailers	25 503.1	24 714.9	21 521.4	23 156.3	24 918.8	25 869.6	28 150.4	31 160.6
30	Other transport equipment	413.3	446.3	356.2	476.9	500.2	564.5	715.8	816.8
31-33	Furniture; repair, installation of machinery and equipment	1 635.3	1 914.1	1 773.0	1 977.6	1 963.4	2 045.0	2 280.9	2 084.3
31	Furniture	145.9	184.0	117.0	93.4	104.7	94.1	91.4	102.2
32	Other manufacturing	1 489.4	1 730.1	1 656.1	1 884.2	1 858.6	1 950.9	2 189.6	1 982.1
33	Repair and installation of machinery and equipment	..	..	..	..	..	..	..	..
35-39	**ELECTRICITY, GAS, WATER AND WASTE MANAGEMENT**	645.0	629.1	556.7	595.6	495.9	483.9	480.9	436.0
35-36	Electricity, gas and water	..	..	..	..	..	..	..	..
37-39	Sewerage, waste management and remediation activities	..	..	..	..	..	..	..	..
41-43	**CONSTRUCTION**	1 019.0	1 045.5	1 014.0	1 023.1	1 004.3	1 024.6	996.1	893.1
45-99	**TOTAL SERVICES**	12 274.9	13 457.0	11 806.9	12 083.8	12 027.6	11 955.5	11 715.1	15 305.7
45-82	**Business sector services**	12 274.9	13 457.0	11 806.9	12 083.8	12 027.6	11 955.5	11 715.1	15 305.7
45-47	Wholesale and retail trade; motor vehicle and motorcycle repairs	278.8	368.1	389.8	360.6	307.0	445.0	459.0	602.0
49-53	Transportation and storage	287.9	343.8	330.9	306.4	320.6	409.1	487.3	527.2
55-56	Accommodation and food service activities	..	..	..	..	..	..	..	..
58-63	Information and communication	4 243.2	5 193.4	4 654.7	4 838.4	5 136.9	4 977.1	4 305.7	6 272.8
58-60	Publishing, audiovisual and broadcasting activities	120.0	128.8	111.5	102.9	8.5	9.1	17.8	15.3
58	Publishing activities	14.2	22.7	8.6	6.7	4.5	6.1	8.1	8.8
59-60	Motion picture, video and TV programme production; broadcasting activities	105.8	106.1	103.0	96.2	4.1	3.0	9.7	6.5
59	Motion picture, video and TV programme production; sound and music	2.8	4.3	2.1	0.4	0.6	0.6	1.7	1.8
60	Programming and broadcasting activities	103.0	101.8	100.9	95.8	3.4	2.4	8.0	4.7
61	Telecommunications	2 133.0	2 853.8	2 311.2	2 277.2	2 726.2	2 721.3	2 594.8	3 461.2
62-63	IT and other information services	1 990.2	2 210.8	2 231.9	2 458.2	2 402.2	2 246.6	1 693.1	2 796.3
62	Computer programming, consultancy and related activities	1 620.2	1 929.4	1 944.9	2 179.3	2 101.0	2 010.6	1 494.3	2 521.5
63	Information service activities	370.1	281.4	287.0	278.9	301.2	236.0	198.7	274.7
64-66	Financial and insurance activities	15.1	21.4	19.8	22.8	30.0	16.9	20.3	29.9
68-82	Real estate; professional, scientific and technical; administrative and support	7 449.9	7 530.3	6 411.7	6 555.7	6 233.2	6 107.5	6 442.8	7 873.8
68	Real estate activities	..	..	..	..	..	..	..	..
69-75x72	Professional, scientific and technical activities, except scientific R&D	435.7	415.4	432.7	387.8	335.4	565.0	667.3	681.3
72	Scientific research and development	6 965.5	7 057.6	5 921.7	6 107.3	5 843.1	5 488.5	5 726.1	7 138.3
77-82	Administrative and support service activities	48.6	57.3	57.3	60.6	54.6	53.9	49.5	54.2
84-99	Community, social and personal services	..	..	..	..	..	..	..	..
84-85	Public administration and defence; compulsory social security and education	..	..	..	..	..	..	..	..
86-88	Human health and social work activities	..	..	..	..	..	..	..	..
90-93	Arts, entertainment and recreation	..	..	..	..	..	..	..	..
94-99	Other services; household-employers; extraterritorial bodies	..	..	..	..	..	..	..	..

.. Not available
Note: Detailed metadata at: http://metalinks.oecd.org/anberd/20170419/301f.
   Information on data for Israel: http://oe.cd/israel-disclaimer.
Disclaimer: http://oe.cd/disclaimer

KOREA

R&D expenditure in industry by main activity of the enterprise, current prices
ISIC Rev. 4

Million USD PPP

Code	Industry	2007	2008	2009	2010	2011	2012	2013	2014
	TOTAL BUSINESS ENTERPRISE	30 985.1	33 090.8	34 150.3	39 025.0	44 680.5	50 559.8	53 679.2	57 272.0
01-03	AGRICULTURE, FORESTRY AND FISHING	15.4	26.1	24.8	31.0	42.3	31.2	30.2	33.0
05-09	MINING AND QUARRYING	8.5	7.8	17.5	22.4	25.7	41.1	29.2	23.3
10-33	MANUFACTURING	27 700.6	29 270.6	29 504.9	34 188.0	39 112.9	44 404.0	47 562.0	50 923.5
10-12	Food products, beverages and tobacco	429.9	445.1	450.1	361.3	472.0	550.9	533.3	561.7
13-15	Textiles, wearing apparel, leather and related products	190.1	194.2	198.6	198.6	334.1	376.0	419.5	424.0
13	Textiles	94.2	94.6	90.1	97.1	142.2	135.5	142.8	148.5
14	Wearing apparel	80.0	83.2	96.7	84.5	164.3	203.9	232.3	227.2
15	Leather and related products, footwear	16.0	16.4	11.7	17.0	27.6	36.6	44.4	48.3
16-18	Wood and paper products and printing	49.8	56.2	74.8	81.0	106.4	141.0	119.7	125.0
16	Wood and wood products, except furniture	7.4	7.4	8.0	7.8	18.8	15.1	15.5	15.1
17	Paper and paper products	18.4	22.6	36.7	42.4	55.6	88.2	63.6	67.4
18	Printing and reproduction of recorded media	24.0	26.2	30.0	30.8	31.9	37.7	40.6	42.5
19-23	Chemical, rubber, plastic, non-metallic mineral products	3 299.6	3 349.6	3 490.3	4 065.1	5 042.5	5 225.5	5 848.5	5 450.3
19	Coke and refined petroleum products	196.2	147.5	166.5	274.4	395.4	317.7	336.0	273.9
20-21	Chemical and pharmaceutical products	2 433.5	2 465.2	2 600.2	2 940.3	3 739.1	3 893.4	4 311.5	4 018.4
20	Chemicals and chemical products	1 658.6	1 657.7	1 763.9	2 062.4	2 729.0	2 671.6	3 063.2	2 729.2
21	Pharmaceuticals, medicinal, chemical and botanical products	774.8	807.5	836.3	877.9	1 010.1	1 221.9	1 248.3	1 289.2
22	Rubber and plastic products	485.7	554.0	435.9	602.9	631.0	634.2	835.7	884.3
23	Other non-metallic mineral products	184.2	182.9	287.6	247.6	277.1	380.1	365.4	273.7
24-25	Basic metals, metal products, except machinery and equipment	762.7	948.8	1 022.0	972.0	1 346.8	1 442.1	1 346.6	1 327.6
24	Basic metals	539.9	651.2	669.2	664.6	721.8	858.4	714.3	745.2
25	Fabricated metal products, except machinery and equipment	222.8	297.5	352.8	307.4	625.0	583.7	632.4	582.5
26-30	Computer, electronic, optical products; electrical machinery, transport equipment	22 778.5	24 053.9	24 040.6	28 258.3	31 402.7	36 303.2	38 924.7	42 598.6
26	Computer, electronic and optical products	14 396.0	16 114.4	16 252.0	19 631.5	21 873.9	25 237.8	27 731.1	30 450.7
27	Electrical equipment	758.7	867.8	932.7	992.7	1 076.2	1 265.4	1 190.7	1 279.7
28	Machinery and equipment n.e.c.	1 950.6	1 996.0	1 943.1	2 184.9	2 413.7	3 184.4	3 072.3	3 244.1
29	Motor vehicles, trailers and semi-trailers	5 032.1	4 381.6	4 283.1	4 758.4	5 309.3	5 724.1	6 083.2	6 750.6
30	Other transport equipment	641.1	694.1	629.8	690.8	729.5	891.5	847.3	873.5
31-33	Furniture; repair, installation of machinery and equipment	190.0	222.9	228.5	251.7	408.6	365.2	369.7	436.1
31	Furniture	38.5	21.7	52.1	52.5	62.7	66.3	74.9	99.5
32	Other manufacturing	151.5	201.2	176.4	199.2	345.9	298.9	294.9	336.6
33	Repair and installation of machinery and equipment	..	..	..	..	..	..	..	..
35-39	ELECTRICITY, GAS, WATER AND WASTE MANAGEMENT	315.8	358.2	355.8	373.9	481.1	509.2	410.6	423.1
35-36	Electricity, gas and water	313.5	329.3	330.8	349.8	444.1	476.5	372.1	383.4
37-39	Sewerage, waste management and remediation activities	2.2	28.9	25.0	24.1	37.0	32.7	38.5	39.7
41-43	CONSTRUCTION	706.8	820.8	1 029.8	886.9	1 063.2	1 156.1	1 106.9	1 139.4
45-99	TOTAL SERVICES	2 238.0	2 607.3	3 217.6	3 522.9	3 955.3	4 418.3	4 540.3	4 729.7
45-82	Business sector services	2 196.0	2 591.1	3 188.6	3 490.7	3 912.0	4 379.9	4 500.2	4 687.3
45-47	Wholesale and retail trade; motor vehicle and motorcycle repairs	105.8	173.0	563.1	641.8	719.9	788.8	815.4	859.3
49-53	Transportation and storage	55.8	70.1	41.6	88.3	144.8	81.6	128.0	45.8
55-56	Accommodation and food service activities	0.9	3.0	9.8	1.0	7.7	1.4	10.0	8.8
58-63	Information and communication	1 405.2	1 644.6	1 592.5	1 827.2	1 978.6	2 378.6	2 251.7	2 461.3
58-60	Publishing, audiovisual and broadcasting activities	814.5	972.0	1 018.3	1 131.6	1 111.1	1 559.1	1 438.8	1 629.7
58	Publishing activities	789.5	945.5	988.1	1 095.7	1 079.0	1 527.5	1 398.7	1 590.8
59-60	Motion picture, video and TV programme production; broadcasting activities	25.0	26.5	30.2	35.9	32.0	31.6	40.1	38.9
59	Motion picture, video and TV programme production; sound and music	3.6	6.3	12.9	13.2	15.4	12.7	9.5	13.7
60	Programming and broadcasting activities	21.4	20.2	17.4	22.7	16.7	18.9	30.6	25.1
61	Telecommunications	422.9	482.2	340.7	412.8	402.6	452.1	469.0	493.3
62-63	IT and other information services	167.8	190.4	233.4	282.8	465.0	367.4	343.9	338.3
62	Computer programming, consultancy and related services	..	97.3	115.8	169.7	319.3	246.7	207.2	223.2
63	Information service activities	..	93.1	117.7	113.1	145.7	120.7	136.7	115.0
64-66	Financial and insurance activities	0.5	0.1	2.0	1.6	1.2	2.1	2.0	5.2
68-82	Real estate; professional, scientific and technical; administrative and support	627.9	700.3	979.5	930.9	1 059.8	1 127.4	1 293.2	1 306.9
68	Real estate activities	0.6	0.7	30.7	21.0	3.5	1.9	1.6	3.7
69-75x72	Professional, scientific and technical activities, except scientific R&D	495.6	517.1	699.3	634.4	679.3	768.7	792.4	867.2
72	Scientific research and development	98.7	147.3	182.3	202.5	305.3	274.8	407.6	342.6
77-82	Administrative and support service activities	33.0	35.2	67.2	73.0	71.7	82.0	91.6	93.3
84-99	Community, social and personal services	42.0	16.2	29.0	32.3	43.3	38.4	40.1	42.4
84-85	Public administration and defence; compulsory social security and education	6.7	9.9	15.0	15.3	19.2	14.6	16.7	16.2
86-88	Human health and social work activities	10.5	0.0	0.2	0.2	0.3	1.1	5.0	5.6
90-93	Arts, entertainment and recreation	9.6	3.4	4.1	4.1	3.2	3.2	3.0	2.2
94-99	Other services; household-employers; extraterritorial bodies	15.3	2.8	9.7	12.6	20.6	19.5	15.4	18.4

.. Not available

Note: Detailed metadata at: http://metalinks.oecd.org/anberd/20170419/301f.
Information on data for Israel: http://oe.cd/israel-disclaimer.
Disclaimer: http://oe.cd/disclaimer

KOREA

R&D expenditure in industry by main activity of the enterprise, constant prices
ISIC Rev. 4

2010 USD PPP

Code	Activity	2007	2008	2009	2010	2011	2012	2013	2014
	TOTAL BUSINESS ENTERPRISE	31 223.1	33 039.7	34 567.4	39 025.0	44 716.9	50 096.2	53 507.2	56 951.4
01-03	AGRICULTURE, FORESTRY AND FISHING	15.5	26.1	25.1	31.0	42.4	30.9	30.1	32.8
05-09	MINING AND QUARRYING	8.6	7.8	17.7	22.4	25.7	40.7	29.1	23.2
10-33	MANUFACTURING	27 913.3	29 225.3	29 865.3	34 188.0	39 144.9	43 996.8	47 409.6	50 638.4
10-12	Food products, beverages and tobacco	433.2	444.4	455.6	361.3	472.4	545.8	531.6	558.6
13-15	Textiles, wearing apparel, leather and related products	191.6	193.9	201.0	198.6	334.3	372.6	418.1	421.7
13	Textiles	95.0	94.4	91.2	97.1	142.3	134.2	142.4	147.7
14	Wearing apparel	80.6	83.1	97.9	84.5	164.4	202.0	231.5	225.9
15	Leather and related products, footwear	16.1	16.4	11.9	17.0	27.6	36.3	44.3	48.0
16-18	Wood and paper products and printing	50.2	56.1	75.7	81.0	106.4	139.7	119.3	124.3
16	Wood and wood products, except furniture	7.4	7.3	8.1	7.8	18.8	15.0	15.4	15.0
17	Paper and paper products	18.6	22.6	37.2	42.4	55.7	87.3	63.4	67.1
18	Printing and reproduction of recorded media	24.2	26.2	30.4	30.8	32.0	37.4	40.4	42.2
19-23	Chemical, rubber, plastic, non-metallic mineral products	3 324.9	3 344.4	3 532.9	4 065.1	5 046.6	5 177.6	5 829.8	5 419.8
19	Coke and refined petroleum products	197.7	147.2	168.5	274.4	395.7	314.8	334.9	272.4
20-21	Chemical and pharmaceutical products	2 452.1	2 461.4	2 632.0	2 940.3	3 742.1	3 857.7	4 297.7	3 995.9
20	Chemicals and chemical products	1 671.4	1 655.1	1 785.5	2 062.4	2 731.2	2 647.1	3 053.3	2 714.0
21	Pharmaceuticals, medicinal, chemical and botanical products	780.8	806.3	846.5	877.9	1 010.9	1 210.7	1 244.3	1 282.0
22	Rubber and plastic products	489.5	553.2	441.3	602.8	631.5	628.4	833.0	879.4
23	Other non-metallic mineral products	185.6	182.6	291.1	247.6	277.3	376.6	364.2	272.2
24-25	Basic metals, metal products, except machinery and equipment	768.6	947.3	1 034.5	972.0	1 347.9	1 428.9	1 342.3	1 320.2
24	Basic metals	544.0	650.2	677.4	664.6	722.4	850.6	712.0	741.0
25	Fabricated metal products, except machinery and equipment	224.5	297.1	357.1	307.4	625.5	578.4	630.4	579.2
26-30	Computer, electronic, optical products; electrical machinery, transport equipment	22 953.4	24 016.7	24 334.2	28 258.3	31 428.3	35 970.3	38 799.9	42 360.1
26	Computer, electronic and optical products	14 506.6	16 089.5	16 450.5	19 631.5	21 891.8	25 006.4	27 642.3	30 280.2
27	Electrical equipment	764.6	866.5	944.1	992.7	1 077.1	1 253.8	1 186.9	1 272.6
28	Machinery and equipment n.e.c.	1 965.5	1 992.9	1 966.8	2 184.9	2 415.7	3 155.2	3 062.5	3 226.0
29	Motor vehicles, trailers and semi-trailers	5 070.8	4 374.8	4 335.4	4 758.4	5 313.7	5 671.6	6 063.7	6 712.8
30	Other transport equipment	646.0	693.0	637.5	690.8	730.1	883.3	844.6	868.6
31-33	Furniture; repair, installation of machinery and equipment	191.5	222.6	231.3	251.7	408.9	361.9	368.5	433.7
31	Furniture	38.8	21.7	52.7	52.5	62.7	65.7	74.6	98.9
32	Other manufacturing	152.7	200.9	178.6	199.2	346.2	296.2	293.9	334.7
33	Repair and installation of machinery and equipment	..	..	..	..	..	..	..	..
35-39	ELECTRICITY, GAS, WATER AND WASTE MANAGEMENT	318.2	357.7	360.1	373.9	481.5	504.5	409.3	420.7
35-36	Electricity, gas and water	315.9	328.8	334.9	349.8	444.4	472.1	370.9	381.2
37-39	Sewerage, waste management and remediation activities	2.3	28.8	25.3	24.1	37.0	32.4	38.4	39.5
41-43	CONSTRUCTION	712.2	819.6	1 042.4	886.9	1 064.0	1 145.5	1 103.4	1 133.0
45-99	TOTAL SERVICES	2 255.2	2 603.3	3 256.9	3 522.9	3 958.5	4 377.8	4 525.8	4 703.2
45-82	Business sector services	2 212.9	2 587.1	3 227.5	3 490.7	3 915.2	4 339.8	4 485.8	4 661.0
45-47	Wholesale and retail trade; motor vehicle and motorcycle repairs	106.6	172.7	570.0	641.8	720.5	781.5	812.8	854.5
49-53	Transportation and storage	56.2	70.0	42.1	88.3	144.9	80.9	127.5	45.6
55-56	Accommodation and food service activities	0.9	3.0	9.9	1.0	7.8	1.4	10.0	8.8
58-63	Information and communication	1 416.0	1 642.1	1 612.0	1 827.2	1 980.3	2 356.8	2 244.5	2 447.5
58-60	Publishing, audiovisual and broadcasting activities	820.8	970.5	1 030.8	1 131.6	1 112.0	1 544.8	1 434.2	1 620.6
58	Publishing activities	795.6	944.0	1 000.2	1 095.7	1 079.9	1 513.5	1 394.2	1 581.9
59-60	Motion picture, video and TV programme production; broadcasting activities	25.2	26.5	30.6	35.9	32.1	31.3	40.0	38.7
59	Motion picture, video and TV programme production; sound and music	3.6	6.3	13.0	13.2	15.4	12.5	9.5	13.7
60	Programming and broadcasting activities	21.6	20.2	17.6	22.7	16.7	18.8	30.5	25.0
61	Telecommunications	426.2	481.5	344.9	412.8	402.9	448.0	467.5	490.5
62-63	IT and other information services	169.0	190.1	236.3	282.8	465.4	364.0	342.8	336.4
62	Computer programming, consultancy and related activities	..	97.1	117.2	169.7	319.6	244.4	206.5	222.0
63	Information service activities	..	93.0	119.1	113.1	145.8	119.6	136.3	114.4
64-66	Financial and insurance activities	0.5	0.1	2.0	1.6	1.2	2.1	2.0	5.1
68-82	Real estate; professional, scientific and technical; administrative and support	632.7	699.2	991.5	930.9	1 060.6	1 117.1	1 289.0	1 299.6
68	Real estate activities	0.6	0.7	31.1	21.0	3.5	1.8	1.6	3.7
69-75x72	Professional, scientific and technical activities, except scientific R&D	499.4	516.3	707.8	634.4	679.9	761.7	789.9	862.3
72	Scientific research and development	99.5	147.1	184.5	202.5	305.6	272.3	406.3	340.7
77-82	Administrative and support service activities	33.3	35.1	68.0	73.0	71.7	81.3	91.3	92.8
84-99	Community, social and personal services	42.3	16.2	29.4	32.3	43.4	38.0	40.0	42.2
84-85	Public administration and defence; compulsory social security and education	6.7	9.9	15.2	15.3	19.2	14.5	16.6	16.2
86-88	Human health and social work activities	10.5	0.0	0.3	0.2	0.3	1.1	5.0	5.6
90-93	Arts, entertainment and recreation	9.6	3.4	4.1	4.1	3.2	3.1	3.0	2.2
94-99	Other services; household-employers; extraterritorial bodies	15.5	2.8	9.8	12.6	20.6	19.3	15.4	18.3

.. Not available

Note: Detailed metadata at: http://metalinks.oecd.org/anberd/20170419/301f.
Information on data for Israel: http://oe.cd/israel-disclaimer.

Disclaimer: http://oe.cd/disclaimer

MEXICO

R&D expenditure in industry by main activity of the enterprise, current prices
ISIC Rev. 4

Million USD PPP

ISIC	Activity	2007	2008	2009	2010	2011	2012	2013	2014
	TOTAL BUSINESS ENTERPRISE	2 717.9	2 547.4	2 878.8	3 274.2	3 410.3	2 909.8	3 215.6	3 549.4
01-03	**AGRICULTURE, FORESTRY AND FISHING**	0.0	5.1	18.6	0.0	0.0	0.0	0.0	0.0
05-09	**MINING AND QUARRYING**	16.3	80.5	93.9	36.4	50.9	6.0	28.3	31.2
10-33	**MANUFACTURING**	1 883.2	1 964.5	2 130.4	1 751.2	2 000.3	1 322.7	1 737.5	1 917.9
10-12	Food products, beverages and tobacco	297.2	182.5	256.5	149.7	173.1	150.6	203.6	224.8
13-15	Textiles, wearing apparel, leather and related products	128.1	32.5	110.3	41.4	41.6	24.7	28.0	30.9
13	Textiles	63.9	26.8	99.3	19.8	22.6	24.3	27.6	30.5
14	Wearing apparel	54.0	0.7	1.3	1.8	0.0	0.3	0.3	0.3
15	Leather and related products, footwear	10.2	5.0	9.6	19.8	19.1	0.1	0.1	0.1
16-18	Wood and paper products and printing	20.0	49.4	31.4	21.7	22.3	25.1	31.3	34.5
16	Wood and wood products, except furniture	0.9	3.5	2.7	4.9	4.8	3.1	6.6	7.3
17	Paper and paper products	9.6	45.7	27.1	16.2	17.2	16.4	21.5	23.8
18	Printing and reproduction of recorded media	9.5	0.3	1.5	0.6	0.2	5.6	3.2	3.5
19-23	Chemical, rubber, plastic, non-metallic mineral products	566.3	570.1	498.6	683.3	795.2	314.4	413.7	456.6
19	Coke and refined petroleum products	62.7	9.3	9.3	10.2	13.5	8.8	11.3	12.5
20-21	Chemical and pharmaceutical products	373.7	470.5	420.2	616.6	721.5	243.7	334.5	369.2
20	Chemicals and chemical products	214.3	288.7	223.2	115.5	137.3	75.7	88.3	97.5
21	Pharmaceuticals, medicinal, chemical and botanical products	159.5	181.8	197.0	501.1	584.2	167.9	246.2	271.7
22	Rubber and plastic products	70.6	16.6	37.9	30.6	39.1	12.8	19.6	21.6
23	Other non-metallic mineral products	59.2	73.7	31.2	25.9	21.1	49.1	48.2	53.2
24-25	Basic metals, metal products, except machinery and equipment	372.7	359.2	288.8	269.4	278.5	169.3	139.6	154.1
24	Basic metals	178.1	194.5	155.8	72.1	105.6	26.4	32.2	35.5
25	Fabricated metal products, except machinery and equipment	194.6	164.7	133.1	197.3	173.0	142.9	107.5	118.6
26-30	Computer, electronic, optical products; electrical machinery, transport equipment	490.4	762.9	939.3	585.0	687.9	636.1	917.2	1 012.4
26	Computer, electronic and optical products	66.0	54.6	61.7	26.1	29.9	80.8	94.4	104.2
27	Electrical equipment	87.1	181.1	218.5	189.4	213.8	163.5	270.5	298.5
28	Machinery and equipment n.e.c.	61.4	93.3	164.3	77.9	68.2	40.6	58.7	64.8
29	Motor vehicles, trailers and semi-trailers	270.5	421.7	474.3	273.3	348.6	330.8	466.0	514.3
30	Other transport equipment	5.4	12.2	20.5	18.3	27.4	20.4	27.6	30.4
31-33	Furniture; repair, installation of machinery and equipment	8.5	7.8	5.4	0.7	1.7	2.4	4.1	4.6
31	Furniture	0.0	2.2	0.8	0.5	1.5	0.1	0.0	0.0
32	Other manufacturing	8.5	5.6	4.6	0.1	0.1	2.3	4.1	4.5
33	Repair and installation of machinery and equipment	..	..	..	..	..	..	..	..
35-39	**ELECTRICITY, GAS, WATER AND WASTE MANAGEMENT**	12.1	13.0	13.5	0.0	0.0	10.4	17.2	18.9
35-36	Electricity, gas and water	..	..	..	..	..	..	..	..
37-39	Sewerage, waste management and remediation activities	..	..	..	..	..	..	..	..
41-43	**CONSTRUCTION**	5.6	6.4	8.7	104.5	1.6	6.3	12.3	13.5
45-99	**TOTAL SERVICES**	800.7	478.1	613.7	1 382.1	1 357.6	1 564.4	1 420.4	1 567.8
45-82	**Business sector services**	213.1	148.9	199.8	1 026.0	967.0	1 035.1	830.8	917.0
45-47	Wholesale and retail trade; motor vehicle and motorcycle repairs	0.0	0.0	0.0	0.0	0.0	0.0	0.0	0.0
49-53	Transportation and storage	0.5	13.5	17.1	..	..	..	..	..
55-56	Accommodation and food service activities	0.0	0.6	0.0	0.5	0.6	1.1	1.8	2.0
58-63	Information and communication	58.7	36.8	68.0	454.1	449.9	478.3	262.7	290.0
58-60	Publishing, audiovisual and broadcasting activities	..	..	..	..	..	..	..	..
58	Publishing activities	..	..	..	..	..	..	..	..
59-60	Motion picture, video and TV programme production; broadcasting activities	..	..	..	..	..	..	..	..
59	Motion picture, video and TV programme production; sound and music	..	..	..	..	..	..	..	..
60	Programming and broadcasting activities	..	..	..	..	..	..	..	..
61	Telecommunications	..	..	..	..	..	..	..	..
62-63	IT and other information services	..	..	..	..	..	..	..	..
62	Computer programming, consultancy and related activities	..	..	..	..	..	..	..	..
63	Information service activities	..	..	..	..	..	..	..	..
64-66	Financial and insurance activities	112.0	34.9	51.3	136.5	145.2	427.7	245.7	271.2
68-82	Real estate; professional, scientific and technical; administrative and support	42.0	63.1	63.5	..	..	..	..	..
68	Real estate activities	..	..	..	..	..	..	..	..
69-75x72	Professional, scientific and technical activities, except scientific R&D	..	..	..	..	..	..	..	..
72	Scientific research and development	40.3	63.1	63.5	419.7	362.6	90.5	115.4	127.3
77-82	Administrative and support service activities	..	..	..	..	..	..	..	..
84-99	**Community, social and personal services**	587.5	329.2	413.8	356.0	390.6	529.3	589.6	650.8
84-85	Public administration and defence; compulsory social security and education	..	..	..	..	..	..	..	..
86-88	Human health and social work activities	..	..	..	..	..	..	..	..
90-93	Arts, entertainment and recreation	..	..	..	..	..	..	..	..
94-99	Other services; household-employers; extraterritorial bodies	..	..	..	..	..	..	..	..

.. Not available

Note: Detailed metadata at: http://metalinks.oecd.org/anberd/20170419/301f.
Information on data for Israel: http://oe.cd/israel-disclaimer.
Disclaimer: http://oe.cd/disclaimer

MEXICO

R&D expenditure in industry by main activity of the enterprise, constant prices
ISIC Rev. 4

2010 USD PPP

		2007	2008	2009	2010	2011	2012	2013	2014
	TOTAL BUSINESS ENTERPRISE	2 983.5	2 680.5	2 913.9	3 274.2	3 238.7	2 742.2	2 989.9	3 198.8
01-03	**AGRICULTURE, FORESTRY AND FISHING**	0.0	5.4	18.9	0.0	0.0	0.0	0.0	0.0
05-09	**MINING AND QUARRYING**	17.9	84.7	95.0	36.4	48.3	5.6	26.3	28.1
10-33	**MANUFACTURING**	2 067.3	2 067.1	2 156.4	1 751.2	1 899.6	1 246.5	1 615.6	1 728.5
10-12	Food products, beverages and tobacco	326.2	192.0	259.7	149.7	164.4	141.9	189.4	202.6
13-15	Textiles, wearing apparel, leather and related products	140.7	34.2	111.6	41.4	39.5	23.3	26.0	27.9
13	Textiles	70.1	28.2	100.5	19.8	21.4	22.9	25.7	27.5
14	Wearing apparel	59.3	0.8	1.3	1.8	0.0	0.3	0.3	0.3
15	Leather and related products, footwear	11.2	5.3	9.7	19.8	18.1	0.1	0.1	0.1
16-18	Wood and paper products and printing	22.0	52.0	31.8	21.7	21.2	23.7	29.1	31.1
16	Wood and wood products, except furniture	1.0	3.6	2.7	4.9	4.6	2.9	6.1	6.5
17	Paper and paper products	10.5	48.1	27.5	16.2	16.3	15.5	20.0	21.4
18	Printing and reproduction of recorded media	10.5	0.3	1.5	0.6	0.2	5.3	3.0	3.2
19-23	Chemical, rubber, plastic, non-metallic mineral products	621.6	599.9	504.7	683.3	755.2	296.3	384.7	411.5
19	Coke and refined petroleum products	68.8	9.8	9.4	10.2	12.8	8.3	10.6	11.3
20-21	Chemical and pharmaceutical products	410.3	495.1	425.3	616.6	685.2	229.6	311.0	332.8
20	Chemicals and chemical products	235.2	303.8	226.0	115.5	130.4	71.4	82.1	87.9
21	Pharmaceuticals, medicinal, chemical and botanical products	175.0	191.3	199.4	501.1	554.8	158.3	228.9	244.9
22	Rubber and plastic products	77.5	17.5	38.4	30.6	37.1	12.1	18.2	19.5
23	Other non-metallic mineral products	65.0	77.5	31.6	25.9	20.0	46.3	44.9	48.0
24-25	Basic metals, metal products, except machinery and equipment	409.1	377.9	292.4	269.4	264.5	159.6	129.8	138.9
24	Basic metals	195.5	204.7	157.7	72.1	100.3	24.9	29.9	32.0
25	Fabricated metal products, except machinery and equipment	213.7	173.3	134.7	197.3	164.3	134.7	99.9	106.9
26-30	Computer, electronic, optical products; electrical machinery, transport equipment	538.4	802.8	950.8	585.0	653.3	599.5	852.8	912.4
26	Computer, electronic and optical products	72.5	57.5	62.5	26.1	28.4	76.1	87.8	93.9
27	Electrical equipment	95.6	190.6	221.1	189.4	203.0	154.1	251.5	269.1
28	Machinery and equipment n.e.c.	67.4	98.2	166.3	77.9	64.8	38.3	54.6	58.4
29	Motor vehicles, trailers and semi-trailers	296.9	443.7	480.1	273.3	331.0	311.8	433.3	463.5
30	Other transport equipment	5.9	12.8	20.7	18.3	26.0	19.2	25.6	27.4
31-33	Furniture; repair, installation of machinery and equipment	9.3	8.3	5.5	0.7	1.6	2.3	3.8	4.1
31	Furniture	0.0	2.3	0.8	0.5	1.5	0.1	0.0	0.0
32	Other manufacturing	9.3	5.9	4.7	0.1	0.1	2.2	3.8	4.1
33	Repair and installation of machinery and equipment	..	..	..	..	..	..	..	..
35-39	**ELECTRICITY, GAS, WATER AND WASTE MANAGEMENT**	13.3	13.7	13.7	0.0	0.0	9.8	16.0	17.1
35-36	Electricity, gas and water	..	..	..	..	..	..	..	..
37-39	Sewerage, waste management and remediation activities	..	..	..	..	..	..	..	..
41-43	**CONSTRUCTION**	6.1	6.7	8.8	104.5	1.5	5.9	11.4	12.2
45-99	**TOTAL SERVICES**	878.9	503.0	621.2	1 382.1	1 289.3	1 474.3	1 320.7	1 413.0
45-82	**Business sector services**	234.0	156.6	202.3	1 026.0	918.3	975.5	772.4	826.4
45-47	Wholesale and retail trade; motor vehicle and motorcycle repairs	0.0	0.0	0.0	0.0	0.0	0.0	0.0	0.0
49-53	Transportation and storage	0.6	14.2	17.3	..	..	..	..	..
55-56	Accommodation and food service activities	0.0	0.7	0.0	0.5	0.5	1.0	1.7	1.8
58-63	Information and communication	64.4	38.7	68.8	454.1	427.2	450.7	244.3	261.3
58-60	Publishing, audiovisual and broadcasting activities	..	..	..	..	..	..	..	..
58	Publishing activities	..	..	..	..	..	..	..	..
59-60	Motion picture, video and TV programme production; broadcasting activities	..	..	..	..	..	..	..	..
59	Motion picture, video and TV programme production; sound and music	..	..	..	..	..	..	..	..
60	Programming and broadcasting activities	..	..	..	..	..	..	..	..
61	Telecommunications	..	..	..	..	..	..	..	..
62-63	IT and other information services	..	..	..	..	..	..	..	..
62	Computer programming, consultancy and related activities	..	..	..	..	..	..	..	..
63	Information service activities	..	..	..	..	..	..	..	..
64-66	**Financial and insurance activities**	122.9	36.8	51.9	136.5	137.9	403.1	228.5	244.4
68-82	Real estate; professional, scientific and technical; administrative and support	46.1	66.4	64.2	..	..	..	..	..
68	Real estate activities	..	..	..	..	..	..	..	..
69-75x72	Professional, scientific and technical activities, except scientific R&D	..	..	..	..	..	..	..	..
72	Scientific research and development	44.2	66.4	64.2	419.7	344.3	85.3	107.3	114.8
77-82	Administrative and support service activities	..	..	..	..	..	..	..	..
84-99	**Community, social and personal services**	645.0	346.4	418.9	356.0	370.9	498.8	548.2	586.5
84-85	Public administration and defence; compulsory social security and education	..	..	..	..	..	..	..	..
86-88	Human health and social work activities	..	..	..	..	..	..	..	..
90-93	Arts, entertainment and recreation	..	..	..	..	..	..	..	..
94-99	Other services; household-employers; extraterritorial bodies	..	..	..	..	..	..	..	..

.. Not available

Note: Detailed metadata at: http://metalinks.oecd.org/anberd/20170419/301f.
Information on data for Israel: http://oe.cd/israel-disclaimer.

Disclaimer: http://oe.cd/disclaimer

NETHERLANDS

R&D expenditure in industry by main activity of the enterprise, current prices
ISIC Rev. 4

Million USD PPP

Code	Activity	2007	2008	2009	2010	2011	2012	2013	2014
	TOTAL BUSINESS ENTERPRISE	..	6 208.0	5 783.1	6 121.1	8 278.9	8 585.1	8 896.9	9 275.6
01-03	AGRICULTURE, FORESTRY AND FISHING	..	75.5	77.9	96.2	210.7	173.7	175.9	214.6
05-09	MINING AND QUARRYING	..	..	..	..	34.9	70.7	72.6	85.9
10-33	MANUFACTURING	..	4 432.8	4 195.7	4 153.8	4 708.0	4 911.0	5 201.1	5 476.5
10-12	Food products, beverages and tobacco	..	294.9	325.7	388.3	456.5	483.7	490.2	469.3
13-15	Textiles, wearing apparel, leather and related products	..	16.5	15.3	15.2	14.2	23.4	23.8	22.5
13	Textiles	..	14.2	13.0	12.9	13.0	19.3	16.9	16.9
14	Wearing apparel	..	0.0	0.0	0.0	0.6	0.5	1.0	1.2
15	Leather and related products, footwear	..	2.4	2.4	1.2	0.7	3.7	5.9	4.5
16-18	Wood and paper products and printing	..	34.2	35.4	24.6	25.6	29.8	29.0	39.3
16	Wood and wood products, except furniture	..	2.4	1.2	4.7	2.3	3.5	2.1	3.0
17	Paper and paper products	..	27.1	28.3	17.6	6.9	18.2	20.4	28.3
18	Printing and reproduction of recorded media	..	4.7	5.9	2.3	16.3	8.1	6.5	8.0
19-23	Chemical, rubber, plastic, non-metallic mineral products	..	1 601.8	1 540.2	1 330.3	1 325.0	1 363.0	1 388.5	1 409.7
19	Coke and refined petroleum products	..	17.7	3.5	16.4	128.9	282.7	295.8	314.2
20-21	Chemical and pharmaceutical products	..	1 513.4	1 465.8	1 251.7	1 048.6	948.7	961.7	984.9
20	Chemicals and chemical products	..	986.1	984.3	803.6	664.1	630.7	656.2	665.3
21	Pharmaceuticals, medicinal, chemical and botanical products	..	527.3	481.5	448.1	384.5	318.0	305.5	319.6
22	Rubber and plastic products	..	47.2	48.4	43.4	117.4	102.5	107.0	89.8
23	Other non-metallic mineral products	..	23.6	22.4	18.8	30.0	29.1	23.9	20.8
24-25	Basic metals, metal products, except machinery and equipment	..	156.6	145.4	164.6	188.9	173.8	207.0	187.2
24	Basic metals	..	77.5	71.0	84.8	95.2	90.1	100.8	83.1
25	Fabricated metal products, except machinery and equipment	..	79.0	74.4	79.8	93.8	83.7	106.2	104.1
26-30	Computer, electronic, optical products; electrical machinery, transport equipment	..	2 057.1	1 847.0	2 172.5	2 538.5	2 751.1	2 980.1	3 254.2
26	Computer, electronic and optical products	..	506.0	469.7	658.1	697.1	742.5	818.9	856.3
27	Electrical equipment	..	678.2	657.4	502.1	576.2	580.8	652.1	581.8
28	Machinery and equipment n.e.c.	..	745.5	607.8	855.2	979.1	1 136.3	1 197.4	1 501.3
29	Motor vehicles, trailers and semi-trailers	..	86.1	73.2	83.3	170.4	168.9	183.1	188.7
30	Other transport equipment	..	41.3	40.1	72.7	115.7	122.7	128.7	126.1
31-33	Furniture; repair, installation of machinery and equipment	..	271.6	286.6	58.3	159.2	86.2	82.5	94.4
31	Furniture	..	13.0	11.8	11.7	105.3	14.7	8.1	14.2
32	Other manufacturing	..	238.3	256.1	24.3	26.6	37.6	35.6	32.5
33	Repair and installation of machinery and equipment	..	20.4	18.7	22.3	27.3	33.9	38.9	47.8
35-39	ELECTRICITY, GAS, WATER AND WASTE MANAGEMENT	..	..	..	..	49.1	37.9	27.3	51.6
35-36	Electricity, gas and water	..	..	..	..	25.7	18.9	14.4	27.3
37-39	Sewerage, waste management and remediation activities	..	..	..	..	23.4	18.9	12.8	24.3
41-43	CONSTRUCTION	..	27.1	38.9	63.3	124.2	158.9	133.6	139.6
45-99	TOTAL SERVICES	..	..	..	..	3 152.1	3 232.9	3 286.5	3 307.4
45-82	Business sector services	..	1 539.3	1 341.9	1 739.7	3 138.2	3 196.8	3 250.0	3 277.6
45-47	Wholesale and retail trade; motor vehicle and motorcycle repairs	..	222.9	218.3	393.0	465.5	513.6	495.7	523.2
49-53	Transportation and storage	..	23.6	46.0	19.9	140.7	142.1	122.1	131.0
55-56	Accommodation and food service activities	..	0.0	0.0	0.0	13.1	2.7	2.2	1.6
58-63	Information and communication	..	370.4	413.1	674.5	944.7	929.2	926.4	1 004.8
58-60	Publishing, audiovisual and broadcasting activities	..	29.5	26.0	7.0	28.8	34.6	24.8	31.8
58	Publishing activities	..	..	..	..	17.6	20.2	16.6	..
59-60	Motion picture, video and TV programme production; broadcasting activities	..	..	..	..	11.3	14.4	8.2	..
59	Motion picture, video and TV programme production; sound and music	..	..	..	..	9.3	14.1	7.9	..
60	Programming and broadcasting activities	..	..	..	..	2.0	0.3	0.3	..
61	Telecommunications	..	18.9	18.9	61.0	76.1	61.4	38.9	60.4
62-63	IT and other information services	..	322.0	368.2	607.6	839.7	833.1	862.7	912.6
62	Computer programming, consultancy and related activities	..	320.8	368.2	583.0	769.3	794.7	815.4	833.6
63	Information service activities	..	1.2	0.0	24.6	70.4	38.4	47.4	79.0
64-66	Financial and insurance activities	..	299.6	23.6	29.3	240.7	329.0	322.1	244.9
68-82	Real estate; professional, scientific and technical; administrative and support	..	622.8	640.9	621.7	1 333.5	1 280.2	1 381.3	1 372.1
68	Real estate activities	..	22.4	0.0	0.0	8.1	5.1	5.9	7.4
69-75x72	Professional, scientific and technical activities, except scientific R&D	..	227.7	174.7	272.2	756.2	633.4	622.4	587.8
72	Scientific research and development	..	362.1	440.2	330.8	453.3	537.5	604.1	629.5
77-82	Administrative and support service activities	..	10.6	26.0	18.8	115.8	104.2	149.0	147.4
84-99	Community, social and personal services	..	..	..	..	13.9	36.1	36.5	29.9
84-85	Public administration and defence; compulsory social security and education	..	..	..	..	..	..	..	..
86-88	Human health and social work activities	..	..	..	..	..	..	..	..
90-93	Arts, entertainment and recreation	..	..	..	..	..	..	..	..
94-99	Other services; household-employers; extraterritorial bodies	..	..	..	..	..	..	..	..

.. Not available

Note: Detailed metadata at: http://metalinks.oecd.org/anberd/20170419/301f.
   Information on data for Israel: http://oe.cd/israel-disclaimer.
Disclaimer: http://oe.cd/disclaimer

NETHERLANDS

R&D expenditure in industry by main activity of the enterprise, constant prices
ISIC Rev. 4

2010 USD PPP

Code	Industry	2007	2008	2009	2010	2011	2012	2013	2014
	TOTAL BUSINESS ENTERPRISE	..	6 251.1	5 796.8	6 121.1	8 108.2	8 174.7	8 083.9	8 457.1
01-03	**AGRICULTURE, FORESTRY AND FISHING**	..	76.0	78.1	96.2	206.4	165.4	159.8	195.7
05-09	**MINING AND QUARRYING**	..	..	..	..	34.2	67.3	66.0	78.3
10-33	**MANUFACTURING**	..	4 463.5	4 205.6	4 153.8	4 610.8	4 676.3	4 725.8	4 993.2
10-12	Food products, beverages and tobacco	..	296.9	326.5	388.3	447.1	460.6	445.4	427.9
13-15	Textiles, wearing apparel, leather and related products	..	16.6	15.4	15.2	14.0	22.3	21.6	20.5
13	Textiles	..	14.3	13.0	12.9	12.7	18.4	15.3	15.4
14	Wearing apparel	..	0.0	0.0	0.0	0.5	0.4	0.9	1.1
15	Leather and related products, footwear	..	2.4	2.4	1.2	0.7	3.5	5.3	4.1
16-18	Wood and paper products and printing	..	34.4	35.5	24.6	25.0	28.4	26.3	35.8
16	Wood and wood products, except furniture	..	2.4	1.2	4.7	2.3	3.3	1.9	2.7
17	Paper and paper products	..	27.3	28.4	17.6	6.8	17.3	18.5	25.8
18	Printing and reproduction of recorded media	..	4.8	5.9	2.3	16.0	7.8	5.9	7.2
19-23	Chemical, rubber, plastic, non-metallic mineral products	..	1 613.0	1 543.8	1 330.3	1 297.7	1 297.8	1 261.6	1 285.3
19	Coke and refined petroleum products	..	17.8	3.5	16.4	126.3	269.2	268.8	286.5
20-21	Chemical and pharmaceutical products	..	1 523.9	1 469.3	1 251.7	1 027.0	903.4	873.8	898.0
20	Chemicals and chemical products	..	993.0	986.6	803.6	650.4	600.6	596.2	606.6
21	Pharmaceuticals, medicinal, chemical and botanical products	..	530.9	482.7	448.1	376.6	302.8	277.6	291.4
22	Rubber and plastic products	..	47.5	48.5	43.4	115.0	97.6	97.2	81.8
23	Other non-metallic mineral products	..	23.8	22.5	18.8	29.4	27.7	21.7	19.0
24-25	Basic metals, metal products, except machinery and equipment	..	157.6	145.7	164.6	185.0	165.5	188.1	170.7
24	Basic metals	..	78.1	71.2	84.8	93.2	85.8	91.6	75.7
25	Fabricated metal products, except machinery and equipment	..	79.6	74.5	79.8	91.8	79.7	96.5	95.0
26-30	Computer, electronic, optical products; electrical machinery, transport equipment	..	2 071.4	1 851.4	2 172.5	2 486.1	2 619.6	2 707.8	2 967.0
26	Computer, electronic and optical products	..	509.5	470.8	658.1	682.7	707.0	744.1	780.7
27	Electrical equipment	..	683.0	658.9	502.1	564.3	553.0	592.5	530.5
28	Machinery and equipment n.e.c.	..	750.7	609.3	855.2	958.9	1 081.9	1 087.9	1 368.8
29	Motor vehicles, trailers and semi-trailers	..	86.7	73.3	83.3	166.8	160.8	166.4	172.0
30	Other transport equipment	..	41.6	40.2	72.7	113.3	116.8	116.9	115.0
31-33	Furniture; repair, installation of machinery and equipment	..	273.5	287.3	58.3	155.9	82.1	75.0	86.1
31	Furniture	..	13.1	11.8	11.7	103.2	14.0	7.4	12.9
32	Other manufacturing	..	239.9	256.7	24.3	26.0	35.8	32.3	29.6
33	Repair and installation of machinery and equipment	..	20.5	18.7	22.3	26.7	32.3	35.3	43.6
35-39	**ELECTRICITY, GAS, WATER AND WASTE MANAGEMENT**	..	..	..	..	48.1	36.0	24.8	47.0
35-36	Electricity, gas and water	..	..	..	..	25.2	18.0	13.1	24.9
37-39	Sewerage, waste management and remediation activities	..	..	..	..	22.9	18.0	11.7	22.2
41-43	**CONSTRUCTION**	..	27.3	39.0	63.3	121.6	151.3	121.4	127.3
45-99	**TOTAL SERVICES**	..	..	..	..	3 087.1	3 078.4	2 986.1	3 015.5
45-82	**Business sector services**	..	1 550.0	1 345.1	1 739.7	3 073.5	3 044.0	2 953.0	2 988.3
45-47	Wholesale and retail trade; motor vehicle and motorcycle repairs	..	224.5	218.9	393.0	455.9	489.0	450.4	477.1
49-53	Transportation and storage	..	23.8	46.1	19.9	137.8	135.3	111.0	119.4
55-56	Accommodation and food service activities	..	0.0	0.0	0.0	12.8	2.6	2.0	1.4
58-63	Information and communication	..	373.0	414.1	674.5	925.2	884.7	841.7	916.2
58-60	Publishing, audiovisual and broadcasting activities	..	29.7	26.0	7.0	28.2	33.0	22.5	29.0
58	Publishing activities	..	..	..	..	17.2	19.2	15.0	..
59-60	Motion picture, video and TV programme production; broadcasting activities	..	..	..	..	11.0	13.7	7.5	..
59	Motion picture, video and TV programme production; sound and music	..	..	..	..	9.1	13.4	7.2	..
60	Programming and broadcasting activities	..	..	..	..	2.0	0.3	0.3	..
61	Telecommunications	..	19.0	18.9	61.0	74.6	58.5	35.4	55.1
62-63	IT and other information services	..	324.3	369.1	607.6	822.4	793.3	783.9	832.1
62	Computer programming, consultancy and related activities	..	323.1	369.1	583.0	753.4	756.7	740.9	760.0
63	Information service activities	..	1.2	0.0	24.6	68.9	36.6	43.0	72.0
64-66	**Financial and insurance activities**	..	301.7	23.7	29.3	235.8	313.3	292.7	223.3
68-82	**Real estate; professional, scientific and technical; administrative and support**	..	627.1	642.4	621.7	1 306.0	1 219.0	1 255.1	1 251.0
68	Real estate activities	..	22.6	0.0	0.0	8.0	4.8	5.4	6.7
69-75x72	Professional, scientific and technical activities, except scientific R&D	..	229.2	175.1	272.2	740.6	603.1	565.5	536.0
72	Scientific research and development	..	364.6	441.3	330.8	444.0	511.8	548.9	574.0
77-82	Administrative and support service activities	..	10.7	26.0	18.8	113.4	99.3	135.4	134.4
84-99	**Community, social and personal services**	..	..	..	..	13.6	34.4	33.1	27.2
84-85	Public administration and defence; compulsory social security and education	..	..	..	..	..	..	..	..
86-88	Human health and social work activities	..	..	..	..	..	..	..	..
90-93	Arts, entertainment and recreation	..	..	..	..	..	..	..	..
94-99	Other services; household-employers; extraterritorial bodies	..	..	..	..	..	..	..	..

.. Not available

Note: Detailed metadata at: http://metalinks.oecd.org/anberd/20170419/301f.
    Information on data for Israel: http://oe.cd/israel-disclaimer.
Disclaimer: http://oe.cd/disclaimer

NEW ZEALAND

R&D expenditure in industry by main activity of the enterprise, current prices
ISIC Rev. 4

Million USD PPP

		2007	2008	2009	2010	2011	2012	2013	2014
	TOTAL BUSINESS ENTERPRISE	613.2	..	690.9	..	802.9	..	861.9	..
01-03	**AGRICULTURE, FORESTRY AND FISHING**	47.8	..	49.6	..	84.1	..	63.6	..
05-09	**MINING AND QUARRYING**	..	..	..	..	..	..	..	..
10-33	**MANUFACTURING**	293.6	..	312.1	..	360.7	..	361.1	..
10-12	Food products, beverages and tobacco	67.8	..	55.1	..	76.7	..	60.9	..
13-15	Textiles, wearing apparel, leather and related products	4.7	..	5.4	..	4.7	..	7.6	..
13	Textiles	..	..	..	..	..	..	..	..
14	Wearing apparel	..	..	..	..	..	..	..	..
15	Leather and related products, footwear	..	..	..	..	..	..	..	..
16-18	Wood and paper products and printing	..	..	..	..	..	..	..	..
16	Wood and wood products, except furniture	..	..	..	..	..	..	..	..
17	Paper and paper products	..	..	..	..	..	..	..	..
18	Printing and reproduction of recorded media	..	..	..	..	..	..	..	..
19-23	Chemical, rubber, plastic, non-metallic mineral products	68.4	..	51.0	..	51.1	..	65.7	..
19	Coke and refined petroleum products	..	..	..	..	..	..	..	..
20-21	Chemical and pharmaceutical products	..	..	..	..	..	..	..	..
20	Chemicals and chemical products	..	..	..	..	..	..	..	..
21	Pharmaceuticals, medicinal, chemical and botanical products	..	..	..	..	..	..	..	..
22	Rubber and plastic products	..	..	..	..	..	..	..	..
23	Other non-metallic mineral products	2.7	..	2.0	..	2.7	..	1.4	..
24-25	Basic metals, metal products, except machinery and equipment	12.6	..	22.4	..	20.9	..	19.4	..
24	Basic metals	..	..	..	..	..	..	..	..
25	Fabricated metal products, except machinery and equipment	..	..	..	..	..	..	..	..
26-30	Computer, electronic, optical products; electrical machinery, transport equipment	116.9	..	147.6	..	177.7	..	179.2	..
26	Computer, electronic and optical products	..	..	..	..	..	..	..	..
27	Electrical equipment	..	..	..	..	..	..	..	..
28	Machinery and equipment n.e.c.	..	..	..	..	..	..	..	..
29	Motor vehicles, trailers and semi-trailers	..	..	..	..	..	..	..	..
30	Other transport equipment	..	..	..	..	..	..	..	..
31-33	Furniture; repair, installation of machinery and equipment	..	..	..	..	..	..	..	..
31	Furniture	..	..	..	..	..	..	..	..
32	Other manufacturing	..	..	..	..	..	..	..	..
33	Repair and installation of machinery and equipment	..	..	..	..	..	..	..	..
35-39	**ELECTRICITY, GAS, WATER AND WASTE MANAGEMENT**	..	..	..	..	..	..	..	..
35-36	Electricity, gas and water	..	..	..	..	..	..	..	..
37-39	Sewerage, waste management and remediation activities	..	..	..	..	..	..	..	..
41-43	**CONSTRUCTION**	..	..	..	..	..	..	..	..
45-99	**TOTAL SERVICES**	271.7	..	329.1	..	358.0	..	437.2	..
45-82	**Business sector services**	..	..	..	..	..	..	..	..
45-47	Wholesale and retail trade; motor vehicle and motorcycle repairs	40.5	..	38.1	..	59.9	..	66.4	..
49-53	Transportation and storage	..	..	..	..	..	..	..	..
55-56	Accommodation and food service activities	..	..	..	..	..	..	..	..
58-63	Information and communication	..	..	..	..	..	..	..	..
58-60	Publishing, audiovisual and broadcasting activities	..	..	..	..	..	..	..	..
58	Publishing activities	..	..	..	..	..	..	..	..
59-60	Motion picture, video and TV programme production; broadcasting activities	..	..	..	..	..	..	..	..
59	Motion picture, video and TV programme production; sound and music	..	..	..	..	..	..	..	..
60	Programming and broadcasting activities	..	..	..	..	..	..	..	..
61	Telecommunications	..	..	..	..	..	..	..	..
62-63	IT and other information services	108.3	..	136.0	..	148.7	..	215.1	..
62	Computer programming, consultancy and related activities	..	..	..	..	..	..	..	..
63	Information service activities	..	..	..	..	..	..	..	..
64-66	**Financial and insurance activities**	..	..	..	..	..	..	..	..
68-82	**Real estate; professional, scientific and technical; administrative and support**	..	..	..	..	..	..	..	..
68	Real estate activities	..	..	..	..	..	..	..	..
69-75x72	Professional, scientific and technical activities, except scientific R&D	..	..	..	..	..	..	..	..
72	Scientific research and development	38.5	..	34.7	..	34.3	..	39.4	..
77-82	Administrative and support service activities	..	..	..	..	..	..	..	..
84-99	Community, social and personal services	..	..	..	..	..	..	..	..
84-85	Public administration and defence; compulsory social security and education	..	..	..	..	..	..	..	..
86-88	Human health and social work activities	..	..	..	..	..	..	..	..
90-93	Arts, entertainment and recreation	..	..	..	..	..	..	..	..
94-99	Other services; household-employers; extraterritorial bodies	..	..	..	..	..	..	..	..

.. Not available

Note: Detailed metadata at: http://metalinks.oecd.org/anberd/20170419/301f.
   Information on data for Israel: http://oe.cd/israel-disclaimer.
Disclaimer: http://oe.cd/disclaimer

NEW ZEALAND

R&D expenditure in industry by main activity of the enterprise, constant prices
ISIC Rev. 4

2010 USD PPP

		2007	2008	2009	2010	2011	2012	2013	2014
	TOTAL BUSINESS ENTERPRISE	663.3	..	704.7	..	781.5	..	781.1	..
01-03	**AGRICULTURE, FORESTRY AND FISHING**	51.7	..	50.6	..	81.9	..	57.7	..
05-09	**MINING AND QUARRYING**	..	..	..	..	..	..	..	..
10-33	**MANUFACTURING**	317.6	..	318.4	..	351.1	..	327.2	..
10-12	Food products, beverages and tobacco	73.3	..	56.2	..	74.7	..	55.2	..
13-15	Textiles, wearing apparel, leather and related products	5.0	..	5.5	..	4.6	..	6.9	..
13	Textiles	..	..	..	..	..	..	..	..
14	Wearing apparel	..	..	..	..	..	..	..	..
15	Leather and related products, footwear	..	..	..	..	..	..	..	..
16-18	Wood and paper products and printing	..	..	..	..	..	..	..	..
16	Wood and wood products, except furniture	..	..	..	..	..	..	..	..
17	Paper and paper products	..	..	..	..	..	..	..	..
18	Printing and reproduction of recorded media	..	..	..	..	..	..	..	..
19-23	Chemical, rubber, plastic, non-metallic mineral products	74.0	..	52.0	..	49.8	..	59.6	..
19	Coke and refined petroleum products	..	..	..	..	..	..	..	..
20-21	Chemical and pharmaceutical products	..	..	..	..	..	..	..	..
20	Chemicals and chemical products	..	..	..	..	..	..	..	..
21	Pharmaceuticals, medicinal, chemical and botanical products	..	..	..	..	..	..	..	..
22	Rubber and plastic products	..	..	..	..	..	..	..	..
23	Other non-metallic mineral products	2.9	..	2.1	..	2.6	..	1.3	..
24-25	Basic metals, metal products, except machinery and equipment	13.7	..	22.9	..	20.3	..	17.6	..
24	Basic metals	..	..	..	..	..	..	..	..
25	Fabricated metal products, except machinery and equipment	..	..	..	..	..	..	..	..
26-30	Computer, electronic, optical products; electrical machinery, transport equipment	126.5	..	150.5	..	172.9	..	162.4	..
26	Computer, electronic and optical products	..	..	..	..	..	..	..	..
27	Electrical equipment	..	..	..	..	..	..	..	..
28	Machinery and equipment n.e.c.	..	..	..	..	..	..	..	..
29	Motor vehicles, trailers and semi-trailers	..	..	..	..	..	..	..	..
30	Other transport equipment	..	..	..	..	..	..	..	..
31-33	Furniture; repair, installation of machinery and equipment	..	..	..	..	..	..	..	..
31	Furniture	..	..	..	..	..	..	..	..
32	Other manufacturing	..	..	..	..	..	..	..	..
33	Repair and installation of machinery and equipment	..	..	..	..	..	..	..	..
35-39	**ELECTRICITY, GAS, WATER AND WASTE MANAGEMENT**	..	..	..	..	..	..	..	..
35-36	Electricity, gas and water	..	..	..	..	..	..	..	..
37-39	Sewerage, waste management and remediation activities	..	..	..	..	..	..	..	..
41-43	**CONSTRUCTION**	..	..	..	..	..	..	..	..
45-99	**TOTAL SERVICES**	293.9	..	335.7	..	348.5	..	396.2	..
45-82	**Business sector services**	..	..	..	..	..	..	..	..
45-47	**Wholesale and retail trade; motor vehicle and motorcycle repairs**	43.8	..	38.8	..	58.3	..	60.2	..
49-53	**Transportation and storage**	..	..	..	..	..	..	..	..
55-56	**Accommodation and food service activities**	..	..	..	..	..	..	..	..
58-63	**Information and communication**	..	..	..	..	..	..	..	..
58-60	Publishing, audiovisual and broadcasting activities	..	..	..	..	..	..	..	..
58	Publishing activities	..	..	..	..	..	..	..	..
59-60	Motion picture, video and TV programme production; broadcasting activities	..	..	..	..	..	..	..	..
59	Motion picture, video and TV programme production; sound and music	..	..	..	..	..	..	..	..
60	Programming and broadcasting activities	..	..	..	..	..	..	..	..
61	Telecommunications	..	..	..	..	..	..	..	..
62-63	IT and other information services	117.1	..	138.7	..	144.8	..	195.0	..
62	Computer programming, consultancy and related activities	..	..	..	..	..	..	..	..
63	Information service activities	..	..	..	..	..	..	..	..
64-66	**Financial and insurance activities**	..	..	..	..	..	..	..	..
68-82	**Real estate; professional, scientific and technical; administrative and support**	..	..	..	..	..	..	..	..
68	Real estate activities	..	..	..	..	..	..	..	..
69-75x72	Professional, scientific and technical activities, except scientific R&D	..	..	..	..	..	..	..	..
72	Scientific research and development	41.7	..	35.4	..	33.4	..	35.7	..
77-82	Administrative and support service activities	..	..	..	..	..	..	..	..
84-99	**Community, social and personal services**	..	..	..	..	..	..	..	..
84-85	Public administration and defence; compulsory social security and education	..	..	..	..	..	..	..	..
86-88	Human health and social work activities	..	..	..	..	..	..	..	..
90-93	Arts, entertainment and recreation	..	..	..	..	..	..	..	..
94-99	Other services; household-employers; extraterritorial bodies	..	..	..	..	..	..	..	..

.. Not available

Note: Detailed metadata at: http://metalinks.oecd.org/anberd/20170419/301f.
Information on data for Israel: http://oe.cd/israel-disclaimer.

Disclaimer: http://oe.cd/disclaimer

NORWAY

R&D expenditure in industry by main activity of the enterprise, current prices
ISIC Rev. 4

Million USD PPP

		2007	2008	2009	2010	2011	2012	2013	2014
	TOTAL BUSINESS ENTERPRISE	2 162.2	2 432.4	2 381.0	2 398.7	2 610.4	2 779.1	2 952.5	3 110.9
01-03	**AGRICULTURE, FORESTRY AND FISHING**	50.9	77.0	79.6	83.5	82.0	92.4	96.1	104.2
05-09	**MINING AND QUARRYING**	211.0	219.9	222.9	229.3	226.1	280.4	333.5	308.3
10-33	**MANUFACTURING**	941.4	1 017.9	962.0	865.3	967.8	1 000.7	1 039.8	1 076.1
10-12	Food products, beverages and tobacco	87.1	102.7	104.4	90.2	90.7	95.8	93.7	104.5
13-15	Textiles, wearing apparel, leather and related products	8.3	9.5	11.4	8.9	13.5	9.7	8.8	7.6
13	Textiles	4.7	5.3	6.2	5.0	7.9	6.5	6.3	6.0
14	Wearing apparel	3.2	3.7	..	..	..	..	..	..
15	Leather and related products, footwear	0.3	0.6	..	..	..	..	..	..
16-18	Wood and paper products and printing	32.1	33.4	37.9	37.0	37.1	40.0	39.3	31.9
16	Wood and wood products, except furniture	11.3	9.4	12.8	15.8	9.9	19.3	19.9	10.5
17	Paper and paper products	17.8	19.0	20.1	17.5	24.5	17.3	15.7	17.3
18	Printing and reproduction of recorded media	3.0	5.0	4.9	3.7	2.8	3.4	3.7	4.0
19-23	Chemical, rubber, plastic, non-metallic mineral products	193.9	216.5	205.1	190.5	218.6	187.3	190.6	184.2
19	Coke and refined petroleum products	..	..	..	..	..	..	..	..
20-21	Chemical and pharmaceutical products	..	..	..	..	..	..	..	..
20	Chemicals and chemical products	..	..	..	..	..	..	..	..
21	Pharmaceuticals, medicinal, chemical and botanical products	57.4	57.4	52.1	55.4	80.9	45.3	44.5	37.0
22	Rubber and plastic products	10.9	12.0	9.1	12.9	11.3	15.6	17.6	16.6
23	Other non-metallic mineral products	13.0	11.9	10.8	11.9	15.0	14.2	14.6	14.8
24-25	Basic metals, metal products, except machinery and equipment	109.9	111.7	117.1	128.3	139.9	165.2	167.7	171.9
24	Basic metals	47.8	47.3	40.5	38.3	28.1	37.0	38.3	35.6
25	Fabricated metal products, except machinery and equipment	62.1	64.5	76.6	89.9	111.8	128.2	129.4	136.3
26-30	Computer, electronic, optical products; electrical machinery, transport equipment	463.7	493.8	436.9	363.0	409.3	444.8	479.1	517.9
26	Computer, electronic and optical products	205.8	214.1	211.0	171.4	188.6	188.1	187.2	200.1
27	Electrical equipment	46.7	42.9	45.3	40.0	42.2	47.0	52.8	61.3
28	Machinery and equipment n.e.c.	102.4	120.4	89.0	84.8	102.5	114.9	141.5	153.0
29	Motor vehicles, trailers and semi-trailers	55.0	51.0	35.1	19.3	28.9	30.9	33.9	35.9
30	Other transport equipment	53.9	65.4	56.5	47.5	47.0	63.9	63.7	67.6
31-33	Furniture; repair, installation of machinery and equipment	46.4	50.2	49.3	47.4	58.7	57.8	60.6	57.9
31	Furniture	..	10.1	11.3	13.7	13.4	15.2	17.6	18.0
32	Other manufacturing	..	19.4	18.1	17.7	28.0	21.3	20.4	19.0
33	Repair and installation of machinery and equipment	..	20.6	19.8	16.0	17.3	21.3	22.6	20.9
35-39	**ELECTRICITY, GAS, WATER AND WASTE MANAGEMENT**	27.7	36.8	44.7	49.8	51.8	56.0	56.6	54.1
35-36	Electricity, gas and water	..	33.2	42.0	41.8	45.8	46.8	48.0	44.9
37-39	Sewerage, waste management and remediation activities	..	3.6	2.8	8.1	5.9	9.2	8.7	9.2
41-43	**CONSTRUCTION**	46.4	64.5	58.8	73.3	63.7	82.2	56.9	45.6
45-99	**TOTAL SERVICES**	884.8	1 016.2	1 013.0	1 097.5	1 219.1	1 267.4	1 369.5	1 522.7
45-82	**Business sector services**	884.8	1 016.2	1 013.0	1 097.5	1 219.1	1 267.4	1 369.5	1 522.7
45-47	Wholesale and retail trade; motor vehicle and motorcycle repairs	67.5	60.3	67.4	49.4	63.0	58.1	75.9	85.7
49-53	Transportation and storage	12.4	16.6	17.9	21.8	22.9	30.1	29.2	36.3
55-56	Accommodation and food service activities	..	..	..	..	..	..	..	..
58-63	Information and communication	434.9	480.2	490.7	528.3	569.8	634.1	691.6	725.0
58-60	Publishing, audiovisual and broadcasting activities	..	146.8	150.5	158.8	165.6	160.9	158.6	209.7
58	Publishing activities	..	146.5	148.3	157.7	164.4	159.3	155.4	206.4
59-60	Motion picture, video and TV programme production; broadcasting activities	..	0.3	2.2	1.1	1.2	1.6	3.2	3.4
59	Motion picture, video and TV programme production; sound and music	..	..	..	1.0	..	..	..	..
60	Programming and broadcasting activities	..	..	..	0.1	..	..	..	..
61	Telecommunications	68.2	76.1	92.6	92.9	82.9	84.6	85.1	88.6
62-63	IT and other information services	..	257.2	247.6	276.6	321.3	388.6	447.9	426.8
62	Computer programming, consultancy and related activities	..	245.1	236.1	263.5	306.6	357.0	420.8	394.9
63	Information service activities	..	12.1	11.5	13.1	14.6	31.6	27.0	31.8
64-66	Financial and insurance activities	108.2	118.8	112.8	114.0	148.3	141.1	153.8	153.3
68-82	Real estate; professional, scientific and technical; administrative and support	261.7	340.4	324.2	384.1	415.1	404.0	419.0	522.3
68	Real estate activities	..	0.0	0.0	0.0	0.0	0.0	0.0	0.0
69-75x72	Professional, scientific and technical activities, except scientific R&D	..	284.1	266.6	318.5	339.8	321.0	346.9	445.4
72	Scientific research and development	38.0	42.0	36.2	49.8	47.2	66.2	56.0	65.2
77-82	Administrative and support service activities	..	14.4	21.5	15.8	28.1	16.8	16.1	11.8
84-99	Community, social and personal services	..	..	..	..	..	..	..	..
84-85	Public administration and defence; compulsory social security and education	..	..	..	..	..	..	..	..
86-88	Human health and social work activities	..	..	..	..	..	..	..	..
90-93	Arts, entertainment and recreation	..	..	..	..	..	..	..	..
94-99	Other services; household-employers; extraterritorial bodies	..	..	..	..	..	..	..	..

.. Not available

Note: Detailed metadata at: http://metalinks.oecd.org/anberd/20170419/301f.
 Information on data for Israel: http://oe.cd/israel-disclaimer.
Disclaimer: http://oe.cd/disclaimer

NORWAY

R&D expenditure in industry by main activity of the enterprise, constant prices
ISIC Rev. 4

2010 USD PPP

		2007	2008	2009	2010	2011	2012	2013	2014
	TOTAL BUSINESS ENTERPRISE	2 361.2	2 513.4	2 449.5	2 398.7	2 519.0	2 602.9	2 689.0	2 853.0
01-03	**AGRICULTURE, FORESTRY AND FISHING**	55.5	79.6	81.9	83.5	79.1	86.5	87.5	95.5
05-09	**MINING AND QUARRYING**	230.4	227.2	229.3	229.3	218.2	262.7	303.8	282.8
10-33	**MANUFACTURING**	1 028.0	1 051.9	989.7	865.3	933.9	937.2	947.0	986.9
10-12	Food products, beverages and tobacco	95.1	106.1	107.4	90.2	87.5	89.8	85.3	95.9
13-15	Textiles, wearing apparel, leather and related products	9.1	9.8	11.8	8.9	13.0	9.1	8.0	7.0
13	Textiles	5.2	5.4	6.4	5.0	7.6	6.1	5.8	5.5
14	Wearing apparel	3.5	3.8	..	..	..	..	..	..
15	Leather and related products, footwear	0.4	0.6	..	..	..	..	..	..
16-18	Wood and paper products and printing	35.0	34.6	38.9	37.0	35.8	37.4	35.8	29.2
16	Wood and wood products, except furniture	12.3	9.8	13.2	15.8	9.5	18.1	18.1	9.7
17	Paper and paper products	19.4	19.6	20.7	17.5	23.6	16.2	14.3	15.9
18	Printing and reproduction of recorded media	3.3	5.2	5.0	3.7	2.7	3.2	3.3	3.7
19-23	Chemical, rubber, plastic, non-metallic mineral products	211.7	223.7	211.0	190.5	210.9	175.4	173.6	169.0
19	Coke and refined petroleum products	..	..	..	..	..	..	..	..
20-21	Chemical and pharmaceutical products	..	..	..	..	..	..	..	..
20	Chemicals and chemical products	..	..	..	..	..	..	..	..
21	Pharmaceuticals, medicinal, chemical and botanical products	62.7	59.3	53.6	55.4	78.1	42.4	40.5	34.0
22	Rubber and plastic products	11.9	12.4	9.3	12.9	10.9	14.6	16.0	15.3
23	Other non-metallic mineral products	14.2	12.3	11.1	11.9	14.5	13.3	13.3	13.6
24-25	Basic metals, metal products, except machinery and equipment	120.0	115.5	120.5	128.3	135.0	154.7	152.7	157.7
24	Basic metals	52.2	48.8	41.7	38.3	27.2	34.7	34.9	32.6
25	Fabricated metal products, except machinery and equipment	67.8	66.6	78.8	89.9	107.9	120.0	117.9	125.0
26-30	Computer, electronic, optical products; electrical machinery, transport equipment	506.4	510.3	449.4	363.0	394.9	416.6	436.3	475.0
26	Computer, electronic and optical products	224.7	221.2	217.0	171.4	182.0	176.1	170.5	183.5
27	Electrical equipment	50.9	44.3	46.6	40.0	40.8	44.1	48.1	56.2
28	Machinery and equipment n.e.c.	111.8	124.4	91.6	84.8	98.9	107.6	128.8	140.4
29	Motor vehicles, trailers and semi-trailers	60.0	52.7	36.1	19.3	27.9	28.9	30.8	33.0
30	Other transport equipment	58.8	67.5	58.1	47.5	45.4	59.8	58.0	62.0
31-33	Furniture; repair, installation of machinery and equipment	50.7	51.9	50.7	47.4	56.6	54.2	55.2	53.1
31	Furniture	..	10.5	11.6	13.7	12.9	14.2	16.1	16.5
32	Other manufacturing	..	20.1	18.6	17.7	27.0	20.0	18.6	17.4
33	Repair and installation of machinery and equipment	..	21.3	20.4	16.0	16.7	20.0	20.6	19.2
35-39	**ELECTRICITY, GAS, WATER AND WASTE MANAGEMENT**	30.3	38.0	46.0	49.8	49.9	52.4	51.6	49.6
35-36	Electricity, gas and water	..	34.3	43.2	41.8	44.2	43.8	43.7	41.2
37-39	Sewerage, waste management and remediation activities	..	3.8	2.8	8.1	5.7	8.6	7.9	8.5
41-43	**CONSTRUCTION**	50.7	66.6	60.5	73.3	61.5	77.0	51.9	41.8
45-99	**TOTAL SERVICES**	966.2	1 050.1	1 042.1	1 097.5	1 176.4	1 187.1	1 247.3	1 396.4
45-82	**Business sector services**	966.2	1 050.1	1 042.1	1 097.5	1 176.4	1 187.1	1 247.3	1 396.4
45-47	Wholesale and retail trade; motor vehicle and motorcycle repairs	73.7	62.3	69.3	49.4	60.8	54.4	69.1	78.6
49-53	Transportation and storage	13.5	17.1	18.4	21.8	22.1	28.2	26.6	33.3
55-56	Accommodation and food service activities	..	..	..	..	..	..	..	..
58-63	Information and communication	474.9	496.2	504.8	528.3	549.9	593.9	629.8	664.9
58-60	Publishing, audiovisual and broadcasting activities	..	151.7	154.8	158.8	159.8	150.7	144.5	192.3
58	Publishing activities	..	151.4	152.6	157.7	158.6	149.2	141.6	189.3
59-60	Motion picture, video and TV programme production; broadcasting activities	..	0.3	2.3	1.1	1.2	1.5	2.9	3.1
59	Motion picture, video and TV programme production; sound and music	..	..	..	1.0	..	..	..	..
60	Programming and broadcasting activities	..	..	..	0.1	..	..	..	..
61	Telecommunications	74.4	78.7	95.2	92.9	80.0	79.2	77.5	81.2
62-63	IT and other information services	..	265.8	254.7	276.6	310.0	364.0	407.9	391.4
62	Computer programming, consultancy and related activities	..	253.3	242.9	263.5	295.9	334.3	383.3	362.2
63	Information service activities	..	12.5	11.8	13.1	14.1	29.6	24.6	29.2
64-66	Financial and insurance activities	118.2	122.7	116.1	114.0	143.1	132.1	140.1	140.6
68-82	Real estate; professional, scientific and technical; administrative and support	285.8	351.8	333.6	384.1	400.6	378.4	381.6	479.0
68	Real estate activities	..	0.0	0.0	0.0	0.0	0.0	0.0	0.0
69-75x72	Professional, scientific and technical activities, except scientific R&D	..	293.6	274.3	318.5	327.9	300.7	315.9	408.5
72	Scientific research and development	41.5	43.4	37.2	49.8	45.5	62.0	51.0	59.8
77-82	Administrative and support service activities	..	14.8	22.1	15.8	27.1	15.8	14.7	10.8
84-99	Community, social and personal services	..	..	..	..	..	..	..	..
84-85	Public administration and defence; compulsory social security and education	..	..	..	..	..	..	..	..
86-88	Human health and social work activities	..	..	..	..	..	..	..	..
90-93	Arts, entertainment and recreation	..	..	..	..	..	..	..	..
94-99	Other services; household-employers; extraterritorial bodies	..	..	..	..	..	..	..	..

.. Not available

Note: Detailed metadata at: http://metalinks.oecd.org/anberd/20170419/301f.
   Information on data for Israel: http://oe.cd/israel-disclaimer.
Disclaimer: http://oe.cd/disclaimer

POLAND

R&D expenditure in industry by main activity of the enterprise, current prices
ISIC Rev. 4

Million USD PPP

		2007	2008	2009	2010	2011	2012	2013	2014
	TOTAL BUSINESS ENTERPRISE	1 091.2	1 293.9	1 384.5	1 539.6	1 954.9	2 973.6	3 573.6	4 283.7
01-03	**AGRICULTURE, FORESTRY AND FISHING**	5.4	9.6	11.0	12.2	15.0	18.5	17.7	19.3
05-09	**MINING AND QUARRYING**	0.4	0.4	0.5	0.6	10.5	122.3	149.7	64.8
10-33	**MANUFACTURING**	548.2	617.8	803.8	783.7	960.9	1 429.5	1 574.4	1 954.2
10-12	Food products, beverages and tobacco	51.2	49.3	94.5	58.6	35.4	33.3	79.4	233.0
13-15	Textiles, wearing apparel, leather and related products	12.8	12.9	6.4	8.1	9.1	12.6	14.8	21.4
13	Textiles	11.7	12.1	5.4	6.3	7.5	7.6	12.3	18.0
14	Wearing apparel	0.9	0.6	0.6	1.0	1.1	3.7	2.0	2.7
15	Leather and related products, footwear	0.1	0.2	0.4	0.8	0.5	1.3	0.5	0.7
16-18	Wood and paper products and printing	8.9	7.4	11.4	17.5	19.5	24.7	40.2	30.0
16	Wood and wood products, except furniture	2.0	3.4	3.7	4.3	6.3	8.7	13.0	7.3
17	Paper and paper products	..	..	..	..	8.3	3.2	3.6	10.5
18	Printing and reproduction of recorded media	..	..	..	..	4.9	12.7	23.6	12.2
19-23	Chemical, rubber, plastic, non-metallic mineral products	140.0	173.8	153.3	203.6	240.9	322.0	322.7	362.3
19	Coke and refined petroleum products	1.1	3.0	3.1	2.8	2.4	5.0	10.4	6.2
20-21	Chemical and pharmaceutical products	94.5	145.9	121.6	142.0	162.9	222.9	227.8	233.6
20	Chemicals and chemical products	27.5	44.7	36.4	55.8	70.1	78.7	104.9	82.2
21	Pharmaceuticals, medicinal, chemical and botanical products	67.0	101.2	85.3	86.2	92.9	144.1	122.9	151.5
22	Rubber and plastic products	35.2	16.7	10.3	33.9	57.1	62.2	57.8	88.5
23	Other non-metallic mineral products	9.2	8.1	18.3	24.9	18.4	31.9	26.7	34.0
24-25	Basic metals, metal products, except machinery and equipment	36.1	44.6	50.0	72.8	119.1	174.3	213.1	248.7
24	Basic metals	8.5	11.2	16.9	26.7	16.3	19.5	16.9	85.7
25	Fabricated metal products, except machinery and equipment	27.6	33.4	33.2	46.1	102.8	154.7	196.2	163.0
26-30	Computer, electronic, optical products; electrical machinery, transport equipment	247.2	274.4	416.5	373.7	480.0	751.2	831.4	963.5
26	Computer, electronic and optical products	33.8	41.6	48.4	84.4	74.0	89.0	84.6	95.1
27	Electrical equipment	80.3	62.5	73.5	108.2	118.7	264.3	186.9	166.8
28	Machinery and equipment n.e.c.	46.9	61.4	67.8	68.3	95.5	160.7	123.7	174.4
29	Motor vehicles, trailers and semi-trailers	54.7	77.8	185.8	50.3	101.2	125.8	310.6	390.6
30	Other transport equipment	31.4	30.9	41.0	62.4	90.4	111.3	125.6	136.5
31-33	Furniture; repair, installation of machinery and equipment	52.0	55.3	71.7	49.3	57.1	111.3	72.8	95.2
31	Furniture	33.0	14.1	17.7	3.9	11.8	31.6	26.9	29.2
32	Other manufacturing	7.2	13.5	19.1	13.9	17.3	36.8	24.7	31.1
33	Repair and installation of machinery and equipment	11.8	27.6	34.9	31.5	28.0	43.0	21.3	34.9
35-39	**ELECTRICITY, GAS, WATER AND WASTE MANAGEMENT**	2.0	1.8	19.9	4.6	12.2	40.0	110.7	72.6
35-36	Electricity, gas and water	..	..	..	..	..	..	69.4	23.1
37-39	Sewerage, waste management and remediation activities	..	..	..	..	..	..	41.3	49.5
41-43	**CONSTRUCTION**	5.8	3.8	7.4	10.4	31.3	30.4	72.0	31.9
45-99	**TOTAL SERVICES**	529.4	660.5	541.8	728.1	925.0	1 332.8	1 649.2	2 140.9
45-82	**Business sector services**	520.7	642.6	539.2	709.4	895.2	1 320.1	1 633.1	2 121.5
45-47	Wholesale and retail trade; motor vehicle and motorcycle repairs	17.3	60.8	70.9	74.0	127.7	209.8	289.0	327.0
49-53	Transportation and storage	..	..	..	..	..	..	..	..
55-56	Accommodation and food service activities	..	..	..	..	..	..	..	..
58-63	Information and communication	100.9	121.0	179.6	380.9	514.4	604.9	682.4	811.6
58-60	Publishing, audiovisual and broadcasting activities	..	..	..	..	100.5	27.8	28.6	40.0
58	Publishing activities	..	..	..	..	..	..	27.4	38.7
59-60	Motion picture, video and TV programme production; broadcasting activities	..	..	..	..	..	..	1.2	1.3
59	Motion picture, video and TV programme production; sound and music	..	..	..	..	..	..	..	..
60	Programming and broadcasting activities	..	..	..	..	..	..	..	..
61	Telecommunications	..	..	..	..	..	..	..	..
62-63	IT and other information services	..	..	..	..	..	..	..	..
62	Computer programming, consultancy and related activities	24.1	..	72.2	179.1	231.8	369.6	409.0	447.7
63	Information service activities	..	..	..	..	..	..	..	..
64-66	Financial and insurance activities	19.6	20.1	20.6	8.4	5.9	18.3	46.3	129.1
68-82	Real estate; professional, scientific and technical; administrative and support	381.4	434.5	266.2	245.2	233.2	483.2	596.9	838.1
68	Real estate activities	0.0	0.0	0.0	0.0	0.0	28.9	42.4	35.8
69-75x72	Professional, scientific and technical activities, except scientific R&D	8.6	4.1	13.0	18.7	30.3	122.3	107.6	234.5
72	Scientific research and development	372.9	430.4	253.2	226.5	202.7	327.7	440.1	558.0
77-82	Administrative and support service activities	0.0	0.0	0.0	0.0	0.3	4.3	6.8	9.7
84-99	Community, social and personal services	8.7	17.9	2.6	18.7	29.9	12.7	16.1	19.4
84-85	Public administration and defence; compulsory social security and education	..	..	..	..	0.7	0.7	0.9	1.4
86-88	Human health and social work activities	..	12.1	..	..	21.1	10.5	8.8	10.6
90-93	Arts, entertainment and recreation	..	..	..	..	6.9	0.3	0.3	0.7
94-99	Other services; household-employers; extraterritorial bodies	..	4.6	..	0.9	1.2	1.2	6.1	6.7

.. Not available

Note: Detailed metadata at: http://metalinks.oecd.org/anberd/20170419/301f.
    Information on data for Israel: http://oe.cd/israel-disclaimer.
Disclaimer: http://oe.cd/disclaimer

POLAND

R&D expenditure in industry by main activity of the enterprise, constant prices
ISIC Rev. 4

2010 USD PPP

Code	Activity	2007	2008	2009	2010	2011	2012	2013	2014
	TOTAL BUSINESS ENTERPRISE	1 232.2	1 395.9	1 458.6	1 539.6	1 893.7	2 806.2	3 295.8	3 926.4
01-03	**AGRICULTURE, FORESTRY AND FISHING**	6.1	10.4	11.6	12.2	14.6	17.5	16.3	17.7
05-09	**MINING AND QUARRYING**	0.4	0.5	0.5	0.6	10.1	115.4	138.1	59.4
10-33	**MANUFACTURING**	619.1	666.5	846.8	783.7	930.8	1 349.0	1 452.0	1 791.2
10-12	Food products, beverages and tobacco	57.8	53.2	99.6	58.6	34.3	31.5	73.2	213.6
13-15	Textiles, wearing apparel, leather and related products	14.4	13.9	6.7	8.1	8.8	11.9	13.6	19.7
13	Textiles	13.3	13.0	5.7	6.3	7.3	7.1	11.3	16.5
14	Wearing apparel	1.0	0.7	0.6	1.0	1.0	3.5	1.8	2.5
15	Leather and related products, footwear	0.1	0.3	0.4	0.8	0.5	1.3	0.5	0.6
16-18	Wood and paper products and printing	10.1	8.0	12.0	17.5	18.9	23.3	37.1	27.5
16	Wood and wood products, except furniture	2.3	3.6	3.9	4.3	6.1	8.2	12.0	6.7
17	Paper and paper products	..	..	..	..	8.0	3.0	3.3	9.6
18	Printing and reproduction of recorded media	..	..	..	..	4.7	12.0	21.8	11.2
19-23	Chemical, rubber, plastic, non-metallic mineral products	158.1	187.4	161.5	203.6	233.3	303.8	297.6	332.1
19	Coke and refined petroleum products	1.2	3.2	3.3	2.8	2.3	4.7	9.6	5.7
20-21	Chemical and pharmaceutical products	106.7	157.4	128.2	142.0	157.8	210.3	210.1	214.1
20	Chemicals and chemical products	31.1	48.3	38.3	55.8	67.9	74.3	96.7	75.3
21	Pharmaceuticals, medicinal, chemical and botanical products	75.6	109.2	89.8	86.2	90.0	136.0	113.4	138.8
22	Rubber and plastic products	39.7	18.0	10.8	33.9	55.3	58.7	53.3	81.1
23	Other non-metallic mineral products	10.4	8.8	19.2	24.9	17.9	30.1	24.6	31.2
24-25	Basic metals, metal products, except machinery and equipment	40.8	48.1	52.7	72.8	115.4	164.4	196.6	228.0
24	Basic metals	9.6	12.1	17.8	26.7	15.8	18.4	15.6	78.6
25	Fabricated metal products, except machinery and equipment	31.2	36.0	34.9	46.1	99.6	146.0	180.9	149.4
26-30	Computer, electronic, optical products; electrical machinery, transport equipment	279.1	296.5	438.8	373.7	464.9	708.9	766.7	883.2
26	Computer, electronic and optical products	38.2	44.9	51.0	84.4	71.7	84.0	78.0	87.2
27	Electrical equipment	90.7	67.5	77.5	108.2	115.0	249.5	172.4	152.9
28	Machinery and equipment n.e.c.	53.0	66.2	71.4	68.3	92.5	151.6	114.0	159.9
29	Motor vehicles, trailers and semi-trailers	61.8	84.0	195.7	50.3	98.0	118.7	286.5	358.0
30	Other transport equipment	35.5	33.4	43.2	62.4	87.6	105.0	115.8	125.1
31-33	Furniture; repair, installation of machinery and equipment	58.7	59.6	75.6	49.3	55.3	105.1	67.2	87.3
31	Furniture	37.3	15.2	18.6	3.9	11.5	29.8	24.8	26.7
32	Other manufacturing	8.2	14.6	20.1	13.9	16.7	34.7	22.7	28.5
33	Repair and installation of machinery and equipment	13.3	29.8	36.8	31.5	27.2	40.6	19.6	32.0
35-39	**ELECTRICITY, GAS, WATER AND WASTE MANAGEMENT**	2.3	1.9	20.9	4.6	11.8	37.8	102.1	66.5
35-36	Electricity, gas and water	..	..	..	..	..	..	64.0	21.2
37-39	Sewerage, waste management and remediation activities	..	..	..	..	..	..	38.1	45.4
41-43	**CONSTRUCTION**	6.5	4.1	7.8	10.4	30.3	28.7	66.4	29.2
45-99	**TOTAL SERVICES**	597.9	712.6	570.8	728.1	896.1	1 257.8	1 521.0	1 962.3
45-82	**Business sector services**	588.0	693.3	568.1	709.4	867.2	1 245.8	1 506.1	1 944.6
45-47	**Wholesale and retail trade; motor vehicle and motorcycle repairs**	19.6	65.6	74.7	74.0	123.7	198.0	266.5	299.7
49-53	**Transportation and storage**	..	..	..	..	..	..	..	..
55-56	**Accommodation and food service activities**	..	..	..	..	..	..	..	..
58-63	**Information and communication**	113.9	130.6	189.2	380.9	498.3	570.8	629.3	743.9
58-60	Publishing, audiovisual and broadcasting activities	..	..	..	..	97.4	26.3	26.4	36.6
58	Publishing activities	..	..	..	..	..	..	25.3	35.4
59-60	Motion picture, video and TV programme production; broadcasting activities	..	..	..	..	..	..	1.2	1.1
59	Motion picture, video and TV programme production; sound and music	..	..	..	..	..	..	..	..
60	Programming and broadcasting activities	..	..	..	..	..	..	..	..
61	Telecommunications	..	..	..	..	..	..	..	..
62-63	IT and other information services	..	..	..	..	..	..	..	..
62	Computer programming, consultancy and related activities	27.3	..	76.0	179.1	224.6	348.8	377.2	410.4
63	Information service activities	..	..	..	..	..	..	..	..
64-66	**Financial and insurance activities**	22.1	21.7	21.7	8.4	5.8	17.3	42.7	118.3
68-82	**Real estate; professional, scientific and technical; administrative and support**	430.7	468.7	280.5	245.2	225.9	456.0	550.5	768.2
68	Real estate activities	0.0	0.0	0.0	0.0	0.0	27.3	39.1	32.8
69-75x72	Professional, scientific and technical activities, except scientific R&D	9.7	4.4	13.7	18.7	29.3	115.4	99.3	214.9
72	Scientific research and development	421.1	464.3	266.7	226.5	196.3	309.2	405.9	511.5
77-82	Administrative and support service activities	0.0	0.0	0.0	0.0	0.3	4.0	6.2	8.9
84-99	Community, social and personal services	9.8	19.3	2.7	18.7	28.9	12.0	14.8	17.8
84-85	Public administration and defence; compulsory social security and education	..	..	..	..	0.7	0.6	0.8	1.3
86-88	Human health and social work activities	..	13.1	..	..	20.4	9.9	8.1	9.7
90-93	Arts, entertainment and recreation	..	..	..	..	6.7	0.3	0.3	0.7
94-99	Other services; household-employers; extraterritorial bodies	..	4.9	..	0.9	1.1	1.2	5.7	6.2

.. Not available

Note: Detailed metadata at: http://metalinks.oecd.org/anberd/20170419/301f.
Information on data for Israel: http://oe.cd/israel-disclaimer.

Disclaimer: http://oe.cd/disclaimer

PORTUGAL

R&D expenditure in industry by main activity of the enterprise, current prices
ISIC Rev. 4

Million USD PPP

		2007	2008	2009	2010	2011	2012	2013	2014
	TOTAL BUSINESS ENTERPRISE	1 560.6	2 035.8	2 092.5	2 035.9	1 952.1	1 905.1	1 840.1	1 794.9
01-03	**AGRICULTURE, FORESTRY AND FISHING**	0.6	2.8	2.9	2.4	4.6	7.9	11.7	7.9
05-09	**MINING AND QUARRYING**	1.3	7.9	4.9	4.9	6.4	4.4	6.5	5.9
10-33	**MANUFACTURING**	561.6	717.5	677.9	663.1	692.7	781.3	727.9	744.6
10-12	Food products, beverages and tobacco	76.9	85.1	74.0	75.5	66.4	117.3	101.1	97.2
13-15	Textiles, wearing apparel, leather and related products	28.2	28.8	31.3	33.2	33.2	38.4	39.0	44.1
13	Textiles	16.7	20.8	19.4	22.3	20.0	23.0	19.0	23.4
14	Wearing apparel	8.9	4.5	5.5	4.8	5.0	5.8	4.4	5.7
15	Leather and related products, footwear	2.6	3.5	6.4	6.1	8.3	9.6	15.6	15.0
16-18	Wood and paper products and printing	24.9	46.1	34.8	40.7	54.8	58.9	61.7	56.6
16	Wood and wood products, except furniture	17.9	16.5	13.7	11.0	15.3	16.0	14.5	15.1
17	Paper and paper products	6.1	11.8	4.8	12.8	21.1	25.7	26.4	19.5
18	Printing and reproduction of recorded media	0.9	17.8	16.3	16.9	18.4	17.1	20.8	22.1
19-23	Chemical, rubber, plastic, non-metallic mineral products	186.5	231.8	234.0	253.6	259.7	297.8	269.7	259.7
19	Coke and refined petroleum products	9.0	10.5	16.1	11.8	8.7	7.1	5.8	3.7
20-21	Chemical and pharmaceutical products	117.1	161.2	139.2	173.7	169.4	188.6	187.0	172.1
20	Chemicals and chemical products	24.5	26.0	30.7	48.4	29.1	40.8	41.9	42.0
21	Pharmaceuticals, medicinal, chemical and botanical products	92.5	135.2	108.5	125.3	140.4	147.8	145.0	130.1
22	Rubber and plastic products	17.6	22.1	38.5	32.1	34.8	38.9	35.6	36.7
23	Other non-metallic mineral products	42.7	38.1	40.3	36.0	46.8	63.1	41.4	47.1
24-25	Basic metals, metal products, except machinery and equipment	45.8	72.4	65.1	63.0	61.3	57.7	59.5	77.9
24	Basic metals	10.4	22.3	18.9	19.6	19.2	19.2	22.0	33.1
25	Fabricated metal products, except machinery and equipment	35.4	50.2	46.2	43.3	42.1	38.5	37.5	44.8
26-30	Computer, electronic, optical products; electrical machinery, transport equipment	175.0	226.2	206.7	177.9	200.9	195.4	177.4	190.0
26	Computer, electronic and optical products	44.6	46.9	33.4	31.1	42.5	43.0	41.0	49.9
27	Electrical equipment	31.9	39.1	43.1	54.8	70.8	62.9	60.0	52.8
28	Machinery and equipment n.e.c.	18.9	24.7	23.3	22.1	25.8	34.6	31.7	32.6
29	Motor vehicles, trailers and semi-trailers	72.6	108.3	100.2	64.9	55.4	47.3	40.9	50.2
30	Other transport equipment	7.0	7.2	6.6	4.9	6.5	7.6	3.8	4.5
31-33	Furniture; repair, installation of machinery and equipment	24.3	26.9	32.0	19.3	16.4	15.8	19.5	19.1
31	Furniture	6.3	7.8	7.4	8.2	6.4	7.3	7.8	8.0
32	Other manufacturing	3.5	4.1	6.3	4.6	4.9	4.1	4.7	3.0
33	Repair and installation of machinery and equipment	14.4	15.0	18.3	6.4	5.0	4.4	7.0	8.1
35-39	**ELECTRICITY, GAS, WATER AND WASTE MANAGEMENT**	68.0	130.8	116.4	90.2	24.3	33.9	17.0	16.2
35-36	Electricity, gas and water	61.2	121.7	109.5	84.7	17.8	15.2	9.1	8.8
37-39	Sewerage, waste management and remediation activities	6.8	9.0	6.9	5.5	6.5	18.7	7.9	7.3
41-43	**CONSTRUCTION**	9.2	12.2	23.8	15.6	16.6	8.5	13.2	14.1
45-99	**TOTAL SERVICES**	919.9	1 164.7	1 266.6	1 259.8	1 207.6	1 069.1	1 063.8	1 006.2
45-82	**Business sector services**	910.5	1 151.2	1 245.2	1 227.4	1 183.6	1 046.5	1 040.1	975.5
45-47	Wholesale and retail trade; motor vehicle and motorcycle repairs	32.4	49.1	49.6	141.5	138.1	129.0	81.5	96.2
49-53	Transportation and storage	79.8	79.8	58.6	46.4	41.7	19.4	23.1	23.2
55-56	Accommodation and food service activities	0.0	0.0	0.0	0.0	0.3	0.2	0.1	0.1
58-63	Information and communication	348.8	460.8	594.8	531.6	532.4	449.1	412.7	337.5
58-60	Publishing, audiovisual and broadcasting activities	25.3	30.1	37.1	37.9	29.4	25.7	23.6	26.7
58	Publishing activities	14.3	26.9	30.2	32.0	22.6	19.6	22.3	..
59-60	Motion picture, video and TV programme production; broadcasting activities	11.0	3.2	6.9	5.9	6.9	6.0	1.3	..
59	Motion picture, video and TV programme production; sound and music	..	..	..	0.5	0.2	0.5	0.1	..
60	Programming and broadcasting activities	..	..	..	5.4	6.7	5.6	1.2	..
61	Telecommunications	184.7	234.8	347.4	294.0	339.1	225.2	184.1	86.1
62-63	IT and other information services	138.8	195.9	210.3	199.7	163.9	198.2	204.9	224.7
62	Computer programming, consultancy and related activities	134.8	189.0	204.5	194.5	158.6	188.9	197.3	216.1
63	Information service activities	4.0	6.9	5.8	5.2	5.2	9.3	7.6	8.6
64-66	Financial and insurance activities	273.0	334.0	258.5	274.5	244.1	246.6	272.2	259.2
68-82	Real estate; professional, scientific and technical; administrative and support	176.5	227.4	283.3	233.3	227.0	202.1	250.5	259.3
68	Real estate activities	0.0	0.0	0.0	0.0	0.0	0.0	0.0	0.0
69-75x72	Professional, scientific and technical activities, except scientific R&D	124.2	180.0	220.6	168.5	138.1	95.2	97.5	89.8
72	Scientific research and development	31.1	36.7	43.8	50.1	73.4	89.0	137.0	149.1
77-82	Administrative and support service activities	21.2	10.7	18.9	14.7	15.5	17.9	15.9	20.4
84-99	**Community, social and personal services**	9.4	13.4	21.4	32.4	24.0	22.6	23.7	30.7
84-85	Public administration and defence; compulsory social security and education	0.9	0.8	2.3	2.2	2.2	1.5	4.0	3.9
86-88	Human health and social work activities	2.4	2.7	3.9	5.0	7.3	6.9	7.7	8.2
90-93	Arts, entertainment and recreation	0.2	0.8	1.1	0.5	1.1	0.6	3.8	1.4
94-99	Other services; household-employers; extraterritorial bodies	5.8	9.1	14.1	24.8	13.3	13.6	8.2	17.2

.. Not available

Note: Detailed metadata at: http://metalinks.oecd.org/anberd/20170419/301f.
   Information on data for Israel: http://oe.cd/israel-disclaimer.
Disclaimer: http://oe.cd/disclaimer

PORTUGAL

R&D expenditure in industry by main activity of the enterprise, constant prices
ISIC Rev. 4

2010 USD PPP

		2007	2008	2009	2010	2011	2012	2013	2014
	TOTAL BUSINESS ENTERPRISE	1 682.3	2 118.6	2 121.5	2 035.9	1 960.9	1 866.8	1 698.1	1 627.4
01-03	**AGRICULTURE, FORESTRY AND FISHING**	0.6	2.9	2.9	2.4	4.6	7.7	10.8	7.1
05-09	**MINING AND QUARRYING**	1.4	8.3	4.9	4.9	6.4	4.3	6.0	5.4
10-33	**MANUFACTURING**	605.4	746.6	687.3	663.1	695.8	765.6	671.8	675.1
10-12	Food products, beverages and tobacco	82.8	88.6	75.1	75.5	66.7	115.0	93.3	88.1
13-15	Textiles, wearing apparel, leather and related products	30.4	30.0	31.7	33.2	33.4	37.6	36.0	40.0
13	Textiles	18.0	21.7	19.7	22.3	20.1	22.5	17.5	21.2
14	Wearing apparel	9.6	4.6	5.5	4.8	5.0	5.7	4.1	5.2
15	Leather and related products, footwear	2.8	3.7	6.5	6.1	8.3	9.4	14.4	13.6
16-18	Wood and paper products and printing	26.9	48.0	35.2	40.7	55.1	57.7	56.9	51.3
16	Wood and wood products, except furniture	19.3	17.1	13.9	11.0	15.4	15.7	13.4	13.7
17	Paper and paper products	6.6	12.3	4.8	12.8	21.2	25.2	24.3	17.6
18	Printing and reproduction of recorded media	0.9	18.5	16.5	16.9	18.5	16.8	19.2	20.0
19-23	Chemical, rubber, plastic, non-metallic mineral products	201.0	241.3	237.3	253.6	260.8	291.8	248.9	235.5
19	Coke and refined petroleum products	9.8	10.9	16.3	11.8	8.7	7.0	5.3	3.4
20-21	Chemical and pharmaceutical products	126.2	167.8	141.1	173.7	170.2	184.8	172.6	156.1
20	Chemicals and chemical products	26.4	27.1	31.1	48.4	29.2	40.0	38.7	38.1
21	Pharmaceuticals, medicinal, chemical and botanical products	99.8	140.7	110.0	125.3	141.0	144.9	133.8	118.0
22	Rubber and plastic products	19.0	23.0	39.0	32.1	35.0	38.2	32.9	33.3
23	Other non-metallic mineral products	46.1	39.6	40.8	36.0	47.0	61.8	38.2	42.7
24-25	Basic metals, metal products, except machinery and equipment	49.4	75.4	66.0	63.0	61.6	56.6	54.9	70.6
24	Basic metals	11.2	23.2	19.2	19.6	19.3	18.8	20.3	30.0
25	Fabricated metal products, except machinery and equipment	38.2	52.2	46.8	43.3	42.3	37.7	34.6	40.6
26-30	Computer, electronic, optical products; electrical machinery, transport equipment	188.7	235.4	209.6	177.9	201.9	191.5	163.8	172.3
26	Computer, electronic and optical products	48.1	48.8	33.9	31.1	42.7	42.2	37.8	45.2
27	Electrical equipment	34.4	40.7	43.7	54.8	71.1	61.6	55.4	47.8
28	Machinery and equipment n.e.c.	20.4	25.7	23.6	22.1	25.9	33.9	29.3	29.6
29	Motor vehicles, trailers and semi-trailers	78.2	112.7	101.6	64.9	55.6	46.4	37.8	45.5
30	Other transport equipment	7.5	7.5	6.7	4.9	6.5	7.4	3.5	4.1
31-33	Furniture; repair, installation of machinery and equipment	26.2	28.0	32.5	19.3	16.4	15.5	18.0	17.3
31	Furniture	6.8	8.1	7.5	8.2	6.4	7.2	7.2	7.2
32	Other manufacturing	3.8	4.3	6.4	4.6	5.0	4.0	4.3	2.7
33	Repair and installation of machinery and equipment	15.6	15.6	18.5	6.4	5.0	4.3	6.5	7.3
35-39	**ELECTRICITY, GAS, WATER AND WASTE MANAGEMENT**	73.3	136.1	118.0	90.2	24.4	33.2	15.7	14.7
35-36	Electricity, gas and water	66.0	126.7	111.0	84.7	17.9	14.9	8.4	8.0
37-39	Sewerage, waste management and remediation activities	7.3	9.4	7.0	5.5	6.5	18.3	7.2	6.7
41-43	**CONSTRUCTION**	10.0	12.7	24.2	15.6	16.7	8.3	12.1	12.8
45-99	**TOTAL SERVICES**	991.6	1 212.0	1 284.2	1 259.8	1 213.0	1 047.5	981.7	912.3
45-82	**Business sector services**	981.5	1 198.0	1 262.5	1 227.4	1 188.9	1 025.4	959.9	884.5
45-47	Wholesale and retail trade; motor vehicle and motorcycle repairs	34.9	51.1	50.3	141.5	138.7	126.4	75.2	87.3
49-53	Transportation and storage	86.0	83.0	59.6	46.4	41.9	19.0	21.3	21.0
55-56	Accommodation and food service activities	0.0	0.0	0.0	0.0	0.3	0.2	0.1	0.1
58-63	Information and communication	376.0	479.5	603.0	531.6	534.8	440.0	380.9	306.0
58-60	Publishing, audiovisual and broadcasting activities	27.3	31.3	37.6	37.9	29.6	25.1	21.8	24.2
58	Publishing activities	15.4	28.0	30.7	32.0	22.7	19.2	20.6	..
59-60	Motion picture, video and TV programme production; broadcasting activities	11.9	3.3	7.0	5.9	6.9	5.9	1.2	..
59	Motion picture, video and TV programme production; sound and music	..	..	..	0.5	0.2	0.5	0.1	..
60	Programming and broadcasting activities	..	..	..	5.4	6.7	5.5	1.1	..
61	Telecommunications	199.1	244.3	352.2	294.0	340.7	220.6	169.9	78.0
62-63	IT and other information services	149.6	203.9	213.2	199.7	164.6	194.3	189.1	203.7
62	Computer programming, consultancy and related activities	145.4	196.7	207.3	194.5	159.4	185.1	182.1	195.9
63	Information service activities	4.3	7.2	5.9	5.2	5.3	9.1	7.0	7.8
64-66	Financial and insurance activities	294.3	347.5	262.1	274.5	245.2	241.7	251.2	235.0
68-82	Real estate; professional, scientific and technical; administrative and support	190.2	236.7	287.3	233.3	228.0	198.0	231.1	235.1
68	Real estate activities	0.0	0.0	0.0	0.0	0.0	0.0	0.0	0.0
69-75x72	Professional, scientific and technical activities, except scientific R&D	133.9	187.3	223.7	168.5	138.7	93.3	90.0	81.4
72	Scientific research and development	33.5	38.2	44.4	50.1	73.7	87.2	126.5	135.2
77-82	Administrative and support service activities	22.9	11.2	19.2	14.7	15.6	17.6	14.7	18.5
84-99	Community, social and personal services	10.1	14.0	21.7	32.4	24.1	22.1	21.8	27.8
84-85	Public administration and defence; compulsory social security and education	0.9	0.8	2.3	2.2	2.2	1.5	3.7	3.5
86-88	Human health and social work activities	2.6	2.8	3.9	5.0	7.3	6.8	7.1	7.4
90-93	Arts, entertainment and recreation	0.2	0.8	1.1	0.5	1.1	0.5	3.5	1.2
94-99	Other services; household-employers; extraterritorial bodies	6.3	9.5	14.3	24.8	13.4	13.3	7.5	15.6

.. Not available

Note: Detailed metadata at: http://metalinks.oecd.org/anberd/20170419/301f.
Information on data for Israel: http://oe.cd/israel-disclaimer.
Disclaimer: http://oe.cd/disclaimer

PORTUGAL

R&D expenditure in industry by product field, current prices
ISIC Rev. 4

Million USD PPP

		2007	2008	2009	2010	2011	2012	2013	2014
	TOTAL BUSINESS ENTERPRISE	..	2 035.8	2 092.5	2 035.9	1 952.1	1 905.1	1 840.1	1 794.9
01-03	**AGRICULTURE, FORESTRY AND FISHING**	..	11.4	12.4	10.3	18.5	27.3	26.2	23.2
05-09	**MINING AND QUARRYING**	..	21.9	32.2	19.1	23.8	13.0	13.0	13.4
10-33	**MANUFACTURING**	..	787.9	723.3	741.7	752.5	844.8	804.9	842.6
10-12	Food products, beverages and tobacco	..	81.5	71.5	75.8	63.8	109.0	89.7	91.0
13-15	Textiles, wearing apparel, leather and related products	..	32.7	35.4	35.5	35.9	40.9	40.9	45.6
13	Textiles	..	22.9	20.3	23.0	20.4	24.3	23.1	28.5
14	Wearing apparel	..	4.8	8.0	6.4	6.9	5.1	3.7	3.7
15	Leather and related products, footwear	..	5.0	7.1	6.1	8.6	11.5	14.1	13.3
16-18	Wood and paper products and printing	..	28.3	23.0	28.5	37.3	44.6	46.7	40.6
16	Wood and wood products, except furniture	..	13.7	13.1	9.8	11.9	15.6	14.1	13.8
17	Paper and paper products	..	12.6	9.6	18.3	25.3	28.2	31.9	25.8
18	Printing and reproduction of recorded media	..	2.0	0.3	0.5	0.1	0.9	0.7	1.0
19-23	Chemical, rubber, plastic, non-metallic mineral products	..	262.9	234.8	269.3	267.7	313.3	283.7	277.3
19	Coke and refined petroleum products	..	5.0	8.5	10.9	0.3	5.9	3.2	2.9
20-21	Chemical and pharmaceutical products	..	193.6	162.2	199.9	195.4	215.4	208.5	199.7
20	Chemicals and chemical products	..	35.1	40.4	54.4	36.7	46.9	45.0	46.8
21	Pharmaceuticals, medicinal, chemical and botanical products	..	158.6	121.9	145.5	158.7	168.5	163.5	152.8
22	Rubber and plastic products	..	24.6	31.3	21.7	26.2	26.5	27.8	28.4
23	Other non-metallic mineral products	..	39.6	32.8	36.8	45.7	65.5	44.2	46.3
24-25	Basic metals, metal products, except machinery and equipment	..	59.7	58.4	55.1	54.8	49.8	54.0	69.2
24	Basic metals	..	23.5	19.4	20.3	21.5	19.8	22.7	34.1
25	Fabricated metal products, except machinery and equipment	..	36.2	39.1	34.8	33.3	30.0	31.3	35.1
26-30	Computer, electronic, optical products; electrical machinery, transport equipment	..	290.3	281.8	253.3	265.5	258.8	262.8	290.1
26	Computer, electronic and optical products	..	67.9	55.2	54.5	62.5	43.5	65.4	81.8
27	Electrical equipment	..	60.5	46.2	68.6	61.3	53.9	56.9	55.0
28	Machinery and equipment n.e.c.	..	31.2	45.4	33.7	44.9	45.6	40.8	44.3
29	Motor vehicles, trailers and semi-trailers	..	111.9	122.5	83.6	77.2	90.1	75.2	83.5
30	Other transport equipment	..	18.8	12.6	12.9	19.6	25.8	24.5	25.5
31-33	Furniture; repair, installation of machinery and equipment	..	32.6	18.4	24.1	27.4	28.4	27.1	28.7
31	Furniture	..	3.9	6.7	8.0	5.8	7.1	8.2	8.0
32	Other manufacturing	..	10.4	9.7	12.3	16.6	14.7	12.2	14.2
33	Repair and installation of machinery and equipment	..	18.2	2.0	3.8	5.0	6.5	6.6	6.6
35-39	**ELECTRICITY, GAS, WATER AND WASTE MANAGEMENT**	..	131.9	134.7	98.3	31.9	38.4	21.4	23.8
35-36	Electricity, gas and water	..	125.0	121.9	90.4	18.8	15.0	8.2	10.7
37-39	Sewerage, waste management and remediation activities	..	6.9	12.7	7.9	13.1	23.3	13.2	13.1
41-43	**CONSTRUCTION**	..	18.4	40.3	15.9	13.7	7.5	12.7	13.3
45-99	**TOTAL SERVICES**	..	1 064.3	1 149.7	1 150.6	1 111.7	974.0	961.9	878.7
45-82	**Business sector services**	..	1 055.9	1 130.2	1 134.5	1 098.6	963.9	942.6	844.6
45-47	Wholesale and retail trade; motor vehicle and motorcycle repairs	..	37.9	53.1	62.4	57.5	71.7	69.8	78.0
49-53	Transportation and storage	..	36.7	29.1	45.4	34.2	12.3	17.7	16.6
55-56	Accommodation and food service activities	..	0.0	0.0	0.0	0.9	6.2	6.2	1.4
58-63	Information and communication	..	627.3	705.4	678.8	702.2	605.0	543.7	462.3
58-60	Publishing, audiovisual and broadcasting activities	..	85.6	67.6	96.5	75.7	90.0	112.1	104.5
58	Publishing activities	..	..	63.9	94.0	70.6	87.1	110.0	104.1
59-60	Motion picture, video and TV programme production; broadcasting activities	..	..	3.7	2.5	5.1	2.9	2.0	0.4
59	Motion picture, video and TV programme production; sound and music	..	..	..	..	2.1	0.8	0.8	0.4
60	Programming and broadcasting activities	..	..	..	..	3.0	2.1	1.3	0.0
61	Telecommunications	..	317.0	428.5	390.1	447.6	328.3	248.7	147.2
62-63	IT and other information services	..	224.7	209.3	192.2	178.9	186.7	183.0	210.6
62	Computer programming, consultancy and related activities	..	196.0	187.8	172.1	131.6	157.5	157.1	182.9
63	Information service activities	..	28.7	21.5	20.1	47.4	29.3	25.9	27.7
64-66	Financial and insurance activities	..	254.1	207.6	180.4	146.7	148.9	151.8	135.4
68-82	Real estate; professional, scientific and technical; administrative and support	..	100.0	135.1	167.5	157.1	119.7	153.5	151.1
68	Real estate activities	..	0.0	2.0	1.5	1.3	0.9	1.6	1.9
69-75x72	Professional, scientific and technical activities, except scientific R&D	..	63.9	94.8	126.1	118.2	73.2	83.1	72.7
72	Scientific research and development	..	32.2	36.3	36.9	33.2	38.6	61.0	69.8
77-82	Administrative and support service activities	..	3.8	2.0	3.0	4.4	7.0	7.7	6.6
84-99	Community, social and personal services	..	8.3	19.4	16.1	13.1	10.2	19.3	34.1
84-85	Public administration and defence; compulsory social security and education	..	2.8	0.1	0.3	0.6	1.2	1.4	1.9
86-88	Human health and social work activities	..	3.4	12.1	5.6	10.2	7.9	14.2	27.6
90-93	Arts, entertainment and recreation	..	0.5	0.4	0.5	0.6	0.5	0.6	1.4
94-99	Other services; household-employers; extraterritorial bodies	..	1.5	6.8	9.7	1.7	0.6	3.1	3.2

.. Not available

Note: Detailed metadata at: http://metalinks.oecd.org/anberd/20170419/301f.
   Information on data for Israel: http://oe.cd/israel-disclaimer.
Disclaimer: http://oe.cd/disclaimer

PORTUGAL

R&D expenditure in industry by product field, constant prices
ISIC Rev. 4

2010 USD PPP

		2007	2008	2009	2010	2011	2012	2013	2014
	TOTAL BUSINESS ENTERPRISE	..	2 118.6	2 121.5	2 035.9	1 960.9	1 866.8	1 698.1	1 627.4
01-03	**AGRICULTURE, FORESTRY AND FISHING**	..	11.8	12.6	10.3	18.6	26.8	24.2	21.1
05-09	**MINING AND QUARRYING**	..	22.8	32.7	19.1	23.9	12.8	12.0	12.1
10-33	**MANUFACTURING**	..	820.0	733.3	741.7	755.9	827.8	742.8	763.9
10-12	Food products, beverages and tobacco	..	84.8	72.5	75.8	64.1	106.8	82.8	82.5
13-15	Textiles, wearing apparel, leather and related products	..	34.0	35.9	35.5	36.0	40.1	37.7	41.3
13	Textiles	..	23.8	20.6	23.0	20.5	23.8	21.3	25.9
14	Wearing apparel	..	5.0	8.1	6.4	6.9	5.0	3.4	3.4
15	Leather and related products, footwear	..	5.2	7.2	6.1	8.6	11.2	13.0	12.1
16-18	Wood and paper products and printing	..	29.5	23.3	28.5	37.5	43.7	43.1	36.8
16	Wood and wood products, except furniture	..	14.3	13.3	9.8	12.0	15.3	13.0	12.5
17	Paper and paper products	..	13.2	9.7	18.3	25.4	27.6	29.4	23.4
18	Printing and reproduction of recorded media	..	2.1	0.3	0.5	0.1	0.9	0.6	0.9
19-23	Chemical, rubber, plastic, non-metallic mineral products	..	273.6	238.1	269.3	268.9	307.0	261.8	251.4
19	Coke and refined petroleum products	..	5.2	8.7	10.9	0.3	5.8	2.9	2.7
20-21	Chemical and pharmaceutical products	..	201.5	164.5	199.9	196.3	211.1	192.4	181.0
20	Chemicals and chemical products	..	36.5	40.9	54.4	36.9	46.0	41.5	42.5
21	Pharmaceuticals, medicinal, chemical and botanical products	..	165.0	123.5	145.5	159.5	165.1	150.9	138.6
22	Rubber and plastic products	..	25.6	31.7	21.7	26.3	26.0	25.7	25.7
23	Other non-metallic mineral products	..	41.2	33.2	36.8	46.0	64.1	40.8	42.0
24-25	Basic metals, metal products, except machinery and equipment	..	62.1	59.2	55.1	55.1	48.8	49.8	62.7
24	Basic metals	..	24.5	19.6	20.3	21.6	19.4	20.9	31.0
25	Fabricated metal products, except machinery and equipment	..	37.7	39.6	34.8	33.4	29.4	28.9	31.8
26-30	Computer, electronic, optical products; electrical machinery, transport equipment	..	302.1	285.7	253.3	266.7	253.6	242.5	263.0
26	Computer, electronic and optical products	..	70.6	55.9	54.5	62.8	42.6	60.4	74.2
27	Electrical equipment	..	63.0	46.8	68.6	61.6	52.8	52.5	49.9
28	Machinery and equipment n.e.c.	..	32.4	46.0	33.7	45.1	44.7	37.7	40.2
29	Motor vehicles, trailers and semi-trailers	..	116.4	124.2	83.6	77.6	88.2	69.4	75.7
30	Other transport equipment	..	19.6	12.8	12.9	19.7	25.2	22.6	23.1
31-33	Furniture; repair, installation of machinery and equipment	..	33.9	18.6	24.1	27.5	27.9	25.0	26.1
31	Furniture	..	4.1	6.8	8.0	5.8	7.0	7.6	7.2
32	Other manufacturing	..	10.8	9.8	12.3	16.7	14.4	11.3	12.9
33	Repair and installation of machinery and equipment	..	19.0	2.0	3.8	5.0	6.4	6.1	6.0
35-39	**ELECTRICITY, GAS, WATER AND WASTE MANAGEMENT**	..	137.3	136.5	98.3	32.1	37.6	19.7	21.6
35-36	Electricity, gas and water	..	130.1	123.6	90.4	18.9	14.7	7.5	9.7
37-39	Sewerage, waste management and remediation activities	..	7.2	12.9	7.9	13.1	22.9	12.2	11.8
41-43	**CONSTRUCTION**	..	19.2	40.8	15.9	13.8	7.4	11.7	12.0
45-99	**TOTAL SERVICES**	..	1 107.5	1 165.6	1 150.6	1 116.7	954.4	887.7	796.7
45-82	**Business sector services**	..	1 098.9	1 145.9	1 134.5	1 103.6	944.5	869.9	765.8
45-47	Wholesale and retail trade; motor vehicle and motorcycle repairs	..	39.4	53.8	62.4	57.8	70.3	64.4	70.7
49-53	Transportation and storage	..	38.2	29.5	45.4	34.3	12.1	16.3	15.0
55-56	Accommodation and food service activities	..	0.0	0.0	0.0	0.9	6.0	5.7	1.2
58-63	Information and communication	..	652.8	715.2	678.8	705.4	592.8	501.8	419.1
58-60	Publishing, audiovisual and broadcasting activities	..	89.1	68.5	96.5	76.0	88.2	103.4	94.7
58	Publishing activities	..	..	64.7	94.0	70.9	85.3	101.6	94.4
59-60	Motion picture, video and TV programme production; broadcasting activities	..	..	3.8	2.5	5.2	2.9	1.9	0.3
59	Motion picture, video and TV programme production; sound and music	..	..	..	..	2.2	0.8	0.7	0.3
60	Programming and broadcasting activities	..	..	..	..	3.0	2.1	1.2	0.0
61	Telecommunications	..	329.9	434.5	390.1	449.6	321.7	229.5	133.4
62-63	IT and other information services	..	233.8	212.2	192.2	179.7	183.0	168.8	190.9
62	Computer programming, consultancy and related activities	..	204.0	190.4	172.1	132.2	154.3	145.0	165.8
63	Information service activities	..	29.8	21.8	20.1	47.6	28.7	23.9	25.1
64-66	Financial and insurance activities	..	264.4	210.5	180.4	147.4	145.9	140.1	122.7
68-82	Real estate; professional, scientific and technical; administrative and support	..	104.1	137.0	167.5	157.8	117.3	141.6	137.0
68	Real estate activities	..	0.0	2.1	1.5	1.3	0.9	1.5	1.7
69-75x72	Professional, scientific and technical activities, except scientific R&D	..	66.5	96.1	126.1	118.7	71.7	76.7	66.0
72	Scientific research and development	..	33.5	36.8	36.9	33.4	37.8	56.3	63.3
77-82	Administrative and support service activities	..	4.0	2.0	3.0	4.4	6.9	7.1	6.0
84-99	Community, social and personal services	..	8.7	19.7	16.1	13.1	10.0	17.8	30.9
84-85	Public administration and defence; compulsory social security and education	..	3.0	0.1	0.3	0.6	1.2	1.3	1.7
86-88	Human health and social work activities	..	3.6	12.3	5.6	10.3	7.8	13.1	25.0
90-93	Arts, entertainment and recreation	..	0.6	0.4	0.5	0.6	0.4	0.6	1.3
94-99	Other services; household-employers; extraterritorial bodies	..	1.6	6.9	9.7	1.7	0.6	2.8	2.9

.. Not available

Note: Detailed metadata at: http://metalinks.oecd.org/anberd/20170419/301f.
Information on data for Israel: http://oe.cd/israel-disclaimer.

Disclaimer: http://oe.cd/disclaimer

SLOVAK REPUBLIC

R&D expenditure in industry by main activity of the enterprise, current prices
ISIC Rev. 4

Million USD PPP

		2007	2008	2009	2010	2011	2012	2013	2014
	TOTAL BUSINESS ENTERPRISE	201.6	252.5	241.5	349.7	343.9	479.6	576.0	511.2
01-03	**AGRICULTURE, FORESTRY AND FISHING**	2.7	2.8	2.5	2.4	2.9	1.9	1.5	1.3
05-09	**MINING AND QUARRYING**	0.0	0.0	0.0	0.0	0.0	0.0	0.0	0.0
10-33	**MANUFACTURING**	99.0	158.0	162.6	241.9	210.0	257.7	330.8	344.3
10-12	Food products, beverages and tobacco	1.5	1.8	1.8	3.4	2.3	2.3	1.4	1.9
13-15	Textiles, wearing apparel, leather and related products	..	..	..	..	..	2.5	0.9	0.5
13	Textiles	..	..	..	..	..	..	..	..
14	Wearing apparel	..	..	..	..	..	..	..	..
15	Leather and related products, footwear	..	..	..	..	..	..	..	..
16-18	Wood and paper products and printing	..	..	..	..	..	..	..	..
16	Wood and wood products, except furniture	..	..	..	..	..	..	..	..
17	Paper and paper products	..	..	..	..	..	..	..	..
18	Printing and reproduction of recorded media	..	..	..	..	..	..	..	..
19-23	Chemical, rubber, plastic, non-metallic mineral products	..	..	..	..	..	..	50.1	57.5
19	Coke and refined petroleum products	..	..	..	..	..	..	6.8	6.3
20-21	Chemical and pharmaceutical products	..	..	..	29.6	32.4	24.4	14.1	14.9
20	Chemicals and chemical products	4.5	6.1	6.2	7.2	7.1	5.8	9.9	6.1
21	Pharmaceuticals, medicinal, chemical and botanical products	..	..	..	22.3	25.3	18.6	4.2	8.7
22	Rubber and plastic products	13.4	15.4	17.9	16.2	11.4	20.3	28.3	33.1
23	Other non-metallic mineral products	5.0	3.2	1.5	1.7	2.1	2.4	0.8	3.3
24-25	Basic metals, metal products, except machinery and equipment	14.9	20.1	18.3	26.0	13.9	17.4	11.2	10.3
24	Basic metals	10.0	9.6	8.6	7.5	7.2	7.3	6.7	6.0
25	Fabricated metal products, except machinery and equipment	4.8	10.5	9.7	18.5	6.7	10.2	4.5	4.3
26-30	Computer, electronic, optical products; electrical machinery, transport equipment	37.8	67.3	74.8	140.0	123.7	163.4	252.2	259.0
26	Computer, electronic and optical products	14.3	3.4	2.2	4.6	5.5	7.2	7.8	7.2
27	Electrical equipment	5.1	36.7	11.6	34.3	35.3	34.5	23.8	35.9
28	Machinery and equipment n.e.c.	15.0	14.9	11.1	20.8	25.6	30.1	29.4	31.4
29	Motor vehicles, trailers and semi-trailers	2.6	9.3	38.1	65.8	47.6	79.4	173.6	153.7
30	Other transport equipment	0.8	2.9	11.9	14.5	9.6	12.3	17.6	30.8
31-33	Furniture; repair, installation of machinery and equipment	..	25.1	25.0	20.0	..	..	..	..
31	Furniture	0.0	0.0	0.0	0.0	0.0	0.0	0.0	0.0
32	Other manufacturing	3.3	3.7	3.2	3.1	..	..	..	..
33	Repair and installation of machinery and equipment	..	21.2	21.7	17.2	16.5	16.4	..	..
35-39	**ELECTRICITY, GAS, WATER AND WASTE MANAGEMENT**	0.0	0.0	0.0	0.0	0.0	0.0	0.0	0.0
35-36	Electricity, gas and water	..	..	..	..	..	..	..	..
37-39	Sewerage, waste management and remediation activities	..	..	..	..	..	..	..	..
41-43	**CONSTRUCTION**	..	..	0.4	1.2	1.1	2.4	2.5	..
45-99	**TOTAL SERVICES**	100.1	90.7	76.0	102.4	126.9	211.6	230.7	..
45-82	**Business sector services**	98.5	89.9	75.1	101.4	124.9	212.4	237.6	163.2
45-47	Wholesale and retail trade; motor vehicle and motorcycle repairs	0.0	0.0	0.0	2.2	2.5	0.6	10.3	7.1
49-53	Transportation and storage	..	..	..	..	..	..	..	..
55-56	Accommodation and food service activities	0.0	0.0	0.0	0.0	0.0	0.0	0.0	0.0
58-63	Information and communication	4.1	3.9	3.7	10.7	11.7	61.2	64.8	65.7
58-60	Publishing, audiovisual and broadcasting activities	..	..	..	..	..	..	..	..
58	Publishing activities	..	..	..	..	..	..	..	..
59-60	Motion picture, video and TV programme production; broadcasting activities	..	..	..	..	..	..	..	..
59	Motion picture, video and TV programme production; sound and music	..	..	..	..	..	..	..	..
60	Programming and broadcasting activities	..	..	..	..	..	..	..	..
61	Telecommunications	..	..	..	..	..	..	..	..
62-63	IT and other information services	4.1	3.0	3.0	9.9	..	..	..	..
62	Computer programming, consultancy and related activities	2.9	3.0	3.0	9.1	9.6	59.2	62.0	64.5
63	Information service activities	..	0.0	0.0	0.7	..	..	..	..
64-66	Financial and insurance activities	..	..	..	..	..	63.5	..	..
68-82	Real estate; professional, scientific and technical; administrative and support	93.4	83.1	68.5	85.1	70.9	78.2	84.0	83.6
68	Real estate activities	0.0	0.0	0.0	0.0	0.0	0.0	0.0	0.0
69-75x72	Professional, scientific and technical activities, except scientific R&D	13.6	7.6	4.1	12.9	17.4	23.8	31.5	29.8
72	Scientific research and development	77.3	72.9	61.4	70.4	51.1	53.4	52.2	52.5
77-82	Administrative and support service activities	1.0	1.7	2.5	3.3	4.2	3.3	4.1	4.9
84-99	**Community, social and personal services**	0.0	0.0	0.9	2.8	4.9	5.1	3.4	..
84-85	Public administration and defence; compulsory social security and education	..	..	..	..	..	..	..	..
86-88	Human health and social work activities	..	..	..	..	..	1.6	0.9	0.4
90-93	Arts, entertainment and recreation	..	..	..	..	..	..	..	..
94-99	Other services; household-employers; extraterritorial bodies	..	..	..	..	..	..	..	..

.. Not available

Note: Detailed metadata at: http://metalinks.oecd.org/anberd/20170419/301f.
  Information on data for Israel: http://oe.cd/israel-disclaimer.
Disclaimer: http://oe.cd/disclaimer

SLOVAK REPUBLIC

R&D expenditure in industry by main activity of the enterprise, constant prices
ISIC Rev. 4

2010 USD PPP

		2007	2008	2009	2010	2011	2012	2013	2014
	TOTAL BUSINESS ENTERPRISE	227.8	268.9	249.4	349.7	341.9	469.1	545.0	476.6
01-03	**AGRICULTURE, FORESTRY AND FISHING**	3.1	3.0	2.6	2.4	2.9	1.9	1.5	1.2
05-09	**MINING AND QUARRYING**	0.0	0.0	0.0	0.0	0.0	0.0	0.0	0.0
10-33	**MANUFACTURING**	111.8	168.2	167.9	241.9	208.7	252.0	313.0	321.0
10-12	Food products, beverages and tobacco	1.7	1.9	1.9	3.4	2.3	2.3	1.3	1.8
13-15	Textiles, wearing apparel, leather and related products	..	..	..	..	..	2.4	0.9	0.5
13	Textiles	..	..	..	..	..	..	..	..
14	Wearing apparel	..	..	..	..	..	..	..	..
15	Leather and related products, footwear	..	..	..	..	..	..	..	..
16-18	Wood and paper products and printing	..	..	..	..	..	..	..	..
16	Wood and wood products, except furniture	..	..	..	..	..	..	..	..
17	Paper and paper products	..	..	..	..	..	..	..	..
18	Printing and reproduction of recorded media	..	..	..	..	..	..	..	..
19-23	Chemical, rubber, plastic, non-metallic mineral products	..	..	..	..	..	..	47.4	53.6
19	Coke and refined petroleum products	..	..	..	..	..	..	6.4	5.8
20-21	Chemical and pharmaceutical products	..	..	..	29.6	32.2	23.8	13.3	13.8
20	Chemicals and chemical products	5.1	6.5	6.4	7.2	7.0	5.6	9.3	5.7
21	Pharmaceuticals, medicinal, chemical and botanical products	..	..	..	22.3	25.1	18.2	4.0	8.1
22	Rubber and plastic products	15.1	16.4	18.5	16.2	11.4	19.8	26.8	30.8
23	Other non-metallic mineral products	5.6	3.4	1.5	1.7	2.1	2.4	0.8	3.0
24-25	Basic metals, metal products, except machinery and equipment	16.8	21.4	18.9	26.0	13.8	17.0	10.6	9.6
24	Basic metals	11.3	10.2	8.9	7.5	7.1	7.1	6.3	5.6
25	Fabricated metal products, except machinery and equipment	5.5	11.2	10.0	18.5	6.7	9.9	4.3	4.0
26-30	Computer, electronic, optical products; electrical machinery, transport equipment	42.7	71.7	77.3	140.0	123.0	159.8	238.6	241.5
26	Computer, electronic and optical products	16.1	3.7	2.3	4.6	5.5	7.0	7.4	6.8
27	Electrical equipment	5.7	39.1	12.0	34.3	35.1	33.7	22.5	33.5
28	Machinery and equipment n.e.c.	17.0	15.9	11.4	20.8	25.5	29.4	27.8	29.3
29	Motor vehicles, trailers and semi-trailers	3.0	9.9	39.3	65.8	47.3	77.7	164.3	143.3
30	Other transport equipment	0.9	3.1	12.3	14.5	9.6	12.0	16.6	28.7
31-33	Furniture; repair, installation of machinery and equipment	..	26.0	25.8	20.0	..	..	..	..
31	Furniture	0.0	0.0	0.0	0.0	0.0	0.0	0.0	0.0
32	Other manufacturing	3.7	3.9	3.3	3.1	..	..	..	..
33	Repair and installation of machinery and equipment	..	22.6	22.4	17.2	16.4	16.0	..	..
35-39	**ELECTRICITY, GAS, WATER AND WASTE MANAGEMENT**	0.0	0.0	0.0	0.0	0.0	0.0	0.0	0.0
35-36	Electricity, gas and water	..	..	..	..	..	..	..	..
37-39	Sewerage, waste management and remediation activities	..	..	..	..	..	..	..	..
41-43	**CONSTRUCTION**	..	..	0.4	1.2	1.1	2.3	2.3	..
45-99	**TOTAL SERVICES**	109.3	94.1	78.5	102.4	126.9	209.1	224.2	..
45-82	**Business sector services**	111.3	95.8	77.6	101.4	124.2	207.7	224.8	152.2
45-47	Wholesale and retail trade; motor vehicle and motorcycle repairs	0.0	0.0	0.0	2.2	2.5	0.6	9.7	6.6
49-53	Transportation and storage	..	..	..	..	..	..	..	..
55-56	Accommodation and food service activities	0.0	0.0	0.0	0.0	0.0	0.0	0.0	0.0
58-63	Information and communication	4.6	4.1	3.8	10.7	11.7	59.9	61.4	61.3
58-60	Publishing, audiovisual and broadcasting activities	..	..	..	..	..	..	..	..
58	Publishing activities	..	..	..	..	..	..	..	..
59-60	Motion picture, video and TV programme production; broadcasting activities	..	..	..	..	..	..	..	..
59	Motion picture, video and TV programme production; sound and music	..	..	..	..	..	..	..	..
60	Programming and broadcasting activities	..	..	..	..	..	..	..	..
61	Telecommunications	..	..	..	..	..	..	..	..
62-63	IT and other information services	4.6	3.2	3.1	9.9	..	..	..	..
62	Computer programming, consultancy and related activities	3.3	3.2	3.1	9.1	9.6	57.9	58.7	60.1
63	Information service activities	..	0.0	0.0	0.7	..	..	..	..
64-66	Financial and insurance activities	..	..	..	..	..	62.1	..	..
68-82	Real estate; professional, scientific and technical; administrative and support	102.0	86.1	69.0	85.1	70.9	77.3	81.6	79.8
68	Real estate activities	0.0	0.0	0.0	0.0	0.0	0.0	0.0	0.0
69-75x72	Professional, scientific and technical activities, except scientific R&D	15.3	8.1	4.3	12.9	17.2	23.3	29.8	27.8
72	Scientific research and development	87.4	77.7	63.4	70.4	50.8	52.2	49.4	48.9
77-82	Administrative and support service activities	1.2	1.9	2.6	3.3	4.1	3.2	3.9	4.6
84-99	Community, social and personal services	0.0	0.0	0.9	2.8	4.9	5.1	3.3	..
84-85	Public administration and defence; compulsory social security and education	..	..	..	..	..	..	..	..
86-88	Human health and social work activities	..	..	..	..	..	1.6	0.8	0.4
90-93	Arts, entertainment and recreation	..	..	..	..	..	..	..	..
94-99	Other services; household-employers; extraterritorial bodies	..	..	..	..	..	..	..	..

.. Not available

Note: Detailed metadata at: http://metalinks.oecd.org/anberd/20170419/301f.
Information on data for Israel: http://oe.cd/israel-disclaimer.
Disclaimer: http://oe.cd/disclaimer

SLOVENIA

R&D expenditure in industry by main activity of the enterprise, current prices
ISIC Rev. 4

Million USD PPP

		2007	2008	2009	2010	2011	2012	2013	2014
	TOTAL BUSINESS ENTERPRISE	474.4	628.4	658.3	794.4	1 058.5	1 158.7	1 213.0	1 179.7
01-03	**AGRICULTURE, FORESTRY AND FISHING**	0.0	0.0	0.4	0.4	0.8	1.0	0.4	0.6
05-09	**MINING AND QUARRYING**	3.6	5.5	8.5	8.3	9.6	7.7	7.9	5.8
10-33	**MANUFACTURING**	425.2	535.9	540.8	642.2	762.9	813.4	875.4	823.5
10-12	Food products, beverages and tobacco	1.7	2.4	2.4	2.8	6.3	7.1	11.8	11.2
13-15	Textiles, wearing apparel, leather and related products	11.8	7.4	9.9	10.7	10.8	13.9	14.1	11.8
13	Textiles	8.5	5.6	6.4	8.4	8.9	10.2	10.2	6.8
14	Wearing apparel	1.4	0.7	0.7	0.3	0.4	2.3	2.4	2.2
15	Leather and related products, footwear	1.9	1.1	2.8	1.9	1.6	1.4	1.5	2.8
16-18	Wood and paper products and printing	0.5	5.6	8.9	9.6	7.0	17.4	25.9	8.9
16	Wood and wood products, except furniture	0.0	1.3	1.9	2.4	2.9	14.0	22.2	4.0
17	Paper and paper products	0.0	3.0	4.4	5.4	3.0	2.2	2.5	3.1
18	Printing and reproduction of recorded media	0.5	1.4	2.7	1.8	1.2	1.2	1.3	1.7
19-23	Chemical, rubber, plastic, non-metallic mineral products	208.5	257.8	251.5	309.1	322.7	336.2	350.5	355.1
19	Coke and refined petroleum products	0.1	0.0	0.0	0.0	0.0	0.0	0.0	0.0
20-21	Chemical and pharmaceutical products	196.3	240.5	234.2	288.8	301.5	310.2	309.9	318.8
20	Chemicals and chemical products	20.7	22.4	24.4	36.7	38.1	38.4	36.6	39.9
21	Pharmaceuticals, medicinal, chemical and botanical products	175.6	218.1	209.8	252.1	263.4	271.8	273.3	279.0
22	Rubber and plastic products	8.9	10.6	13.0	15.4	16.5	16.4	16.2	23.8
23	Other non-metallic mineral products	3.3	6.6	4.2	4.9	4.7	9.6	24.4	12.4
24-25	Basic metals, metal products, except machinery and equipment	25.6	32.0	34.7	48.1	59.0	74.4	71.2	68.0
24	Basic metals	4.3	11.4	10.8	13.8	15.0	10.4	16.4	17.1
25	Fabricated metal products, except machinery and equipment	21.4	20.6	23.9	34.3	44.0	64.0	54.8	50.9
26-30	Computer, electronic, optical products; electrical machinery, transport equipment	162.1	214.8	220.6	245.5	333.3	338.0	377.8	344.6
26	Computer, electronic and optical products	70.3	76.4	68.8	69.3	77.3	80.3	98.0	83.8
27	Electrical equipment	36.6	51.1	66.7	77.1	112.6	104.9	153.5	138.8
28	Machinery and equipment n.e.c.	22.1	25.8	26.3	34.6	54.6	26.5	33.3	34.7
29	Motor vehicles, trailers and semi-trailers	29.2	57.0	52.6	54.0	79.1	123.3	84.0	84.2
30	Other transport equipment	3.8	4.5	6.3	10.5	9.7	3.0	9.0	3.2
31-33	Furniture; repair, installation of machinery and equipment	15.0	15.9	12.8	16.4	23.8	26.5	24.1	23.8
31	Furniture	..	1.1	1.9	4.1	4.5	5.9	3.1	2.8
32	Other manufacturing	..	4.4	5.8	6.9	12.2	17.2	11.6	12.1
33	Repair and installation of machinery and equipment	..	10.4	5.1	5.4	7.1	3.3	9.4	8.9
35-39	**ELECTRICITY, GAS, WATER AND WASTE MANAGEMENT**	0.0	0.6	2.3	2.0	5.9	8.7	12.9	11.4
35-36	Electricity, gas and water	..	0.6	2.2	1.9	4.7	6.7	9.8	7.1
37-39	Sewerage, waste management and remediation activities	..	0.1	0.1	0.1	1.1	2.0	3.1	4.3
41-43	**CONSTRUCTION**	0.2	0.6	0.3	0.8	2.4	2.5	3.3	3.8
45-99	**TOTAL SERVICES**	45.3	85.8	106.0	140.6	276.8	325.3	313.2	334.6
45-82	**Business sector services**	45.2	85.1	105.3	139.2	271.0	318.0	308.0	330.6
45-47	Wholesale and retail trade; motor vehicle and motorcycle repairs	1.4	3.1	10.6	9.3	9.9	9.7	12.5	15.8
49-53	Transportation and storage	0.2	0.1	2.1	2.4	3.3	1.3	0.3	0.3
55-56	Accommodation and food service activities	0.0	0.0	0.0	0.0	0.0	0.0	0.0	0.1
58-63	Information and communication	13.1	29.7	36.5	43.7	77.7	78.7	71.5	91.3
58-60	Publishing, audiovisual and broadcasting activities	..	4.0	2.7	1.7	6.3	21.7	6.6	6.0
58	Publishing activities	..	4.0	2.7	1.7	6.2	6.5	6.6	6.0
59-60	Motion picture, video and TV programme production; broadcasting activities	..	0.0	0.0	0.0	0.1	15.1	0.0	0.0
59	Motion picture, video and TV programme production; sound and music	..	0.0	0.0	0.0	0.1	0.0	0.0	0.0
60	Programming and broadcasting activities	..	0.0	0.0	0.0	0.0	15.1	0.0	0.0
61	Telecommunications	..	1.5	3.1	7.5	7.3	4.4	3.5	12.4
62-63	IT and other information services	11.1	24.1	30.7	34.5	64.2	52.6	61.4	72.9
62	Computer programming, consultancy and related activities	..	21.7	29.7	31.2	59.9	47.5	57.2	66.5
63	Information service activities	..	2.4	1.0	3.2	4.3	5.1	4.2	6.4
64-66	Financial and insurance activities	0.3	0.9	1.0	2.3	19.9	11.8	16.9	6.7
68-82	Real estate; professional, scientific and technical; administrative and support	30.2	51.3	55.0	81.5	160.1	216.5	206.8	216.4
68	Real estate activities	..	0.0	0.0	0.0	0.0	0.1	1.1	1.5
69-75x72	Professional, scientific and technical activities, except scientific R&D	..	35.2	40.1	42.1	70.1	69.7	80.7	62.8
72	Scientific research and development	10.1	14.1	12.9	38.7	89.9	146.7	123.6	151.0
77-82	Administrative and support service activities	..	2.0	2.1	0.7	0.1	0.1	1.4	1.0
84-99	**Community, social and personal services**	0.2	0.7	0.8	1.4	5.8	7.2	5.2	4.0
84-85	Public administration and defence; compulsory social security and education	..	0.1	0.1	0.5	1.2	1.8	1.4	1.4
86-88	Human health and social work activities	..	0.6	0.6	0.9	2.7	2.3	0.9	0.7
90-93	Arts, entertainment and recreation	..	0.0	0.0	0.0	0.1	0.2	0.7	0.3
94-99	Other services; household-employers; extraterritorial bodies	..	0.0	0.0	0.0	1.8	2.9	2.3	1.7

.. Not available

Note: Detailed metadata at: http://metalinks.oecd.org/anberd/20170419/301f.
      Information on data for Israel: http://oe.cd/israel-disclaimer.
Disclaimer: http://oe.cd/disclaimer

SLOVENIA

R&D expenditure in industry by main activity of the enterprise, constant prices
ISIC Rev. 4

2010 USD PPP

		2007	2008	2009	2010	2011	2012	2013	2014
	TOTAL BUSINESS ENTERPRISE	**503.0**	**640.1**	**660.0**	**794.4**	**1 025.8**	**1 089.0**	**1 098.9**	**1 048.9**
01-03	**AGRICULTURE, FORESTRY AND FISHING**	**0.0**	**0.0**	**0.4**	**0.4**	**0.8**	**1.0**	**0.4**	**0.5**
05-09	**MINING AND QUARRYING**	**3.8**	**5.6**	**8.5**	**8.3**	**9.3**	**7.3**	**7.2**	**5.2**
10-33	**MANUFACTURING**	**450.9**	**545.8**	**542.2**	**642.2**	**739.4**	**764.5**	**793.0**	**732.1**
10-12	Food products, beverages and tobacco	1.8	2.4	2.4	2.8	6.1	6.6	10.7	10.0
13-15	Textiles, wearing apparel, leather and related products	12.5	7.5	9.9	10.7	10.4	13.1	12.8	10.5
13	Textiles	9.1	5.7	6.5	8.4	8.6	9.5	9.2	6.1
14	Wearing apparel	1.5	0.7	0.7	0.3	0.3	2.2	2.1	1.9
15	Leather and related products, footwear	2.0	1.2	2.8	1.9	1.5	1.4	1.4	2.5
16-18	Wood and paper products and printing	0.5	5.7	8.9	9.6	6.8	16.4	23.5	7.9
16	Wood and wood products, except furniture	0.0	1.3	1.9	2.4	2.8	13.2	20.1	3.6
17	Paper and paper products	0.0	3.0	4.4	5.4	2.9	2.0	2.2	2.8
18	Printing and reproduction of recorded media	0.5	1.4	2.7	1.8	1.1	1.1	1.1	1.5
19-23	Chemical, rubber, plastic, non-metallic mineral products	221.1	262.6	252.1	309.1	312.7	316.0	317.5	315.7
19	Coke and refined petroleum products	0.1	0.0	0.0	0.0	0.0	0.0	0.0	0.0
20-21	Chemical and pharmaceutical products	208.1	245.0	234.8	288.8	292.2	291.6	280.7	283.5
20	Chemicals and chemical products	21.9	22.8	24.5	36.7	37.0	36.1	33.1	35.4
21	Pharmaceuticals, medicinal, chemical and botanical products	186.2	222.2	210.3	252.1	255.2	255.5	247.6	248.0
22	Rubber and plastic products	9.4	10.8	13.0	15.4	16.0	15.4	14.7	21.2
23	Other non-metallic mineral products	3.5	6.7	4.2	4.9	4.5	9.0	22.1	11.0
24-25	Basic metals, metal products, except machinery and equipment	27.2	32.6	34.8	48.1	57.2	69.9	64.5	60.5
24	Basic metals	4.5	11.6	10.8	13.8	14.6	9.8	14.8	15.2
25	Fabricated metal products, except machinery and equipment	22.7	21.0	23.9	34.3	42.7	60.2	49.7	45.2
26-30	Computer, electronic, optical products; electrical machinery, transport equipment	171.9	218.8	221.2	245.5	323.0	317.6	342.3	306.4
26	Computer, electronic and optical products	74.5	77.8	69.0	69.3	74.9	75.4	88.7	74.5
27	Electrical equipment	38.8	52.1	66.9	77.1	109.1	98.6	139.1	123.4
28	Machinery and equipment n.e.c.	23.5	26.3	26.4	34.6	53.0	24.9	30.2	30.9
29	Motor vehicles, trailers and semi-trailers	31.0	58.1	52.7	54.0	76.7	115.8	76.1	74.8
30	Other transport equipment	4.0	4.6	6.3	10.5	9.4	2.9	8.1	2.8
31-33	Furniture; repair, installation of machinery and equipment	15.9	16.2	12.9	16.4	23.1	24.9	21.8	21.2
31	Furniture	..	1.1	1.9	4.1	4.4	5.6	2.8	2.5
32	Other manufacturing	..	4.5	5.9	6.9	11.8	16.2	10.5	10.8
33	Repair and installation of machinery and equipment	..	10.6	5.1	5.4	6.9	3.1	8.5	7.9
35-39	**ELECTRICITY, GAS, WATER AND WASTE MANAGEMENT**	**0.0**	**0.6**	**2.3**	**2.0**	**5.7**	**8.2**	**11.6**	**10.1**
35-36	Electricity, gas and water	..	0.6	2.2	1.9	4.6	6.3	8.9	6.3
37-39	Sewerage, waste management and remediation activities	..	0.1	0.1	0.1	1.1	1.9	2.8	3.8
41-43	**CONSTRUCTION**	**0.2**	**0.6**	**0.3**	**0.8**	**2.3**	**2.4**	**2.9**	**3.4**
45-99	**TOTAL SERVICES**	**48.1**	**87.4**	**106.3**	**140.6**	**268.3**	**305.7**	**283.8**	**297.5**
45-82	**Business sector services**	**47.9**	**86.7**	**105.5**	**139.2**	**262.6**	**298.9**	**279.0**	**293.9**
45-47	**Wholesale and retail trade; motor vehicle and motorcycle repairs**	**1.5**	**3.2**	**10.6**	**9.3**	**9.6**	**9.1**	**11.3**	**14.0**
49-53	**Transportation and storage**	**0.2**	**0.1**	**2.1**	**2.4**	**3.2**	**1.2**	**0.3**	**0.3**
55-56	**Accommodation and food service activities**	**0.0**	**0.0**	**0.0**	**0.0**	**0.0**	**0.0**	**0.0**	**0.1**
58-63	**Information and communication**	**13.9**	**30.2**	**36.6**	**43.7**	**75.3**	**74.0**	**64.8**	**81.2**
58-60	Publishing, audiovisual and broadcasting activities	..	4.1	2.7	1.7	6.1	20.4	6.0	5.3
58	Publishing activities	..	4.1	2.7	1.7	6.0	6.1	6.0	5.3
59-60	Motion picture, video and TV programme production; broadcasting activities	..	0.0	0.0	0.0	0.1	14.2	0.0	0.0
59	Motion picture, video and TV programme production; sound and music	..	0.0	0.0	0.0	0.1	0.0	0.0	0.0
60	Programming and broadcasting activities	..	0.0	0.0	0.0	0.0	14.2	0.0	0.0
61	Telecommunications	..	1.6	3.1	7.5	7.1	4.1	3.2	11.1
62-63	IT and other information services	11.8	24.5	30.7	34.5	62.2	49.5	55.7	64.8
62	Computer programming, consultancy and related activities	..	22.1	29.7	31.2	58.1	44.7	51.9	59.1
63	Information service activities	..	2.5	1.0	3.2	4.1	4.8	3.8	5.7
64-66	**Financial and insurance activities**	**0.3**	**0.9**	**1.0**	**2.3**	**19.3**	**11.1**	**15.3**	**6.0**
68-82	**Real estate; professional, scientific and technical; administrative and support**	**32.0**	**52.3**	**55.2**	**81.5**	**155.2**	**203.5**	**187.3**	**192.4**
68	Real estate activities	..	0.0	0.0	0.0	0.0	0.1	1.0	1.4
69-75x72	Professional, scientific and technical activities, except scientific R&D	..	35.8	40.2	42.1	68.0	65.5	73.1	55.9
72	Scientific research and development	10.7	14.4	12.9	38.7	87.1	137.9	111.9	134.3
77-82	Administrative and support service activities	..	2.0	2.1	0.7	0.1	0.0	1.3	0.9
84-99	**Community, social and personal services**	**0.2**	**0.7**	**0.8**	**1.4**	**5.7**	**6.8**	**4.7**	**3.6**
84-85	Public administration and defence; compulsory social security and education	..	0.1	0.1	0.5	1.2	1.7	1.3	1.2
86-88	Human health and social work activities	..	0.6	0.6	0.9	2.6	2.2	0.8	0.6
90-93	Arts, entertainment and recreation	..	0.0	0.0	0.0	0.1	0.2	0.6	0.3
94-99	Other services; household-employers; extraterritorial bodies	..	0.0	0.0	0.0	1.8	2.7	2.1	1.5

.. Not available

Note: Detailed metadata at: http://metalinks.oecd.org/anberd/20170419/301f.
Information on data for Israel: http://oe.cd/israel-disclaimer.

Disclaimer: http://oe.cd/disclaimer

SPAIN

R&D expenditure in industry by main activity of the enterprise, current prices
ISIC Rev. 4

Million USD PPP

		2007	2008	2009	2010	2011	2012	2013	2014
	TOTAL BUSINESS ENTERPRISE	10 163.4	11 122.7	10 542.8	10 345.4	10 357.2	10 208.0	10 244.0	10 243.9
01-03	**AGRICULTURE, FORESTRY AND FISHING**	154.0	125.1	102.6	143.1	136.5	138.5	146.4	155.2
05-09	**MINING AND QUARRYING**	188.3	36.2	25.0	27.9	39.3	33.0	28.5	23.5
10-33	**MANUFACTURING**	5 638.4	5 760.6	5 637.6	5 616.3	5 769.0	5 591.2	5 648.4	5 755.7
10-12	Food products, beverages and tobacco	333.6	348.2	326.0	302.9	312.2	328.0	337.6	338.8
13-15	Textiles, wearing apparel, leather and related products	171.3	170.4	140.6	135.2	131.8	151.7	163.3	228.8
13	Textiles	82.4	69.1	52.8	53.6	53.6	52.1	49.9	55.2
14	Wearing apparel	64.2	71.8	62.0	53.5	52.5	75.9	88.6	145.2
15	Leather and related products, footwear	24.8	29.5	25.7	28.1	25.7	23.7	24.8	28.4
16-18	Wood and paper products and printing	91.4	123.9	89.2	67.5	72.1	58.8	55.3	60.5
16	Wood and wood products, except furniture	19.3	33.1	21.9	25.8	23.5	17.5	18.6	21.7
17	Paper and paper products	34.6	45.1	44.0	24.6	35.2	24.4	21.6	19.5
18	Printing and reproduction of recorded media	37.5	45.7	23.2	17.1	13.3	16.9	15.1	19.2
19-23	Chemical, rubber, plastic, non-metallic mineral products	1 844.1	1 917.6	1 835.4	1 762.0	1 781.9	1 724.2	1 816.5	1 793.2
19	Coke and refined petroleum products	103.6	86.5	72.5	84.0	97.5	100.0	105.3	105.3
20-21	Chemical and pharmaceutical products	1 407.8	1 490.8	1 437.7	1 371.1	1 392.0	1 337.4	1 419.6	1 420.9
20	Chemicals and chemical products	361.0	437.3	365.8	374.9	367.8	370.2	392.7	405.7
21	Pharmaceuticals, medicinal, chemical and botanical products	1 046.7	1 053.5	1 071.9	996.2	1 024.2	967.2	1 026.9	1 015.2
22	Rubber and plastic products	160.1	192.7	193.4	183.1	176.3	188.8	188.3	168.5
23	Other non-metallic mineral products	172.7	147.6	131.7	123.8	116.1	98.0	103.2	98.6
24-25	Basic metals, metal products, except machinery and equipment	346.7	400.8	343.4	347.6	381.3	339.0	322.2	333.0
24	Basic metals	138.6	145.0	114.4	124.8	154.3	123.4	116.0	108.4
25	Fabricated metal products, except machinery and equipment	208.1	255.8	229.0	222.8	227.0	215.5	206.2	224.5
26-30	Computer, electronic, optical products; electrical machinery, transport equipment	2 703.8	2 616.0	2 734.4	2 871.6	2 957.1	2 865.3	2 821.2	2 868.0
26	Computer, electronic and optical products	530.6	393.4	343.4	336.7	303.3	266.9	268.8	275.8
27	Electrical equipment	298.9	359.0	339.5	341.2	347.1	371.8	333.4	323.1
28	Machinery and equipment n.e.c.	455.8	415.3	462.7	421.6	409.6	437.9	418.4	418.0
29	Motor vehicles, trailers and semi-trailers	824.1	780.0	870.8	904.4	839.9	835.6	848.1	973.1
30	Other transport equipment	594.5	668.3	718.0	867.7	1 057.3	953.1	952.6	878.0
31-33	Furniture; repair, installation of machinery and equipment	147.5	183.7	168.6	129.4	132.6	124.3	132.4	133.5
31	Furniture	..	35.7	36.0	28.5	27.8	23.9	22.8	28.0
32	Other manufacturing	..	107.9	98.2	80.6	86.4	82.1	90.8	82.1
33	Repair and installation of machinery and equipment	..	40.1	34.4	20.3	18.5	18.3	18.8	23.4
35-39	**ELECTRICITY, GAS, WATER AND WASTE MANAGEMENT**	230.8	264.7	296.2	340.2	396.0	415.3	388.6	360.6
35-36	Electricity, gas and water	..	218.2	244.1	295.4	353.9	380.4	356.1	325.0
37-39	Sewerage, waste management and remediation activities	..	46.5	52.2	44.7	42.1	34.9	32.5	35.5
41-43	**CONSTRUCTION**	498.1	398.9	335.0	298.6	231.8	209.4	192.6	208.0
45-99	**TOTAL SERVICES**	3 453.8	4 537.2	4 146.2	3 919.3	3 784.5	3 820.5	3 839.4	3 741.0
45-82	**Business sector services**	3 051.2	4 077.3	3 784.5	3 592.7	3 478.5	3 470.9	3 510.1	3 411.3
45-47	Wholesale and retail trade; motor vehicle and motorcycle repairs	220.9	611.2	442.9	378.6	378.9	377.6	362.9	356.1
49-53	Transportation and storage	88.6	134.0	111.5	131.3	95.3	96.6	78.3	78.3
55-56	Accommodation and food service activities	17.0	18.2	16.8	9.1	3.3	11.9	7.0	6.1
58-63	Information and communication	1 531.7	1 755.0	1 618.5	1 460.0	1 427.8	1 432.5	1 556.3	1 521.6
58-60	Publishing, audiovisual and broadcasting activities	..	168.0	109.2	112.9	98.4	85.4	63.1	67.3
58	Publishing activities	..	106.0	62.5	66.1	55.2	48.2	42.9	52.6
59-60	Motion picture, video and TV programme production; broadcasting activities	..	62.1	46.6	46.8	43.2	37.2	20.2	14.7
59	Motion picture, video and TV programme production; sound and music	..	41.6	20.7	22.9	18.1	20.0	13.1	10.8
60	Programming and broadcasting activities	..	20.5	25.9	23.8	25.1	17.2	7.1	3.9
61	Telecommunications	577.2	653.9	566.1	436.4	399.4	377.9	508.2	425.4
62-63	IT and other information services	..	933.0	943.3	910.8	930.0	969.2	985.0	1 028.9
62	Computer programming, consultancy and related activities	..	891.0	893.3	857.3	855.1	899.0	929.4	970.2
63	Information service activities	..	42.0	49.9	53.5	74.9	70.2	55.5	58.7
64-66	Financial and insurance activities	174.7	186.7	256.8	271.4	214.3	136.0	134.8	130.5
68-82	Real estate; professional, scientific and technical; administrative and support	1 018.2	1 372.2	1 338.0	1 342.3	1 358.8	1 416.3	1 370.8	1 318.6
68	Real estate activities	..	10.0	12.7	11.4	8.9	8.7	3.2	8.0
69-75x72	Professional, scientific and technical activities, except scientific R&D	..	977.3	908.5	916.2	1 082.4	1 079.1	1 096.6	1 021.1
72	Scientific research and development	66.0	318.5	349.9	356.5	214.0	251.5	197.4	225.6
77-82	Administrative and support service activities	..	66.3	66.9	58.2	53.5	77.0	73.6	63.8
84-99	Community, social and personal services	402.6	459.9	361.7	326.6	306.1	349.5	329.3	329.8
84-85	Public administration and defence; compulsory social security and education	..	160.8	101.6	73.7	52.1	48.4	42.7	37.3
86-88	Human health and social work activities	..	243.4	218.4	215.5	213.7	257.1	245.7	252.7
90-93	Arts, entertainment and recreation	..	12.1	7.8	11.0	6.8	16.6	16.5	15.8
94-99	Other services; household-employers; extraterritorial bodies	..	43.5	33.8	26.5	33.5	27.5	24.4	24.0

.. Not available

Note: Detailed metadata at: http://metalinks.oecd.org/anberd/20170419/301f.
   Information on data for Israel: http://oe.cd/israel-disclaimer.
Disclaimer: http://oe.cd/disclaimer

SPAIN

R&D expenditure in industry by main activity of the enterprise, constant prices
ISIC Rev. 4

2010 USD PPP

		2007	2008	2009	2010	2011	2012	2013	2014
	TOTAL BUSINESS ENTERPRISE	10 535.8	11 173.0	10 446.4	10 345.4	10 190.8	9 767.9	9 475.7	9 332.9
01-03	**AGRICULTURE, FORESTRY AND FISHING**	159.6	125.7	101.7	143.1	134.3	132.6	135.5	141.4
05-09	**MINING AND QUARRYING**	195.2	36.4	24.8	27.9	38.7	31.6	26.4	21.4
10-33	**MANUFACTURING**	5 845.0	5 786.6	5 586.1	5 616.3	5 676.3	5 350.2	5 224.8	5 243.8
10-12	Food products, beverages and tobacco	345.8	349.7	323.1	302.9	307.2	313.9	312.3	308.6
13-15	Textiles, wearing apparel, leather and related products	177.6	171.1	139.3	135.2	129.6	145.1	151.1	208.4
13	Textiles	85.4	69.4	52.3	53.6	52.7	49.9	46.2	50.3
14	Wearing apparel	66.5	72.1	61.4	53.5	51.7	72.6	81.9	132.2
15	Leather and related products, footwear	25.7	29.6	25.5	28.1	25.2	22.7	23.0	25.9
16-18	Wood and paper products and printing	94.8	124.5	88.4	67.5	71.0	56.3	51.1	55.1
16	Wood and wood products, except furniture	20.0	33.3	21.7	25.8	23.2	16.8	17.2	19.8
17	Paper and paper products	35.9	45.3	43.6	24.6	34.7	23.3	19.9	17.8
18	Printing and reproduction of recorded media	38.9	45.9	23.0	17.1	13.1	16.2	14.0	17.5
19-23	Chemical, rubber, plastic, non-metallic mineral products	1 911.7	1 926.3	1 818.6	1 762.0	1 753.3	1 649.8	1 680.3	1 633.7
19	Coke and refined petroleum products	107.4	86.9	71.9	84.0	95.9	95.7	97.4	95.9
20-21	Chemical and pharmaceutical products	1 459.3	1 497.5	1 424.6	1 371.1	1 369.6	1 279.7	1 313.2	1 294.5
20	Chemicals and chemical products	374.3	439.2	362.5	374.9	361.9	354.2	363.3	369.6
21	Pharmaceuticals, medicinal, chemical and botanical products	1 085.1	1 058.3	1 062.1	996.2	1 007.7	925.5	949.9	924.9
22	Rubber and plastic products	166.0	193.6	191.7	183.1	173.5	180.7	174.2	153.5
23	Other non-metallic mineral products	179.0	148.3	130.5	123.8	114.2	93.7	95.5	89.8
24-25	Basic metals, metal products, except machinery and equipment	359.4	402.6	340.2	347.6	375.2	324.4	298.0	303.4
24	Basic metals	143.6	145.6	113.3	124.8	151.8	118.1	107.3	98.8
25	Fabricated metal products, except machinery and equipment	215.8	257.0	226.9	222.8	223.4	206.3	190.7	204.6
26-30	Computer, electronic, optical products; electrical machinery, transport equipment	2 802.9	2 627.9	2 709.4	2 871.6	2 909.6	2 741.8	2 609.6	2 613.0
26	Computer, electronic and optical products	550.0	395.2	340.2	336.7	298.4	255.4	248.7	251.3
27	Electrical equipment	309.9	360.7	336.4	341.2	341.5	355.8	308.4	294.3
28	Machinery and equipment n.e.c.	472.5	417.2	458.5	421.6	403.0	419.0	387.0	380.8
29	Motor vehicles, trailers and semi-trailers	854.3	783.5	862.9	904.4	826.4	799.6	784.5	886.6
30	Other transport equipment	616.2	671.4	711.5	867.7	1 040.3	912.0	881.1	799.9
31-33	Furniture; repair, installation of machinery and equipment	152.9	184.6	167.1	129.4	130.5	118.9	122.4	121.6
31	Furniture	..	35.9	35.7	28.5	27.3	22.8	21.1	25.5
32	Other manufacturing	..	108.4	97.3	80.6	85.0	78.5	84.0	74.8
33	Repair and installation of machinery and equipment	..	40.3	34.1	20.3	18.2	17.6	17.4	21.3
35-39	**ELECTRICITY, GAS, WATER AND WASTE MANAGEMENT**	239.3	265.9	293.5	340.2	389.7	397.4	359.5	328.5
35-36	Electricity, gas and water	..	219.2	241.8	295.4	348.2	364.0	329.4	296.1
37-39	Sewerage, waste management and remediation activities	..	46.7	51.7	44.7	41.5	33.4	30.1	32.4
41-43	**CONSTRUCTION**	516.4	400.7	332.0	298.6	228.0	200.4	178.2	189.5
45-99	**TOTAL SERVICES**	3 580.3	4 557.7	4 108.3	3 919.3	3 723.7	3 655.8	3 551.5	3 408.3
45-82	**Business sector services**	3 163.0	4 095.7	3 750.0	3 592.7	3 422.6	3 321.3	3 246.9	3 107.9
45-47	Wholesale and retail trade; motor vehicle and motorcycle repairs	229.0	614.0	438.8	378.6	372.9	361.3	335.7	324.4
49-53	Transportation and storage	91.8	134.6	110.5	131.3	93.8	92.5	72.4	71.3
55-56	Accommodation and food service activities	17.7	18.3	16.6	9.1	3.2	11.4	6.5	5.6
58-63	Information and communication	1 587.8	1 763.0	1 603.8	1 460.0	1 404.9	1 370.7	1 439.6	1 386.3
58-60	Publishing, audiovisual and broadcasting activities	..	168.8	108.2	112.9	96.9	81.7	58.4	61.3
58	Publishing activities	..	106.4	62.0	66.1	54.3	46.1	39.7	48.0
59-60	Motion picture, video and TV programme production; broadcasting activities	..	62.4	46.2	46.8	42.5	35.6	18.7	13.4
59	Motion picture, video and TV programme production; sound and music	..	41.8	20.5	22.9	17.9	19.1	12.1	9.9
60	Programming and broadcasting activities	..	20.6	25.6	23.8	24.7	16.5	6.6	3.5
61	Telecommunications	598.3	656.9	560.9	436.4	392.9	361.6	470.1	387.6
62-63	IT and other information services	..	937.3	934.7	910.8	915.1	927.4	911.1	937.4
62	Computer programming, consultancy and related activities	..	895.0	885.2	857.3	841.3	860.2	859.7	883.9
63	Information service activities	..	42.2	49.5	53.5	73.7	67.2	51.4	53.5
64-66	Financial and insurance activities	181.1	187.5	254.5	271.4	210.8	130.1	124.7	118.9
68-82	Real estate; professional, scientific and technical; administrative and support	1 055.5	1 378.4	1 325.8	1 342.3	1 337.0	1 355.3	1 268.0	1 201.3
68	Real estate activities	..	10.0	12.6	11.4	8.8	8.3	3.0	7.3
69-75x72	Professional, scientific and technical activities, except scientific R&D	..	981.7	900.2	916.2	1 065.0	1 032.6	1 014.3	930.3
72	Scientific research and development	68.4	319.9	346.7	356.5	210.5	240.6	182.6	205.6
77-82	Administrative and support service activities	..	66.6	66.3	58.2	52.6	73.7	68.1	58.1
84-99	**Community, social and personal services**	417.3	462.0	358.4	326.6	301.2	334.5	304.6	300.4
84-85	Public administration and defence; compulsory social security and education	..	161.5	100.7	73.7	51.3	46.3	39.5	34.0
86-88	Human health and social work activities	..	244.5	216.4	215.5	210.2	246.0	227.3	230.2
90-93	Arts, entertainment and recreation	..	12.2	7.8	11.0	6.7	15.9	15.3	14.4
94-99	Other services; household-employers; extraterritorial bodies	..	43.7	33.5	26.5	32.9	26.3	22.6	21.9

.. Not available

Note: Detailed metadata at: http://metalinks.oecd.org/anberd/20170419/301f.
Information on data for Israel: http://oe.cd/israel-disclaimer.
Disclaimer: http://oe.cd/disclaimer

SWEDEN

R&D expenditure in industry by main activity of the enterprise, current prices
ISIC Rev. 4

Million USD PPP

		2007	2008	2009	2010	2011	2012	2013	2014
	TOTAL BUSINESS ENTERPRISE	8 818.5	9 987.6	8 905.5	8 639.7	9 175.1	9 470.3	10 004.1	..
01-03	**AGRICULTURE, FORESTRY AND FISHING**	18.9	22.0	20.0	20.4	22.7	22.9	23.7	..
05-09	**MINING AND QUARRYING**	15.7	18.3	16.7	17.0	18.9	19.1	19.7	..
10-33	**MANUFACTURING**	6 127.5	7 226.4	6 695.7	6 350.4	6 592.8	6 737.3	7 049.7	..
10-12	Food products, beverages and tobacco	45.9	49.7	42.3	42.6	46.8	47.4	49.2	..
13-15	Textiles, wearing apparel, leather and related products	8.4	9.9	9.2	6.9	5.2	5.5	5.9	..
13	Textiles	..	..	..	..	..	..	..	..
14	Wearing apparel	..	..	..	..	..	..	..	..
15	Leather and related products, footwear	..	..	..	..	..	..	..	..
16-18	Wood and paper products and printing	255.3	352.3	369.7	228.3	107.1	124.7	145.9	..
16	Wood and wood products, except furniture	..	..	..	..	..	..	..	..
17	Paper and paper products	246.0	..	365.7	..	102.8	..	136.9	..
18	Printing and reproduction of recorded media	..	..	..	..	..	..	..	..
19-23	Chemical, rubber, plastic, non-metallic mineral products	1 191.8	1 212.2	959.7	987.4	1 107.0	1 086.2	1 090.9	..
19	Coke and refined petroleum products	..	..	..	..	..	..	..	..
20-21	Chemical and pharmaceutical products	..	..	..	..	..	..	..	..
20	Chemicals and chemical products	..	..	..	..	..	..	..	..
21	Pharmaceuticals, medicinal, chemical and botanical products	958.6	939.6	709.2	757.5	876.5	834.0	810.4	..
22	Rubber and plastic products	19.6	26.2	26.8	24.3	24.0	26.6	30.0	..
23	Other non-metallic mineral products	9.0	11.8	12.0	12.7	14.6	15.3	16.4	..
24-25	Basic metals, metal products, except machinery and equipment	308.6	391.6	386.2	309.5	261.0	308.5	364.8	..
24	Basic metals	157.3	187.5	175.4	164.3	168.4	206.5	250.6	..
25	Fabricated metal products, except machinery and equipment	151.3	204.1	210.8	145.2	92.6	102.0	114.2	..
26-30	Computer, electronic, optical products; electrical machinery, transport equipment	4 123.0	4 977.5	4 709.2	4 589.0	4 894.0	4 998.2	5 225.9	..
26	Computer, electronic and optical products	1 791.6	2 185.9	2 087.1	2 024.4	2 149.1	2 071.2	2 040.9	..
27	Electrical equipment	226.3	271.4	255.2	252.7	273.5	298.5	331.3	..
28	Machinery and equipment n.e.c.	550.0	668.5	636.2	630.0	682.3	704.4	744.1	..
29	Motor vehicles, trailers and semi-trailers	1 069.6	1 188.7	1 040.0	1 010.7	1 075.1	1 156.2	1 267.6	..
30	Other transport equipment	485.5	663.0	690.7	671.3	714.0	767.9	841.9	..
31-33	Furniture; repair, installation of machinery and equipment	194.4	233.1	219.2	186.6	171.2	166.8	164.4	..
31	Furniture	10.5	14.8	15.7	12.2	9.7	13.4	17.6	..
32	Other manufacturing	118.6	126.2	105.3	107.6	120.0	127.5	138.3	..
33	Repair and installation of machinery and equipment	65.3	92.2	98.2	66.9	41.5	25.9	10.5	..
35-39	**ELECTRICITY, GAS, WATER AND WASTE MANAGEMENT**	10.6	13.4	13.2	11.4	10.6	24.0	38.4	..
35-36	Electricity, gas and water	..	..	..	..	..	..	..	..
37-39	Sewerage, waste management and remediation activities	..	..	..	..	..	..	..	..
41-43	**CONSTRUCTION**	45.0	36.1	19.1	17.5	17.6	22.7	28.5	..
45-99	**TOTAL SERVICES**	2 600.7	2 671.5	2 140.8	2 223.0	2 512.4	2 644.2	2 844.0	..
45-82	**Business sector services**	2 568.2	2 638.4	2 114.6	2 204.7	2 500.3	2 606.9	2 780.0	..
45-47	Wholesale and retail trade; motor vehicle and motorcycle repairs	264.6	292.6	254.3	380.4	542.5	571.0	614.2	..
49-53	Transportation and storage	16.9	17.7	14.6	15.0	16.7	26.7	37.6	..
55-56	Accommodation and food service activities	0.0	0.0	0.0	0.0	0.0	0.0	0.0	..
58-63	Information and communication	659.8	660.9	512.4	427.0	380.4	447.0	526.4	..
58-60	Publishing, audiovisual and broadcasting activities	122.2	..	85.0	..	80.2	..	130.5	..
58	Publishing activities	..	..	..	..	..	..	..	..
59-60	Motion picture, video and TV programme production; broadcasting activities	..	..	..	..	..	..	..	..
59	Motion picture, video and TV programme production; sound and music	..	..	..	..	..	..	..	..
60	Programming and broadcasting activities	..	..	..	..	..	..	..	..
61	Telecommunications	..	..	..	..	..	..	..	..
62-63	IT and other information services	..	..	..	..	..	..	..	..
62	Computer programming, consultancy and related activities	..	..	..	..	..	..	..	..
63	Information service activities	..	..	..	..	..	..	..	..
64-66	Financial and insurance activities	89.8	90.3	70.3	77.4	91.8	95.7	102.1	..
68-82	Real estate; professional, scientific and technical; administrative and support	1 535.1	1 576.9	1 261.8	1 304.9	1 468.7	1 466.5	1 499.7	..
68	Real estate activities	0.0	0.0	0.0	0.0	0.0	0.0	0.0	..
69-75x72	Professional, scientific and technical activities, except scientific R&D	173.2	160.2	111.7	149.3	201.6	323.0	455.9	..
72	Scientific research and development	1 356.7	1 409.6	1 149.9	1 147.5	1 255.1	1 132.9	1 034.5	..
77-82	Administrative and support service activities	7.9	7.1	4.8	8.0	12.0	10.5	9.3	..
84-99	Community, social and personal services	32.5	33.1	26.2	18.3	12.1	37.2	64.0	..
84-85	Public administration and defence; compulsory social security and education	..	..	..	..	..	..	..	..
86-88	Human health and social work activities	..	..	..	..	..	..	..	..
90-93	Arts, entertainment and recreation	..	..	..	..	..	..	..	..
94-99	Other services; household-employers; extraterritorial bodies	..	..	..	..	..	..	..	..

.. Not available

Note: Detailed metadata at: http://metalinks.oecd.org/anberd/20170419/301f.
Information on data for Israel: http://oe.cd/israel-disclaimer.
Disclaimer: http://oe.cd/disclaimer

SWEDEN

R&D expenditure in industry by main activity of the enterprise, constant prices
ISIC Rev. 4

2010 USD PPP

		2007	2008	2009	2010	2011	2012	2013	2014
	TOTAL BUSINESS ENTERPRISE	9 292.4	10 064.5	8 895.7	8 639.7	8 902.7	8 898.1	9 231.7	..
01-03	**AGRICULTURE, FORESTRY AND FISHING**	20.0	22.1	20.0	20.4	22.1	21.6	21.9	..
05-09	**MINING AND QUARRYING**	16.6	18.4	16.6	17.0	18.3	17.9	18.2	..
10-33	**MANUFACTURING**	6 456.8	7 282.0	6 688.3	6 350.4	6 397.1	6 330.2	6 505.4	..
10-12	Food products, beverages and tobacco	48.4	50.1	42.3	42.6	45.4	44.6	45.4	..
13-15	Textiles, wearing apparel, leather and related products	8.9	10.0	9.2	6.9	5.0	5.2	5.5	..
13	Textiles	..	..	..	..	..	..	..	..
14	Wearing apparel	..	..	..	..	..	..	..	..
15	Leather and related products, footwear	..	..	..	..	..	..	..	..
16-18	Wood and paper products and printing	269.0	355.0	369.3	228.3	103.9	117.2	134.6	..
16	Wood and wood products, except furniture	..	..	..	..	..	..	..	..
17	Paper and paper products	259.3	..	365.3	..	99.7	..	126.3	..
18	Printing and reproduction of recorded media	..	..	..	..	..	..	..	..
19-23	Chemical, rubber, plastic, non-metallic mineral products	1 255.8	1 221.6	958.7	987.4	1 074.1	1 020.5	1 006.7	..
19	Coke and refined petroleum products	..	..	..	..	..	..	..	..
20-21	Chemical and pharmaceutical products	..	..	..	..	..	..	..	..
20	Chemicals and chemical products	..	..	..	..	..	..	..	..
21	Pharmaceuticals, medicinal, chemical and botanical products	1 010.1	946.9	708.4	757.5	850.5	783.6	747.8	..
22	Rubber and plastic products	20.6	26.4	26.8	24.3	23.3	25.0	27.7	..
23	Other non-metallic mineral products	9.5	11.9	12.0	12.7	14.2	14.4	15.1	..
24-25	Basic metals, metal products, except machinery and equipment	325.2	394.6	385.8	309.5	253.2	289.8	336.7	..
24	Basic metals	165.8	189.0	175.2	164.3	163.4	194.0	231.3	..
25	Fabricated metal products, except machinery and equipment	159.4	205.6	210.5	145.2	89.9	95.9	105.4	..
26-30	Computer, electronic, optical products; electrical machinery, transport equipment	4 344.6	5 015.9	4 704.1	4 589.0	4 748.8	4 696.2	4 822.4	..
26	Computer, electronic and optical products	1 887.8	2 202.8	2 084.9	2 024.4	2 085.3	1 946.1	1 883.3	..
27	Electrical equipment	238.5	273.5	254.9	252.7	265.4	280.4	305.7	..
28	Machinery and equipment n.e.c.	579.6	673.6	635.5	630.0	662.0	661.8	686.7	..
29	Motor vehicles, trailers and semi-trailers	1 127.0	1 197.9	1 038.8	1 010.7	1 043.2	1 086.4	1 169.8	..
30	Other transport equipment	511.6	668.1	690.0	671.3	692.8	721.5	776.9	..
31-33	Furniture; repair, installation of machinery and equipment	204.8	234.9	219.0	186.6	166.1	156.7	153.5	..
31	Furniture	11.0	14.9	15.7	12.2	9.4	12.6	16.2	..
32	Other manufacturing	125.0	127.1	105.2	107.6	116.4	119.8	127.6	..
33	Repair and installation of machinery and equipment	68.8	92.9	98.1	66.9	40.3	24.3	9.7	..
35-39	**ELECTRICITY, GAS, WATER AND WASTE MANAGEMENT**	11.1	13.5	13.2	11.4	10.3	22.6	35.5	..
35-36	Electricity, gas and water	..	..	..	..	..	..	..	..
37-39	Sewerage, waste management and remediation activities	..	..	..	..	..	..	..	..
41-43	**CONSTRUCTION**	47.4	36.4	19.1	17.5	17.1	21.4	26.3	..
45-99	**TOTAL SERVICES**	2 740.4	2 692.0	2 138.5	2 223.0	2 437.8	2 484.4	2 624.5	..
45-82	**Business sector services**	2 706.2	2 658.7	2 112.3	2 204.7	2 426.1	2 449.4	2 565.4	..
45-47	Wholesale and retail trade; motor vehicle and motorcycle repairs	278.8	294.9	254.0	380.4	526.4	536.5	566.8	..
49-53	Transportation and storage	17.8	17.9	14.6	15.0	16.2	25.1	34.7	..
55-56	Accommodation and food service activities	0.0	0.0	0.0	0.0	0.0	0.0	0.0	..
58-63	Information and communication	695.2	665.9	511.8	427.0	369.1	420.0	485.8	..
58-60	Publishing, audiovisual and broadcasting activities	128.8	..	84.9	..	77.8	..	120.4	..
58	Publishing activities	..	..	..	..	..	..	..	..
59-60	Motion picture, video and TV programme production; broadcasting activities	..	..	..	..	..	..	..	..
59	Motion picture, video and TV programme production; sound and music	..	..	..	..	..	..	..	..
60	Programming and broadcasting activities	..	..	..	..	..	..	..	..
61	Telecommunications	..	..	..	..	..	..	..	..
62-63	IT and other information services	..	..	..	..	..	..	..	..
62	Computer programming, consultancy and related activities	..	..	..	..	..	..	..	..
63	Information service activities	..	..	..	..	..	..	..	..
64-66	Financial and insurance activities	94.6	90.9	70.2	77.4	89.1	90.0	94.2	..
68-82	Real estate; professional, scientific and technical; administrative and support	1 617.6	1 589.1	1 260.4	1 304.9	1 425.1	1 377.9	1 383.9	..
68	Real estate activities	0.0	0.0	0.0	0.0	0.0	0.0	0.0	..
69-75x72	Professional, scientific and technical activities, except scientific R&D	182.5	161.4	111.6	149.3	195.6	303.5	420.7	..
72	Scientific research and development	1 429.6	1 420.5	1 148.6	1 147.5	1 217.8	1 064.4	954.6	..
77-82	Administrative and support service activities	8.3	7.2	4.8	8.0	11.6	9.9	8.6	..
84-99	Community, social and personal services	34.3	33.3	26.1	18.3	11.7	35.0	59.1	..
84-85	Public administration and defence; compulsory social security and education	..	..	..	..	..	..	..	..
86-88	Human health and social work activities	..	..	..	..	..	..	..	..
90-93	Arts, entertainment and recreation	..	..	..	..	..	..	..	..
94-99	Other services; household-employers; extraterritorial bodies	..	..	..	..	..	..	..	..

.. Not available

Note: Detailed metadata at: http://metalinks.oecd.org/anberd/20170419/301f.
Information on data for Israel: http://oe.cd/israel-disclaimer.
Disclaimer: http://oe.cd/disclaimer

SWITZERLAND

R&D expenditure in industry by main activity of the enterprise, current prices
ISIC Rev. 4

Million USD PPP

		2007	2008	2009	2010	2011	2012	2013	2014
	TOTAL BUSINESS ENTERPRISE	..	8 023.8	..	..	..	9 466.8	..	..
01-03	**AGRICULTURE, FORESTRY AND FISHING**	..	..	..	..	..	..	..	..
05-09	**MINING AND QUARRYING**	..	..	..	..	..	..	..	..
10-33	**MANUFACTURING**	..	5 991.8	..	..	..	6 492.8	..	..
10-12	Food products, beverages and tobacco	..	83.1	..	..	..	45.0	..	..
13-15	Textiles, wearing apparel, leather and related products	..	..	..	..	..	..	..	..
13	Textiles	..	..	..	..	..	..	..	..
14	Wearing apparel	..	..	..	..	..	..	..	..
15	Leather and related products, footwear	..	..	..	..	..	..	..	..
16-18	Wood and paper products and printing	..	..	..	..	..	..	..	..
16	Wood and wood products, except furniture	..	..	..	..	..	..	..	..
17	Paper and paper products	..	..	..	..	..	..	..	..
18	Printing and reproduction of recorded media	..	..	..	..	..	..	..	..
19-23	Chemical, rubber, plastic, non-metallic mineral products	..	3 481.5	..	..	..	3 180.0	..	..
19	Coke and refined petroleum products	..	..	..	..	..	..	..	..
20-21	Chemical and pharmaceutical products	..	..	..	..	..	..	..	..
20	Chemicals and chemical products	..	..	..	..	..	..	..	..
21	Pharmaceuticals, medicinal, chemical and botanical products	..	3 099.7	..	..	..	2 805.6	..	..
22	Rubber and plastic products	..	..	..	..	..	..	..	..
23	Other non-metallic mineral products	..	..	..	..	..	..	..	..
24-25	Basic metals, metal products, except machinery and equipment	..	173.5	..	..	..	336.8	..	..
24	Basic metals	..	..	..	..	..	..	..	..
25	Fabricated metal products, except machinery and equipment	..	..	..	..	..	..	..	..
26-30	Computer, electronic, optical products; electrical machinery, transport equipment	..	2 034.8	..	..	..	2 677.1	..	..
26	Computer, electronic and optical products	..	1 156.7	..	..	..	1 525.8	..	..
27	Electrical equipment	..	..	..	..	..	..	..	..
28	Machinery and equipment n.e.c.	..	..	..	..	..	..	..	..
29	Motor vehicles, trailers and semi-trailers	..	..	..	..	..	..	..	..
30	Other transport equipment	..	..	..	..	..	..	..	..
31-33	Furniture; repair, installation of machinery and equipment	..	..	..	..	..	..	..	..
31	Furniture	..	..	..	..	..	..	..	..
32	Other manufacturing	..	..	..	..	..	..	..	..
33	Repair and installation of machinery and equipment	..	..	..	..	..	..	..	..
35-39	**ELECTRICITY, GAS, WATER AND WASTE MANAGEMENT**	..	..	..	..	..	..	..	..
35-36	Electricity, gas and water	..	..	..	..	..	..	..	..
37-39	Sewerage, waste management and remediation activities	..	..	..	..	..	..	..	..
41-43	**CONSTRUCTION**	..	..	..	..	..	..	..	..
45-99	**TOTAL SERVICES**	..	2 032.1	..	..	..	2 974.0	..	..
45-82	**Business sector services**	..	..	..	..	..	..	..	..
45-47	Wholesale and retail trade; motor vehicle and motorcycle repairs	..	..	..	..	..	..	..	..
49-53	Transportation and storage	..	..	..	..	..	..	..	..
55-56	Accommodation and food service activities	..	..	..	..	..	..	..	..
58-63	Information and communication	..	..	..	..	..	..	..	..
58-60	Publishing, audiovisual and broadcasting activities	..	..	..	..	..	..	..	..
58	Publishing activities	..	..	..	..	..	..	..	..
59-60	Motion picture, video and TV programme production; broadcasting activities	..	..	..	..	..	..	..	..
59	Motion picture, video and TV programme production; sound and music	..	..	..	..	..	..	..	..
60	Programming and broadcasting activities	..	..	..	..	..	..	..	..
61	Telecommunications	..	..	..	..	..	..	..	..
62-63	IT and other information services	..	..	..	..	..	..	..	..
62	Computer programming, consultancy and related activities	..	..	..	..	..	..	..	..
63	Information service activities	..	..	..	..	..	..	..	..
64-66	Financial and insurance activities	..	..	..	..	..	..	..	..
68-82	Real estate; professional, scientific and technical; administrative and support	..	..	..	..	..	..	..	..
68	Real estate activities	..	..	..	..	..	..	..	..
69-75x72	Professional, scientific and technical activities, except scientific R&D	..	..	..	..	..	..	..	..
72	Scientific research and development	..	722.0	..	..	..	2 721.4	..	..
77-82	Administrative and support service activities	..	..	..	..	..	..	..	..
84-99	Community, social and personal services	..	..	..	..	..	..	..	..
84-85	Public administration and defence; compulsory social security and education	..	..	..	..	..	..	..	..
86-88	Human health and social work activities	..	..	..	..	..	..	..	..
90-93	Arts, entertainment and recreation	..	..	..	..	..	..	..	..
94-99	Other services; household-employers; extraterritorial bodies	..	..	..	..	..	..	..	..

.. Not available

Note: Detailed metadata at: http://metalinks.oecd.org/anberd/20170419/301f.
    Information on data for Israel: http://oe.cd/israel-disclaimer.
Disclaimer: http://oe.cd/disclaimer

SWITZERLAND

R&D expenditure in industry by main activity of the enterprise, constant prices
ISIC Rev. 4

2010 USD PPP

		2007	2008	2009	2010	2011	2012	2013	2014
	TOTAL BUSINESS ENTERPRISE	..	8 244.1	..	..	..	8 759.0	..	..
01-03	AGRICULTURE, FORESTRY AND FISHING	..	..	..	..	..	..	..	..
05-09	MINING AND QUARRYING	..	..	..	..	..	..	..	..
10-33	MANUFACTURING	..	6 156.2	..	..	..	6 007.4	..	..
10-12	Food products, beverages and tobacco	..	85.3	..	..	..	41.7	..	..
13-15	Textiles, wearing apparel, leather and related products	..	..	..	..	..	..	..	..
13	Textiles	..	..	..	..	..	..	..	..
14	Wearing apparel	..	..	..	..	..	..	..	..
15	Leather and related products, footwear	..	..	..	..	..	..	..	..
16-18	Wood and paper products and printing	..	..	..	..	..	..	..	..
16	Wood and wood products, except furniture	..	..	..	..	..	..	..	..
17	Paper and paper products	..	..	..	..	..	..	..	..
18	Printing and reproduction of recorded media	..	..	..	..	..	..	..	..
19-23	Chemical, rubber, plastic, non-metallic mineral products	..	3 577.0	..	..	..	2 942.3	..	..
19	Coke and refined petroleum products	..	..	..	..	..	..	..	..
20-21	Chemical and pharmaceutical products	..	..	..	..	..	..	..	..
20	Chemicals and chemical products	..	..	..	..	..	..	..	..
21	Pharmaceuticals, medicinal, chemical and botanical products	..	3 184.8	..	..	..	2 595.9	..	..
22	Rubber and plastic products	..	..	..	..	..	..	..	..
23	Other non-metallic mineral products	..	..	..	..	..	..	..	..
24-25	Basic metals, metal products, except machinery and equipment	..	178.2	..	..	..	311.6	..	..
24	Basic metals	..	..	..	..	..	..	..	..
25	Fabricated metal products, except machinery and equipment	..	..	..	..	..	..	..	..
26-30	Computer, electronic, optical products; electrical machinery, transport equipment	..	2 090.6	..	..	..	2 477.0	..	..
26	Computer, electronic and optical products	..	1 188.4	..	..	..	1 411.7	..	..
27	Electrical equipment	..	..	..	..	..	..	..	..
28	Machinery and equipment n.e.c.	..	..	..	..	..	..	..	..
29	Motor vehicles, trailers and semi-trailers	..	..	..	..	..	..	..	..
30	Other transport equipment	..	..	..	..	..	..	..	..
31-33	Furniture; repair, installation of machinery and equipment	..	..	..	..	..	..	..	..
31	Furniture	..	..	..	..	..	..	..	..
32	Other manufacturing	..	..	..	..	..	..	..	..
33	Repair and installation of machinery and equipment	..	..	..	..	..	..	..	..
35-39	ELECTRICITY, GAS, WATER AND WASTE MANAGEMENT	..	..	..	..	..	..	..	..
35-36	Electricity, gas and water	..	..	..	..	..	..	..	..
37-39	Sewerage, waste management and remediation activities	..	..	..	..	..	..	..	..
41-43	CONSTRUCTION	..	..	..	..	..	..	..	..
45-99	TOTAL SERVICES	..	2 087.9	..	..	..	2 751.6	..	..
45-82	Business sector services	..	..	..	..	..	..	..	..
45-47	Wholesale and retail trade; motor vehicle and motorcycle repairs	..	..	..	..	..	..	..	..
49-53	Transportation and storage	..	..	..	..	..	..	..	..
55-56	Accommodation and food service activities	..	..	..	..	..	..	..	..
58-63	Information and communication	..	..	..	..	..	..	..	..
58-60	Publishing, audiovisual and broadcasting activities	..	..	..	..	..	..	..	..
58	Publishing activities	..	..	..	..	..	..	..	..
59-60	Motion picture, video and TV programme production; broadcasting activities	..	..	..	..	..	..	..	..
59	Motion picture, video and TV programme production; sound and music	..	..	..	..	..	..	..	..
60	Programming and broadcasting activities	..	..	..	..	..	..	..	..
61	Telecommunications	..	..	..	..	..	..	..	..
62-63	IT and other information services	..	..	..	..	..	..	..	..
62	Computer programming, consultancy and related activities	..	..	..	..	..	..	..	..
63	Information service activities	..	..	..	..	..	..	..	..
64-66	Financial and insurance activities	..	..	..	..	..	..	..	..
68-82	Real estate; professional, scientific and technical; administrative and support	..	..	..	..	..	..	..	..
68	Real estate activities	..	..	..	..	..	..	..	..
69-75x72	Professional, scientific and technical activities, except scientific R&D	..	..	..	..	..	..	..	..
72	Scientific research and development	..	741.8	..	..	..	2 518.0	..	..
77-82	Administrative and support service activities	..	..	..	..	..	..	..	..
84-99	Community, social and personal services	..	..	..	..	..	..	..	..
84-85	Public administration and defence; compulsory social security and education	..	..	..	..	..	..	..	..
86-88	Human health and social work activities	..	..	..	..	..	..	..	..
90-93	Arts, entertainment and recreation	..	..	..	..	..	..	..	..
94-99	Other services; household-employers; extraterritorial bodies	..	..	..	..	..	..	..	..

.. Not available

Note: Detailed metadata at: http://metalinks.oecd.org/anberd/20170419/301f.
Information on data for Israel: http://oe.cd/israel-disclaimer.
Disclaimer: http://oe.cd/disclaimer

TURKEY

R&D expenditure in industry by main activity of the enterprise, current prices
ISIC Rev. 4

Million USD PPP

		2007	2008	2009	2010	2011	2012	2013	2014
	TOTAL BUSINESS ENTERPRISE	2 948.5	3 464.4	3 580.7	4 292.3	4 985.9	5 776.5	6 575.6	7 634.8
01-03	**AGRICULTURE, FORESTRY AND FISHING**	5.0	7.0	8.5	9.9	13.3	12.4	16.9	17.9
05-09	**MINING AND QUARRYING**	9.7	10.2	13.0	14.5	19.8	17.1	30.6	17.5
10-33	**MANUFACTURING**	2 110.6	2 347.1	2 229.8	2 215.7	2 659.4	3 063.3	3 376.6	3 957.9
10-12	Food products, beverages and tobacco	60.8	76.6	83.3	66.3	78.4	80.8	115.7	114.4
13-15	Textiles, wearing apparel, leather and related products	53.6	63.1	70.2	70.2	99.3	106.8	93.0	114.3
13	Textiles	44.4	51.3	54.9	55.7	83.0	88.6	73.3	91.2
14	Wearing apparel	6.2	7.8	13.8	12.7	13.7	15.3	16.3	17.7
15	Leather and related products, footwear	3.0	4.0	1.5	1.8	2.6	2.9	3.4	5.3
16-18	Wood and paper products and printing	6.0	7.4	11.8	9.5	11.3	12.5	12.0	16.9
16	Wood and wood products, except furniture	1.5	1.7	3.3	1.6	3.5	3.2	1.8	3.5
17	Paper and paper products	0.5	0.6	4.7	4.7	4.5	5.7	4.7	4.8
18	Printing and reproduction of recorded media	4.1	5.1	3.8	3.2	3.3	3.6	5.4	8.6
19-23	Chemical, rubber, plastic, non-metallic mineral products	279.9	292.0	334.4	383.4	550.3	601.2	723.4	657.3
19	Coke and refined petroleum products	0.0	0.6	9.2	12.6	16.4	19.2	29.5	25.3
20-21	Chemical and pharmaceutical products	183.9	187.3	205.8	243.6	387.6	406.1	531.6	478.0
20	Chemicals and chemical products	..	..	104.2	143.3	186.6	218.3	335.0	287.0
21	Pharmaceuticals, medicinal, chemical and botanical products	..	..	101.6	100.3	201.0	187.8	196.7	191.0
22	Rubber and plastic products	47.2	54.9	63.0	69.8	80.1	98.2	80.6	83.0
23	Other non-metallic mineral products	48.8	49.1	56.5	57.4	66.1	77.7	81.7	71.0
24-25	Basic metals, metal products, except machinery and equipment	51.6	49.3	82.9	209.3	206.7	246.3	252.9	368.1
24	Basic metals	20.2	16.1	22.2	30.2	55.0	59.4	55.7	93.3
25	Fabricated metal products, except machinery and equipment	31.4	33.1	60.7	179.1	151.6	187.0	197.2	274.8
26-30	Computer, electronic, optical products; electrical machinery, transport equipment	1 611.0	1 803.3	1 581.6	1 431.3	1 654.4	1 945.1	2 110.3	2 610.3
26	Computer, electronic and optical products	424.2	480.8	496.6	133.3	153.7	196.5	264.2	228.3
27	Electrical equipment	130.4	168.5	225.4	236.4	322.7	328.8	344.3	405.2
28	Machinery and equipment n.e.c.	100.1	153.7	161.0	186.7	242.4	295.6	313.9	298.3
29	Motor vehicles, trailers and semi-trailers	816.1	816.9	495.3	637.4	676.7	773.4	909.7	1 338.7
30	Other transport equipment	140.2	183.5	203.4	237.6	258.9	350.8	278.1	339.9
31-33	Furniture; repair, installation of machinery and equipment	47.8	55.5	65.6	45.7	59.1	70.6	69.3	76.5
31	Furniture	..	..	14.1	14.5	15.9	13.6	14.7	12.4
32	Other manufacturing	..	..	18.5	18.4	26.8	36.9	28.8	39.6
33	Repair and installation of machinery and equipment	..	..	33.1	12.8	16.4	20.2	25.8	24.5
35-39	**ELECTRICITY, GAS, WATER AND WASTE MANAGEMENT**	10.8	12.4	18.0	11.7	17.5	30.1	34.4	37.2
35-36	Electricity, gas and water	..	..	..	..	12.8	25.0	30.6	33.0
37-39	Sewerage, waste management and remediation activities	..	..	..	..	4.7	5.1	3.8	4.2
41-43	**CONSTRUCTION**	7.4	8.6	14.2	22.4	30.3	41.6	25.3	26.2
45-99	**TOTAL SERVICES**	804.9	1 079.0	1 297.2	2 018.0	2 245.6	2 612.1	3 091.8	3 578.3
45-82	**Business sector services**	780.8	1 054.7	1 268.4	2 005.9	2 230.6	2 590.2	3 075.8	3 557.3
45-47	Wholesale and retail trade; motor vehicle and motorcycle repairs	52.5	59.8	153.0	117.4	183.4	153.6	180.9	190.2
49-53	Transportation and storage	2.9	4.3	4.8	10.6	10.3	17.6	25.8	29.0
55-56	Accommodation and food service activities	0.0	0.0	0.7	0.0	0.0	0.5	0.4	0.6
58-63	Information and communication	475.6	634.9	741.3	1 207.3	1 176.8	1 449.5	1 655.4	2 018.2
58-60	Publishing, audiovisual and broadcasting activities	..	..	102.0	189.7	68.1	22.7	30.1	53.5
58	Publishing activities	..	..	..	..	..	21.1	28.4	50.6
59-60	Motion picture, video and TV programme production; broadcasting activities	..	..	..	..	..	1.7	1.7	2.8
59	Motion picture, video and TV programme production; sound and music	..	..	..	..	..	..	..	..
60	Programming and broadcasting activities	..	..	..	..	..	..	..	..
61	Telecommunications	52.8	74.3	79.7	279.9	215.9	310.1	333.1	446.1
62-63	IT and other information services	..	..	559.6	737.6	892.8	1 116.6	1 292.3	1 518.7
62	Computer programming, consultancy and related activities	..	..	550.3	728.0	881.8	1 100.2	1 283.8	1 509.9
63	Information service activities	..	..	9.3	9.6	11.0	16.4	8.5	8.7
64-66	Financial and insurance activities	172.1	208.3	152.8	66.5	96.9	93.9	130.8	116.6
68-82	Real estate; professional, scientific and technical; administrative and support	77.7	147.4	215.8	604.1	763.1	875.1	1 082.4	1 202.8
68	Real estate activities	..	..	0.0	0.0	0.0	0.0	0.0	0.0
69-75x72	Professional, scientific and technical activities, except scientific R&D	..	..	60.8	17.3	28.4	31.7	37.2	39.4
72	Scientific research and development	60.6	112.4	151.9	584.2	732.5	840.8	1 040.5	1 155.3
77-82	Administrative and support service activities	..	..	3.1	2.6	2.2	2.6	4.8	8.1
84-99	**Community, social and personal services**	24.1	24.3	28.8	12.1	15.0	21.9	16.1	20.9
84-85	Public administration and defence; compulsory social security and education	..	..	24.1	5.5	8.5	15.0	12.0	13.2
86-88	Human health and social work activities	..	..	2.1	3.9	3.4	3.8	2.2	6.2
90-93	Arts, entertainment and recreation	..	..	..	..	..	..	..	..
94-99	Other services; household-employers; extraterritorial bodies	..	..	..	..	..	..	..	..

.. Not available

Note: Detailed metadata at: http://metalinks.oecd.org/anberd/20170419/301f.
    Information on data for Israel: http://oe.cd/israel-disclaimer.
Disclaimer: http://oe.cd/disclaimer

TURKEY

R&D expenditure in industry by main activity of the enterprise, constant prices
ISIC Rev. 4

2010 USD PPP

		2007	2008	2009	2010	2011	2012	2013	2014
	TOTAL BUSINESS ENTERPRISE	3 409.8	3 692.6	3 721.8	4 292.3	4 829.8	5 525.2	6 211.4	7 143.1
01-03	**AGRICULTURE, FORESTRY AND FISHING**	5.8	7.5	8.8	9.9	12.9	11.8	16.0	16.7
05-09	**MINING AND QUARRYING**	11.2	10.9	13.5	14.5	19.2	16.3	28.9	16.4
10-33	**MANUFACTURING**	2 440.8	2 501.8	2 317.6	2 215.7	2 576.2	2 930.1	3 189.5	3 702.9
10-12	Food products, beverages and tobacco	70.3	81.7	86.6	66.3	75.9	77.3	109.2	107.1
13-15	Textiles, wearing apparel, leather and related products	62.0	67.2	73.0	70.2	96.2	102.1	87.9	106.9
13	Textiles	51.4	54.7	57.1	55.7	80.4	84.8	69.2	85.4
14	Wearing apparel	7.1	8.3	14.4	12.7	13.3	14.6	15.4	16.6
15	Leather and related products, footwear	3.5	4.2	1.5	1.8	2.5	2.8	3.2	5.0
16-18	Wood and paper products and printing	7.0	7.9	12.2	9.5	11.0	11.9	11.3	15.8
16	Wood and wood products, except furniture	1.7	1.8	3.4	1.6	3.4	3.1	1.7	3.2
17	Paper and paper products	0.5	0.7	4.9	4.7	4.4	5.4	4.5	4.5
18	Printing and reproduction of recorded media	4.7	5.4	4.0	3.2	3.2	3.4	5.1	8.1
19-23	Chemical, rubber, plastic, non-metallic mineral products	323.6	311.2	347.5	383.4	533.0	575.0	683.3	615.0
19	Coke and refined petroleum products	0.0	0.7	9.5	12.6	15.9	18.4	27.9	23.7
20-21	Chemical and pharmaceutical products	212.6	199.7	213.9	243.6	375.5	388.4	502.2	447.2
20	Chemicals and chemical products	..	..	108.3	143.3	180.7	208.8	316.4	268.5
21	Pharmaceuticals, medicinal, chemical and botanical products	..	..	105.6	100.3	194.7	179.6	185.8	178.7
22	Rubber and plastic products	54.6	58.5	65.5	69.8	77.6	93.9	76.1	77.7
23	Other non-metallic mineral products	56.4	52.3	58.7	57.4	64.1	74.3	77.1	66.4
24-25	Basic metals, metal products, except machinery and equipment	59.7	52.5	86.2	209.3	200.2	235.6	238.9	344.4
24	Basic metals	23.3	17.2	23.1	30.2	53.3	56.8	52.7	87.3
25	Fabricated metal products, except machinery and equipment	36.3	35.3	63.0	179.1	146.9	178.8	186.3	257.1
26-30	Computer, electronic, optical products; electrical machinery, transport equipment	1 863.0	1 922.1	1 643.9	1 431.3	1 602.6	1 860.5	1 993.4	2 442.2
26	Computer, electronic and optical products	490.5	512.4	516.1	133.3	148.9	188.0	249.5	213.6
27	Electrical equipment	150.9	179.6	234.3	236.4	312.5	314.5	325.3	379.1
28	Machinery and equipment n.e.c.	115.8	163.8	167.3	186.7	234.9	282.7	296.5	279.1
29	Motor vehicles, trailers and semi-trailers	943.8	870.7	514.8	637.4	655.5	739.8	859.3	1 252.4
30	Other transport equipment	162.1	195.6	211.4	237.6	250.8	335.5	262.7	318.0
31-33	Furniture; repair, installation of machinery and equipment	55.3	59.2	68.2	45.7	57.2	67.5	65.5	71.6
31	Furniture	..	..	14.6	14.5	15.4	13.0	13.9	11.6
32	Other manufacturing	..	..	19.2	18.4	25.9	35.3	27.2	37.1
33	Repair and installation of machinery and equipment	..	..	34.4	12.8	15.9	19.3	24.4	22.9
35-39	**ELECTRICITY, GAS, WATER AND WASTE MANAGEMENT**	12.4	13.2	18.7	11.7	17.0	28.8	32.5	34.8
35-36	Electricity, gas and water	..	..	..	..	12.4	23.9	28.9	30.9
37-39	Sewerage, waste management and remediation activities	..	..	..	..	4.5	4.9	3.6	3.9
41-43	**CONSTRUCTION**	8.6	9.2	14.8	22.4	29.3	39.7	23.9	24.5
45-99	**TOTAL SERVICES**	930.9	1 150.1	1 348.3	2 018.0	2 175.3	2 498.4	2 920.6	3 347.8
45-82	**Business sector services**	903.0	1 124.2	1 318.4	2 005.9	2 160.7	2 477.5	2 905.4	3 328.2
45-47	Wholesale and retail trade; motor vehicle and motorcycle repairs	60.7	63.8	159.1	117.4	177.7	147.0	170.9	177.9
49-53	Transportation and storage	3.4	4.5	5.0	10.6	10.0	16.8	24.4	27.1
55-56	Accommodation and food service activities	0.0	0.0	0.7	0.0	0.0	0.5	0.4	0.5
58-63	Information and communication	550.0	676.7	770.5	1 207.3	1 140.0	1 386.4	1 563.7	1 888.2
58-60	Publishing, audiovisual and broadcasting activities	..	..	106.0	189.7	66.0	21.8	28.4	50.0
58	Publishing activities	..	..	..	..	..	20.2	26.8	47.4
59-60	Motion picture, video and TV programme production; broadcasting activities	..	..	..	..	..	1.6	1.6	2.7
59	Motion picture, video and TV programme production; sound and music	..	..	..	..	..	..	..	..
60	Programming and broadcasting activities	..	..	..	..	..	..	..	..
61	Telecommunications	61.1	79.2	82.9	279.9	209.1	296.6	314.6	417.3
62-63	IT and other information services	..	..	581.6	737.6	864.9	1 068.0	1 220.7	1 420.8
62	Computer programming, consultancy and related activities	..	..	572.0	728.0	854.2	1 052.3	1 212.7	1 412.7
63	Information service activities	..	..	9.6	9.6	10.7	15.7	8.0	8.2
64-66	Financial and insurance activities	199.1	222.0	158.8	66.5	93.8	89.8	123.5	109.1
68-82	Real estate; professional, scientific and technical; administrative and support	89.9	157.1	224.3	604.1	739.2	837.0	1 022.5	1 125.3
68	Real estate activities	..	..	0.0	0.0	0.0	0.0	0.0	0.0
69-75x72	Professional, scientific and technical activities, except scientific R&D	..	..	63.2	17.3	27.5	30.3	35.1	36.9
72	Scientific research and development	70.1	119.8	157.8	584.2	709.6	804.2	982.8	1 080.9
77-82	Administrative and support service activities	..	..	3.3	2.6	2.1	2.5	4.5	7.6
84-99	Community, social and personal services	27.9	25.9	30.0	12.1	14.6	20.9	15.2	19.6
84-85	Public administration and defence; compulsory social security and education	..	..	25.0	5.5	8.2	14.3	11.3	12.4
86-88	Human health and social work activities	..	..	2.2	3.9	3.3	3.6	2.1	5.8
90-93	Arts, entertainment and recreation	..	..	..	..	..	..	..	..
94-99	Other services; household-employers; extraterritorial bodies	..	..	..	..	..	..	..	..

.. Not available

Note: Detailed metadata at: http://metalinks.oecd.org/anberd/20170419/301f.
Information on data for Israel: http://oe.cd/israel-disclaimer.

Disclaimer: http://oe.cd/disclaimer

UNITED KINGDOM

R&D expenditure in industry by main activity of the enterprise, current prices
ISIC Rev. 4

Million USD PPP

Code	Activity	2007	2008	2009	2010	2011	2012	2013	2014
	TOTAL BUSINESS ENTERPRISE	22 008.8	22 653.9	22 030.4	22 922.5	24 655.7	24 381.2	26 558.1	28 797.1
01-03	**AGRICULTURE, FORESTRY AND FISHING**	37.6	29.2	11.1	19.4	17.6	20.0	14.8	19.4
05-09	**MINING AND QUARRYING**	92.8	103.9	126.1	194.7	245.0	243.7	274.1	263.6
10-33	**MANUFACTURING**	9 363.4	8 833.2	8 480.9	8 515.8	9 097.9	9 745.8	10 538.6	11 244.4
10-12	Food products, beverages and tobacco	..	..	366.7	330.7	393.2	391.7	471.5	476.7
13-15	Textiles, wearing apparel, leather and related products	..	..	14.7	15.4	36.0	45.5	31.7	32.4
13	Textiles	..	..	11.1	13.3	32.4	38.9	23.8	24.0
14	Wearing apparel	..	..	2.0	1.1	1.7	3.8	4.2	4.9
15	Leather and related products, footwear	..	..	1.6	1.0	1.8	2.7	3.7	3.5
16-18	Wood and paper products and printing	..	..	23.8	25.8	21.4	31.2	51.4	58.1
16	Wood and wood products, except furniture	..	..	3.9	5.1	2.0	4.0	9.5	9.0
17	Paper and paper products	..	..	10.4	12.8	12.5	11.4	15.1	17.8
18	Printing and reproduction of recorded media	..	..	9.4	7.8	6.9	15.8	26.8	31.3
19-23	Chemical, rubber, plastic, non-metallic mineral products	..	..	1 250.7	1 283.0	1 350.5	1 310.1	1 391.7	1 383.2
19	Coke and refined petroleum products	..	..	123.2	18.5	26.8	31.6	27.5	48.2
20-21	Chemical and pharmaceutical products	..	..	963.9	1 110.4	1 151.0	1 093.2	1 178.6	1 106.2
20	Chemicals and chemical products	..	..	384.5	457.5	402.4	374.6	519.6	528.6
21	Pharmaceuticals, medicinal, chemical and botanical products	..	..	579.4	652.8	748.7	718.6	659.1	577.7
22	Rubber and plastic products	..	..	104.8	95.2	115.1	140.4	136.9	159.8
23	Other non-metallic mineral products	..	..	58.8	58.9	57.5	44.9	48.7	68.9
24-25	Basic metals, metal products, except machinery and equipment	..	..	948.0	918.3	903.9	796.1	803.2	868.8
24	Basic metals	..	..	65.6	70.5	123.5	90.2	63.9	102.3
25	Fabricated metal products, except machinery and equipment	..	..	882.4	847.9	780.4	705.9	739.3	766.5
26-30	Computer, electronic, optical products; electrical machinery, transport equipment	..	..	5 444.4	5 458.4	6 048.1	6 853.0	7 384.0	8 005.2
26	Computer, electronic and optical products	..	..	1 372.7	1 179.6	1 384.5	1 391.9	1 469.6	1 453.8
27	Electrical equipment	..	..	193.5	233.0	215.7	242.1	230.9	261.9
28	Machinery and equipment n.e.c.	..	..	887.1	886.8	897.4	1 106.3	1 079.9	1 079.1
29	Motor vehicles, trailers and semi-trailers	..	..	1 360.5	1 507.5	1 834.9	2 106.7	2 510.3	2 913.2
30	Other transport equipment	..	..	1 629.2	1 651.6	1 715.6	2 006.0	2 093.4	2 297.3
31-33	Furniture; repair, installation of machinery and equipment	..	..	432.6	484.2	344.9	318.3	405.1	420.2
31	Furniture	..	..	38.5	46.7	70.8	51.6	73.1	56.3
32	Other manufacturing	..	..	121.3	204.7	166.0	147.7	181.7	178.7
33	Repair and installation of machinery and equipment	..	..	272.8	232.8	108.1	119.0	150.3	185.2
35-39	**ELECTRICITY, GAS, WATER AND WASTE MANAGEMENT**	45.1	35.5	43.9	42.7	46.6	118.6	163.0	157.2
35-36	Electricity, gas and water	..	..	32.3	32.2	37.1	102.8	141.1	140.4
37-39	Sewerage, waste management and remediation activities	..	..	11.6	10.4	9.5	15.8	21.9	16.8
41-43	**CONSTRUCTION**	28.6	39.8	76.6	54.2	53.1	85.8	100.3	151.7
45-99	**TOTAL SERVICES**	12 441.4	13 612.4	13 291.8	14 095.8	15 195.6	14 167.4	15 467.3	16 960.8
45-82	**Business sector services**	..	..	13 069.6	13 791.7	14 852.7	13 816.3	15 023.6	16 646.8
45-47	Wholesale and retail trade; motor vehicle and motorcycle repairs	..	..	827.7	1 074.8	1 084.8	996.8	994.4	1 013.1
49-53	Transportation and storage	..	..	40.9	40.9	41.9	14.0	43.9	66.6
55-56	Accommodation and food service activities	..	..	12.0	26.7	36.0	41.6	23.2	42.2
58-63	Information and communication	..	..	3 208.1	2 981.0	3 317.3	3 450.7	3 787.8	4 239.9
58-60	Publishing, audiovisual and broadcasting activities	..	..	111.8	102.0	120.4	98.1	174.3	284.4
58	Publishing activities	..	..	71.3	63.5	87.0	73.5	126.8	119.5
59-60	Motion picture, video and TV programme production; broadcasting activities	..	..	40.5	38.4	33.4	24.5	47.5	165.0
59	Motion picture, video and TV programme production; sound and music	..	..	29.2	33.8	24.8	15.0	32.0	111.0
60	Programming and broadcasting activities	..	..	11.3	4.6	8.6	9.5	15.5	54.0
61	Telecommunications	..	..	1 427.9	1 177.7	1 018.1	999.8	1 054.0	1 149.9
62-63	IT and other information services	..	..	1 668.4	1 701.3	2 178.9	2 352.9	2 559.5	2 805.6
62	Computer programming, consultancy and related activities	..	..	1 553.4	1 637.4	2 116.3	2 228.9	2 321.3	2 361.6
63	Information service activities	..	..	114.9	63.9	62.6	124.0	238.3	444.1
64-66	Financial and insurance activities	..	..	534.7	497.0	430.0	380.3	476.2	541.3
68-82	Real estate; professional, scientific and technical; administrative and support	..	..	8 446.2	9 171.1	9 942.8	8 933.0	9 698.1	10 743.7
68	Real estate activities	..	..	15.1	14.3	14.0	16.0	23.8	31.3
69-75x72	Professional, scientific and technical activities, except scientific R&D	..	..	1 105.6	1 212.2	1 377.1	1 821.9	2 277.5	2 875.7
72	Scientific research and development	6 182.0	7 085.6	7 207.5	7 750.1	8 276.0	6 681.7	6 998.8	7 186.7
77-82	Administrative and support service activities	..	..	118.0	194.5	275.6	413.6	398.1	650.1
84-99	Community, social and personal services	..	..	222.2	304.2	342.9	351.0	443.7	314.0
84-85	Public administration and defence; compulsory social security and education	..	..	22.8	12.4	11.0	27.2	47.7	22.4
86-88	Human health and social work activities	..	..	4.2	36.0	24.8	23.9	45.3	57.5
90-93	Arts, entertainment and recreation	..	..	173.9	216.4	272.1	264.5	304.3	196.5
94-99	Other services; household-employers; extraterritorial bodies	..	..	21.3	39.4	35.0	35.3	46.4	37.7

.. Not available

Note: Detailed metadata at: http://metalinks.oecd.org/anberd/20170419/301f.
   Information on data for Israel: http://oe.cd/israel-disclaimer.
Disclaimer: http://oe.cd/disclaimer

UNITED KINGDOM

R&D expenditure in industry by main activity of the enterprise, constant prices
ISIC Rev. 4

2010 USD PPP

ISIC	Activity	2007	2008	2009	2010	2011	2012	2013	2014
	TOTAL BUSINESS ENTERPRISE	23 639.2	23 380.2	22 633.7	22 922.5	24 345.7	23 561.4	24 933.7	26 507.4
01-03	**AGRICULTURE, FORESTRY AND FISHING**	40.4	30.2	11.4	19.4	17.3	19.3	13.9	17.8
05-09	**MINING AND QUARRYING**	99.7	107.2	129.5	194.7	241.9	235.5	257.3	242.7
10-33	**MANUFACTURING**	10 057.0	9 116.4	8 713.2	8 515.8	8 983.5	9 418.1	9 894.0	10 350.4
10-12	Food products, beverages and tobacco	..	..	376.8	330.7	388.2	378.5	442.6	438.8
13-15	Textiles, wearing apparel, leather and related products	..	..	15.1	15.4	35.5	43.9	29.7	29.8
13	Textiles	..	..	11.4	13.3	32.0	37.6	22.3	22.1
14	Wearing apparel	..	..	2.0	1.1	1.7	3.7	3.9	4.5
15	Leather and related products, footwear	..	..	1.6	1.0	1.8	2.6	3.5	3.2
16-18	Wood and paper products and printing	..	..	24.5	25.8	21.1	30.2	48.3	53.5
16	Wood and wood products, except furniture	..	..	4.1	5.1	2.0	3.9	8.9	8.2
17	Paper and paper products	..	..	10.7	12.8	12.3	11.0	14.2	16.4
18	Printing and reproduction of recorded media	..	..	9.7	7.8	6.9	15.3	25.1	28.9
19-23	Chemical, rubber, plastic, non-metallic mineral products	..	..	1 285.0	1 283.0	1 333.5	1 266.0	1 306.6	1 273.2
19	Coke and refined petroleum products	..	..	126.6	18.5	26.4	30.6	25.8	44.4
20-21	Chemical and pharmaceutical products	..	..	990.3	1 110.4	1 136.6	1 056.4	1 106.5	1 018.3
20	Chemicals and chemical products	..	..	395.0	457.5	397.3	362.0	487.8	486.5
21	Pharmaceuticals, medicinal, chemical and botanical products	..	..	595.2	652.8	739.3	694.4	618.8	531.7
22	Rubber and plastic products	..	..	107.6	95.2	113.7	135.7	128.5	147.1
23	Other non-metallic mineral products	..	..	60.4	58.9	56.8	43.4	45.7	63.4
24-25	Basic metals, metal products, except machinery and equipment	..	..	973.9	918.3	892.5	769.4	754.0	799.7
24	Basic metals	..	..	67.4	70.5	122.0	87.2	60.0	94.1
25	Fabricated metal products, except machinery and equipment	..	..	906.6	847.9	770.6	682.2	694.0	705.5
26-30	Computer, electronic, optical products; electrical machinery, transport equipment	..	..	5 593.5	5 458.4	5 972.1	6 622.6	6 932.4	7 368.7
26	Computer, electronic and optical products	..	..	1 410.3	1 179.6	1 367.1	1 345.1	1 379.7	1 338.2
27	Electrical equipment	..	..	198.8	233.0	213.0	234.0	216.8	241.1
28	Machinery and equipment n.e.c.	..	..	911.3	886.8	886.1	1 069.1	1 013.8	993.3
29	Motor vehicles, trailers and semi-trailers	..	..	1 397.8	1 507.5	1 811.8	2 035.8	2 356.7	2 681.6
30	Other transport equipment	..	..	1 673.8	1 651.6	1 694.0	1 938.6	1 965.3	2 114.6
31-33	Furniture; repair, installation of machinery and equipment	..	..	444.4	484.2	340.5	307.6	380.3	386.8
31	Furniture	..	..	39.5	46.7	69.9	49.9	68.7	51.9
32	Other manufacturing	..	..	124.6	204.7	163.9	142.7	170.6	164.5
33	Repair and installation of machinery and equipment	..	..	280.3	232.8	106.7	115.0	141.1	170.5
35-39	**ELECTRICITY, GAS, WATER AND WASTE MANAGEMENT**	48.4	36.6	45.1	42.7	46.0	114.6	153.0	144.7
35-36	Electricity, gas and water	..	..	33.2	32.2	36.6	99.3	132.5	129.2
37-39	Sewerage, waste management and remediation activities	..	..	11.9	10.4	9.4	15.3	20.5	15.4
41-43	**CONSTRUCTION**	30.7	41.0	78.7	54.2	52.4	82.9	94.2	139.6
45-99	**TOTAL SERVICES**	13 363.0	14 048.8	13 655.8	14 095.8	15 004.5	13 691.0	14 521.2	15 612.3
45-82	**Business sector services**	..	..	13 427.5	13 791.7	14 666.0	13 351.7	14 104.7	15 323.2
45-47	Wholesale and retail trade; motor vehicle and motorcycle repairs	..	..	850.4	1 074.8	1 071.1	963.3	933.5	932.5
49-53	Transportation and storage	..	..	42.0	40.9	41.4	13.5	41.2	61.3
55-56	Accommodation and food service activities	..	..	12.3	26.7	35.5	40.2	21.8	38.8
58-63	Information and communication	..	..	3 296.0	2 981.0	3 275.6	3 334.6	3 556.1	3 902.8
58-60	Publishing, audiovisual and broadcasting activities	..	..	114.9	102.0	118.9	94.8	163.7	261.8
58	Publishing activities	..	..	73.3	63.5	85.9	71.1	119.1	110.0
59-60	Motion picture, video and TV programme production; broadcasting activities	..	..	41.6	38.4	33.0	23.7	44.6	151.9
59	Motion picture, video and TV programme production; sound and music	..	..	30.0	33.8	24.5	14.5	30.0	102.2
60	Programming and broadcasting activities	..	..	11.6	4.6	8.5	9.2	14.6	49.7
61	Telecommunications	..	..	1 467.0	1 177.7	1 005.3	966.2	989.5	1 058.4
62-63	IT and other information services	..	..	1 714.0	1 701.3	2 151.5	2 273.8	2 403.0	2 582.5
62	Computer programming, consultancy and related activities	..	..	1 596.0	1 637.4	2 089.7	2 154.0	2 179.3	2 173.8
63	Information service activities	..	..	118.1	63.9	61.8	119.8	223.7	408.7
64-66	Financial and insurance activities	..	..	549.3	497.0	424.6	367.5	447.1	498.2
68-82	Real estate; professional, scientific and technical; administrative and support	..	..	8 677.5	9 171.1	9 817.7	8 632.6	9 104.9	9 889.5
68	Real estate activities	..	..	15.5	14.3	13.8	15.4	22.3	28.9
69-75x72	Professional, scientific and technical activities, except scientific R&D	..	..	1 135.9	1 212.2	1 359.8	1 760.6	2 138.2	2 647.0
72	Scientific research and development	6 640.0	7 312.8	7 404.9	7 750.1	8 172.0	6 457.0	6 570.7	6 615.3
77-82	Administrative and support service activities	..	..	121.2	194.5	272.2	399.6	373.7	598.4
84-99	Community, social and personal services	..	..	228.3	304.2	338.6	339.2	416.6	289.1
84-85	Public administration and defence; compulsory social security and education	..	..	23.5	12.4	10.9	26.3	44.7	20.6
86-88	Human health and social work activities	..	..	4.3	36.0	24.5	23.1	42.6	52.9
90-93	Arts, entertainment and recreation	..	..	178.6	216.4	268.7	255.6	285.7	180.8
94-99	Other services; household-employers; extraterritorial bodies	..	..	21.9	39.4	34.5	34.2	43.5	34.7

.. Not available

Note: Detailed metadata at: http://metalinks.oecd.org/anberd/20170419/301f.
Information on data for Israel: http://oe.cd/israel-disclaimer.
Disclaimer: http://oe.cd/disclaimer

UNITED KINGDOM

R&D expenditure in industry by product field, current prices
ISIC Rev. 4

Million USD PPP

		2007	2008	2009	2010	2011	2012	2013	2014
	TOTAL BUSINESS ENTERPRISE	22 008.8	22 653.9	22 030.4	22 922.5	24 655.7	24 381.2	26 558.1	28 797.1
01-03	**AGRICULTURE, FORESTRY AND FISHING**	133.2	135.5	157.5	145.7	188.2	188.7	177.9	172.3
05-09	**MINING AND QUARRYING**	126.4	127.9	157.0	162.2	275.3	306.0	324.2	455.5
10-33	**MANUFACTURING**	16 307.1	16 721.7	16 277.8	16 603.0	17 778.0	17 438.2	18 456.0	19 252.3
10-12	Food products, beverages and tobacco	461.2	435.3	414.6	435.8	495.9	509.2	611.1	621.0
13-15	Textiles, wearing apparel, leather and related products	27.0	21.8	14.7	15.4	18.6	28.8	31.8	32.4
13	Textiles	..	..	..	..	..	..	..	..
14	Wearing apparel	..	..	..	..	..	..	..	..
15	Leather and related products, footwear	..	..	..	..	..	..	..	..
16-18	Wood and paper products and printing	75.2	70.1	36.7	39.5	30.3	39.6	70.4	69.3
16	Wood and wood products, except furniture	..	..	6.1	7.9	2.8	5.1	13.0	10.7
17	Paper and paper products	..	..	16.1	19.6	17.7	14.4	20.7	21.2
18	Printing and reproduction of recorded media	..	..	14.5	12.0	9.8	20.1	36.7	37.4
19-23	Chemical, rubber, plastic, non-metallic mineral products	6 965.0	7 548.6	7 669.9	7 848.0	8 168.2	7 168.6	7 077.0	7 053.9
19	Coke and refined petroleum products	..	..	..	104.7	102.3	108.5	100.1	125.0
20-21	Chemical and pharmaceutical products	6 496.0	7 053.0	7 119.6	7 550.5	7 844.7	6 836.0	6 763.7	6 654.4
20	Chemicals and chemical products	942.1	894.8	869.6	939.3	975.7	841.6	889.0	985.6
21	Pharmaceuticals, medicinal, chemical and botanical products	5 553.9	6 158.2	6 250.0	6 611.2	6 869.0	5 994.4	5 874.7	5 668.7
22	Rubber and plastic products	111.7	108.9	81.9	112.7	136.8	159.8	145.0	186.1
23	Other non-metallic mineral products	..	..	..	80.0	84.4	64.3	68.2	88.6
24-25	Basic metals, metal products, except machinery and equipment	193.3	186.4	196.9	295.3	338.8	275.6	293.1	341.8
24	Basic metals	..	..	..	162.8	171.0	138.0	125.7	183.0
25	Fabricated metal products, except machinery and equipment	..	..	..	132.5	167.8	137.7	167.4	158.8
26-30	Computer, electronic, optical products; electrical machinery, transport equipment	8 547.1	8 411.9	7 807.2	7 778.4	8 518.2	9 218.6	10 128.4	10 845.0
26	Computer, electronic and optical products	1 804.1	1 907.5	1 764.6	1 732.4	1 820.0	2 105.4	2 298.2	2 478.7
27	Electrical equipment	764.1	811.1	830.2	730.2	720.5	663.9	562.9	664.9
28	Machinery and equipment n.e.c.	1 519.4	1 188.9	1 256.0	1 191.1	1 374.0	1 423.0	1 495.6	1 433.3
29	Motor vehicles, trailers and semi-trailers	1 313.7	1 793.4	1 605.0	1 790.7	2 160.0	2 468.8	2 965.6	3 327.4
30	Other transport equipment	3 145.9	2 711.0	2 351.3	2 334.0	2 443.7	2 557.6	2 806.0	2 940.7
31-33	Furniture; repair, installation of machinery and equipment	38.3	47.7	137.8	190.6	208.1	197.7	244.2	288.9
31	Furniture	..	..	..	..	..	..	..	..
32	Other manufacturing	..	..	..	..	..	..	..	..
33	Repair and installation of machinery and equipment	..	..	..	..	..	..	..	..
35-39	**ELECTRICITY, GAS, WATER AND WASTE MANAGEMENT**	53.1	50.1	113.7	102.4	95.2	168.6	199.5	208.3
35-36	Electricity, gas and water	..	..	106.1	90.9	80.3	151.5	175.3	191.7
37-39	Sewerage, waste management and remediation activities	..	..	7.6	11.6	14.9	17.1	24.2	16.6
41-43	**CONSTRUCTION**	19.2	20.5	24.8	10.4	31.3	83.2	103.5	191.0
45-99	**TOTAL SERVICES**	5 369.7	5 598.2	5 299.6	5 898.8	6 287.6	6 196.5	7 296.9	8 517.7
45-82	**Business sector services**	5 295.0	5 554.3	5 191.2	5 781.2	6 193.5	6 099.6	7 144.9	8 376.6
45-47	Wholesale and retail trade; motor vehicle and motorcycle repairs	52.5	106.8	107.5	249.7	334.5	261.7	240.7	353.5
49-53	Transportation and storage	29.1	17.2	34.5	24.8	25.9	30.1	50.2	55.2
55-56	Accommodation and food service activities	..	..	..	..	..	..	..	..
58-63	Information and communication	..	..	..	3 883.9	4 103.7	4 060.1	4 210.5	4 869.3
58-60	Publishing, audiovisual and broadcasting activities	..	..	..	49.6	37.7	42.5	92.1	90.1
58	Publishing activities	..	..	..	..	..	..	..	..
59-60	Motion picture, video and TV programme production; broadcasting activities	..	..	..	..	..	..	..	..
59	Motion picture, video and TV programme production; sound and music	..	..	..	..	..	..	..	..
60	Programming and broadcasting activities	..	..	..	..	..	..	..	..
61	Telecommunications	2 126.9	2 011.3	1 537.0	1 480.7	1 489.1	1 267.6	1 210.0	1 382.9
62-63	IT and other information services	2 114.9	2 132.4	2 050.5	2 353.5	2 576.9	2 750.0	2 908.4	3 396.3
62	Computer programming, consultancy and related activities	..	..	..	..	..	..	..	..
63	Information service activities	..	..	..	..	..	..	..	..
64-66	Financial and insurance activities	..	..	..	214.9	191.2	59.7	182.0	251.4
68-82	Real estate; professional, scientific and technical; administrative and support	..	..	..	1 408.0	1 538.1	1 688.1	2 461.5	2 847.2
68	Real estate activities	..	..	..	14.3	14.0	0.0	0.0	31.3
69-75x72	Professional, scientific and technical activities, except scientific R&D	..	..	..	..	..	..	..	..
72	Scientific research and development	235.0	573.9	619.3	805.5	965.8	872.1	1 337.0	1 189.3
77-82	Administrative and support service activities	..	..	..	..	..	..	..	..
84-99	Community, social and personal services	74.8	43.9	108.4	117.6	94.2	96.9	152.0	141.1
84-85	Public administration and defence; compulsory social security and education	..	..	..	..	..	..	..	..
86-88	Human health and social work activities	..	..	..	..	..	..	..	..
90-93	Arts, entertainment and recreation	..	..	..	..	..	..	..	..
94-99	Other services; household-employers; extraterritorial bodies	..	..	..	..	..	..	..	..

.. Not available

Note: Detailed metadata at: http://metalinks.oecd.org/anberd/20170419/301f.
Information on data for Israel: http://oe.cd/israel-disclaimer.
Disclaimer: http://oe.cd/disclaimer

UNITED KINGDOM

R&D expenditure in industry by product field, constant prices
ISIC Rev. 4

2010 USD PPP

Code	Industry	2007	2008	2009	2010	2011	2012	2013	2014
	TOTAL BUSINESS ENTERPRISE	23 639.2	23 380.2	22 633.7	22 922.5	24 345.7	23 561.4	24 933.7	26 507.4
01-03	**AGRICULTURE, FORESTRY AND FISHING**	143.1	139.8	161.8	145.7	185.9	182.4	167.1	158.6
05-09	**MINING AND QUARRYING**	135.8	132.0	161.3	162.2	271.9	295.7	304.4	419.3
10-33	**MANUFACTURING**	17 515.1	17 257.8	16 723.6	16 603.0	17 554.5	16 851.8	17 327.1	17 721.6
10-12	Food products, beverages and tobacco	495.3	449.2	425.9	435.8	489.6	492.1	573.7	571.6
13-15	Textiles, wearing apparel, leather and related products	29.0	22.5	15.1	15.4	18.3	27.8	29.9	29.8
13	Textiles	..	..	..	..	..	..	..	..
14	Wearing apparel	..	..	..	..	..	..	..	..
15	Leather and related products, footwear	..	..	..	..	..	..	..	..
16-18	Wood and paper products and printing	80.8	72.3	37.7	39.5	29.9	38.3	66.1	63.8
16	Wood and wood products, except furniture	..	..	6.2	7.9	2.8	4.9	12.2	9.8
17	Paper and paper products	..	..	16.5	19.6	17.4	13.9	19.4	19.5
18	Printing and reproduction of recorded media	..	..	14.9	12.0	9.7	19.4	34.4	34.5
19-23	Chemical, rubber, plastic, non-metallic mineral products	7 480.9	7 790.6	7 879.9	7 848.0	8 065.5	6 927.5	6 644.1	6 493.1
19	Coke and refined petroleum products	..	..	..	104.7	101.0	104.8	93.9	115.0
20-21	Chemical and pharmaceutical products	6 977.2	7 279.1	7 314.6	7 550.5	7 746.1	6 606.2	6 350.0	6 125.3
20	Chemicals and chemical products	1 011.9	923.4	893.4	939.3	963.4	813.3	834.6	907.3
21	Pharmaceuticals, medicinal, chemical and botanical products	5 965.3	6 355.6	6 421.2	6 611.2	6 782.7	5 792.9	5 515.4	5 218.0
22	Rubber and plastic products	120.0	112.4	84.2	112.7	135.1	154.4	136.1	171.3
23	Other non-metallic mineral products	..	..	..	80.0	83.4	62.1	64.1	81.5
24-25	Basic metals, metal products, except machinery and equipment	207.7	192.4	202.3	295.3	334.5	266.4	275.2	314.6
24	Basic metals	..	..	..	162.8	168.8	133.3	118.0	168.5
25	Fabricated metal products, except machinery and equipment	..	..	..	132.5	165.7	133.0	157.2	146.1
26-30	Computer, electronic, optical products; electrical machinery, transport equipment	9 180.3	8 681.6	8 021.0	7 778.4	8 411.1	8 908.6	9 508.9	9 982.7
26	Computer, electronic and optical products	1 937.7	1 968.7	1 812.9	1 732.4	1 797.1	2 034.6	2 157.7	2 281.6
27	Electrical equipment	820.7	837.1	852.9	730.2	711.4	641.6	528.5	612.1
28	Machinery and equipment n.e.c.	1 631.9	1 227.0	1 290.4	1 191.1	1 356.7	1 375.1	1 404.2	1 319.3
29	Motor vehicles, trailers and semi-trailers	1 411.0	1 850.9	1 649.0	1 790.7	2 132.9	2 385.8	2 784.3	3 062.8
30	Other transport equipment	3 378.9	2 797.9	2 415.7	2 334.0	2 413.0	2 471.6	2 634.4	2 706.9
31-33	Furniture; repair, installation of machinery and equipment	41.1	49.2	141.6	190.6	205.4	191.0	229.2	265.9
31	Furniture	..	..	..	..	..	..	..	..
32	Other manufacturing	..	..	..	..	..	..	..	..
33	Repair and installation of machinery and equipment	..	..	..	..	..	..	..	..
35-39	**ELECTRICITY, GAS, WATER AND WASTE MANAGEMENT**	57.0	51.7	116.8	102.4	94.0	162.9	187.3	191.7
35-36	Electricity, gas and water	..	..	109.0	90.9	79.3	146.4	164.6	176.5
37-39	Sewerage, waste management and remediation activities	..	..	7.8	11.6	14.7	16.5	22.7	15.3
41-43	**CONSTRUCTION**	20.6	21.2	25.5	10.4	30.9	80.4	97.2	175.8
45-99	**TOTAL SERVICES**	5 767.5	5 777.7	5 444.7	5 898.8	6 208.6	5 988.2	6 850.6	7 840.4
45-82	**Business sector services**	5 687.2	5 732.3	5 333.3	5 781.2	6 115.6	5 894.5	6 707.9	7 710.5
45-47	Wholesale and retail trade; motor vehicle and motorcycle repairs	56.4	110.2	110.5	249.7	330.3	252.9	226.0	325.4
49-53	Transportation and storage	31.3	17.7	35.4	24.8	25.6	29.1	47.2	50.8
55-56	Accommodation and food service activities	..	..	..	..	..	..	..	..
58-63	Information and communication	..	..	..	3 883.9	4 052.1	3 923.6	3 953.0	4 482.2
58-60	Publishing, audiovisual and broadcasting activities	..	..	..	49.6	37.2	41.0	86.5	83.0
58	Publishing activities	..	..	..	..	..	..	..	..
59-60	Motion picture, video and TV programme production; broadcasting activities	..	..	..	..	..	..	..	..
59	Motion picture, video and TV programme production; sound and music	..	..	..	..	..	..	..	..
60	Programming and broadcasting activities	..	..	..	..	..	..	..	..
61	Telecommunications	2 284.5	2 075.8	1 579.1	1 480.7	1 470.4	1 225.0	1 136.0	1 272.9
62-63	IT and other information services	2 271.6	2 200.8	2 106.6	2 353.5	2 544.5	2 657.5	2 730.5	3 126.3
62	Computer programming, consultancy and related activities	..	..	..	..	..	..	..	..
63	Information service activities	..	..	..	..	..	..	..	..
64-66	Financial and insurance activities	..	..	..	214.9	188.8	57.7	170.8	231.4
68-82	Real estate; professional, scientific and technical; administrative and support	..	..	..	1 408.0	1 518.8	1 631.3	2 310.9	2 620.8
68	Real estate activities	..	..	..	14.3	13.8	0.0	0.0	28.9
69-75x72	Professional, scientific and technical activities, except scientific R&D	..	..	..	..	..	..	..	..
72	Scientific research and development	252.4	592.3	636.3	805.5	953.6	842.8	1 255.2	1 094.7
77-82	Administrative and support service activities	..	..	..	..	..	..	..	..
84-99	Community, social and personal services	80.3	45.3	111.4	117.6	93.0	93.7	142.7	129.9
84-85	Public administration and defence; compulsory social security and education	..	..	..	..	..	..	..	..
86-88	Human health and social work activities	..	..	..	..	..	..	..	..
90-93	Arts, entertainment and recreation	..	..	..	..	..	..	..	..
94-99	Other services; household-employers; extraterritorial bodies	..	..	..	..	..	..	..	..

.. Not available

Note: Detailed metadata at: http://metalinks.oecd.org/anberd/20170419/301f.
Information on data for Israel: http://oe.cd/israel-disclaimer.

Disclaimer: http://oe.cd/disclaimer

UNITED STATES

R&D expenditure in industry by main activity of the enterprise, current prices
ISIC Rev. 4

Million USD PPP

		2007	2008	2009	2010	2011	2012	2013	2014
	TOTAL BUSINESS ENTERPRISE	269 267.0	290 680.0	282 393.0	278 977.0	294 093.0	302 250.0	322 528.0	340 728.0
01-03	AGRICULTURE, FORESTRY AND FISHING	..	..	..	..	..	..	..	..
05-09	**MINING AND QUARRYING**	1 445.0	1 502.0	2 706.7	2 542.0	2 733.0	2 815.0	3 997.0	4 703.0
10-33	**MANUFACTURING**	187 477.0	203 755.0	195 144.0	196 711.0	201 361.0	208 415.0	221 476.0	232 815.0
10-12	Food products, beverages and tobacco	2 943.0	2 880.0	4 669.0	4 544.7	5 085.9	4 860.0	5 855.0	6 212.0
13-15	Textiles, wearing apparel, leather and related products	806.0	815.0	428.0	489.0	634.0	560.0	662.0	631.0
13	Textiles	..	..	..	..	..	..	..	..
14	Wearing apparel	..	..	..	..	..	..	..	..
15	Leather and related products, footwear	..	..	..	..	..	..	..	..
16-18	Wood and paper products and printing	2 800.1	1 789.0	1 956.0	1 752.0	1 732.0	1 469.0	1 392.0	1 319.0
16	Wood and wood products, except furniture	204.1	273.0	512.0	247.0	211.0	461.0	220.0	362.0
17	Paper and paper products	..	1 167.0	1 249.0	1 274.0	1 346.0	752.0	920.0	723.0
18	Printing and reproduction of recorded media	..	349.0	195.0	231.0	175.0	256.0	252.0	234.0
19-23	Chemical, rubber, plastic, non-metallic mineral products	60 513.5	62 981.0	57 502.0	62 589.0	60 267.2	62 956.0	66 885.0	71 553.0
19	Coke and refined petroleum products	1 719.2	1 358.0	606.0	1 154.0	1 484.2	894.0	242.0	234.0
20-21	Chemical and pharmaceutical products	55 572.1	58 250.0	53 328.0	58 038.0	55 324.0	57 226.0	61 664.0	66 300.0
20	Chemicals and chemical products	7 840.1	10 119.0	8 392.0	8 623.0	9 375.0	9 080.0	9 238.0	9 688.0
21	Pharmaceuticals, medicinal, chemical and botanical products	47 732.0	48 131.0	44 936.0	49 415.0	45 949.0	48 146.0	52 426.0	56 612.0
22	Rubber and plastic products	2 097.2	1 817.0	2 468.0	2 121.0	2 280.0	3 509.0	3 650.0	3 574.0
23	Other non-metallic mineral products	1 125.0	1 556.0	1 100.0	1 276.0	1 179.0	1 327.0	1 329.0	1 445.0
24-25	Basic metals, metal products, except machinery and equipment	2 605.0	3 114.0	2 877.0	2 356.0	2 508.0	2 574.0	2 836.0	2 808.0
24	Basic metals	896.0	695.0	837.0	653.0	655.0	741.0	624.0	677.0
25	Fabricated metal products, except machinery and equipment	1 709.0	2 419.0	2 040.0	1 703.0	1 853.0	1 833.0	2 212.0	2 131.0
26-30	Computer, electronic, optical products; electrical machinery, transport equipment	110 818.4	124 264.0	117 244.0	116 063.0	121 888.0	124 715.0	129 963.0	137 129.0
26	Computer, electronic and optical products	58 599.0	60 464.0	56 435.0	59 875.0	62 704.0	65 068.0	67 205.0	73 891.0
27	Electrical equipment	2 708.0	3 143.0	3 334.0	3 320.0	3 595.0	3 087.0	4 136.0	4 365.0
28	Machinery and equipment n.e.c.	9 865.0	10 104.0	9 138.0	9 955.0	14 709.0	14 254.0	12 650.0	12 128.0
29	Motor vehicles, trailers and semi-trailers	16 102.8	13 140.0	11 364.0	10 109.1	11 694.8	14 587.6	16 729.0	18 404.0
30	Other transport equipment	23 543.5	37 413.0	36 973.0	32 803.9	29 185.2	27 717.4	29 244.0	28 342.0
31-33	Furniture; repair, installation of machinery and equipment	6 992.0	7 914.0	10 466.0	8 917.3	9 245.9	11 281.0	13 883.0	13 162.0
31	Furniture	582.0	477.0	396.0	373.0	319.0	348.0	374.0	373.0
32	Other manufacturing	6 410.0	7 437.0	10 070.0	8 544.3	8 926.9	10 933.0	13 509.0	12 789.0
33	Repair and installation of machinery and equipment	..	..	..	..	..	..	..	..
35-39	**ELECTRICITY, GAS, WATER AND WASTE MANAGEMENT**	235.0	226.0	246.0	425.0	386.0	348.0	294.0	310.0
35-36	Electricity, gas and water	..	..	..	..	..	..	..	..
37-39	Sewerage, waste management and remediation activities	..	..	..	..	..	..	..	..
41-43	**CONSTRUCTION**	386.0	1 346.7	115.0	1 079.0	775.0	760.0	248.0	204.0
45-99	**TOTAL SERVICES**	79 724.0	83 850.3	84 181.3	78 220.0	88 838.0	89 912.0	96 513.0	102 696.0
45-82	**Business sector services**	76 589.0	80 243.0	82 998.3	75 089.9	86 633.0	88 352.0	94 979.0	101 538.0
45-47	Wholesale and retail trade; motor vehicle and motorcycle repairs	4 824.0	3 115.0	1 893.3	2 013.9	2 617.0	3 177.0	1 886.0	1 727.0
49-53	Transportation and storage	166.0	135.0	178.0	96.0	81.0	178.0	411.0	679.0
55-56	Accommodation and food service activities	..	..	..	..	..	..	..	..
58-63	Information and communication	43 452.0	49 841.0	46 366.0	47 902.0	55 124.0	58 056.0	66 475.0	74 792.0
58-60	Publishing, audiovisual and broadcasting activities	..	..	..	..	..	..	..	..
58	Publishing activities	20 900.0	28 426.0	27 077.0	26 982.0	28 435.0	28 987.0	35 675.0	36 140.0
59-60	Motion picture, video and TV programme production; broadcasting activities	..	..	..	..	..	..	..	..
59	Motion picture, video and TV programme production; sound and music	..	..	..	..	..	..	..	..
60	Programming and broadcasting activities	..	..	..	..	..	..	..	..
61	Telecommunications	3 264.0	1 684.0	1 496.0	1 868.0	2 157.0	2 824.0	3 041.0	3 755.0
62-63	IT and other information services	18 696.0	18 713.0	15 295.0	13 588.0	17 544.0	16 164.0	15 714.0	20 048.0
62	Computer programming, consultancy and related activities	14 407.0	12 146.0	12 560.0	11 050.0	13 259.0	11 251.0	9 268.0	11 019.0
63	Information service activities	4 289.0	6 567.0	2 735.0	2 538.0	4 285.0	4 913.0	6 446.0	9 029.0
64-66	Financial and insurance activities	1 640.6	1 091.0	1 911.0	2 109.0	3 457.0	3 519.0	4 308.0	4 122.0
68-82	Real estate; professional, scientific and technical; administrative and support	26 506.4	26 061.0	32 650.0	22 969.0	25 355.0	23 421.0	21 899.0	20 218.0
68	Real estate activities	68.4	45.5	47.5	59.1	71.0	21.0	92.0	207.0
69-75x72	Professional, scientific and technical activities, except scientific R&D	9 277.0	7 895.0	15 116.0	7 822.0	9 659.0	6 514.0	7 548.0	7 149.0
72	Scientific research and development	16 849.0	17 913.0	17 270.0	14 818.0	15 301.0	16 544.0	14 201.0	12 807.0
77-82	Administrative and support service activities	312.1	207.5	216.5	269.9	324.0	342.0	58.0	55.0
84-99	**Community, social and personal services**	..	..	..	..	..	..	..	..
84-85	Public administration and defence; compulsory social security and education	..	..	..	..	..	..	..	..
86-88	Human health and social work activities	1 280.0	1 313.0	537.0	1 232.0	741.0	675.0	526.0	501.0
90-93	Arts, entertainment and recreation	..	..	..	..	..	..	..	..
94-99	Other services; household-employers; extraterritorial bodies	..	..	..	..	..	..	..	..

.. Not available

Note: Detailed metadata at: http://metalinks.oecd.org/anberd/20170419/301f.
Information on data for Israel: http://oe.cd/israel-disclaimer.
Disclaimer: http://oe.cd/disclaimer

UNITED STATES

R&D expenditure in industry by main activity of the enterprise, constant prices
ISIC Rev. 4

2010 USD PPP

		2007	2008	2009	2010	2011	2012	2013	2014
	TOTAL BUSINESS ENTERPRISE	280 012.7	296 464.7	285 842.0	278 977.0	288 143.9	290 779.6	305 356.5	316 913.7
01-03	AGRICULTURE, FORESTRY AND FISHING	..	..	..	..	..	..	..	..
05-09	**MINING AND QUARRYING**	1 502.7	1 531.9	2 739.8	2 542.0	2 677.7	2 708.2	3 784.2	4 374.3
10-33	**MANUFACTURING**	194 958.7	207 809.8	197 527.4	196 711.0	197 287.7	200 505.6	209 684.5	216 543.0
10-12	Food products, beverages and tobacco	3 060.5	2 937.3	4 726.0	4 544.7	4 983.0	4 675.6	5 543.3	5 777.8
13-15	Textiles, wearing apparel, leather and related products	838.2	831.2	433.2	489.0	621.2	538.7	626.8	586.9
13	Textiles	..	..	..	..	..	..	..	..
14	Wearing apparel	..	..	..	..	..	..	..	..
15	Leather and related products, footwear	..	..	..	..	..	..	..	..
16-18	Wood and paper products and printing	2 911.8	1 824.6	1 979.9	1 752.0	1 697.0	1 413.3	1 317.9	1 226.8
16	Wood and wood products, except furniture	212.2	278.4	518.3	247.0	206.7	443.5	208.3	336.7
17	Paper and paper products	..	1 190.2	1 264.3	1 274.0	1 318.8	723.5	871.0	672.5
18	Printing and reproduction of recorded media	..	355.9	197.4	231.0	171.5	246.3	238.6	217.6
19-23	Chemical, rubber, plastic, non-metallic mineral products	62 928.4	64 234.4	58 204.3	62 589.0	59 048.1	60 566.8	63 324.0	66 552.0
19	Coke and refined petroleum products	1 787.8	1 385.0	613.4	1 154.0	1 454.2	860.1	229.1	217.6
20-21	Chemical and pharmaceutical products	57 789.8	59 409.2	53 979.3	58 038.0	54 204.9	55 054.3	58 381.0	61 666.1
20	Chemicals and chemical products	8 153.0	10 320.4	8 494.5	8 623.0	9 185.4	8 735.4	8 746.2	9 010.9
21	Pharmaceuticals, medicinal, chemical and botanical products	49 636.8	49 088.8	45 484.8	49 415.0	45 019.5	46 318.9	49 634.8	52 655.2
22	Rubber and plastic products	2 180.9	1 853.2	2 498.1	2 121.0	2 233.9	3 375.8	3 455.7	3 324.2
23	Other non-metallic mineral products	1 169.9	1 587.0	1 113.4	1 276.0	1 155.2	1 276.6	1 258.2	1 344.0
24-25	Basic metals, metal products, except machinery and equipment	2 709.0	3 176.0	2 912.1	2 356.0	2 457.3	2 476.3	2 685.0	2 611.7
24	Basic metals	931.8	708.8	847.2	653.0	641.8	712.9	590.8	629.7
25	Fabricated metal products, except machinery and equipment	1 777.2	2 467.1	2 064.9	1 703.0	1 815.5	1 763.4	2 094.2	1 982.1
26-30	Computer, electronic, optical products; electrical machinery, transport equipment	115 240.8	126 736.9	118 676.0	116 063.0	119 422.4	119 982.1	123 043.7	127 544.7
26	Computer, electronic and optical products	60 937.5	61 667.3	57 124.3	59 875.0	61 435.6	62 598.7	63 627.0	68 726.6
27	Electrical equipment	2 816.1	3 205.5	3 374.7	3 320.0	3 522.3	2 969.8	3 915.8	4 059.9
28	Machinery and equipment n.e.c.	10 258.7	10 305.1	9 249.6	9 955.0	14 411.5	13 713.1	11 976.5	11 280.3
29	Motor vehicles, trailers and semi-trailers	16 745.4	13 401.5	11 502.8	10 109.1	11 458.2	14 034.0	15 838.3	17 117.7
30	Other transport equipment	24 483.1	38 157.5	37 424.6	32 803.9	28 594.9	26 665.5	27 687.0	26 361.1
31-33	Furniture; repair, installation of machinery and equipment	7 271.0	8 071.5	10 593.8	8 917.3	9 058.9	10 852.9	13 143.9	12 242.1
31	Furniture	605.2	486.5	400.8	373.0	312.5	334.8	354.1	346.9
32	Other manufacturing	6 665.8	7 585.0	10 193.0	8 544.3	8 746.3	10 518.1	12 789.8	11 895.1
33	Repair and installation of machinery and equipment	..	..	..	..	..	..	..	..
35-39	**ELECTRICITY, GAS, WATER AND WASTE MANAGEMENT**	244.4	230.5	249.0	425.0	378.2	334.8	278.3	288.3
35-36	Electricity, gas and water	..	..	..	..	..	..	..	..
37-39	Sewerage, waste management and remediation activities	..	..	..	..	..	..	..	..
41-43	**CONSTRUCTION**	401.4	1 373.5	116.4	1 079.0	759.3	731.2	234.8	189.7
45-99	**TOTAL SERVICES**	82 905.6	85 519.0	85 209.4	78 220.0	87 040.9	86 499.8	91 374.6	95 518.3
45-82	**Business sector services**	79 645.4	81 839.9	84 012.0	75 089.9	84 880.5	84 999.0	89 922.3	94 441.3
45-47	Wholesale and retail trade; motor vehicle and motorcycle repairs	5 016.5	3 177.0	1 916.4	2 013.9	2 564.1	3 056.4	1 785.6	1 606.3
49-53	Transportation and storage	172.6	137.7	180.2	96.0	79.4	171.2	389.1	631.5
55-56	Accommodation and food service activities	..	..	..	..	..	..	..	..
58-63	Information and communication	45 186.0	50 832.9	46 932.3	47 902.0	54 008.9	55 852.8	62 935.8	69 564.6
58-60	Publishing, audiovisual and broadcasting activities	..	..	..	..	..	..	..	..
58	Publishing activities	21 734.1	28 991.7	27 407.7	26 982.0	27 859.8	27 886.9	33 775.7	33 614.1
59-60	Motion picture, video and TV programme production; broadcasting activities	..	..	..	..	..	..	..	..
59	Motion picture, video and TV programme production; sound and music	..	..	..	..	..	..	..	..
60	Programming and broadcasting activities	..	..	..	..	..	..	..	..
61	Telecommunications	3 394.3	1 717.5	1 514.3	1 868.0	2 113.4	2 716.8	2 879.1	3 492.6
62-63	IT and other information services	19 442.1	19 085.4	15 481.8	13 588.0	17 189.1	15 550.6	14 877.4	18 646.8
62	Computer programming, consultancy and related activities	14 981.9	12 387.7	12 713.4	11 050.0	12 990.8	10 824.0	8 774.6	10 248.9
63	Information service activities	4 460.2	6 697.7	2 768.4	2 538.0	4 198.3	4 726.6	6 102.8	8 397.9
64-66	Financial and insurance activities	1 706.0	1 112.7	1 934.3	2 109.0	3 387.1	3 385.5	4 078.6	3 833.9
68-82	Real estate; professional, scientific and technical; administrative and support	27 564.2	26 579.6	33 048.8	22 969.0	24 842.1	22 532.2	20 733.1	18 804.9
68	Real estate activities	71.1	46.4	48.0	59.1	69.6	20.2	87.1	192.5
69-75x72	Professional, scientific and technical activities, except scientific R&D	9 647.2	8 052.1	15 300.6	7 822.0	9 463.6	6 266.8	7 146.1	6 649.3
72	Scientific research and development	17 521.4	18 269.5	17 480.9	14 818.0	14 991.5	15 916.2	13 444.9	11 911.9
77-82	Administrative and support service activities	324.5	211.7	219.2	269.9	317.4	329.0	54.9	51.2
84-99	Community, social and personal services	..	..	..	..	..	..	..	..
84-85	Public administration and defence; compulsory social security and education	..	..	..	..	..	..	..	..
86-88	Human health and social work activities	1 331.1	1 339.1	543.6	1 232.0	726.0	649.4	498.0	466.0
90-93	Arts, entertainment and recreation	..	..	..	..	..	..	..	..
94-99	Other services; household-employers; extraterritorial bodies	..	..	..	..	..	..	..	..

.. Not available

Note: Detailed metadata at: http://metalinks.oecd.org/anberd/20170419/301f.
    Information on data for Israel: http://oe.cd/israel-disclaimer.
Disclaimer: http://oe.cd/disclaimer

CHINA

R&D expenditure in industry by main activity of the enterprise, current prices
ISIC Rev. 4

Million USD PPP

		2007	2008	2009	2010	2011	2012	2013	2014
	TOTAL BUSINESS ENTERPRISE	89 768.4	107 052.0	135 661.9	156 726.1	187 684.1	222 508.3	255 985.9	286 086.9
01-03	**AGRICULTURE, FORESTRY AND FISHING**	..	235.8	363.8	425.2	483.3	461.2	..	..
05-09	**MINING AND QUARRYING**	..	3 485.6	5 437.1	6 539.2	7 206.5	7 946.0	7 725.0	7 820.9
10-33	**MANUFACTURING**	..	92 731.9	114 034.3	134 532.3	162 466.1	194 233.3	224 237.6	252 534.8
10-12	Food products, beverages and tobacco	..	3 518.4	4 816.8	5 713.9	6 846.1	9 148.3	10 615.3	12 179.6
13-15	Textiles, wearing apparel, leather and related products	..	2 564.5	3 445.9	3 949.9	5 146.7	6 272.1	7 380.4	8 302.0
13	Textiles	..	1 931.4	2 592.0	3 016.1	3 880.2	3 916.3	4 470.2	5 053.1
14	Wearing apparel	..	..	..	..	..	..	..	..
15	Leather and related products, footwear	..	..	..	..	..	..	..	..
16-18	Wood and paper products and printing	..	1 380.0	1 856.2	2 012.7	2 549.4	3 379.5	4 099.3	4 645.8
16	Wood and wood products, except furniture	..	256.7	330.5	334.5	412.8	531.3	766.0	930.3
17	Paper and paper products	..	895.2	1 175.4	1 234.9	1 594.3	2 150.8	2 476.2	2 742.0
18	Printing and reproduction of recorded media	..	228.1	350.4	443.3	542.4	697.5	857.1	973.6
19-23	Chemical, rubber, plastic, non-metallic mineral products	..	16 568.1	20 463.8	24 897.8	30 750.1	37 407.5	44 525.5	50 980.5
19	Coke and refined petroleum products	..	954.1	1 184.3	1 397.2	1 784.2	2 316.3	2 519.3	3 030.6
20-21	Chemical and pharmaceutical products	..	11 457.3	13 941.1	16 615.9	21 107.3	25 545.5	30 315.4	34 460.8
20	Chemicals and chemical products	..	8 201.4	9 645.1	11 581.2	15 081.2	17 507.2	20 509.8	23 361.6
21	Pharmaceuticals, medicinal, chemical and botanical products	..	3 255.8	4 295.9	5 034.7	6 026.1	8 038.2	9 805.7	11 099.1
22	Rubber and plastic products	..	2 236.3	2 734.6	3 567.1	3 872.9	4 904.8	5 625.7	6 480.7
23	Other non-metallic mineral products	..	1 920.5	2 603.8	3 317.6	3 985.7	4 641.0	6 065.0	7 008.5
24-25	Basic metals, metal products, except machinery and equipment	..	14 566.6	15 733.0	19 226.6	23 224.2	30 825.7	32 835.4	34 801.2
24	Basic metals	..	12 801.7	13 630.1	16 564.8	20 049.5	25 507.4	26 347.7	27 657.0
25	Fabricated metal products, except machinery and equipment	..	1 764.9	2 102.9	2 661.9	3 174.7	5 318.3	6 487.7	7 144.2
26-30	Computer, electronic, optical products; electrical machinery, transport equipment	..	53 472.5	66 687.1	77 706.0	92 525.3	105 135.8	122 120.1	138 177.2
26	Computer, electronic and optical products	..	18 242.9	21 575.1	25 186.3	30 292.6	33 719.1	39 537.7	44 404.6
27	Electrical equipment	..	10 124.6	12 782.8	15 236.7	17 800.7	19 979.0	22 998.2	26 242.5
28	Machinery and equipment n.e.c.	..	12 690.7	16 676.1	18 425.5	22 031.7	25 522.7	29 903.4	33 028.0
29	Motor vehicles, trailers and semi-trailers	..	..	..	..	..	16 190.0	19 185.8	22 384.2
30	Other transport equipment	..	..	..	..	..	9 724.9	10 495.0	12 118.0
31-33	Furniture; repair, installation of machinery and equipment	..	661.9	1 031.4	1 025.3	1 424.2	2 064.3	2 661.6	3 448.4
31	Furniture	..	144.7	221.2	160.7	257.7	412.2	633.6	769.8
32	Other manufacturing	..	517.2	792.4	815.1	1 083.0	1 514.2	1 808.4	2 393.2
33	Repair and installation of machinery and equipment	..	0.0	17.8	49.4	83.5	137.9	219.6	285.5
35-39	**ELECTRICITY, GAS, WATER AND WASTE MANAGEMENT**	..	1 052.8	1 100.3	1 174.7	1 333.9	1 479.1	..	..
35-36	Electricity, gas and water	..	..	..	..	..	..	..	..
37-39	Sewerage, waste management and remediation activities	..	..	..	..	..	..	..	..
41-43	**CONSTRUCTION**	..	2 794.2	4 310.7	4 226.7	4 144.7	4 274.1	..	..
45-99	**TOTAL SERVICES**	..	6 751.6	10 415.7	9 828.0	12 049.6	14 114.5	..	..
45-82	**Business sector services**	..	..	10 398.2	..	..	..	..	..
45-47	Wholesale and retail trade; motor vehicle and motorcycle repairs	..	..	0.0	..	..	..	..	..
49-53	Transportation and storage	..	..	338.7	..	..	..	..	..
55-56	Accommodation and food service activities	..	..	0.0	..	..	..	..	..
58-63	Information and communication	..	..	5 005.2	..	..	..	..	..
58-60	Publishing, audiovisual and broadcasting activities	..	..	2.8	..	..	..	..	..
58	Publishing activities	..	..	2.2	..	..	..	..	..
59-60	Motion picture, video and TV programme production; broadcasting activities	..	..	0.6	..	..	..	..	..
59	Motion picture, video and TV programme production; sound and music	..	..	..	..	..	..	..	..
60	Programming and broadcasting activities	..	..	..	..	..	..	..	..
61	Telecommunications	..	..	1 238.1	..	..	..	..	..
62-63	IT and other information services	..	..	3 764.4	..	..	..	..	..
62	Computer programming, consultancy and related activities	..	..	2 485.2	..	..	..	..	..
63	Information service activities	..	..	1 279.2	..	..	..	..	..
64-66	**Financial and insurance activities**	..	..	34.0	..	..	..	..	..
68-82	**Real estate; professional, scientific and technical; administrative and support**	..	..	5 020.3	..	..	..	..	..
68	Real estate activities	..	..	0.0	..	..	..	..	..
69-75x72	Professional, scientific and technical activities, except scientific R&D	..	..	..	..	..	..	..	..
72	Scientific research and development	..	..	2 337.7	..	..	..	..	..
77-82	Administrative and support service activities	..	..	..	..	..	..	..	..
84-99	**Community, social and personal services**	..	..	17.6	..	..	..	..	..
84-85	Public administration and defence; compulsory social security and education	..	..	0.0	..	..	..	..	..
86-88	Human health and social work activities	..	..	17.3	..	..	..	..	..
90-93	Arts, entertainment and recreation	..	..	0.2	..	..	..	..	..
94-99	Other services; household-employers; extraterritorial bodies	..	..	0.0	..	..	..	..	..

.. Not available

Note: Detailed metadata at: http://metalinks.oecd.org/anberd/20170419/301f.
      Information on data for Israel: http://oe.cd/israel-disclaimer.

Disclaimer: http://oe.cd/disclaimer

CHINA

R&D expenditure in industry by main activity of the enterprise, constant prices
ISIC Rev. 4

2010 USD PPP

ISIC	Activity	2007	2008	2009	2010	2011	2012	2013	2014
	TOTAL BUSINESS ENTERPRISE	93 352.9	109 161.3	137 328.0	156 726.1	183 870.0	214 044.1	242 323.3	266 403.2
01-03	AGRICULTURE, FORESTRY AND FISHING	..	240.5	368.3	425.2	473.5	443.7	..	..
05-09	MINING AND QUARRYING	..	3 554.3	5 503.9	6 539.2	7 060.0	7 643.8	7 312.7	7 282.8
10-33	MANUFACTURING	..	94 559.1	115 434.8	134 532.3	159 164.5	186 844.7	212 269.5	235 159.6
10-12	Food products, beverages and tobacco	..	3 587.7	4 876.0	5 713.9	6 707.0	8 800.3	10 048.8	11 341.6
13-15	Textiles, wearing apparel, leather and related products	..	2 615.0	3 488.2	3 949.9	5 042.1	6 033.5	6 986.5	7 730.8
13	Textiles	..	1 969.5	2 623.8	3 016.1	3 801.4	3 767.3	4 231.6	4 705.4
14	Wearing apparel	..	..	..	..	..	..	..	..
15	Leather and related products, footwear	..	..	..	..	..	..	..	..
16-18	Wood and paper products and printing	..	1 407.2	1 879.0	2 012.7	2 497.6	3 251.0	3 880.5	4 326.2
16	Wood and wood products, except furniture	..	261.7	334.6	334.5	404.4	511.1	725.1	866.3
17	Paper and paper products	..	912.8	1 189.8	1 234.9	1 561.9	2 069.0	2 344.0	2 553.3
18	Printing and reproduction of recorded media	..	232.6	354.7	443.3	531.3	670.9	811.4	906.6
19-23	Chemical, rubber, plastic, non-metallic mineral products	..	16 894.6	20 715.1	24 897.8	30 125.2	35 984.5	42 149.1	47 472.9
19	Coke and refined petroleum products	..	972.9	1 198.9	1 397.2	1 747.9	2 228.2	2 384.8	2 822.1
20-21	Chemical and pharmaceutical products	..	11 683.0	14 112.3	16 615.9	20 678.4	24 573.7	28 697.4	32 089.7
20	Chemicals and chemical products	..	8 363.0	9 763.6	11 581.2	14 774.7	16 841.2	19 415.1	21 754.3
21	Pharmaceuticals, medicinal, chemical and botanical products	..	3 320.0	4 348.7	5 034.7	5 903.6	7 732.5	9 282.3	10 335.5
22	Rubber and plastic products	..	2 280.4	2 768.2	3 567.1	3 794.2	4 718.2	5 325.5	6 034.8
23	Other non-metallic mineral products	..	1 958.3	2 635.8	3 317.6	3 904.7	4 464.5	5 741.3	6 526.3
24-25	Basic metals, metal products, except machinery and equipment	..	14 853.6	15 926.2	19 226.6	22 752.3	29 653.1	31 082.9	32 406.8
24	Basic metals	..	13 054.0	13 797.5	16 564.8	19 642.1	24 537.1	24 941.5	25 754.1
25	Fabricated metal products, except machinery and equipment	..	1 799.7	2 128.7	2 661.9	3 110.2	5 116.0	6 141.4	6 652.6
26-30	Computer, electronic, optical products; electrical machinery, transport equipment	..	54 526.1	67 506.1	77 706.0	90 645.1	101 136.4	115 602.3	128 670.2
26	Computer, electronic and optical products	..	18 602.4	21 840.0	25 186.3	29 677.0	32 436.4	37 427.5	41 349.4
27	Electrical equipment	..	10 324.1	12 939.8	15 236.7	17 438.9	19 219.0	21 770.7	24 436.9
28	Machinery and equipment n.e.c.	..	12 940.7	16 880.9	18 425.5	21 584.0	24 551.8	28 307.4	30 755.6
29	Motor vehicles, trailers and semi-trailers	..	..	..	..	..	15 574.2	18 161.8	20 844.1
30	Other transport equipment	..	..	..	..	..	9 355.0	9 934.8	11 284.3
31-33	Furniture; repair, installation of machinery and equipment	..	674.9	1 044.1	1 025.3	1 395.3	1 985.8	2 519.5	3 211.1
31	Furniture	..	147.5	223.9	160.7	252.5	396.5	599.8	716.2
32	Other manufacturing	..	527.4	802.2	815.1	1 061.0	1 456.6	1 711.8	2 228.5
33	Repair and installation of machinery and equipment	..	0.0	18.0	49.4	81.8	132.7	207.9	265.8
35-39	ELECTRICITY, GAS, WATER AND WASTE MANAGEMENT	..	1 073.6	1 113.8	1 174.7	1 306.8	1 422.8	..	..
35-36	Electricity, gas and water	..	..	..	..	..	..	..	..
37-39	Sewerage, waste management and remediation activities	..	..	..	..	..	..	..	..
41-43	CONSTRUCTION	..	2 849.3	4 363.6	4 226.7	4 060.5	4 111.5	..	..
45-99	TOTAL SERVICES	..	6 884.6	10 543.7	9 828.0	11 804.7	13 577.6	..	..
45-82	Business sector services	..	..	10 525.9	..	..	..	..	..
45-47	Wholesale and retail trade; motor vehicle and motorcycle repairs	..	..	0.0	..	..	..	..	..
49-53	Transportation and storage	..	..	342.8	..	..	..	..	..
55-56	Accommodation and food service activities	..	..	0.0	..	..	..	..	..
58-63	Information and communication	..	..	5 066.7	..	..	..	..	..
58-60	Publishing, audiovisual and broadcasting activities	..	..	2.8	..	..	..	..	..
58	Publishing activities	..	..	2.2	..	..	..	..	..
59-60	Motion picture, video and TV programme production; broadcasting activities	..	..	0.6	..	..	..	..	..
59	Motion picture, video and TV programme production; sound and music	..	..	..	..	..	..	..	..
60	Programming and broadcasting activities	..	..	..	..	..	..	..	..
61	Telecommunications	..	..	1 253.3	..	..	..	..	..
62-63	IT and other information services	..	..	3 810.6	..	..	..	..	..
62	Computer programming, consultancy and related activities	..	..	2 515.7	..	..	..	..	..
63	Information service activities	..	..	1 294.9	..	..	..	..	..
64-66	Financial and insurance activities	..	..	34.4	..	..	..	..	..
68-82	Real estate; professional, scientific and technical; administrative and support	..	..	5 081.9	..	..	..	..	..
68	Real estate activities	..	..	0.0	..	..	..	..	..
69-75x72	Professional, scientific and technical activities, except scientific R&D	..	..	..	..	..	..	..	..
72	Scientific research and development	..	..	2 366.4	..	..	..	..	..
77-82	Administrative and support service activities	..	..	..	..	..	..	..	..
84-99	Community, social and personal services	..	..	17.8	..	..	..	..	..
84-85	Public administration and defence; compulsory social security and education	..	..	0.0	..	..	..	..	..
86-88	Human health and social work activities	..	..	17.5	..	..	..	..	..
90-93	Arts, entertainment and recreation	..	..	0.2	..	..	..	..	..
94-99	Other services; household-employers; extraterritorial bodies	..	..	0.0	..	..	..	..	..

.. Not available

Note: Detailed metadata at: http://metalinks.oecd.org/anberd/20170419/301f.
Information on data for Israel: http://oe.cd/israel-disclaimer.
Disclaimer: http://oe.cd/disclaimer

ROMANIA

R&D expenditure in industry by main activity of the enterprise, current prices
ISIC Rev. 4

Million USD PPP

		2007	2008	2009	2010	2011	2012	2013	2014
	TOTAL BUSINESS ENTERPRISE	598.9	559.2	600.0	581.1	622.2	677.4	445.5	625.1
01-03	**AGRICULTURE, FORESTRY AND FISHING**	66.6	78.3	56.6	85.3	3.3	5.7	6.5	7.7
05-09	**MINING AND QUARRYING**	21.6	12.9	12.0	0.8	0.0	0.1	0.4	17.2
10-33	**MANUFACTURING**	305.3	244.4	271.6	235.4	323.1	283.8	234.3	323.1
10-12	Food products, beverages and tobacco	5.5	5.8	3.7	1.5	4.0	10.2	10.8	30.5
13-15	Textiles, wearing apparel, leather and related products	3.6	4.3	1.2	2.2	0.9	5.4	2.5	2.5
13	Textiles	..	3.4	0.3	0.5	0.1	0.6	0.1	0.3
14	Wearing apparel	..	0.4	0.5	0.1	0.2	0.6	0.3	1.2
15	Leather and related products, footwear	..	0.6	0.4	1.5	0.6	4.1	2.1	0.4
16-18	Wood and paper products and printing	1.0	0.5	0.1	0.1	0.0	0.0	0.1	0.8
16	Wood and wood products, except furniture	..	..	..	..	..	..	..	..
17	Paper and paper products	..	..	..	..	..	..	..	..
18	Printing and reproduction of recorded media	..	..	..	..	..	..	..	..
19-23	Chemical, rubber, plastic, non-metallic mineral products	87.5	50.9	50.4	50.1	94.6	33.4	31.1	44.1
19	Coke and refined petroleum products	41.1	3.1	1.2	0.8	0.0	0.0	0.0	0.0
20-21	Chemical and pharmaceutical products	42.9	44.9	45.7	46.1	82.8	28.7	26.9	43.3
20	Chemicals and chemical products	7.9	39.1	39.7	38.3	58.9	3.3	3.1	6.1
21	Pharmaceuticals, medicinal, chemical and botanical products	35.0	5.7	6.0	7.8	23.9	25.4	23.8	37.3
22	Rubber and plastic products	2.2	1.3	2.3	1.8	11.7	3.0	3.9	0.2
23	Other non-metallic mineral products	1.2	1.6	1.1	1.5	0.2	1.7	0.3	0.6
24-25	Basic metals, metal products, except machinery and equipment	23.5	17.3	13.0	10.5	15.4	8.1	9.1	10.2
24	Basic metals	18.3	10.4	6.2	5.5	11.0	3.8	4.6	4.7
25	Fabricated metal products, except machinery and equipment	5.2	6.8	6.7	5.0	4.4	4.3	4.5	5.5
26-30	Computer, electronic, optical products; electrical machinery, transport equipment	184.0	152.8	186.9	157.6	206.9	219.6	178.5	229.5
26	Computer, electronic and optical products	10.9	19.6	14.1	13.4	13.2	57.5	38.0	15.6
27	Electrical equipment	34.1	18.6	16.0	16.5	44.2	17.7	13.8	13.0
28	Machinery and equipment n.e.c.	48.2	24.0	17.4	16.8	6.6	19.5	12.4	12.7
29	Motor vehicles, trailers and semi-trailers	77.1	64.5	115.5	92.4	136.2	117.6	108.6	179.8
30	Other transport equipment	13.5	26.1	24.0	18.6	6.7	7.4	5.6	8.5
31-33	Furniture; repair, installation of machinery and equipment	0.4	12.7	16.4	13.5	1.3	7.1	2.2	6.0
31	Furniture	..	0.6	0.2	0.2	0.1	0.1	0.1	0.5
32	Other manufacturing	..	5.8	9.9	10.2	0.0	2.2	0.8	1.2
33	Repair and installation of machinery and equipment	..	6.3	6.3	3.1	1.2	4.8	1.3	4.3
35-39	**ELECTRICITY, GAS, WATER AND WASTE MANAGEMENT**	43.8	54.4	43.9	66.3	0.6	3.2	1.5	1.3
35-36	Electricity, gas and water	..	54.3	43.8	65.9	0.2	2.6	..	..
37-39	Sewerage, waste management and remediation activities	..	0.1	0.1	0.3	0.4	0.6	..	..
41-43	**CONSTRUCTION**	6.6	15.8	12.5	7.7	6.3	0.5	0.4	1.1
45-99	**TOTAL SERVICES**	155.0	153.4	203.3	185.6	288.9	384.1	202.3	274.8
45-82	**Business sector services**	147.0	152.2	202.7	184.3	288.8	381.4	202.3	272.0
45-47	Wholesale and retail trade; motor vehicle and motorcycle repairs	..	..	6.2	..	14.1	28.0	16.9	31.9
49-53	Transportation and storage	..	..	..	..	4.0	..	..	11.7
55-56	Accommodation and food service activities	..	..	..	..	..	1.7	1.2	0.6
58-63	Information and communication	53.8	17.2	86.3	70.7	109.7	120.5	43.5	66.9
58-60	Publishing, audiovisual and broadcasting activities	..	8.7	44.2	47.3	53.6	2.0	0.0	9.3
58	Publishing activities	..	..	..	..	..	2.0	..	..
59-60	Motion picture, video and TV programme production; broadcasting activities	..	..	..	..	..	0.1	..	..
59	Motion picture, video and TV programme production; sound and music	..	..	..	..	..	..	..	..
60	Programming and broadcasting activities	..	..	..	..	..	..	..	..
61	Telecommunications	..	..	..	..	..	12.4	1.2	2.3
62-63	IT and other information services	..	..	..	..	..	106.1	42.4	55.2
62	Computer programming, consultancy and related activities	..	..	40.7	23.4	54.6	72.4	30.3	55.1
63	Information service activities	..	..	..	..	..	33.6	12.0	0.1
64-66	Financial and insurance activities	..	..	..	..	..	..	..	..
68-82	Real estate; professional, scientific and technical; administrative and support	89.2	134.4	110.2	112.8	159.6	231.2	..	..
68	Real estate activities	..	0.0	0.0	0.0	0.0	2.6	..	..
69-75x72	Professional, scientific and technical activities, except scientific R&D	..	15.1	8.1	17.9	28.5	44.6	15.0	14.4
72	Scientific research and development	83.2	105.7	100.8	87.0	130.9	181.4	124.6	144.5
77-82	Administrative and support service activities	..	13.7	1.2	7.9	0.3	2.5	..	1.9
84-99	Community, social and personal services	8.0	1.2	0.6	1.3	0.1	2.7	0.0	2.7
84-85	Public administration and defence; compulsory social security and education	..	..	..	..	..	..	..	..
86-88	Human health and social work activities	..	..	..	..	..	..	..	..
90-93	Arts, entertainment and recreation	..	..	..	..	..	..	..	..
94-99	Other services; household-employers; extraterritorial bodies	..	..	..	..	..	..	..	..

.. Not available

Note: Detailed metadata at: http://metalinks.oecd.org/anberd/20170419/301f.
Information on data for Israel: http://oe.cd/israel-disclaimer.
Disclaimer: http://oe.cd/disclaimer

ROMANIA

R&D expenditure in industry by main activity of the enterprise, constant prices
ISIC Rev. 4

2010 USD PPP

		2007	2008	2009	2010	2011	2012	2013	2014
	TOTAL BUSINESS ENTERPRISE	727.2	619.7	627.4	581.1	602.7	641.6	418.8	577.4
01-03	**AGRICULTURE, FORESTRY AND FISHING**	80.9	86.8	59.2	85.3	3.2	5.4	6.1	7.1
05-09	**MINING AND QUARRYING**	26.2	14.3	12.6	0.8	0.0	0.1	0.4	15.9
10-33	**MANUFACTURING**	370.7	270.8	284.0	235.4	312.9	268.8	220.3	298.4
10-12	Food products, beverages and tobacco	6.6	6.4	3.8	1.5	3.9	9.7	10.2	28.1
13-15	Textiles, wearing apparel, leather and related products	4.3	4.8	1.3	2.2	0.8	5.1	2.3	2.3
13	Textiles	..	3.8	0.4	0.5	0.1	0.6	0.1	0.3
14	Wearing apparel	..	0.4	0.5	0.1	0.2	0.6	0.3	1.1
15	Leather and related products, footwear	..	0.6	0.4	1.5	0.5	3.9	1.9	0.3
16-18	Wood and paper products and printing	1.2	0.6	0.1	0.1	0.0	0.0	0.1	0.7
16	Wood and wood products, except furniture	..	..	..	..	..	..	..	..
17	Paper and paper products	..	..	..	..	..	..	..	..
18	Printing and reproduction of recorded media	..	..	..	..	..	..	..	..
19-23	Chemical, rubber, plastic, non-metallic mineral products	106.2	56.4	52.7	50.1	91.6	31.7	29.3	40.8
19	Coke and refined petroleum products	49.9	3.5	1.2	0.8	0.0	0.0	0.0	0.0
20-21	Chemical and pharmaceutical products	52.1	49.7	47.8	46.1	80.2	27.2	25.3	40.0
20	Chemicals and chemical products	9.6	43.4	41.5	38.3	57.0	3.1	2.9	5.6
21	Pharmaceuticals, medicinal, chemical and botanical products	42.5	6.4	6.3	7.8	23.1	24.1	22.4	34.4
22	Rubber and plastic products	2.7	1.4	2.4	1.8	11.3	2.9	3.6	0.2
23	Other non-metallic mineral products	1.5	1.8	1.2	1.5	0.2	1.6	0.3	0.5
24-25	Basic metals, metal products, except machinery and equipment	28.5	19.1	13.6	10.5	14.9	7.6	8.6	9.5
24	Basic metals	22.2	11.6	6.5	5.5	10.6	3.6	4.3	4.4
25	Fabricated metal products, except machinery and equipment	6.3	7.6	7.0	5.0	4.2	4.1	4.2	5.1
26-30	Computer, electronic, optical products; electrical machinery, transport equipment	223.4	169.4	195.5	157.6	200.4	208.0	167.8	212.0
26	Computer, electronic and optical products	13.3	21.7	14.7	13.4	12.8	54.5	35.8	14.4
27	Electrical equipment	41.4	20.7	16.7	16.5	42.9	16.8	13.0	12.0
28	Machinery and equipment n.e.c.	58.6	26.6	18.2	16.8	6.4	18.4	11.7	11.7
29	Motor vehicles, trailers and semi-trailers	93.7	71.5	120.7	92.4	131.9	111.4	102.1	166.0
30	Other transport equipment	16.4	28.9	25.1	18.6	6.5	7.0	5.3	7.8
31-33	Furniture; repair, installation of machinery and equipment	0.4	14.1	17.2	13.5	1.3	6.8	2.0	5.5
31	Furniture	..	0.6	0.2	0.2	0.1	0.1	0.1	0.5
32	Other manufacturing	..	6.5	10.4	10.2	0.0	2.1	0.7	1.1
33	Repair and installation of machinery and equipment	..	7.0	6.6	3.1	1.1	4.6	1.3	3.9
35-39	**ELECTRICITY, GAS, WATER AND WASTE MANAGEMENT**	53.2	60.3	45.9	66.3	0.6	3.0	1.4	1.2
35-36	Electricity, gas and water	..	60.2	45.8	65.9	0.2	2.5	..	..
37-39	Sewerage, waste management and remediation activities	..	0.1	0.1	0.3	0.4	0.6	..	..
41-43	**CONSTRUCTION**	8.0	17.5	13.1	7.7	6.1	0.4	0.4	1.0
45-99	**TOTAL SERVICES**	188.3	170.0	212.5	185.6	279.8	363.8	190.2	253.8
45-82	**Business sector services**	178.5	168.7	211.9	184.3	279.8	361.2	190.2	251.2
45-47	Wholesale and retail trade; motor vehicle and motorcycle repairs	..	..	6.5	..	13.7	26.5	15.9	29.4
49-53	Transportation and storage	..	..	..	..	..	3.8	..	10.9
55-56	Accommodation and food service activities	..	..	..	..	..	1.6	1.2	0.6
58-63	Information and communication	65.3	19.1	90.2	70.7	106.3	114.2	40.9	61.8
58-60	Publishing, audiovisual and broadcasting activities	..	9.7	46.3	47.3	51.9	1.9	0.0	8.6
58	Publishing activities	..	..	..	..	..	1.9	..	..
59-60	Motion picture, video and TV programme production; broadcasting activities	..	..	..	..	..	0.1	..	..
59	Motion picture, video and TV programme production; sound and music	..	..	..	..	..	..	..	..
60	Programming and broadcasting activities	..	..	..	..	..	..	..	..
61	Telecommunications	..	..	..	..	..	11.8	1.1	2.2
62-63	IT and other information services	..	..	..	..	..	100.5	39.8	51.0
62	Computer programming, consultancy and related activities	..	..	42.5	23.4	52.9	68.6	28.5	50.9
63	Information service activities	..	..	..	..	..	31.9	11.3	0.1
64-66	Financial and insurance activities	..	..	..	..	..	..	..	..
68-82	Real estate; professional, scientific and technical; administrative and support	108.3	149.0	115.2	112.8	154.6	218.9	..	..
68	Real estate activities	..	0.0	0.0	0.0	0.0	2.4	..	..
69-75x72	Professional, scientific and technical activities, except scientific R&D	..	16.7	8.5	17.9	27.6	42.3	14.1	13.3
72	Scientific research and development	101.1	117.1	105.4	87.0	126.8	171.8	117.1	133.4
77-82	Administrative and support service activities	..	15.2	1.3	7.9	0.3	2.4	..	1.7
84-99	**Community, social and personal services**	9.7	1.3	0.6	1.3	0.1	2.6	0.0	2.5
84-85	Public administration and defence; compulsory social security and education	..	..	..	..	..	..	..	..
86-88	Human health and social work activities	..	..	..	..	..	..	..	..
90-93	Arts, entertainment and recreation	..	..	..	..	..	..	..	..
94-99	Other services; household-employers; extraterritorial bodies	..	..	..	..	..	..	..	..

.. Not available

Note: Detailed metadata at: http://metalinks.oecd.org/anberd/20170419/301f.
Information on data for Israel: http://oe.cd/israel-disclaimer.
Disclaimer: http://oe.cd/disclaimer

SINGAPORE

R&D expenditure in industry by main activity of the enterprise, current prices
ISIC Rev. 4

Million USD PPP

		2007	2008	2009	2010	2011	2012	2013	2014
	TOTAL BUSINESS ENTERPRISE	4 613.3	5 772.3	4 088.4	4 386.2	5 194.4	5 005.9	5 215.9	..
01-03	**AGRICULTURE, FORESTRY AND FISHING**	0.3	0.0	0.0	0.0	0.0	0.0	0.0	..
05-09	**MINING AND QUARRYING**	0.0	0.0	0.0	0.0	0.0	0.0	0.0	..
10-33	**MANUFACTURING**	3 253.5	4 227.3	2 527.9	2 674.1	2 467.5	3 014.4	3 003.1	..
10-12	Food products, beverages and tobacco	16.6	26.4	22.5	20.7	19.5	24.9	24.1	..
13-15	Textiles, wearing apparel, leather and related products	0.0	0.3	1.0	1.1	1.0	0.9	0.6	..
13	Textiles	0.0	0.0	0.0	0.0	0.0	..	..	..
14	Wearing apparel	0.0	0.0	0.8	0.8	0.7	..	..	..
15	Leather and related products, footwear	0.0	0.3	0.2	0.3	0.3	..	..	..
16-18	Wood and paper products and printing	3.6	2.7	5.3	4.3	3.5	3.6	3.2	..
16	Wood and wood products, except furniture	0.2	0.0	0.0	0.1	0.0	0.0	0.0	..
17	Paper and paper products	1.3	1.2	3.2	3.3	2.7	2.9	2.8	..
18	Printing and reproduction of recorded media	2.0	1.5	2.1	0.9	0.8	0.6	0.4	..
19-23	Chemical, rubber, plastic, non-metallic mineral products	237.8	147.1	177.3	229.0	248.7	272.4	351.0	..
19	Coke and refined petroleum products	1.3	1.4	1.6	0.8	1.2	1.4	1.0	..
20-21	Chemical and pharmaceutical products	218.1	115.4	153.1	210.0	229.4	264.7	344.3	..
20	Chemicals and chemical products	78.2	79.7	67.2	89.2	97.6	111.9	201.8	..
21	Pharmaceuticals, medicinal, chemical and botanical products	139.9	35.6	85.9	120.8	131.8	152.8	142.5	..
22	Rubber and plastic products	10.4	24.7	7.7	4.2	14.3	2.7	3.0	..
23	Other non-metallic mineral products	8.0	5.6	14.9	14.0	3.8	3.6	2.7	..
24-25	Basic metals, metal products, except machinery and equipment	207.9	184.2	145.2	195.1	23.1	30.0	43.7	..
24	Basic metals	9.0	13.0	3.6	4.6	1.6	1.6	3.1	..
25	Fabricated metal products, except machinery and equipment	198.9	171.2	141.6	190.5	21.5	28.4	40.6	..
26-30	Computer, electronic, optical products; electrical machinery, transport equipment	2 777.8	3 852.5	2 148.8	2 185.6	2 094.1	2 547.6	2 446.7	..
26	Computer, electronic and optical products	2 488.1	3 531.7	1 797.3	1 804.8	1 644.2	2 052.1	1 801.4	..
27	Electrical equipment	33.4	22.1	73.5	29.8	24.7	15.6	31.8	..
28	Machinery and equipment n.e.c.	137.6	138.3	117.6	182.0	209.4	219.8	308.1	..
29	Motor vehicles, trailers and semi-trailers	76.0	94.8	98.1	44.1	49.6	54.9	61.5	..
30	Other transport equipment	42.7	65.7	62.2	124.9	166.1	205.2	243.8	..
31-33	Furniture; repair, installation of machinery and equipment	9.7	14.0	27.8	38.3	77.5	135.0	133.9	..
31	Furniture	..	..	..	12.7	17.1	16.9	16.3	..
32	Other manufacturing	..	..	..	25.7	60.5	118.1	117.6	..
33	Repair and installation of machinery and equipment	..	..	..	0.0	0.0	0.0	0.0	..
35-39	**ELECTRICITY, GAS, WATER AND WASTE MANAGEMENT**	0.0	1.0	0.0	15.7	13.9	10.9	15.1	..
35-36	Electricity, gas and water	..	..	..	0.3	0.1	0.0	0.0	..
37-39	Sewerage, waste management and remediation activities	..	..	..	15.5	13.8	10.9	15.1	..
41-43	**CONSTRUCTION**	1.9	4.0	2.2	1.2	2.5	1.5	1.8	..
45-99	**TOTAL SERVICES**	1 357.6	1 540.1	1 558.2	1 695.2	2 710.4	1 979.2	2 195.8	..
45-82	**Business sector services**	1 312.5	1 464.5	1 465.9	1 684.8	2 700.6	1 969.7	2 160.0	..
45-47	Wholesale and retail trade; motor vehicle and motorcycle repairs	315.9	389.4	374.6	439.7	575.1	611.2	822.3	..
49-53	Transportation and storage	21.1	25.0	27.5	56.2	46.6	31.0	46.2	..
55-56	Accommodation and food service activities	1.1	1.1	0.0	0.0	0.0	0.0	0.0	..
58-63	Information and communication	152.2	144.0	141.4	156.1	160.7	169.2	173.7	..
58-60	Publishing, audiovisual and broadcasting activities	..	..	..	26.3	39.4	54.4	45.3	..
58	Publishing activities	..	..	..	24.6	37.6	54.0	45.2	..
59-60	Motion picture, video and TV programme production; broadcasting activities	..	..	..	1.6	1.8	0.3	0.2	..
59	Motion picture, video and TV programme production; sound and music	..	..	..	1.6	1.8	0.3	0.2	..
60	Programming and broadcasting activities	..	..	..	0.0	0.0	0.0	0.0	..
61	Telecommunications	17.7	15.8	8.5	3.9	5.7	3.5	6.7	..
62-63	IT and other information services	..	..	..	125.9	115.6	111.4	121.7	..
62	Computer programming, consultancy and related activities	..	..	..	123.6	112.9	108.5	115.8	..
63	Information service activities	..	..	..	2.3	2.7	2.9	5.9	..
64-66	Financial and insurance activities	108.7	122.0	102.4	100.0	105.3	102.3	107.4	..
68-82	Real estate; professional, scientific and technical; administrative and support	713.4	782.9	819.9	932.8	1 812.9	1 056.0	1 010.4	..
68	Real estate activities	..	..	..	0.0	0.0	0.0	0.0	..
69-75x72	Professional, scientific and technical activities, except scientific R&D	..	..	..	156.9	319.6	265.8	191.1	..
72	Scientific research and development	527.8	546.4	598.4	765.0	810.2	785.0	812.7	..
77-82	Administrative and support service activities	..	..	..	10.9	683.1	5.2	6.6	..
84-99	Community, social and personal services	45.0	75.6	92.4	10.4	9.9	9.6	35.8	..
84-85	Public administration and defence; compulsory social security and education	..	..	..	3.3	4.3	3.2	2.3	..
86-88	Human health and social work activities	..	..	..	6.1	4.5	6.1	33.3	..
90-93	Arts, entertainment and recreation	..	..	..	0.0	0.0	0.0	0.0	..
94-99	Other services; household-employers; extraterritorial bodies	..	..	..	1.1	1.1	0.3	0.2	..

.. Not available

Note: Detailed metadata at: http://metalinks.oecd.org/anberd/20170419/301f.
Information on data for Israel: http://oe.cd/israel-disclaimer.
Disclaimer: http://oe.cd/disclaimer

SINGAPORE

R&D expenditure in industry by main activity of the enterprise, constant prices
ISIC Rev. 4

2010 USD PPP

Code	Activity	2007	2008	2009	2010	2011	2012	2013	2014
	TOTAL BUSINESS ENTERPRISE	4 796.3	5 886.5	4 136.4	4 386.2	5 086.0	4 816.7	4 939.5	..
01-03	**AGRICULTURE, FORESTRY AND FISHING**	0.3	0.0	0.0	0.0	0.0	0.0	0.0	..
05-09	**MINING AND QUARRYING**	0.0	0.0	0.0	0.0	0.0	0.0	0.0	..
10-33	**MANUFACTURING**	3 382.6	4 310.9	2 557.7	2 674.1	2 416.0	2 900.5	2 844.0	..
10-12	Food products, beverages and tobacco	17.3	27.0	22.7	20.7	19.1	24.0	22.8	..
13-15	Textiles, wearing apparel, leather and related products	0.0	0.3	1.0	1.1	1.0	0.8	0.6	..
13	Textiles	0.0	0.0	0.0	0.0	0.0	..	..	..
14	Wearing apparel	0.0	0.0	0.8	0.8	0.7	..	..	..
15	Leather and related products, footwear	0.0	0.3	0.2	0.3	0.3	..	..	..
16-18	Wood and paper products and printing	3.7	2.7	5.4	4.3	3.4	3.4	3.0	..
16	Wood and wood products, except furniture	0.2	0.0	0.0	0.1	0.0	0.0	0.0	..
17	Paper and paper products	1.4	1.3	3.3	3.3	2.6	2.8	2.6	..
18	Printing and reproduction of recorded media	2.1	1.5	2.1	0.9	0.8	0.6	0.4	..
19-23	Chemical, rubber, plastic, non-metallic mineral products	247.2	150.0	179.4	229.0	243.5	262.1	332.4	..
19	Coke and refined petroleum products	1.4	1.4	1.7	0.8	1.2	1.4	1.0	..
20-21	Chemical and pharmaceutical products	226.8	117.7	154.9	210.0	224.6	254.7	326.1	..
20	Chemicals and chemical products	81.3	81.3	68.0	89.2	95.6	107.6	191.1	..
21	Pharmaceuticals, medicinal, chemical and botanical products	145.5	36.3	86.9	120.8	129.0	147.1	135.0	..
22	Rubber and plastic products	10.8	25.2	7.8	4.2	14.0	2.6	2.9	..
23	Other non-metallic mineral products	8.3	5.7	15.1	14.0	3.7	3.5	2.5	..
24-25	Basic metals, metal products, except machinery and equipment	216.2	187.9	146.9	195.1	22.6	28.9	41.4	..
24	Basic metals	9.4	13.3	3.7	4.6	1.5	1.5	2.9	..
25	Fabricated metal products, except machinery and equipment	206.8	174.6	143.2	190.5	21.1	27.3	38.5	..
26-30	Computer, electronic, optical products; electrical machinery, transport equipment	2 888.0	3 928.8	2 174.0	2 185.6	2 050.4	2 451.3	2 317.0	..
26	Computer, electronic and optical products	2 586.9	3 601.5	1 818.4	1 804.8	1 609.9	1 974.5	1 705.9	..
27	Electrical equipment	34.8	22.5	74.4	29.8	24.2	15.0	30.1	..
28	Machinery and equipment n.e.c.	143.0	141.0	119.0	182.0	205.1	211.5	291.8	..
29	Motor vehicles, trailers and semi-trailers	79.0	96.6	99.2	44.1	48.6	52.8	58.3	..
30	Other transport equipment	44.4	67.0	63.0	124.9	162.6	197.5	230.9	..
31-33	Furniture; repair, installation of machinery and equipment	10.1	14.3	28.1	38.3	75.9	129.9	126.8	..
31	Furniture	..	..	..	12.7	16.7	16.2	15.4	..
32	Other manufacturing	..	..	..	25.7	59.2	113.6	111.4	..
33	Repair and installation of machinery and equipment	..	..	..	0.0	0.0	0.0	0.0	..
35-39	**ELECTRICITY, GAS, WATER AND WASTE MANAGEMENT**	0.0	1.0	0.0	15.7	13.6	10.5	14.3	..
35-36	Electricity, gas and water	..	..	..	0.3	0.1	0.0	0.0	..
37-39	Sewerage, waste management and remediation activities	..	..	..	15.5	13.5	10.5	14.3	..
41-43	**CONSTRUCTION**	2.0	4.1	2.2	1.2	2.4	1.4	1.7	..
45-99	**TOTAL SERVICES**	1 411.4	1 570.5	1 576.5	1 695.2	2 653.9	1 904.4	2 079.4	..
45-82	**Business sector services**	1 364.6	1 493.4	1 483.1	1 684.8	2 644.2	1 895.2	2 045.5	..
45-47	**Wholesale and retail trade; motor vehicle and motorcycle repairs**	328.5	397.2	379.0	439.7	563.1	588.1	778.7	..
49-53	**Transportation and storage**	22.0	25.5	27.8	56.2	45.6	29.8	43.7	..
55-56	**Accommodation and food service activities**	1.1	1.1	0.0	0.0	0.0	0.0	0.0	..
58-63	**Information and communication**	158.3	146.9	143.1	156.1	157.4	162.8	164.5	..
58-60	Publishing, audiovisual and broadcasting activities	..	..	..	26.3	38.6	52.3	42.9	..
58	Publishing activities	..	..	..	24.6	36.8	52.0	42.8	..
59-60	Motion picture, video and TV programme production; broadcasting activities	..	..	..	1.6	1.8	0.3	0.2	..
59	Motion picture, video and TV programme production; sound and music	..	..	..	1.6	1.8	0.3	0.2	..
60	Programming and broadcasting activities	..	..	..	0.0	0.0	0.0	0.0	..
61	Telecommunications	18.4	16.1	8.6	3.9	5.6	3.3	6.3	..
62-63	IT and other information services	..	..	..	125.9	113.2	107.2	115.3	..
62	Computer programming, consultancy and related activities	..	..	..	123.6	110.6	104.4	109.7	..
63	Information service activities	..	..	..	2.3	2.6	2.8	5.6	..
64-66	**Financial and insurance activities**	113.0	124.4	103.6	100.0	103.1	98.4	101.7	..
68-82	**Real estate; professional, scientific and technical; administrative and support**	741.7	798.4	829.6	932.8	1 775.1	1 016.1	956.9	..
68	Real estate activities	..	..	..	0.0	0.0	0.0	0.0	..
69-75x72	Professional, scientific and technical activities, except scientific R&D	..	..	..	156.9	313.0	255.8	181.0	..
72	Scientific research and development	548.7	557.2	605.4	765.0	793.3	755.3	769.6	..
77-82	Administrative and support service activities	..	..	..	10.9	668.8	5.0	6.3	..
84-99	**Community, social and personal services**	46.8	77.1	93.5	10.4	9.7	9.2	33.9	..
84-85	Public administration and defence; compulsory social security and education	..	..	..	3.3	4.2	3.0	2.2	..
86-88	Human health and social work activities	..	..	..	6.1	4.4	5.9	31.5	..
90-93	Arts, entertainment and recreation	..	..	..	0.0	0.0	0.0	0.0	..
94-99	Other services; household-employers; extraterritorial bodies	..	..	..	1.1	1.1	0.3	0.2	..

.. Not available

Note: Detailed metadata at: http://metalinks.oecd.org/anberd/20170419/301f.
Information on data for Israel: http://oe.cd/israel-disclaimer.

Disclaimer: http://oe.cd/disclaimer

CHINESE TAIPEI

R&D expenditure in industry by main activity of the enterprise, current prices
ISIC Rev. 4

Million USD PPP

		2007	2008	2009	2010	2011	2012	2013	2014
	TOTAL BUSINESS ENTERPRISE	13 418.1	15 230.6	15 891.0	17 943.7	19 949.5	21 589.2	23 238.4	25 060.1
01-03	AGRICULTURE, FORESTRY AND FISHING	..	..	..	..	..	..	..	..
05-09	MINING AND QUARRYING	..	..	..	..	..	..	..	..
10-33	MANUFACTURING	12 447.9	14 097.7	14 645.9	16 522.4	18 440.2	19 760.3	21 228.2	22 929.5
10-12	Food products, beverages and tobacco	101.9	116.5	109.4	125.2	141.5	166.5	145.7	154.0
13-15	Textiles, wearing apparel, leather and related products	231.3	234.4	240.4	221.9	246.6	265.3	260.9	291.2
13	Textiles	102.2	124.1	121.9	118.9	126.6	125.7	117.2	127.0
14	Wearing apparel	13.3	13.2	12.7	11.6	12.6	11.3	13.1	13.3
15	Leather and related products, footwear	115.8	97.1	105.8	91.4	107.4	128.3	130.6	150.9
16-18	Wood and paper products and printing	25.4	38.2	40.8	41.5	38.9	41.9	55.3	42.3
16	Wood and wood products, except furniture	0.1	0.0	0.0	0.3	1.0	0.9	1.4	4.0
17	Paper and paper products	13.2	20.3	17.1	17.8	16.7	17.8	12.3	10.5
18	Printing and reproduction of recorded media	12.1	17.8	23.7	23.3	21.2	23.2	41.6	27.8
19-23	Chemical, rubber, plastic, non-metallic mineral products	847.3	973.1	986.8	1 149.7	1 293.6	1 405.4	1 482.7	1 600.5
19	Coke and refined petroleum products	71.7	66.9	70.3	75.9	80.4	97.7	137.9	148.4
20-21	Chemical and pharmaceutical products	584.0	702.3	726.6	844.5	970.5	1 039.5	1 096.7	1 172.1
20	Chemicals and chemical products	435.5	497.6	503.6	583.7	643.2	689.6	702.4	683.9
21	Pharmaceuticals, medicinal, chemical and botanical products	148.5	204.7	223.0	260.8	327.3	349.9	394.3	488.2
22	Rubber and plastic products	148.1	162.2	167.2	197.6	198.9	225.5	208.9	226.3
23	Other non-metallic mineral products	43.4	41.8	22.7	31.8	43.7	42.7	39.2	53.7
24-25	Basic metals, metal products, except machinery and equipment	241.0	276.3	286.1	311.9	324.3	325.1	349.5	354.3
24	Basic metals	146.1	157.5	159.2	180.0	169.9	168.1	177.2	173.9
25	Fabricated metal products, except machinery and equipment	94.9	118.8	126.9	131.9	154.5	157.0	172.2	180.5
26-30	Computer, electronic, optical products; electrical machinery, transport equipment	10 872.1	12 282.5	12 836.7	14 490.6	16 229.2	17 367.1	18 725.1	20 274.3
26	Computer, electronic and optical products	9 484.9	10 781.8	11 380.6	12 826.8	14 473.2	15 594.4	16 820.8	18 214.5
27	Electrical equipment	423.1	493.6	528.9	609.3	610.7	631.9	638.5	635.4
28	Machinery and equipment n.e.c.	418.9	467.0	396.9	473.0	573.9	520.6	588.2	676.8
29	Motor vehicles, trailers and semi-trailers	351.1	304.2	267.0	299.2	307.1	343.0	374.5	438.5
30	Other transport equipment	194.1	236.0	263.3	282.3	264.4	277.1	303.1	309.1
31-33	Furniture; repair, installation of machinery and equipment	129.0	176.7	145.8	181.6	166.1	189.0	209.1	212.9
31	Furniture	10.8	10.9	12.4	10.3	8.4	10.7	7.2	9.1
32	Other manufacturing	118.2	165.7	133.4	171.3	157.7	178.3	201.9	203.7
33	Repair and installation of machinery and equipment	0.0	0.0	0.0	0.0	0.0	0.0	0.0	0.0
35-39	ELECTRICITY, GAS, WATER AND WASTE MANAGEMENT	53.1	41.2	38.5	46.7	44.2	48.6	38.8	37.6
35-36	Electricity, gas and water	50.9	40.8	37.5	45.3	42.6	47.4	37.5	36.4
37-39	Sewerage, waste management and remediation activities	2.2	0.4	1.0	1.4	1.6	1.2	1.2	1.3
41-43	CONSTRUCTION	8.6	11.9	10.8	10.4	10.0	12.1	14.0	17.9
45-99	TOTAL SERVICES	908.5	1 079.8	1 195.8	1 364.2	1 455.0	1 768.1	1 957.4	2 075.1
45-82	Business sector services	761.7	921.8	1 018.1	1 168.2	1 276.0	1 566.8	1 753.6	1 841.6
45-47	Wholesale and retail trade; motor vehicle and motorcycle repairs	31.7	40.1	55.1	54.6	51.3	99.1	103.7	119.0
49-53	Transportation and storage	22.3	11.6	9.9	13.1	12.1	12.6	16.0	17.5
55-56	Accommodation and food service activities	1.3	3.8	2.6	0.2	0.7	0.3	0.5	0.1
58-63	Information and communication	557.2	678.1	719.5	817.2	871.8	874.8	993.2	1 027.0
58-60	Publishing, audiovisual and broadcasting activities	13.5	15.6	10.3	10.7	13.3	18.5	28.6	30.7
58	Publishing activities	2.8	9.8	8.9	8.4	11.3	15.4	23.1	22.3
59-60	Motion picture, video and TV programme production; broadcasting activities	10.7	5.8	1.3	2.2	2.0	3.0	5.5	8.4
59	Motion picture, video and TV programme production; sound and music	5.1	1.6	0.5	1.1	0.2	0.4	4.1	3.0
60	Programming and broadcasting activities	5.6	4.2	0.9	1.1	1.8	2.6	1.4	5.4
61	Telecommunications	171.8	195.0	202.0	245.0	257.6	262.2	260.1	253.1
62-63	IT and other information services	371.9	467.4	507.2	561.6	600.8	594.0	704.5	743.2
62	Computer programming, consultancy and related activities	304.7	392.6	435.7	514.0	536.5	557.0	663.9	694.3
63	Information service activities	67.1	74.8	71.5	47.6	64.3	37.0	40.6	48.8
64-66	Financial and insurance activities	62.5	76.6	95.0	108.8	124.2	150.5	159.5	182.7
68-82	Real estate; professional, scientific and technical; administrative and support	86.7	111.6	136.0	174.3	216.0	429.6	480.7	495.3
68	Real estate activities	0.2	0.3	0.3	0.0	0.8	1.2	1.6	2.4
69-75x72	Professional, scientific and technical activities, except scientific R&D	39.5	50.6	53.5	94.2	128.4	337.9	388.9	399.4
72	Scientific research and development	41.8	54.8	76.3	73.5	80.4	82.8	80.7	83.7
77-82	Administrative and support service activities	5.1	5.9	5.9	6.6	6.4	7.6	9.5	9.8
84-99	Community, social and personal services	146.7	158.0	177.7	196.1	179.0	201.4	203.8	233.5
84-85	Public administration and defence; compulsory social security and education	0.0	0.0	0.0	0.2	0.0	0.1	0.1	0.2
86-88	Human health and social work activities	144.2	153.0	174.3	192.1	176.4	199.4	201.9	231.5
90-93	Arts, entertainment and recreation	0.2	0.1	0.0	0.0	0.0	0.0	0.0	0.0
94-99	Other services; household-employers; extraterritorial bodies	2.3	4.9	3.5	3.8	2.6	1.9	1.9	1.9

.. Not available

Note: Detailed metadata at: http://metalinks.oecd.org/anberd/20170419/301f.
   Information on data for Israel: http://oe.cd/israel-disclaimer.

Disclaimer: http://oe.cd/disclaimer

CHINESE TAIPEI

R&D expenditure in industry by main activity of the enterprise, constant prices
ISIC Rev. 4

2010 USD PPP

		2007	2008	2009	2010	2011	2012	2013	2014
	TOTAL BUSINESS ENTERPRISE	13 954.2	15 534.1	16 085.7	17 943.7	19 545.9	20 770.9	22 001.6	23 309.7
01-03	**AGRICULTURE, FORESTRY AND FISHING**	..	..	..	..	..	..	..	..
05-09	**MINING AND QUARRYING**	..	..	..	..	..	..	..	..
10-33	**MANUFACTURING**	12 945.2	14 378.6	14 825.3	16 522.4	18 067.2	19 011.3	20 098.4	21 327.9
10-12	Food products, beverages and tobacco	105.9	118.8	110.7	125.2	138.6	160.2	137.9	143.2
13-15	Textiles, wearing apparel, leather and related products	240.5	239.1	243.3	221.9	241.6	255.2	247.0	270.8
13	Textiles	106.2	126.6	123.4	118.9	124.1	120.9	111.0	118.1
14	Wearing apparel	13.9	13.5	12.9	11.6	12.4	10.9	12.4	12.4
15	Leather and related products, footwear	120.4	99.1	107.0	91.4	105.2	123.4	123.7	140.3
16-18	Wood and paper products and printing	26.4	38.9	41.3	41.5	38.1	40.3	52.3	39.4
16	Wood and wood products, except furniture	0.1	0.0	0.0	0.3	1.0	0.8	1.3	3.7
17	Paper and paper products	13.8	20.7	17.3	17.8	16.3	17.1	11.6	9.7
18	Printing and reproduction of recorded media	12.5	18.2	24.0	23.3	20.8	22.4	39.4	25.9
19-23	Chemical, rubber, plastic, non-metallic mineral products	881.2	992.5	998.9	1 149.7	1 267.4	1 352.1	1 403.8	1 488.7
19	Coke and refined petroleum products	74.6	68.2	71.2	75.9	78.8	94.0	130.5	138.0
20-21	Chemical and pharmaceutical products	607.3	716.3	735.5	844.5	950.9	1 000.1	1 038.4	1 090.2
20	Chemicals and chemical products	452.9	507.5	509.8	583.7	630.2	663.5	665.0	636.1
21	Pharmaceuticals, medicinal, chemical and botanical products	154.4	208.7	225.7	260.8	320.6	336.6	373.3	454.1
22	Rubber and plastic products	154.1	165.4	169.2	197.6	194.9	217.0	197.8	210.5
23	Other non-metallic mineral products	45.2	42.6	23.0	31.8	42.9	41.1	37.1	49.9
24-25	Basic metals, metal products, except machinery and equipment	250.6	281.8	289.6	311.9	317.8	312.8	330.9	329.6
24	Basic metals	151.9	160.7	161.1	180.0	166.4	161.8	167.8	161.7
25	Fabricated metal products, except machinery and equipment	98.7	121.1	128.5	131.9	151.4	151.0	163.1	167.9
26-30	Computer, electronic, optical products; electrical machinery, transport equipment	11 306.5	12 527.3	12 994.0	14 490.6	15 900.9	16 708.8	17 728.5	18 858.2
26	Computer, electronic and optical products	9 863.9	10 996.6	11 520.0	12 826.8	14 180.4	15 003.3	15 925.5	16 942.3
27	Electrical equipment	440.0	503.5	535.3	609.3	598.3	608.0	604.5	591.0
28	Machinery and equipment n.e.c.	435.6	476.3	401.7	473.0	562.3	500.9	556.9	629.6
29	Motor vehicles, trailers and semi-trailers	365.2	310.2	270.3	299.2	300.8	330.0	354.6	407.9
30	Other transport equipment	201.8	240.7	266.6	282.3	259.1	266.6	287.0	287.5
31-33	Furniture; repair, installation of machinery and equipment	134.1	180.2	147.6	181.6	162.8	181.8	197.9	198.0
31	Furniture	11.2	11.2	12.6	10.3	8.2	10.3	6.8	8.5
32	Other manufacturing	122.9	169.0	135.0	171.3	154.5	171.5	191.1	189.5
33	Repair and installation of machinery and equipment	0.0	0.0	0.0	0.0	0.0	0.0	0.0	0.0
35-39	**ELECTRICITY, GAS, WATER AND WASTE MANAGEMENT**	55.2	42.0	39.0	46.7	43.3	46.8	36.7	35.0
35-36	Electricity, gas and water	52.9	41.6	38.0	45.3	41.7	45.6	35.5	33.8
37-39	Sewerage, waste management and remediation activities	2.3	0.4	1.0	1.4	1.5	1.2	1.2	1.2
41-43	**CONSTRUCTION**	9.0	12.1	10.9	10.4	9.8	11.7	13.3	16.6
45-99	**TOTAL SERVICES**	944.8	1 101.3	1 210.5	1 364.2	1 425.6	1 701.1	1 853.2	1 930.2
45-82	**Business sector services**	792.1	940.2	1 030.6	1 168.2	1 250.2	1 507.4	1 660.2	1 712.9
45-47	Wholesale and retail trade; motor vehicle and motorcycle repairs	33.0	40.9	55.7	54.6	50.2	95.3	98.2	110.7
49-53	Transportation and storage	23.2	11.8	10.0	13.1	11.8	12.1	15.1	16.3
55-56	Accommodation and food service activities	1.4	3.9	2.7	0.2	0.7	0.3	0.5	0.1
58-63	Information and communication	579.5	691.6	728.3	817.2	854.1	841.6	940.3	955.2
58-60	Publishing, audiovisual and broadcasting activities	14.1	15.9	10.4	10.7	13.0	17.8	27.1	28.6
58	Publishing activities	2.9	10.0	9.1	8.4	11.1	14.9	21.8	20.8
59-60	Motion picture, video and TV programme production; broadcasting activities	11.1	5.9	1.4	2.2	2.0	2.9	5.2	7.8
59	Motion picture, video and TV programme production; sound and music	5.3	1.6	0.5	1.1	0.2	0.4	3.9	2.8
60	Programming and broadcasting activities	5.8	4.3	0.9	1.1	1.8	2.5	1.3	5.0
61	Telecommunications	178.7	198.9	204.5	245.0	252.4	252.3	246.2	235.4
62-63	IT and other information services	386.7	476.8	513.4	561.6	588.7	571.5	667.0	691.3
62	Computer programming, consultancy and related activities	316.9	400.5	441.0	514.0	525.6	535.9	628.5	645.8
63	Information service activities	69.8	76.3	72.4	47.6	63.0	35.6	38.5	45.4
64-66	Financial and insurance activities	65.0	78.1	96.2	108.8	121.7	144.8	151.0	169.9
68-82	Real estate; professional, scientific and technical; administrative and support	90.1	113.8	137.6	174.3	211.7	413.3	455.1	460.7
68	Real estate activities	0.2	0.3	0.3	0.0	0.8	1.2	1.6	2.3
69-75x72	Professional, scientific and technical activities, except scientific R&D	41.1	51.6	54.1	94.2	125.8	325.1	368.2	371.5
72	Scientific research and development	43.5	55.9	77.2	73.5	78.8	79.7	76.4	77.9
77-82	Administrative and support service activities	5.3	6.0	6.0	6.6	6.3	7.3	9.0	9.1
84-99	**Community, social and personal services**	152.6	161.1	179.9	196.1	175.4	193.7	193.0	217.2
84-85	Public administration and defence; compulsory social security and education	0.0	0.0	0.0	0.2	0.0	0.1	0.1	0.2
86-88	Human health and social work activities	150.0	156.1	176.4	192.1	172.8	191.8	191.2	215.3
90-93	Arts, entertainment and recreation	0.2	0.1	0.0	0.0	0.0	0.0	0.0	0.0
94-99	Other services; household-employers; extraterritorial bodies	2.4	5.0	3.5	3.8	2.6	1.8	1.8	1.7

.. Not available

Note: Detailed metadata at: http://metalinks.oecd.org/anberd/20170419/301f.
Information on data for Israel: http://oe.cd/israel-disclaimer.
Disclaimer: http://oe.cd/disclaimer

ORGANISATION FOR ECONOMIC CO-OPERATION AND DEVELOPMENT

The OECD is a unique forum where governments work together to address the economic, social and environmental challenges of globalisation. The OECD is also at the forefront of efforts to understand and to help governments respond to new developments and concerns, such as corporate governance, the information economy and the challenges of an ageing population. The Organisation provides a setting where governments can compare policy experiences, seek answers to common problems, identify good practice and work to co-ordinate domestic and international policies.

The OECD member countries are: Australia, Austria, Belgium, Canada, Chile, the Czech Republic, Denmark, Estonia, Finland, France, Germany, Greece, Hungary, Iceland, Ireland, Israel, Italy, Japan, Korea, Latvia, Luxembourg, Mexico, the Netherlands, New Zealand, Norway, Poland, Portugal, the Slovak Republic, Slovenia, Spain, Sweden, Switzerland, Turkey, the United Kingdom and the United States. The European Union takes part in the work of the OECD.

OECD Publishing disseminates widely the results of the Organisation's statistics gathering and research on economic, social and environmental issues, as well as the conventions, guidelines and standards agreed by its members.

www.ingramcontent.com/pod-product-compliance
Lightning Source LLC
Chambersburg PA
CBHW082353220526
45470CB00008B/2732